EDI DEVELOPMENT STUDIES

Corporate Governance in Transitional Economies

Insider Control and the Role of Banks

Edited by

Masahiko Aoki
Hyung-Ki Kim

The World Bank
Washington, D. C.

First printing February 1995

The Economic Development Institute (EDI) was established by the World Bank in 1955 to train officials concerned with development planning, policymaking, investment analysis, and project implementation in member developing countries. At present the substance of the EDI's work emphasizes macroeconomic and sectoral economic policy analysis. Through a variety of courses, seminars, and workshops, most of which are given overseas in cooperation with local institutions, the EDI seeks to sharpen analytical skills used in policy analysis and to broaden understanding of the experience of individual countries with economic development. Although the EDI's publications are designed to support its training activities, many are of interest to a much broader audience. EDI materials, including any findings, interpretations, and conclusions, are entirely those of the authors and should not be attributed in any manner to the World Bank, to its affiliated organizations, or to members of its Board of Executive Directors or the countries they represent.

Because of the informality of this series and to make the publication available with the least possible delay, the manuscript has not been edited as fully as would be the case with a more formal document, and the World Bank accepts no responsibility for errors. Some sources cited in this book may be informal documents that are not readily available.

The backlist of publications by the World Bank is shown in the annual *Index of Publications*, which is available from Distribution Unit, Office of the Publisher, The World Bank, 1818 H Street, N.W., Washington, D.C. 20433, U.S.A., or from Publications, Banque mondiale, 66, avenue d'Iéna, 75116 Paris, France.

Masahiko Aoki is professor of Japanese studies in Stanford University's department of economics. Hyung-Ki Kim is chief of the Studies and Training Design Division in the World Bank's Economic Development Institute

Library of Congress Cataloging-in-Publication Data

Corporate governance in transitional economies : insider control and the role of banks / edited by Masahiko Aoki, Hyung-Ki Kim.
p. cm.—(EDI development studies, ISSN 1020-105X)
Includes bibliographical references and index.
ISBN 0-8213-2990-1
1. Corporate governance—Case studies. 2. Banks and banking—Case studies. 3. Economic development—Case studies. I. Aoki, Masahiko, 1938– . II. Kim, Hyung-Ki, 1936– . III. International Bank for Reconstruction and Development. IV. Series.
HD2741.C776 1994
658.4—dc20 94-42709
CIP

Contents

Foreword

This book presents the results of a research project on corporate governance issues in transitional economies from a new perspective based on comparative institutional analysis. The project grew out of a concern about three issues: the emerging phenomenon of insider control, the possible role of banks in corporate governance, and the desirability of taking a comparative analytic approach to finding solutions.

By examining and comparing individual country studies, policymakers may be able to avoid simplistic generalizations or theories based on the observation of a single economy. By analyzing the workings of diverse systems, they may also be able to uncover those factors that contribute to or constrain the effectiveness of particular governance structures. This kind of comparative analysis may serve in the social sciences as a kind of proxy for laboratory experimentation.

This work was prepared as part of the Economic Development Institute's (EDI) multiyear Program for the Study of the Japanese Development Management Experience, which is financed by the Policy and Human Resources Development Trust Fund established at the World Bank by the Government of Japan. The program is managed by EDI's Studies and Training Design Division.

Vinod Thomas
Director
Economic Development Institute
The World Bank

Acknowledgments

We would like to express our appreciation to our colleagues both in and outside the World Bank for their invaluable contributions to this project. As we set out to identify and articulate the relevant issues during two design and review workshops, many World Bank staff working on corporate governance issues in transitional economies helped to shape this study. In particular, we would like to thank Cheryl Gray, Djordjija Petkoski, Gerhard Pohl, Inderjit Singh, and Alexander Tsapin. We also benefited from the wisdom of the discussants at the workshops and the reviewers of the draft manuscript, including John Earle, Millard Long, John McMillan, Gerhard Pohl, and Dimitri Slavnov. Their challenging comments helped to clarify our thoughts and analysis. Elizabeth Goldstein and Bruce Donald served as rapporteurs at the workshops and produced faithful records of complex discussions. We are also grateful to Yushiru Yamamuro, chairman of the Board of the International University of Japan, who shared with us his experiences in dealing with the recapitalization of Japanese banks after World War II. Caroline McEuen provided valuable editorial and production support in preparing the manuscript for publication. Finally, the two workshops were skillfully organized by Deborah Carvalho at the Stanford Center for Economic Policy Research and by Latifah Alsegaf at the World Bank. We are also grateful to the Stanford Center for Economic Policy Research for cosponsoring this project.

Overview

During the initial phase of transforming socialist planned economies, there was a naive optimism that the transition to a market economy could be readily achieved by the privatization of the state-owned enterprise, combined with the introduction of the equity market, which would also serve as the market for corporate control. This belief reflected a textbook notion of the capitalist economy, but recommendations for economic reforms based on such theological belief have proven to be unrealistic or simplistic. It has been increasingly recognized that the issue of the transition or evolution of the system has not been well understood because of economists' preoccupation with the idealized model of the market economy, as well as their naiveté regarding the effects of the political economy and the broad diversity of transformation issues. Further, it has come to be recognized that advanced market economies are not necessarily structured according to the textbook description.

The Anglo-American economy is perhaps the closest to the textbook model of market economies, but the economies of continental Europe and Japan operate very differently from the Anglo-American model. In Japan and Germany, banks, rather than the market for corporate control, have played unique roles in the corporate governance structure. The three largest banks in Germany own a large share of the stocks of publicly traded corporations. They also vote on behalf of individual stockholders. They normally sit in the *Aufsichtsrats* (supervisory boards) of large, publicly traded corporations, which select the management boards. In Japan, the size of stockholdings and the extent of board participation by the banks are, on the surface, not as large as in Germany. Yet it has been observed that the financial difficulties experienced by large corporations have almost surely triggered bank intervention and, very often, the shift of management control to the bank.

The coexistence of the alternative models for corporate control in the developed countries suggests that their possible "lessons" for the transitional economies are not so obvious. It makes little sense to judge the merits of each corporate governance model and its applicability to the transitional economies without noting a country's development stage and the history of its institutions and conventions. In designing corporate governance structures for the transitional economies, economists are required to identify the specific conditions under which each corporate control model (or the combination of different models) works, the availability of these conditions in the transitional economies, and the most efficient approach to achieve these conditions.

This volume presents the results of a research project on corporate governance issues in transitional economies from the perspective of the new comparative institutional analysis. In this approach, banks and other outside institutions can play an important role in corporate governance. This contrasts with the traditional approach, where enabling stockholders to exercise control is the goal of efficient corporate governance. The traditional analysis suggests that the problem of creating corporate governance in transitional economies should be addressed by promoting the development of efficient securities markets, nurturing the growth of active and influential stockholders, and legislating corporate laws that would assure stockholders a controlling position on corporate boards. But a series of events in transitional economies has made it clear that the matter is not so simple. We cannot ignore the path-dependent, or evolutionary, nature of the transition process. The legacies of socialism, the increased autonomy of managers of state-owned enterprises in the last phase of the communist regime, and the strong political power of the workers in many transitional economies, including Russia, Poland, and China, seem to have left strong constraints on the privatization process of the succeeding transitional economies and the nature of the evolving corporate control structure.

In many transitional economies the phenomena of insider control are becoming evident. By insider control we mean de facto or de jure capture of controlling rights by the managers and the strong representation of their interests in corporate strategic decisionmaking, often in collusion with the workers. Some recent privatization programs have, in effect, legitimized the de facto control of insiders by transferring the majority of the ownership of many large enterprises to incumbent managers and workers. In Russia, by November 1993, 91 percent of the privatized enterprises had adopted the so-called type II privatization program, in which employees (including managers) buy up to 51 percent of shares at the pre-inflation book value. In many privatized firms, board meetings and shareholders' meetings are dominated by the management, who also find ways to prevent workers from selling their equity holdings (see Chapter 6). In Poland, widespread asset stripping by state enterprise managers took place when the government started to loosen control over the state-owned enterprises in the late 1980s (Lipton and Sachs 1990). After privatization, insiders, especially the management, continued to preserve their privileged status, and workers' representatives on the supervisory board continued their activist Solidarity tradition and played an important role in enterprise decisions. In China, evidence from some 4,000 experimental shareholding companies suggests that employee-shareholders have benefited greatly from unfair profit division between themselves and the state, and employee-shareholders have continued to demand excessive wage increases and in-kind benefits. In many collectively owned Chinese enterprises, spontaneous and formal privatization—unauthorized transfer of assets to formal or de facto private ownership—has become common (see Chapter 7).

In the orthodox stockholder sovereignty model, the problems of management slack, incompetence, and moral hazard are corrected by outside stockholders through an efficient capital market for corporate valuation and control, as well as institutions such as competitive labor markets for managers and for workers' labor services. In the transitional economies, however, both competitive capital and labor markets are lacking. Managers have established strong control within their enterprises; there is no external agent with the decisive power to dismiss them for poor management performance or moral hazard behavior. Workers have strong attachments to their employing enterprises, which protect their vested interests and jobs. Insider control has evolved out of this relationship. Outsiders would then anticipate substantial agency costs to investing in insider-controlled enterprises. Therefore, the funds necessary for restructuring formerly state-owned enterprises would be difficult to come by from the capital market ("insiders' dilemma"—see Chapter 3). Faced with a majority or substantial share ownership by the insiders (managers and workers), any external pressure over strategic decisions that might adversely affect the job security and other benefits of the insiders would surely face tremendous resistance. If the securities market is thin and the workers and managers have strong attachments to their employing firms, market signals of corporate valuation would be garbled and full of noise. Further, exercising corporate control through the market (the takeover mechanism) would simply not be feasible unless insiders gave up their shares. The design of the corporate governance structure in transitional economies must face this reality.

Recognition of the strong tendency toward insider control compels us to search for an alternative external monitoring mechanism over enterprises, which may work even if outsiders are not the dominant stockholders and managers and workers do not voluntarily give up their vested interests and rights. An obvious candidate to implement such a mechanism would be the bank. In the postwar high-growth stage of both the German and Japanese economies, banks maintained continuous relationships with corporate clients and occupied unique positions in corporate governance. Their role has been somewhat different from that played by anonymous stockholders. There are phenomena in both economies that would suggest that bank monitoring might be consistent with, even complementary to, a certain degree of insider control. In Germany, worker representation on the supervisory board (*Aufsichtsrat*) through codetermination is matched by the high concentration of voting rights in a few large, universal banks. In Japan, the main bank system, in which investors delegate the monitoring of the enterprise to a single bank, emerged after the demise of the planned war economy and the massive sales of stock of major *Zaibatsu* corporations to insiders. This bank, called the main bank, selectively intervened in the internal management in the event of financial distress.

The idea of applying the bank-oriented monitoring system of the German and Japanese model to transitional economies has been proposed rather casually in many writings and public discourses. Its genuine applicability to transitional economies is, as yet, far from obvious. The German and Japanese systems evolved in different historical and institutional circumstances and there are major differences between the two. The role of banks in the corporate governance structure in each economy may be complementary to other institutional facets that may not exist in the transitional economies (for example, participatory work organizations, competitive product markets, or neutral government regulatory power).

The old banking institutions inherited by the transitional economies from the planned era suffer from bad debts and bad reputations. Can the spin-offs of the former state banking sector, privatized and recapitalized, be transformed into a solid banking system? Will the emerging new banks evolve, eventually, into accountable financial intermediaries to which monitoring of enterprises may be delegated and trusted? Alternatively, should the nonbank intermediaries, such as mutual funds, be nurtured as potential corporate monitors in spite of the temporary phenomena of insider control, or should the banking sector and the securities markets be developed in complementary ways?

These questions do not seem to be readily answerable by mechanically extrapolating the experiences of existing bank-oriented systems to the financial system design of transitional economies. On one hand, we need to carefully identify the historical conditions prevailing in existing bank-oriented economies that were conducive to the evolution of such systems, and the institutional environments that might have been complementary to their effective operation. On the other hand, we need to carefully observe current developments in transitional economies and identify conditions that may (or may not) call for, and facilitate the development of, the banks as potentially active players in corporate governance.

By pooling rich individual country studies and cross-examining and comparing their implications, we may be able to avoid premature generalizations or theorizing based on the observation of a single economy. By comparing the workings of diverse systems, we may also be able to uncover latent factors that are conducive to, or constrain, the workability of particular governance structures. Comparative analysis may thus serve as a substitute for the laboratory experiments difficult in the social sciences, although the potential sample numbers are extremely limited.

A concern with three points—the emergent phenomena of insider control, the possible role of banks in corporate governance, and the desirability of a comparative analytic approach—sets the common ground for our collective research, which resulted in this volume. The volume is composed of three parts. Part I contains three chapters that deal with generic and theoretical issues of corporate governance in transitional economies from the perspective of comparative institutional analysis.

The five chapters comprising Part II deal in depth with various aspects of the corporate governance problem in three transitional economies: Russia, China, and the former German Democratic Republic. Part III contains four contributions dealing with aspects of Japanese and German experiences relevant to the transitional issues. Let us briefly introduce each chapter.

In Chapter 1, entitled "Controlling Insider Control: Issues of Corporate Governance in Transition Economies," Masahiko Aoki first reviews the tendency toward insider control in transitional economies and explains why the model of stockholder sovereignty may be ineffective in coping with this problem. He emphasizes complementary relationships between corporate governance structure and other facets of institutional arrangements of the economy, especially internal organization of the enterprise. He presents a theoretical possibility of contingent governance in which the control rights can shift automatically from the insider to the outsider (the lead bank of a consortium) contingent on the financial distress of the enterprise, and indicates how the expectation that such an intervention can occur effectively controls various incentive issues for the insider-controlled enterprise. This scheme appears to be more applicable to financially viable insider-controlled firms in the posttransition period rather than as a solution to the transition problem itself. Since the direction of the institutional development of internal organization in transition economies remains full of uncertainty, the paper advocates an evolutionary approach to corporate governance design in the transition. It argues that only the organic development of an institutional cluster will ultimately determine the relative importance of the banking institutions and capital markets in corporate governance.

In Chapter 2, "Political Economy Issues of Ownership Transformation in Eastern Europe," Gérard Roland takes up the issue of political constraints on privatization and restructuring arising from the legacies of the socialist system. He makes an important analytical distinction, not necessarily mutually exclusive in practice, between the strong government, with agenda-setting power, and the weak government, susceptible to the rent-seeking activities of various groups. Using this framework, he argues for the importance of correctly sequencing the privatization procedure so that the transition is politically irreversible and restructuring is effective. Massive giveaways or distribution of corporate assets may well result in insider control (as in Russia and Poland) or the concentration of economic power (as in the Czech Republic), the result of which may be the deterrence of economically viable restructuring and de facto renationalization (rescue by the government). He recognizes advantages of the gradualism in privatization pursued by the agenda-setting Chinese government. He concludes with several concrete proposals for banking reform from both agenda-setting and rent-seeking perspectives.

Recent academic thoughts on the subject of corporate governance are much more subtle than the single-minded advocacy of stockholder control over corporate governance. Unique roles for debt contracts and bank intermediaries are increasingly recognized. In Chapter 3, entitled "Corporate Governance in Transition Economies: The Theory and Its Policy Implications," Erik Berglöf introduces a valuable conceptual distinction between "arm's-length" and "control-oriented" financing and argues that these two kinds of financing are actually complementary and mixed in various ways, depending on national conditions. Under the condition of the illiquidity of asset markets and ambiguity about property rights, he predicts that control-oriented financing will play a dominant, albeit not exclusive, role in the transition. He presents a nuanced and balanced argument for positive and gradualist intervention by the government to transform the fragile banking sector into credible financial institutions.

In Chapter 4, "Corporate Governance, Banks, and Fiscal Reform in Russia," John Litwack argues that the commitment and trust in economic relationships developed through long-run personal and mutually beneficial ties have a long tradition in Russia, which may favor the development of a bank-oriented financial system as opposed to an American-type arm's-length model. He notes, however, that the current practice of using the commercial banking system for the administration of implicit subsidization distorts the incentives of banks to monitor, while discretionary taxation encourages managers of enterprises to minimize legal profits by diverting resources to hidden consumption by insiders. He argues that, given the magnitude and scope of the necessary restructuring in Russia, the reduction of subsidies should be gradual and based on optimal sequencing, but for an accountable banking system to develop, subsidies should not be made through the commercial bank network.

Chapter 5 by Noritaka Akamatsu, "Enterprise Governance and Investment Funds in Russian Privatization," provides detailed, up-to-date institutional descriptions of privatization schemes, Voucher Investment Funds (VIFs), corporate and bankruptcy laws, and the emergent industrial financial conglomerates in Russia. In conjunction with Chapter 6, it gives a most comprehensive overview of the current Russian situation surrounding enterprises and the financial system. He describes the rivalry between the GKI (the State Property Management Committee), responsible for privatization schemes and capital market regulation, and the Ministry of Finance, responsible for commercial banking regulation. He makes an interesting point that, as the former tries to promote investment banking and restrict commercial banks' activities in capital markets, the mixture of Anglo-American-style capital markets and a German-style banking system may well result in the Japanese model.

Chapter 6 by Elena Belyanova and Ivan Rozinsky, "Evolution of Commercial Banking in Russia and Its Implications for Corporate Governance," is a rare contribution by academicians-cum-practitioners from Russia regarding the recent development of the banking sector in Russia. Based on recent statistical data and questionnaire studies, the chapter provides a valuable glimpse into the relatively unknown workings of the newly emergent banks, as well as spin-offs of former state banks. It depicts the Russian banks as becoming much more important financial institutions in comparison with investment funds, and predicts that the best part of the banking sector, the so-called "hard currency islands," will play a significant role in mid-term investment financing and corporate governance in the future. Because of situational and historical differences from Japan, however, they argue that a German-style system, based on more formal controlling instruments, is more likely to be viable in Russia. From this perspective, they criticize the recent regulation on banks' holding of industrial shares.

Chapter 7 by Yingyi Qian, "Reforming Corporate Governance and Finance in China," provides a comprehensive description and analytical discussion of the most recent corporate governance reforms in China. He portrays the paradox of Chinese reform: that the communist leadership was able to delegate more decisionmaking authority to managers precisely because of their retention of control over personnel appointments, and thus control of managers' career incentives, but that this increased delegation leads to a tendency toward de facto insider control.

He compares proposals for reforming corporate governance in China within the political constraints of gradualist privatization. He concludes that reforming corporate governance should not follow a single model in China, although a sound banking system would certainly constitute an important element of any reform to counterbalance insider control. From this perspective he outlines a proposal to spin off the vast network of the existing central bank as multiple regional commercial banks.

Chapter 8 by Ernst-Ludwig von Thadden, "Centralized Decentralization: Corporate Governance in the German Economic Transition," describes and assesses the privatization process mediated by the *Treuhandanstalt*, which had privatized about 18,000 businesses or parts of businesses by the end of March 1994. More than half of these new entities were purchased by western German firms in a manner analogous to the working of takeovers in competitive capital markets. The presence of strong centralized control by the *Treuhandanstalt* prior to privatization was instrumental in curbing the insider control problem. The chapter argues that the complete independence of, and institutional time limit imposed on, the activity of the *Treuhandanstalt* (it will cease its operations at the end of 1994 by law) and the career concerns of its managers effectively precluded any long-term gains possible from collusion and lobbying by interest groups. Another interesting point is that West German banks did not play any significant role in the provision of risky restructuring finance to *Treuhandanstalt* firms prior to privatization. That this is the case, even under the exceptionally favorable institutional environment of East Germany, suggests that the role of banks may be limited in the transition process, if not in posttransition corporate governance.

Part III turns to the experience of Japan and Germany. After a brief introductory note concerning broad historical contexts for the emergence of a bank-oriented system in Japan, Chapter 9 by Takeo Hoshi, "Cleaning Up the Balance Sheets: Japanese Experience in the Postwar Reconstruction Period," describes how Japanese banks and enterprises resolved a serious postwar, economywide insolvency problem caused by the repudiation of wartime compensation by the government. His careful case traces how the bad loans of banks and losses of enterprises were cleaned up without interfering with ongoing business through the separation of old and new accounts, the cancellation of debts and capital in the old accounts against losses (bad loans), and the subsequent recapitalization through new equity issues. Because the balance sheet clean-up was performed in close cooperation between enterprises and single partner banks, sometimes against the interests of workers, the reorganization process had a significant impact on the subsequent development of the corporate governance structure. Since the insolvency and recapitalization problem is an important issue in today's transitional economies, this chapter may be very suggestive and relevant for policymakers.

In Chapter 10, "The Privatization of Ex-*Zaibatsu* Holding Stocks and the Emergence of Bank-Centered Corporate Groups in Japan," Hideaki Miyajima utilizes hitherto unused original documents of the privatization following *Zaibatsu* dissolution in the postwar period of Japan and describes its consequences. As in the current privatization process in Russia, the initial objective of the occupation army was the democratization of stockholding, supplemented by employee ownership. The subsequent slump of the stock market and the managerial effort to fend off outsiders' control eventually led to the formation of bank-centered cross-holding among related enterprises. He presents some empirical evidence to indicate that the main bank, which had a multidimensional, close relationship with the client enterprise, functioned as an effective monitoring device to counteract insider control in the reconstruction period.

In Chapter 11, "Savings Mobilization and Investment Financing during Japan's Postwar Economic Recovery," Juro Teranishi discusses how the banking sector evolved as an effective intermediary, channeling savings into investible funds in the high-growth period after the mid-1950s. He argues that the interim period (1950–55) between the immediate postwar period (as dealt with by Hoshi) and the high-growth period was characterized by a low share of investment to GNP and a heavy reliance by large enterprises on internal financing. Using rich statistical data, he shows that the establishment of an effective system of maturity transformation of short-term savings to long-term financing was instrumental and responsible for ushering in the period of high growth. He analyzes the workings of this system, in which rationing of corporate bonds to the banks and the accommodating supply of Bank of Japan credits to the banks at below market rates played very important roles. From this analysis he opposes the view that the postwar system is a simple inheritance of the wartime system.

Chapter 12, "Shareholder Voting and Corporate Governance: The German Experience and a New Approach," is by corporate and banking law scholars in Germany, Theodor Baums and Philipp v. Randow. They describe the German experience, in which a substantial proportion of voting rights in large corporations are exercised by leading banks on the basis of their own shares, their custodial shares, and shares held by investment companies that are bank subsidiaries. They point to the danger of conflict of interest inherent in such a system and propose an institutional solution—the creation of a specialized proxy agent. The conflict may arise between the bank's interest as the representative of value-maximizing small shareholders and the bank managers' own interests in expanding their business with corporations through underwriting syndicates, lending, and so forth. As Akamatsu indicates in Chapter 5, there is already a similar potential conflict in Russia and other Eastern European economies, where banks also control investment funds through subsidiaries, and this analysis of the German experience may be relevant and instructive.

These introductory paragraphs only touch the surface of the analyses and presentations of empirical evidence in what is a set of deep and richly nuanced studies of the issues. Without flinching from too bold a generalization, we may succinctly summarize the consensus view drawn from the project as follows:

- Sole reliance on the stockholder control model of corporate governance would be of limited merit in transitional economies because of the evolutionary tendency toward strong insider control.
- The comparative analysis indicates that, while the tendency toward insider control is generic in transitional economies, its degree and scope varies across economies, depending upon evolutionary and institutional factors (the strength of the government authority before and after the demise of communist control, the development stage and the historical legacy of the economy, and the political-economic processes involving many interest groups during the transition, to name but a few influ-

ences). Therefore, institutional responses to insider control should also be diverse. At least on a theoretical level, however, strong banking institutions can be considered effective for controlling insider control, and public policies encouraging such developments need to be recommended. But the effectiveness of the banking sector may depend upon the simultaneous development of other complementary institutions. Because there is much uncertainty in this regard, the banking system and the capital markets should not be taken as alternative choices in the transition.

- Although sound banking institutions can be designed to play an effective monitoring role in the corporate governance structure of viable insider-controlled firms, the role of banks in the transition may be limited because of their undercapitalization, the low level of monitoring capacity, the legacy of soft budgeting, and so forth. Therefore, government subsides may need to be continued in the restructuring process, but they should be separated from the commercial banking sector for its sound development.
- Many subtle lessons can be drawn for corporate governance and financial system design in transitional economies from the experiences of Japan—particularly in how insider control can be controlled, how banks are to be motivated to monitor, how bad debts of banks and enterprises are to be resolved through their recapitalization at the time of restructuring, and how the banking institutions are to be nurtured as an effective vehicle for transforming saving into long-term financing. Obviously, however, the direct transplantation of the Japanese system is out of the question. The developmental, historical, institutional, and international conditions are different in many important respects between postwar Japan and the current transitional economies.

Masahiko Aoki
Hyung-Ki Kim

Reference

Lipton, David, and Jeffrey Sachs. 1990. "Privatization in Eastern Europe: The Case of Poland." *Brookings Papers on Economic Activities* 2: 293–341.

Part I

Generic and Comparative Issues: Theory and Policy Implications

1

Controlling Insider Control: Issues of Corporate Governance in Transition Economies

Masahiko Aoki

This chapter identifies and discusses some fundamental issues of corporate governance in the transition economy. In the first part we present an overview of the generic tendency toward insider control in transitional economies. By insider control, we mean the capture of substantial control rights by the manager or the workers of a formerly state-owned enterprise (SOE) in the process of its corporatization. There are variations in the degree and scope of insider control across transitional economies, depending on national conditions. The tendency is generic, however, in the sense that it is an evolutionary outcome of communist legacies. We argue that the mechanical application of the neoclassical model of stockholder sovereignty for corporate governance

---

In writing this chapter, I benefited from comments and discussions by Erik Berglöf, John Earle, Hyung-Ki Kim, Gérard Roland, Dimitri Slavnov, Yingyi Qian, and other participants in the project on "Corporate Governance in Transition Economies: Insider Control and the Role of Bank" sponsored by Economic Development Institute of the World Bank and the Center for Economic Policy Research at Stanford University. Bruce Donnell provided research assistance.

design in the transition is not effective in coping with the insider control problem; worse, it may even prolong the transition process.

The second part of the chapter shows that there can be an alternative model of corporate governance to monitor and control incentive issues unique to the insider-controlled enterprise. The essential idea is to rely on the development of banking institutions that can selectively intervene in the insider-controlled enterprise at the time of financial distress. The model considers the problem of how the bank is motivated to monitor the insider-controlled enterprise while diversifying lending risk to some extent.

The second part of the chapter is purely theoretical; the preconditions assumed for the workability of the model do not seem to exist in transition economies. The fundamental question of which model is superior—the model of stockholder sovereignty with competitive capital markets or the model of the governance in which control rights shift from the insider to the outsider (the bank), contingent on the financial state of the enterprise—cannot be answered in isolation from other institutional characteristics of the economy, particularly the mode of internal organization of enterprises. We argue that the future course of the transition economy in this respect is too uncertain to predict. Therefore, we advocate an eclectic approach to corporate governance in the transition, including the simultaneous development of the capital markets and banking institutions. They are presumably complementary in their roles in the development of sound corporate governance in transitional economies.

It seems certain, however, that sole reliance on the neoclassical model of stockholder sovereignty will be untenable. With this in mind, the last part of the chapter discusses banking reform in transition economies.

Setting a Conceptual Framework

In order to discuss issues of corporate governance in transitional economies, let us first make clear what we mean by the transition: transition from which regime to which regime? In orthodox neoclassical economics, the latter should be something close to the neoclassical ideal of a regime of perfectly competitive markets. If all marketable factors of production are valued in competitive markets, the allocative efficiency of the economy would be assured by the maximization of residual after payments to those marketable factors. If the claimant of residual is identified with the stockholders, who do not gain any benefits other than the residual, they would be unanimously interested in maximizing the stock value of enterprises as reflecting the discounted sum of expected future flow of residual. Therefore, what is needed is to value enterprises competitively and effectively correct the management of enterprises if their values are lowered. The corporate governance structure that assures the sovereignty of the stockholders, combined with the competitive stock market, provides the necessary and sufficient institutional framework for that purpose. The task of the transition is to jump as quickly as possible to the regime in which such a framework prevails.

This neoclassical paradigm is crystal clear in its logic and useful for some purposes, but in our opinion its mechanical application to transitional policy may not always yield good results because of its incompatibility with historical constraints. We want to propose more practical and inclusive definitions of the transition and the posttransition that allow for more diverse approaches. We believe it important to recognize two central issues in considering corporate governance.

First, the conditions inherited from the communist regime and those extant at the outset of the transition constrain the feasible options for corporate governance design in the transition process both politically and economically. Second, the neoclassical stockholder-sovereignty model of corporate governance may not be the only efficient solution. Any corporate governance structure may be in complementary relationships with other institutional arrangements of the economy—such as the internal work organization of the enterprise, the labor market and financial market institutions, and so forth—and the performance of a governance structure cannot be judged independently of how those other institutions are arranged. More specifically, the stockholder-sovereignty model can be efficient when it is surrounded by a cluster of complementary institutions of a particular kind, such as the hierarchical work organization and competitive labor and capital markets. We cannot preclude the possibility that for another cluster of institutions including the team-oriented work organization, another type of corporate governance could be more efficient. Recent results of comparative institutional analysis indicate that these two systems may not be efficiency-rankable independent of technological parameters of the economy. Accordingly, the transition path could also be diverse. We will elaborate these points gradually.

Anticipating the diversity of institutional arrangements, we begin with a less specific definition of the time-line, composed of the *communist regime*, the *posttransition regime*, and the intermediate *transition process*. Because our immediate concern is about corporate governance, we deal only with ownership and management of enterprises as defining factors. First, we refer to the communist regime as the period when the following conditions prevail:

- (C1) All enterprises are owned by the state, and their continuity is at the discretion of the state.
- (C2) The management (directors) of enterprises are appointed by the state organ controlled by the Communist Party.

The transition process is defined as the time period characterized by the following conditions.

- (T1) All enterprises are transformed into corporations (corporatization or "commercialization"), but their ownership structures are in the process of being defined.
- (T2) The state has lost the discretionary power to appoint and dismiss the management of enterprises, yet no definite power to do so has emerged.

Finally, the posttransition regime is defined as the one satisfying the following conditions.

- (P1) The corporate governance structure has been well defined for each enterprise and the share ownership structure has become stable in a statistical sense.
- (P2) The management of enterprises is chosen through due process, defined by the corporate law. There is a credible mechanism operating to replace poorly performing management.

This time-line construction is purely conceptual and its mechanical application to any economy may entail some classification problems. For instance, Poland introduced the State Enterprise Law in 1981, while the Communist Party still held political control. It enabled the workers to appoint the managing director of enterprises through democratically elected workers' councils. At the same time, the state retained the power to create and liquidate enterprises. In China enterprises are now being corporatized, and varied ownership structures are being tried (see the chapter by Qian in this volume). The selection of the management, however, is still placed under the personnel administration of the Communist Party. According to the above definitions, we cannot say whether or not Poland in 1981 and China today are in the transition process. Ad hoc and somewhat inconsistent it may be, but we say that both Poland after 1981 and China today are in the transition process. We expect that the mass corporatization of enterprises in China will eventually lead to depoliticization of management appointments.

Note that we do not necessarily identify the transition with the privatization of enterprises. The majority stocks of a significant number of corporatized enterprises may remain owned by the state (as in Hungary). Also note that we do not include the market control of corporate governance as a condition for the arrival of the posttransition regime (for example, we do not observe it in Japan). We intend to include in that regime cases in which the majority or minority blocks of the stock of enterprises are stably owned by the state or insiders (workers, managers, enterprise pension funds, and the like) when there is a credible mechanism to punish poor management, if not through takeover. We deem that the existence of such a mechanism is imperative for an economic system to be viable without discretionary state intervention.

One of the purposes of this chapter is to inquire: If insider control is likely to evolve in many enterprises in the transition process because of conditions prevailing at the demise of the communist regime, what public policies would be desirable and politically feasible for transiting to an efficient posttransition regime? This inquiry will inevitably entail another important question: Is it possible for a posttransition regime to include a significant number of enterprises efficiently controlled by insiders?

Emergent Insider Control in the Transition

Insider control (either by the manager or the worker) appears to be a generic potential in the transition process, evolving out of inheritances of the communist regime. When the stagnation of communist regimes deepened in the 1970s and 1980s in Central and Eastern Europe, central planning bureaucrats tried to cope with the problem by relinquishing most of the planning instruments to the management of SOEs. The directors built up an irreversible jurisdictional authority within their own SOEs. The gradual retreat of the central planning authority ended with its sudden dismantling. The managers of the SOEs who had already carved out substantial controlling rights from the planning apparatus further enhanced their rights in the vacuum created by the collapse of the communist state. There seems to be nobody who has obvious legal or political power to dismiss the managers of ex-SOEs while they have the support of their workers.

The other quality of the communist regime that constrained the worker's freedom of job choice was their de facto job security. They were provided with medicare, child care, leisure facilities, housing, pensions, and so forth by the employing SOEs or the state. Workers had strong stakes at the employing enterprise. After the collapse of communism and the end of its "egalitarian" ideology, the workers were threatened by the possibility of losing those vested interests. Their fear may be greater the more uncertain the outcome of corporatization of their enterprises. Their possible opposition to massive privatization may have to be overcome by virtually giving them a substantial portion of enterprise assets.

Needless to say, the actualization of the potential of insider control varies across economies. We define insider control as a majority or substantial block-holding by the insiders in the case of privatization, or strong assertion of insider interests in strategic enterprise decision-making when the enterprises remain owned by the state. Among possible factors conditioning the extent of insider control, the most important ones are the degree of management autonomy and the workers' strength against communist control in the final stage of the communist regime, and the political autonomy of the privatization authority against the various interest groups in the transition process.

At one end of this continuum, there is Poland. As already noted, even before the fall of the communist regime, the workers councils, composed of fifteen members elected by the employees, had attained a powerful position analogous to the board of directors in capitalist corporations, including the right to appoint the director and approve the annual plans of the enterprise. Once the transition phase began, the workers quickly moved to capture control of the assets of the enterprises before any market-based privatization plan was to be put into effect. The most common form of state property transformation worked as follows. Rather than corporatizing, the viable SOE was "liquidated" and a new company, in which the majority of the workers of the liquidated SOE became stockholders, leased or bought the assets. The much-publicized massive privatization through state-sponsored investment funds, an artifact of the neoclassical dogma of stockholder sovereignty, has thus been virtually defeated by the coalition of workers and managers of the better enterprises.

Russia is a case of strong manager control. The director of the SOE, who had already built a virtually autonomous empire in the communist regime, became almost invincible after the dismantling of the party and its planning apparatus. For any privatization plan to be implemented, it would have had to recognize this de facto control power of the director (see the chapter by Litwack in this volume). The State Committee on Property Administration (GKI), which was charged with mass privatization, has become the most politically successful reform authority in Russia through its generous accommodation of insiders' interests.

The details of the scheme are described in the chapter by Akamatsu in this volume. Simply put, according to the scheme the privatization of the SOE proceeds through three stages. In the first stage, mandated by a Yeltsin decree of July 1991, the SOEs were to be corporatized and made legally autonomous entities, although all the shares were held initially by the state (the Federal Property Foundation) and administered by GKI. In the second stage, the insiders (the workers) chose an option for their privatization benefits from three variants specified by GKI, and the local committee of GKI approved an adopted plan. At this stage, the managers and the workers obtained a large share free-of-charge, or a majority share purchased at discounted value, depending on the adopted variant. In the third stage, the remaining shares were auctioned for vouchers that had been given to every citizen of Russia, sold in a package to investment tenders, and kept by state control for the next several years.

The full implications of the scheme have not been worked out yet, but so far the insiders have overwhelmingly selected an option to guarantee them a majority share—that is, the option that gives managers and workers together individual ownership of 51 percent of the equity at a low purchase price (at 1.7 times the July 1992 book value of assets). The managers can also increase their shares by purchasing vouchers in the market or by buying back shares from their own workers and markets (the workers are now given incentives to sell their shares tax-free). At the same time, investment funds that participate in voucher auctioning are limited initially in their ownership in one privatized SOE to 10 percent (raised to 25 percent after January 1994). The board of directors of the newly privatized SOE, before the first meeting of shareholders (which has to take place within one year after privatization), is composed exclusively of the general manager and worker representatives, except for representatives of the local GKI and the Property Foundation. As a result, the insiders, particularly the managers, have built solid controlling power in their enterprises.[1]

At the other end of spectrum is the former German Democratic Republic (East Germany), whose privatization process under the centralized privatization authority, the *Treuhandanstaldt* (THA), is described in detail in the chapter by von Thadden in this volume. Even in East Germany, however, asset stripping by the insiders was an imminent danger at the time of the demise of the communist regime. The only factor that prevented the subsequent development of insider control was the authority given to the THA. von Thadden shows that the institutional commitment to complete privatization by the end of 1994 prevented the THA from being susceptible to influence by the insiders. The recruitment of professionally capable THA managers from western Germany is also a positive factor unique to East Germany. The

1. In a decree issued by Yeltsin on December 24, 1993 (N2284), some measures were introduced to curb the tendency toward strong insider control. Requirements for worker payment for benefit options were made somewhat stringent (for example, the amount of the first installment for stocks bought with a discount was increased). It was also stipulated that the number of representatives of employee-stockholders may not be more than one-third of the board of directors, and that managers or workers may not sit on the board representing the interests of the state. That these provisions were thought necessary may suggest that such practices had been widespread, without check.

privatization of the SOEs was to be completed predominantly through the partial or whole acquisition of assets by West German (former Federal Republic of Germany) corporations. In that sense, the privatization in East Germany may be said to be comparable to a takeover in capital markets, although it was mediated by the centralized privatization agency. Even in this case, however, the end result of the transition would be the absorption of the SOEs into the West German corporate governance structure, which is different from the neoclassical model of stockholder sovereignty. This governance structure is characterized by insider (worker) participation in the supervisory councils through the legal requirement of codetermination.

The Czech Republic and Hungary provide intermediate cases. The insiders were weaker in the era of the communist regime in comparison with Poland or Russia, and the political power of the state (the privatization agency) in the transition process is weaker in comparison with East Germany. As a result, the tendency toward insider control has not been clearly resolved. Privatization in the Czech Republic is widely viewed as an ideal example of an approximation of the neoclassical model of outside stockholders' control through "voucher" privatization. The matter does not seem to be so simple, however. The privatization process is initiated with the decentralized submissions of a "privatization project," which can be done by anybody. The Ministry of Privatization has the centralized power to select a project. The Ministry has a political preference for projects including the competitive bidding of shares for vouchers. Nevertheless, project proposals for direct sales of assets to a new company formed by a group of insiders are also possible. According to data from the Ministry of Privatization, and quoted in Frydman, Rapaczynski, and Earle (1993, p. 84), only 53 percent of the total book value of privatized enterprises have gone to vouchers. The first preference of managers who were able to submit the most informative plans is said to be buyout (Frydman, Rapaczynski, and Earle 1993 p. 81). The tendency toward insider control surely exists, but has been moderated by the centralization of project selection.

In Hungary, a self-management system similar to the 1981 Polish scheme was introduced in 1984 (Law on Enterprise Councils), although the relative authority of managers in relation of the workers was stronger. The free-market-oriented postcommunist government adopted a decentralized privatization scheme that gave the initiative to privatize to the enterprise councils, subject to approval of the State Property Agency (SPA). In contrast to the semicentralized Czech approach, this scheme seems to have provided more room for maneuvering by the managers to retain control and to fend off "outsider" intervention. Privatized enterprises tend to be cross-owned by other enterprises, banks, and the state (SPA). Unfortunately, because of the unavailability of data, the extent of cross-holding is not precisely known, but something similar to the corporate grouping in Japan may be emergent.

Thus, although there is a variation in its degree, the tendency toward insider control is manifested everywhere in Eastern and Central Europe except for the newly emergent entrepreneurial enterprises and joint ventures with foreign corporations. This is an evolutionary outcome of legacies of the communist regime, which can be moderated only by a strong privatization agency. But an attempt to introduce outside stockholder control does not seem to effectively counteract this tide. Privatization of SOEs is ex ante constrained by the legacy of socialism, and in most it is cases ex post constrained by the weakness of the privatization agency in relation to the inside interest groups (see the chapter by Roland in this volume).

This lesson may be instructive for China, which has now begun experimenting with various corporate governance structures. Even in China, where the Communist Party has retained solid control over the personnel selection and dismissal of management of the SOEs, the evolutionary tendency toward insider control is not unknown. The chapter by Qian illustrates this point in detail. One commonly observed method for enhancing insider control is the spin-off of subsidiaries by the management of the SOEs and the leasing or sale of assets to these subsidiaries, created for this purpose. The "non-state-owned" enterprises thus created, together with smaller township and village enterprises, constitute the essential carriers of vital entrepreneurial initiatives in present-day China. This state asset stripping by insiders is often regarded as illegitimate by citizens and, unless placed under a transparent due process, this "privatization" process may provoke political backlash. The mechanical application of the neoclassical paradigm, however, such as voucher privatization by investment funds, does not seem to be an alternative solution. We next present theoretical reasons for this.

Inadequacy of the Investment Fund Scheme for the Transition

Many economists have argued that the creation of investment funds (IF) that hold a substantial block of shares of the privatized enterprise may serve as an effective external check on insider control. The hope is that the IF would be interested in capital gains made possible by efficiency-enhancing restructuring, while at the same time being capable of exercising sufficient pressure or control over the management to implement the restructuring (see the chapter by Akamatsu for a detailed description of the IF in Russia and a comparison with those in the Czech Republic).

Nevertheless, it generally seems to be the case that the effectiveness of IFs in external monitoring has been limited. First of all, facing a substantial insider holding of shares, even a block of shares held by the IF may not be sufficient for effectively controlling the privatized SOE (as in Russia). To advance the case for the active role of the IF in corporate governance, a well-known proposition by Shleifer-Vishny, which points to the importance of a blockholder, is often mentioned. What the proposition asserts, however, is that the existence of a blockholder is "necessary" for overcoming free-riding by small, passive shareholders in disciplining inefficient management by a takeover. Differing from the presumption of the Shleifer-Vishny model, the Russian situation is characterized by the existence of a large body of inside shareholders. How can the minority IF overcome this imbalance of power at a critical moment when the possible dismissal of the inside managers (and massive labor shearing) should be placed on the agenda?

Second, the IFs were formed as privatization intermediaries and funded primarily by vouchers that were entrusted by investors or purchased by the IF. They are therefore under pressure to realize reasonable dividends for investors. If the markets for shares develop, however, they paradoxically may not be interested in monitoring and restructuring individual enterprises. By investing in the market index, like funds in developed, securities-oriented economies, the IF would be able to perform at least as well as the market (this possibility is also emphasized by Phelps and others 1993). To respond to this concern, it has been proposed that the range of portfolio selection of the IF be restricted. But such a move would be inconsistent with the IF function of expected profit maximization, and it would effectively transform the

IF into a holding company. The next issue raises a question about the ability of the IF to function as a holding company.

Third, the privatized SOE may be in desperate need of additional funding for restructuring, but the IF, as a share redistributing intermediary, may not be able to readily mobilize financial resources to meet such needs. Even if the IF could mobilize new financial resources, the insider majority control may imply tremendous agency costs for equity financing. The management and the workers may be interested in consuming on-the-job potential residual before it is distributed as dividends. The IF may be able to mediate bank loans because the IF is often controlled by a holding company that also controls a bank (as in Russia) or is owned by a bank (as in the Czech Republic). In this case, however, the conflict of interest issue needs to be addressed (see the chapter by Akamatsu). For example, the assets of the IF may have been heavily invested in a failing enterprise and the holding company/bank may be interested in funneling funds to salvage it at the depositors' risk.

These discussions are not intended to deny any role for the IF in the governance structure in the transition process. On the contrary, it may be an indispensable institutional component in counteracting the ill-effects of insider control. The point is to argue that the IF *alone* may not effectively resolve the problem of corporate governance design in the transition process posed by the evolutionary tendency toward insider control. To attempt to rely solely on the IF may actually prolong the transitional process by encouraging inefficient influence of insiders to reduce outside intervention. The management may sabotage restructuring by colluding with the workers to fend off the outsider intervention. Further, public policy that may be needed to foster the development of other institutions, such as the banks, may lag behind.

The transition economy has to face the evolutionary tendency toward insider control, and to do so an application of the abstract neoclassical model or the straightforward transplant of the Anglo-American model seems to be of limited value. In the next section, we propose an alternative model of external control of the insider control enterprise based on the idea of "selective intervention." Following the presentation of the theoretical model, we discuss whether it suggests any public policy approach toward the insider control problem in the transition process.

Bank Syndication and Contingent Governance

The insider-controlled enterprise may have unique incentive problems, even if it is potentially productive. The management may try to borrow to build an empire (in the case of management control), to spend on nonproductive projects to enhance worker benefits, or to construct plants excessively equipped with machines to increase per capita outputs, while staying away from risky entrepreneurial projects (adverse selection problems). The workers may shirk to free ride on each others' efforts when team work is involved (moral hazard problem). The insiders may have incentives to consume as much of the revenue of the enterprise as possible on the job or in the form of supracompetitive compensation before repayments to lenders or dividend payments to shareholders are made. Poor management may be tolerated out of collegial compassion.

To cope with the possible inefficiencies of such incentive problems, some external agents must play active roles in monitoring the insider-controlled enterprises. To facilitate the following discussion, it is useful to distinguish conceptually three phases of investors' monitoring in reference to the timing of investment: *ex ante* monitoring, in which potential new projects and/or new clients are evaluated to cope with the problem of adverse selection; interim (ongoing) monitoring, to uncover moral hazard problems arising from the divergence of interests between outside investors and the insiders, as well as free-riding among the insiders; and, finally, *ex post* monitoring, to verify the true financial state of the enterprise, to assure the (re)payment of debts or dividends, and to punish the management in the event of a failure to do so.

This section presents a purely theoretical model of corporate governance that resolves incentive problems of insider control by integrating the three stages of monitoring by a single bank, while other investors can diversify risk. The model is derived by a modification of the bankruptcy procedure proposed by Bebchuck (1988) and Aghion, Hart, and Moore (1992), which attempts to strike a balance between the merits of equity and debt contracts as controlling instruments. The novelty of the model presented below is to explicitly consider the incentives of the monitor—in this case, a bank—to monitor the insider-controlled enterprise in an integrative way, while preserving the essential feature of their model.

Suppose that when the viable insider-controlled enterprise is in need of external long-term investment funds, a bank that has had a long-term relationship with the enterprise organizes a loan syndicate with many other banks. This lead bank (LB) may own a minority share of the borrowing enterprise up to a certain limit (say, 5 percent). The LB is assumed to perform the commercial banking function by running the major payment system accounts as well as the deposit accounts of the borrowing enterprise. These two attributes may provide the information advantage necessary for the bank to be an LB. The question is how this advantage can be utilized for the reduction of agency costs of the external financing and monitoring costs, rather than allowing the LB to exploit its private benefits at the cost of other banks and investors.

Suppose that the LB is limited to provide only a minority share, say 20 percent, of the syndicate loans, but the LB must guarantee the repayment of the claims of other member banks (this stringent requirement will be relaxed later). This imposes a heavy responsibility on the LB. In return, however, the LB may charge a syndicate management premium, as well as enjoying the benefits of running the payment settlement and deposit accounts of the borrowing enterprise. Meanwhile, the IF and other investors may be active in share markets, evaluating the performance of the enterprise through trading on the basis of their own interim monitoring.

When the enterprise becomes unable to meet repayment obligations, the LB is obliged to buy the defaulted claims of syndicate member banks. The LB then completely writes off these debts and converts them into new equity. The LB either auctions off the new equity rights to reorganization specialists or holds them for a specified period of time (for instance, three years). In the latter case, the LB is engaged in restructuring the defaulting enterprise by replacing the managers, laying off workers, liquidating some assets, and so forth. If the insiders refuse to cooperate, the LB could threaten to invoke the liquidation procedure. After restructuring within the said period, the LB may sell the amount of shares beyond the normal limit (5 percent, for example) for possible capital gains from restructuring. In either case, the restructured enterprise would be transformed into an outsider-controlled enterprise, while the insiders are penalized for debt default by the loss of their share values, and possibly the loss of employment continuation values as well. If there is no prospect for capital gains from restructuring, the LB may decide to liquidate the enterprise. In this case the uncovered value of debts would be born by the LB.

The scheme has merit. First, in contrast to the Aghion-Hart-Moore model, the postbankruptcy procedure is administered by the LB rather than by the court, which may lack expertise in ex post management of the bankrupt enterprise. The LB is clearly advantaged in information useful for ex post management, but prevented from using it at the expense of other creditors' interests because of its repayment guarantee.

In our scheme the LB is also responsible for ex ante monitoring to cope with adverse selection of the borrowing enterprise and for interim monitoring to control its moral hazard. The LB would be motivated to earnestly perform ex ante and interim monitoring in order to avoid the heavy costs of liquidation and/or restructuring arising from debt guarantees for other member banks.

Second, generally speaking, from the point of view of the bank, there are tradeoffs between the diversification of lending risk and incentives to monitor. An arm's-length relationship between the bank and the borrower may allow the bank to diversify risk, provided that risk is distributed independently of bank action. But risk diversification may dilute the incentives of the bank to monitor the enterprise ex ante and interim. At the same time, the exclusive lending relationship will not only expose the bank to idiosyncratic risk, but may also dilute its commitment to ex post monitoring because once lending is made, the continuation of the enterprise may become ex post desirable even for the bank.

As noted above, in our scheme the LB is certainly motivated to monitor. But what about the risk diversification opportunities of the LB? Does the proposed scheme not amount to the same thing as the LB bearing full risk costs, as in exclusive relational lending? That is, is the LB not exposed to the same degree of idiosyncratic risk as the relational bank? Why then is syndication worth the trouble?

Suppose that a sufficient number of qualified banks that have the required monitoring capability exist to allow for workable competition among them (roughly, the number is not too small nor too large). Suppose that each of them has a mutually exclusive group of customer enterprises for which they function as LBs. These banks become ordinary syndicate members for nonaffiliated enterprises for which other banks act as LBs. In other words, there is "reciprocal delegation of monitoring" (Sheard 1994) among the banks. Other minor banks may participate in any syndicate as ordinary members. Responsible monitoring by the LB saves the duplication of monitoring costs, particularly by minor banks.

Now let us modify the described scheme in such a way that the group of qualified banks mutually agree to rebate a fraction of the LB's guaranteed repayment to them in case the revenue of the LB from liquidation of assets or the prerestructuring auction falls short of a certain level. Such reciprocal arrangements may spread the cost of risk-bearing among qualified banks, while somewhat diluting the incentives for the LB to monitor. The modified syndicate arrangement is a device to strike a balance between the conflicting requirements of risk diversification and incentive provision.

The third advantage of the scheme is that the risk of bad performance by the borrowing enterprise is not distributed independently of insider and bank actions. The risk may be reduced by more intensive ex ante and interim monitoring of the LB. The requirement of syndication severs qualified banks from exclusive relationships with the borrowing enterprise. This would reduce the hazard of the banks being captured by the interests of the customer enterprises and make them more independent in their judgements at the ex ante monitoring stage.

Fourth, after the initial investment is sunk, the continuation of a bad project might become ex post profitable, if bad debt were written off. In such a situation, if the relationship between the bank and the enterprise is that of the exclusive relational bank, they would be induced to renegotiate. The enterprise's insiders may have strong motives to negotiate for the survival of the enterprise to save the loss of employment continuation values if the labor market is imperfectly competitive. The bank may be induced to accept an insider's concession, while keeping the insider's control intact. Such a prospect would dilute the ex ante and interim incentives of the insiders. In our scheme, the shift of control rights can be automatically triggered by a debt-equity swap when the insider-controlled enterprise defaults. Insider control is maintained contingent only on the financial viability of the enterprise. The corporate governance structure implied by the scheme may thus be called *contingent*.

The LB or the reorganizer (IFs, or another enterprise) that acquires the shares in the restructuring auction has incentives to restructure for capital gains. As opposed to the creditor rescue operation, the restructuring agent can secure future returns to restructuring costs without fearing the emancipation of the rescued enterprise. Thus, premature liquidation (Type I error) may be avoided, while the threat of punishing poorly performing insiders is made credible. This is the essential feature of the Aghion-Hart-Moore model.

The fifth major advantage of the scheme is that the contingent governance structure may have positive incentive effects on the insiders. The contingent governance implies that as long as the insider-controlled enterprise is financially healthy and able to repay its debts without any problem, the insiders remain as residual claimants. If they always remain residual claimants, regardless of the financial state of the enterprise, the moral hazard of free-riding among insiders would become a problem, or sheer bad luck might make the insiders lose large asset values (in financial and human capital) in liquidation. These possibilities may be prevented by the participation of the LB, which may restructure the failed yet viable enterprise, but imposes harsh penalties when the postbankruptcy situation is hopeless.

If the contingent governance is efficiently designed, the insiders may develop incentives to accumulate the internal financial resources to become autonomous from possible external intervention. The relative autonomy of the enterprise from external loans would in turn stimulate insiders' incentives for greater effort, because the fruit of their effort would accrue to them as residual claimants. Thus, once the contingent governance is put in effect, the virtuous cycle of insider control and enterprise growth may be generated up to a certain threshold point. (The possibility of such dynamics, together with the efficiency property of the contingent governance structure, is analyzed in Aoki 1994.)

Eclectic Approach—Probably the Best in the Transition

We have shown a theoretical possibility of a governance structure that can cope with the unique incentive problems arising from insider control. But we have assumed that the insider control enterprise is viable and that there is a banking sector comprising a sufficient number of banks capable of assuming the heavy responsibility of lead banks. These last two conditions do not hold in the transition process. The privatized enterprise may need to be restructured, for which outside financing is needed. Nevertheless, incentive problems of insider control may be rampant and any bank may consider it too risky to assume the responsibility of the LB. First of all, no bank may have either the financial resources to bear the responsibility or the capacity to monitor.

The merit of the theoretical exercise in the last section was to show that a corporate governance structure alternative to the neoclassical model of stockholder sovereignty is conceptually possible in the post-transition regime. The contingent governance structure may not be just a passive reaction to the insider control problem. Rather, it may have an active *raison d'etre*: to facilitate the development of a team-oriented production organization characterized by lateral cross-functional coordination, joint task responsibilities, mutual help, and the like in which worker skills and shared knowledge become specific to the organization. According to a recent achievement of comparative institutional analysis, we cannot unequivocally rank the team-oriented work organization and the traditional hierarchical organization according to efficiency criteria. The former may perform better in an industry where coordination among tasks is relatively more important because tasks are complementary, while the latter organization may perform better in the industry where flexible reallocation of scarce corporate assets among tasks is important (Aoki 1994b).

The kind of financial institution that would be desirable to develop would depend on the prevailing work organization. If workers' skills and shared knowledge become organization-specific, and thus not individually marketable, stock value maximization may not be consistent with internal and allocative efficiency. This is because the value maximization criteria presupposes that all factors of production other than fixed factors are market valued. If the insiders constitute an immobile factor of production as a team, the enterprise ought to strike a balance between insiders' interests and outsiders' interests. Games between them may no longer be zero-sum, however, and there may be gains from cooperation (Aoki 1984). Insiders' shared rights of control in corporate governance (as in West Germany) or outsiders' selective intervention through the contingent governance (as in Japan) may facilitate an approximation of the cooperative solution. Thus the bank-oriented financial system may be complementary to the team-oriented organization, while the market-oriented financial system is complementary to the hierarchical organization, as the neoclassical paradigm asserts.

In what direction will the evolution of the transitional economies lead? One scenario may be that the hierarchical aspect of the work organization in the SOE would reform itself so that task assignments in the organization are made more on the basis of individual skills. For this direction, the complementary development of the capital market institutions would be necessary, because the efficiency of such an organization can be best valued by residual after competitive payments for individual skills. Another scenario may be that the collegial aspect of the work organization in the SOE would develop into an efficient, team-oriented work organization. For this direction, the development of banking institutions might be complementary. Still other scenarios may be feasible. The transition economy may take advantage of the latecomer being able to develop a hybrid by combining the two types of organizations. Or, if the transition economy fails to develop proper governance and financial institutions, it might be locked in permanent stagnation. Nobody seems to be able to predict with certainty which scenario is the most likely.

We may posit that an eclectic approach is an option in the transition process. That is, instead of pursuing solely the possibility of external control of the enterprise through the development of capital markets, or that of banking institutions, it is better to foster their simultaneous development in the transition. Only spontaneous development of organizations through competition would determine the dominant system in the posttransition regime.

Other Reasons to Develop Banking Institutions in the Transition

In the model of syndicate lending presented above, ex ante, interim, and ex post monitoring of the enterprises are all integrated and delegated to a single LB. In contrast, in a highly advanced securities-oriented financial system, such as the Anglo-American economy, these three phases of monitoring are dispersed among various intermediaries, information-processing agents, and corporate and legal institutions possessed of different specialized expertise. For example, ex ante monitoring is performed by investment banks for large enterprises, venture capitalists for entrepreneurial start-ups, and commercial banks for smaller firms; interim monitoring is performed by rating firms, commercial banks, funds of various types, market arbitrageurs, and so forth; ex post monitoring is done by accounting firms, the bankruptcy court and reorganization specialists, takeover raiders, LBO partners, and the like. In general, the transition economy that has evolved from a state of an absence of financial markets initially lacks the accumulation of such diverse monitoring resources. The integrated delegation of the three phases of monitoring to a single bank is a way to economize in the use of scarce monitoring resources.

Further, there is a positive reason for the integration of the three phases of monitoring, rather than their decentralization, to bring about better results. In the transition process, ex ante monitoring of the corporatized SOE, if not that of a new, innovative start-up, would be unlikely to require highly sophisticated project analysis. The urgent problem with the corporatized SOE, privatized or not, is to restructure itself rather than to initiate new projects at the technological and commercial frontier. If this is so, the relevant ex ante monitoring would be more on the organizational capability of the corporatized SOE to absorb, adapt, and improve the existing organizational, engineering, and commercialization know-how. For that, the bank that would maintain a long-run relationship with the borrowing enterprise may be in an informationally advantageous position because it can feed back information available from interim monitoring to the assessment of relevant organizational capability.

It may also be the case that ex ante monitoring and interim monitoring are complementary to ex post monitoring. Even if the financial state of the enterprise is critically worsened, the IF may be less adept at finding the problem when the accounting methods are not very informative and disclosure requirements are lax. Even if they are competent enough to find problems at an early stage, they may encounter resistance in the insiders to yielding control power. In contrast, the bank would mediate daily payment settlements for the customer enterprise as well as roll over short-term loans or discount trade bills necessary for financing working capital. Such operations would give the bank a power similar to that of being able to partially open the books. At the time of automatic transfer of control triggered by debt contracts in the event of repayment default, the bank may utilize knowledge accumulated through interim monitoring to exercise its judgement of whether the enterprise has a chance to survive or would be better served by liquidation.

The merits discussed of the integration of the three phases of monitoring presume that a single bank would credibly commit ex ante to interim and ex post monitoring. Such a commitment is not credible in the highly developed, market-oriented system where debt instruments are easily marketed. The initial investors may get rid of their claims in the market rather than bear bankruptcy or rescue costs ex post if they are in a position to find possible problems with borrowers at an early phase.

As already noted, however, the necessity of developing a sound banking sector should not be taken as precluding the simultaneous functioning of financial markets. On the contrary, competitive and informative financial markets can be complementary to bank monitoring. Instead of the formation of syndicates, the bank may underwrite and guarantee bond issues of the customer enterprise. The price formation of the securities of the enterprise in the market can compete with the interim monitoring of the bank, pointing out its mistakes or remedying possible moral hazard. If the IF develops restructuring expertise in the posttransition regime, it can bid for the equity that the LB auctions off after the debt-equity swap operation. The point is, however, that the role of a sound banking sector, composed of a reasonable number of qualified banks, could not be fully substituted for the financial markets when the magnitude of insider control is substantial.

Banking Reform Needed in the Transition

Although the case for the development of a sound banking system in the transition process appears to be strong, the current state of banking institutions in transition economies seems to be far from that needed to perform the kind of tasks suggested above. Is there any hope that they will develop the capacity and incentives to do so? What kind of banking regulations are to be instituted in the transition process to encourage such developments?

In transitional economies, most of the banks are either successors or spin-offs of the former state banks or newly established agent banks of corporatized SOEs. Large commercial banks in Central Europe were created in the last few years with the split of the former state mono-bank into a central bank and a number of commercial banks. The loan portfolio was distributed to the new commercial banks along regional (Poland) or sectoral lines (Czech Republic, Hungary). Most of the deposits are with specialized savings institutions, channeled to commercial banks in the form of refinancing credits through central banks. The spin-offs of the former state banks are still owned by the state and their privatization is under preparation (Poland, Hungary), or their majority ownership has now been privatized (Czech Republic). Private commercial banks have been established recently, yet the former state banks are still dominant in assets. In Russia there are now approximately 1,700 independent commercial banks (see the chapter by Belyanova and Rozinsky for a detailed account of the present-day Russian banking institutions). Among them, about 700 banks, including most of the larger banks, are spin-offs of the former Soviet specialized banks, which are now primarily owned by former SOEs. For these banks the sets of shareholders and borrowers are the same.

The state bank in the centrally planned economy was not an autonomous financial institution, but an administrative instrument of centralized planning to control the SOE. As is well known, one of the most important causes of the failure of centrally planned economies was the soft budget constraint on the SOE because of the lack of commitment by the state bank not to refinance ex post inefficient projects. Financing the existing SOE became automatic because of the political necessity of maintaining employment (latent insider control problem), the rising bargaining power of managers, and possibly because refinancing made economic sense once the initial investment was sunk. Insolvency criteria did not exist in the communist regime, and thus soft credits could not be distinguished from outright giveaways. A possible problem with the spin-offs of former state banks is the continuation of soft credits as a form of inertia. Half of all commercial bank loans extended in 1992 in Russia were in the form of directed credits funded by the Central Bank or the budget and channeled through these banks (World Bank 1993, p. 2).

The newly created agent banks may have their own problems. In Russia more than 1,000 agent banks have been created from nothing since 1990. They were usually created by enterprises or by groups of enterprises to manage their cash flows and to perform payment system transactions on their behalf. These banks also make loans, primarily with funds from enterprise deposits and interbank markets, as well as funds in the process of collection. A possible problem with the agent bank is that, as with most relational banks in developing economies, they are captured by the interests of the parent enterprise and cannot act as independent sources of monitoring. Their credits may be exposed to risks that are too idiosyncratic.

For banks to operate on a sound basis, it is necessary that their assets are sufficiently diversified. When the funding basis of the bank is thin, however, as is the case with most agent banks, it is difficult to diversify lending while meeting the funds requirements of the parent enterprises. The formation of a loan syndicate may be a possible response. The difficulty is that the sheer number of agent banks and their small size seems to prevent the development of syndicates, because the question of which bank ought to bear the responsibility for syndicate organization (ex ante monitoring), interim monitoring, and how to set the priority for claims cannot be settled easily.

In spite these problems, however, the banking sector in transitional economies appears to be gradually evolving as a viable institution. Peter Dittus (1994) recognized the increasing spread between the deposit and lending rate and the recent noticeable decline of net lending to enterprises in Central European economies. By careful examination, he tentatively concludes that the decline of lending is not a result of a credit crunch from the government deficit, and it can be regarded as a hardening of budget constraints for the enterprises. He cautiously notes: "clearly, the environment in which banks are operating and their behavior have changed much more than seems to be commonly acknowledged. It has also become evident, however, that the difficulties remain to be overcome are substantial" (p. 34). The chapter by Belyanova and Rozinsky in this volume indicates that the difference between better spin-offs of the ex state banks and newly created banks are beginning to be blurred, and some of them seem to be evolving as viable institutions in spite of the problems.

What difficulties are to be overcome in order for better banks to evolve into active monitors of insider control? Let us try to identify some basic problems to be addressed.

The first is the dilemma between risk diversification and monitoring. In order to be free from soft credits and the excessive exposure to idiosyncratic risks associated with relational lending, it is desirable that the bank diversify its loans. As noted earlier, one method to achieve this is to form syndicates. At the same time, the formation of loan syndicates may dilute incentives for the bank to monitor. How can we resolve this dilemma?

The second problem is related to the social costs of bankruptcy. As we have hinted, one possible advantage of a bank-centered monitoring mechanism is that the default of debt repayment can trigger the automatic shift of control rights from the insider to the creditor bank, even if the latter does not own a block of shares. The mechanical application of bankruptcy procedures would be unproductive given the current state of transitional economies.[2] The newly corporatized SOE seems to need outside financing, and sometimes subsidies, to be viable and perform the necessary restructuring. How can such finance and subsidy be made without perpetuating the soft credit relationship between the bank and the enterprise?

As previously noted, there are some 1,700 banks today in Russia. This number is simply too large, and the average size of banks is too small to induce risk diversification and delegate responsible monitoring to single banks. Nevertheless, that more than 1,000 banks devoid of the traits of the old state bank system have emerged from scratch in only a few years may be considered as a positive sign of the potential for vigorous evolutionary change. It is said that some of the new banks were

---

2. Factors pointed out by many authors as working against the mechanical application of the bankruptcy procedure in the transition: without a sound payment system, many viable enterprises may be forced into bankruptcy by a mere chain reaction; the asset registry does not exist and private ownership in land is not legally well defined; the bankruptcy procedure may involve costs of maintaining a system of commercial courts; and the lack of expertise and discipline in receivership, and the absence of clear rules regarding claim subordination, may also incur additional social costs of bankruptcy.

organized and run by young, competent people (see the chapter by Belyanova and Rozinsky in this volume). Such a situation may suggest that, once a prudent and competitive regulatory framework is provided and a stable macroeconomic policy environment is set, some of the existing banks may be given an opportunity to develop as banks accountable for external monitoring.

To emancipate banks from fragmented, exclusive relational banking, there is a need to drastically increase the minimum capital requirements of banks. Such regulation would provide an impetus for acquisition and mergers among banks. Further, it would be desirable to limit the lending of the bank to a single enterprise—for example, to one-quarter of the bank's capital. Such measures would induce banks to restrain the volume of relational lending. Nevertheless, our purpose is not to promote arm's-length banking. If portfolio diversification by banks were merely to accelerate arm's-length relationships, a vacuum would remain for external monitoring of the insider control enterprise. Because many banks are now owned by (a group of) enterprises, the movement toward arm's-length banking following the Anglo-American system may not be likely. Through the process of merger and acquisition, originally close bank-enterprise relationships may be diluted, but maintained with some distance. The enterprise would likely hold major payment system accounts only with a few banks. Those banks would be likely candidates for the role of lead banks if lending diversification should lead to organized syndication.

In the process of past hyperinflation, bad debts of enterprises appear to have been largely wiped out in Central and Eastern European transitional economies, but it has not solved the recapitalization problem of banks. On one hand, enterprises appear to rely upon intricate networks of trade credits rather than banks credits. Default on trade credits by one large enterprise may trigger chain reactions. On the other hand, banks appear to rely on lending based on interbank markets and funds in the collection process, but they have not acquired a solid deposit basis yet, except for deposits by foreign currencies. Spin-offs of state banks also rely upon the central bank's directed credits as lending sources. One solution to cope with all these problems may be to induce the development of an interbank payment settlement system based on trade bills drawable on partner banks by enterprises. The central bank should then gradually limit its capital infusion to the banking sector to "neutral" rediscounting of eligible trade bills at the window rather than directing credits to particular enterprises by discretion. Such a development would not only resolve the problem of supplying money on a sound basis, but also increase the capacity and incentives of the banks to monitor customer enterprises. Nevertheless, necessary state subsidies should be made through the budgetary process, separated from the commercial banking sector. Only through such a neutral stance of the central bank and insulation of the commercial banking sector from discretionary subsidization can the soft credits of banks be reduced.

Bibliography

Aghion, Philippe, Oliver Hart, and John Moore. 1992. "The Economics of Bankruptcy Reform." *Journal of Law, Economics and Organization* 8: 523–46.

Aoki, Masahiko. 1984. *The Co-Operative Game Theory of the Firm.* Oxford, U.K.: Clarendon.

Aoki, Masahiko. 1994a. "Contingent Governance of Teams: Analysis of Institutional Complementarity." *International Economic Review* 35: 657–76.

———. 1994b. "An Evolutionary Parable of the Gains from International Organizational Diversity." Stanford University. Mimeo.

Bebchuk, L. 1988. "A New Approach to Corporate Reorganizations." *Harvard Law Review* 101: 775–804.

Berg, Andrew. 1994. "The Logistics of Privatization in Poland." In Olivier Jean Blanchard, Kenneth A. Froot, and Jeffrey D. Sachs, eds., *The Transition in Eastern Europe.* Chicago, Illinois: The University of Chicago Press.

Dittus, Peter. 1994. "Corporate Governance in Central Europe: The Role of Banks." Bank of International Settlements, Basle. Mimeo.

Frydman, Roman, Andrzej Rapaczynski, and John S. Earle. 1993. *The Privatization Process in Europe*. Prague: Central European University Press.

Phelps, E. S., Roman Frydman, A. Rapaczynski, and A. Scheifer. 1993. "Needed Mechanisms of Corporate Governance and Finance in Eastern Europe." European Bank for Reconstruction and Development, Working Paper #1, London.

Sheard, Paul. 1994. "Reciprocal Delegated Monitoring in the Japanese Main Bank System." *Journal of the Japanese and International Economies* 8: 1–21.

World Bank. 1993. "The Banking System in Transition—Russia." Europe and Central Asia Department Report 12763. Washington, D.C.

2

Political Economy Issues of Ownership Transformation in Eastern Europe

Gérard Roland

It is probably no exaggeration to state that analysts of transition in Eastern Europe have strongly underestimated the political constraints to reform. The fall of communism and the advent of democratic regimes in 1989 were widely applauded by the people of these countries, raising the general level of expectations. Analysts thought that a drastic and rapid move to the market economy would most likely be accepted, despite the inevitable transitional pains imposed on the population. In practice, things have been much more difficult and signs of political opposition and backlash have increased, as witnessed by recent elections in Poland, Russia, and Hungary. Understanding correctly some of the basic political economy issues of transition is thus crucial for formulating realistic policies of transition in these countries.

In this chapter we focus on the political economy issues of privatization and restructuring. Various questions are raised in that context. How serious are the political constraints to reform? What is their influ-

This paper was written for the World Bank project, "The Role of Banks in Corporate Governance in Transforming Economies." An important part of this paper is derived from joint work with Mathias Dewatripont. I benefited from discussions with Erik Berglöf and Janos Kornai. I thank John Litwack and Juro Teranishi for their helpful comments and suggestions.

ence on the design of reform programs? To what extent can the differences in privatization policies in various countries be explained by differences in political constraints? The answers to these questions depend very much on the view one has of political decisionmaking, and in particular of the relative power or weakness of governments. We define strong governments as governments with the power to set the agenda: they are free to design and propose reform packages submitted to a democratic vote. An agenda-setting government faces political constraints but is strong in the sense that, by virtue of its agenda-setting power, its proposals are not subject to amendment but only to approval or rejection. We define weak governments as governments that are continuously the prey of rent-seeking activities by all sorts of lobbies and interest groups. In that case, the lobbies tend to set the political agenda and succeed in influencing the government to adopt measures they put on the agenda. Fewer policy conclusions can be drawn if one adopts the rent-seeking perspective, but it offers a positive analysis that can be relatively sobering to policy expectations.

It is important to emphasize that our definition of "strong" and "weak" governments encompasses only one of the many dimensions of political institutions—the relative autonomy of government in relation to pressure groups. Strong government usually is associated with dictatorship, to a large span of control over the economy, or to commitment power. Our definition is different and does not coincide with those categories. An agenda-setting government can be democratically elected and submit its proposals to a vote in parliament. Its agenda-setting power means it has the power to submit "take it or leave it" packages to a vote. Conversely, a dictatorship can be weak if it is the prey of rent-seeking activity by all sorts of groups. A government may have agenda-setting power in an economy with a small government; conversely, a government may be the prey to rent-seeking in an economy with a large state sector. An agenda-setting government may have commitment power in the sense that it may not have to fear policy reversals dictated by powerful interest groups, but it may lack precommitment power with respect to its own actions. A reformist government may, for example, decide on a partial reform at a given time because of political constraints, but renege on its commitment and go ahead with reforms once political constraints are less stringent. Finally, rent-seeking and agenda-setting are not mutually exclusive. We view these as polar cases. In practice, every government has some agenda-setting power and is also prey to some rent-seeking activity. Strong governments have, according to our definition, relatively more agenda-setting power and are largely immune from rent-seeking; and the reverse is true for weak governments.

In the next section of this chapter we define what we view as the basic political economy issues of privatization and restructuring. In the third section, we discuss privatization and restructuring in the context of the agenda-setting model. In the fourth section, we look at the same questions from the rent-seeking perspective. In the last two sections, we use both political economy frameworks to ask two questions. In the fifth section, we ask how relevant the Chinese reform experience is for understanding political economy issues of the Eastern European transition. In the sixth section, we look at the role of banks in ownership transformation against the background of political constraints to restructuring.

Political Economy Issues of Ownership Transformation

One of the most important legacies of the socialist system's imposition of political constraints on privatization and restructuring is the high degree of *job security*, which provides, in practice, a full income insurance. Unemployment was quasi-inexistent under socialism, and the labor markets were characterized by net excess demand for labor (Kornai 1992). Income insurance was thus provided by the enterprise.

A second legacy is the importance of the *benefits in kind and social services* provided by the enterprise, such as daycare, vacations, and other services that affect individual welfare. The amount of benefits in kind received by workers varied greatly across enterprises and had little connection with the labor services provided. Having a job in a big enterprise meant having *ipso facto* access to the more important benefits in kind provided by that enterprise. When quitting, the worker lost access to the benefits. They were thus used by enterprises to reduce voluntary labor mobility because of the shortage on the labor market (Kahan and Ruble 1979).

A third important legacy is the relatively *egalitarian distribution of income*. Studies on income distribution under socialism differ in many of their conclusions, but there is a general agreement that the distribution of income was relatively egalitarian compared with Western economies, for example (see Atkinson and Micklewright 1992).

Viewed from the perspective of modern incentive theory, we may say that workers under socialism benefited from a high level of insurance, but with low incentives, and thus a high level of inefficiency. The change toward the market system is meant to lead to a huge improvement in overall efficiency, which requires a stronger role for incentives, and thus a marked decrease in income insurance for workers.

This implies first that unemployment risks will generally increase compared with what they were under socialism because the steady-state unemployment rates tend to be higher under capitalism than under socialism.

Second, associated with possible job losses is the potential loss of many of the social services people received in the enterprises. Many enterprise services, such as housing facilities and vacation tickets, will disappear with privatization and restructuring. Labor markets will become more characterized by excess supply of labor, and there will be less need to retain workers in the enterprise by offering benefits in kind.

Third, the distribution of income will be more inegalitarian. Unemployment risks will be associated with higher income risks and increasing poverty risks for many people.

Most economists would agree that the higher unemployment and income risks will be more than compensated, after transition, by a much higher level of expected income made possible by the efficiency gains from higher incentives under the market system.

How serious are the political economy problems of transition then likely to be? The increased inequality in income distribution may not be too serious if it is associated with a general increase in average income. The political economic problems of transition, however, are much more important than one might expect by simply looking at the tradeoffs implied by the change from socialism to capitalism. Indeed, the higher income level one may expect from capitalism is not likely to materialize at the early stages of transition, if at all, whereas the increase of uncertainty that people will have to face is very likely to precede any important increase in efficiency.

In that context, job uncertainty represents a very serious political economy problem. Nobody expected the huge output shock these countries have experienced at the beginning of transition when prices were liberalized and the Council for Mutual Economic Assistance (CMEA) broke down (Kornai 1993). The big output fall was not accompanied by a corresponding fall in employment, which indicates that the resistance to job losses is a very important problem. In Poland, the increase in unemployment has followed with delay. When the economy started to recover in 1992, unemployment continued to increase. The former coalition of ex-communists and the Peasant Party won the elections despite the recovery.

Any transition policy that is likely to increase job uncertainty is also likely to meet important political constraints. This is particularly true for privatization and restructuring of enterprises.

Political Economy Problems Facing an Agenda-Setting Government

An agenda-setting government with the power to propose reform packages subject to a democratic vote is going to face *ex ante* and *ex post* political constraints.

Ex ante political constraints mean that some measures cannot be adopted because a majority is not ready to vote for them, whether in parliament, inside government, or within the ruling coalition. In order to be implementable, reform packages must satisfy the *ex ante* political feasibility constraints.

Ex post political constraints refer to the danger of political backlash. There is a problem of political commitment related to a potential change in the balance of power following, for example, a negative economic shock. Such a shock might change the majority in a country, and thus potentially lead to policy reversals. Policy reversals can also be endogenous and result from measures that turn out hurting a majority.

Combining the *ex ante* and the *ex post* political constraints leads to two simple implications. First, only politically feasible measures can be implemented. There is no use criticizing a government for not implementing given policies that are economically sensible but cannot get through the political decisionmaking process. Second, it is crucial to create irreversibility to reduce *ex post* political constraints.

How are political feasibility and irreversibility taken into account in policies of privatization and restructuring? Two basic policy options are available in transition economies. One is the option taken by most countries, which is a policy of mass privatization, with the implication that the restructuring is "privatized"—that is, the responsibility of restructuring is taken over by the private sector. The second policy option is one of gradual privatization and restructuring. Let us discuss these two policies in terms of how they deal with *ex ante* and *ex post* political constraints.

Mass Privatization and Political Constraints

Political feasibility of mass privatization is achieved through the popularity of giveaway privatization, where state assets are redistributed for free to the population.

A first possible reason for the popularity of giveaway privatization is related to socialist ideology. During more than forty years, people were brought up with the idea that socialism meant "ownership of the people." Giveaway privatization has been presented by noncommunist politicians as "real ownership of the people," compared with "pseudo" ownership of the people that was, in reality, communist-controlled state ownership.

A second, and probably more serious, reason for the popularity of mass privatization is that by giving away state assets, one "buys" potential popular resistance to privatization. Giveaway privatization can be understood as a policy package combining standard privatization with transfers to the population. The median voter may benefit from these transfers even if he would otherwise be fearful of the job uncertainty associated with privatization.

Irreversibility is built into mass privatization policies for many reasons. One important idea is that if shares are distributed to people at large, the population becomes interested in the political success of privatization because everybody then has a stake in the success of privatization (see Roland and Verdier, forthcoming). For this to be true, shares must be nontradable against money, because any backlash against privatization hurts shareholders. If shares given away are exchangeable against money, it is possible for individuals to cash in their shares and to oppose privatization *ex post*. Indeed, it is reasonable to assume that those who sell their shares (low-income workers) are also those who are the most likely to be hurt by the consequences of privatization. In countries where mass privatization policies were chosen, there was a debate about whether privatization vouchers should be made exchangeable against money. In the Czech Republic and Poland, governments chose to make vouchers nontradable during an initial period. In Russia, it was decided that vouchers could be immediately tradable for money.

According to Boycko, Shleifer, and Vishny (1993), another element of irreversibility present in mass privatization policies is that the political cost of taking back assets given away for free may be higher than the cost of renationalizing enterprises privatized through sale. Irreversibility is also enhanced because mass privatization represents a form of "scorched earth" politics. By transferring state wealth to the population and making its reappropriation costly, one constrains future conservative governments by reducing considerably the budgetary means available to them. Under this view of irreversibility, the probability of having a proreform government replaced by a conservative government is exogenous, but the policies that can be chosen by a conservative government are constrained.

How have mass privatization policies met with political constraints in practice?

The Czech and Russian programs have passed the political feasibility tests, but the Polish mass privatization plan has not. Designed in late 1990 and early 1991, the Polish mass privatization plan was widely advertised in the economics profession and beyond as the fastest and best thought-out mass privatization plan. Unlike the Czech program, where adult citizens were to receive (against a symbolic price) vouchers to purchase shares directly in privatized enterprises, under the Polish program, citizens would receive vouchers to buy shares in a limited number of mutual funds (twenty, initially), each of which would be lead shareholder in twenty large firms. Fears were indeed expressed that the Czech program would lead to dispersed ownership and thus to weak shareholder monitoring. The Polish scheme combined free distribution of assets to the population with strong monitoring of firms by mutual funds. More than three years after its design, however, the Polish mass privatization program has not reached the implementation stage. It took more than two years of fierce debate in Parliament before the plan was brought to a vote, and since the new coalition came to power, there is widespread skepticism with respect to implementation of the program. Political constraints are the main reason for the delay in Polish mass privatization. Earle, Frydman, and Rapaczynski (1993) claim that privatization has become politically more difficult than in the early transition period. The main blocking forces in Poland are those representing coalitions of workers and managers, hostile to a redistribution of assets to the population at large.

One sees here how political constraints vary across economies in transition. The Czech mass privatization plan also represents a redistribution to the population at large. It was not blocked by workers and managers, because unlike other countries such as Hungary, Poland, and Russia, Czechoslovakia had not experienced economic reforms that gave more power to worker coalitions. In Russia, a Czech-style mass privatization would probably also have been blocked, and the Russian plan was designed to take this constraint explicitly into account. Not surprisingly, the Russian plan essentially involves a giveaway of assets to insiders of firms. Boycko, Shleifer, and Vishny (1993) justify the Russian privatization policy not in economic but in purely political terms, by stating that all other plans would have been politically unfeasible. Differences in initial conditions before transition lead to differences in political constraints.

It is too soon to judge whether the mass privatization plans in the different countries have achieved irreversibility. One should, however, emphasize that there is no foolproof method to obtain irreversibility, only ways to make it more costly. Outright renationalization of privatized assets was probably excluded from the beginning because governments have generally not been able to reassert their ownership rights over firms before privatization. Indeed, this process, called *commercialization*, generally has proved much more difficult than expected. In Poland and Hungary, the number of enterprises privatized without being commercialized tends to exceed the number of commercialized enterprises. In Poland, by March 1993, 1,661 enterprises had been privatized through liquidation, a procedure where commercialization is bypassed, compared to 495 enterprises commercialized and 17 enterprises sold through direct sales. In Hungary, the most successful form of privatization has appeared to be the "self-privatization" program, where enterprises take upon themselves the initiative of privatization without undergoing commercialization, and where the only form of government control consists of checking through an audit (conducted by private consultants) whether the sale value is not too low.

There is, however, a danger of a political backlash against privatization in the name of fairness. Fairness has been put forward as an argument to justify privatization policies, certainly in the Czech Republic and in Poland. In the Czech Republic, for example, the ideology of "popular capitalism," with widespread and relatively egalitarian shareholder ownership, has been invoked to justify privatization. The government has imposed a 20 percent limit on the percentage of shares a single shareholder can hold in a given firm. In practice, a high level of concentration has been observed. The initial fears of dispersed ownership were displaced as mutual funds sprang from the earth to collect the vouchers of the population, promising a tenfold return on the initial price of the voucher. In this way, more than half of the voucher points ended up in the hands of the largest thirteen investment funds (Kotrba and Svejnar 1994). Even though concentrated ownership is desirable from the point of view of incentives, the outcome of Czech privatization may generate political backlash if people realize that an important part of the economy has been given nearly free to a very small number of people. This may not lead to renationalization, but to popular claims to redistribute parts of the concentrated ownership.

Even if mass privatization programs are successful, there will be political constraints associated with restructuring once the firms are privatized, implying important redundancies. Under mass privatization policies, the government is not expected to play a role in enterprise restructuring, leaving to the new private owners the responsibility for laying off workers. If, however, the private investors know that there are political uncertainties surrounding restructuring and laying off, they may shy away from investing in those countries. The distribution of assets to the population at large through mass privatization may partly mitigate these negative effects by the irreversibility effects created by widespread distribution of shares to the population (see Roland and Verdier, forthcoming). The tradeoff, however, is that if one wants to prevent political opposition to inevitable restructuring, a great number of shares will have to be distributed to buy away resistance, and if there are sunk costs to restructuring, private investors may be less willing to engage in restructuring investments if they have to share the benefits of those investments with workers.

Another problem is related to the restructuring of firms privatized to insiders, which is the case in Russia. New private firms are already going to face a high cost of raising capital. In economies in transition, informational asymmetries are going to be very important. New private firms will have no track record of past performance. Bank lending will also be difficult to obtain because of the absence of collateral related to the low liquidation value of firms brought about by the very low level of private wealth, the illiquidity of financial markets, and the big recession in Eastern Europe. All these problems will be exacerbated for firms privatized to insiders, primarily because of the usual argument that insider-controlled firms cannot credibly commit to pay back investors (see the chapter by E. Berglöf in this volume). Many firms will thus be denied access to private sources of finance and will face the choice of closing down or turning to the government for financial help. Because of the political constraints to closing down firms, the government will be tempted to rescue a substantial number of those firms, especially in the case of big firms that play a role in regional employment. Firms rescued by government in this way would have been *de facto*, if not formally, renationalized.

Some formal renationalization may thus be the inevitable result of the political constraints on restructuring. To the extent that firms privatized to insiders will have less easy access to private sources of finance, there may be more renationalizations in a country such as Russia.

Gradual Privatization and Restructuring

Gradualism is, in general, a way of reducing *ex ante* political feasibility constraints compared with more radical big bang policies (for a formal analysis, see Dewatripont and Roland 1993). With respect to privatization and restructuring, it implies that a policy of gradual privatization and restructuring is less likely to violate political feasibility constraints. One may say that Hungary and Poland are, in practice, following a policy of gradual privatization and restructuring. Privatization is proceeding more slowly than expected, but there is also evidence of restructuring in privatized firms and in firms preparing for privatization (see Pinto, Belka, and Krajewski 1993; Estrin, Schaffer, and Singh 1992; Carlin, Van Reenen, and Wolfe 1994).

What about creating irreversibility? The general idea is that irreversibility of a gradual policy of privatization associated with restructuring may be obtained if constituencies are built gradually in favor of further reform (see Dewatripont and Roland 1992a,b, 1993).

In Eastern Europe, gradualism may reinforce irreversibility to the extent that there is a big option value of waiting to invest. Transition involves, by definition, transitional uncertainty, thereby creating an incentive for investors to wait for uncertainty resolution before investing. Indeed, their investments may be lost if there is a policy reversal. Therefore, it pays for them to wait and invest only when the outcome of transition appears sufficiently positive. The option value of waiting is greater the quicker the uncertainty resolution. Indeed, under a big bang program, uncertainty is supposed to be resolved more quickly than under a gradual program because the speed of reforms is by definition faster.[1] This, however, means that the benefits of waiting one more period before investing are also higher. Other things being equal, this reasoning suggests a higher investment response under gradualism. This is consistent with the observed pattern of foreign direct investment, where Hungary has been able to attract a substantial share of total investment in Eastern Europe ($6 out of $18 billion in 1993). To the extent that a higher investment level leads to a general increase in welfare and endogenously broadens the support for reform, this may lead to more irreversibility (see Dewatripont and Roland 1993).

Nevertheless, under gradualism, as under the big bang, there is no foolproof method of creating irreversibility. Reform outcomes may turn out to be negative because of the generic aggregate uncertainty affecting transition countries where the whole social, political, and economic system is subject to radical changes.

In order to enhance *ex post* irreversibility by creating constituencies for reform, it is important to observe a correct sequencing of reforms (see Dewatripont and Roland 1993). With respect to privatization and restructuring, correct sequencing implies that it is better to privatize first the good enterprises because this creates momentum and positive

1. We abstract here from the possibility that a big bang program may by itself bring about chaotic disturbances, leading to increased uncertainty.

experiences. It allows the creation of strong coalitions to overcome later opposition on restructuring. Similarly, gradual restructuring creates room for "divide and rule" policies that can be implemented even with fully rational and forward-looking agents. Assume, for example, that two-thirds of the workers must be made redundant in a sector and that political constraints require that restructuring plans be accepted by a majority. It is possible to make one-third redundant today and the next third redundant in a later period, without fully compensating either group. Such a plan can be accepted by a majority, including those who are laid off today, provided compensation given to that group makes them *better off than under rejection of the plan*. If agents in that group know that rejection would lead to a status quo, followed in the second period by the adoption of a redundancy plan that would hurt them *even more*, they may prefer to accept being made redundant today with better conditions. This point is developed more fully in Dewatripont and Roland (1992a).

Convergence of Mass Privatization to Gradualism?

Despite the important conceptual differences between mass privatization policies and a policy of gradual privatization and restructuring, one cannot exclude the possibility that the former will turn out to be equivalent to the latter. In a sense, both policies address similar *ex ante* and *ex post* political constraints. Mass privatization may achieve a faster transfer of control to private hands, but the design of the program will have been adapted to *ex ante* political constraints—for example, by privileged giveaways to insiders, as in Russia. Nevertheless, the political constraints of restructuring will be the same, independent of the privatization policies adopted. This means that gradual restructuring will be a likely outcome because of the important political constraints of restructuring. As stated in the preceding section, this is likely to induce some inevitable renationalization. Gradual restructuring thus may end up indirectly transforming mass privatization policies into forms of gradual privatization.

The danger, however, is that partial renationalization may discredit mass privatization and create political instability. A potentially greater danger associated with mass privatization is that it may lead to slower restructuring than a gradual policy. The government may indeed be tempted, in order to avoid outright renationalization and to ensure the political success of privatization, to guarantee bank loans to privatized firms to alleviate credit rationing. This could be a recipe for generalized soft budget constraints. Government guarantees reduce the incentives of creditors to monitor the firms because they will be insured against bad risks. There is thus a danger of generalized creditor passivity associated with soft budget constraints in the banking sector. Generalized bailouts of banks will reduce incentives in all firms and lead to widespread moral hazard. Firms that would have made the effort to restructure in order to survive would realize that those who exerted no effort will get bailed out anyway and benefit from a higher government subsidy. It thus pays to remain passive and not to restructure. With low incentives to restructure, the necessary restructuring would certainly be delayed, even compared with what is politically possible. Despite the success of Czech mass privatization, restructuring does not seem to be moving faster there than in other countries. The scenario depicted here cannot be excluded, and the Czech government's commitment not to intervene to subsidize firms privatized through vouchers will be tested repeatedly in the future.

Another reason for a possible slower restructuring under mass privatization policies is related to fiscal equilibrium. Policies of giveaway have a high fiscal cost because governments give away their wealth and are likely to face difficulties in tax collection in the early years of transition. Policies of sales, especially against noncash bids, as advocated in Bolton and Roland (1992) and increasingly used in Poland and Hungary, may generate a regular flow of revenues during the transition period. Governments opting for giveaway policies may then find it more difficult to finance banking reform, involving the inevitable bailing out and recapitalization of banks, riddled with nonperforming bank loans of loss-making state-owned enterprises. The budgetary cost of writing off the stock of existing enterprise debt is in principle compensated by a higher sale price when the enterprises or the banks are sold. Such a compensation does not exist if assets are given away. Governments that choose mass privatization policies may thus be much more reluctant to write off debts of enterprises and recapitalize banks. This may have very adverse consequences for the development of financial systems.

Rent-Seeking and Ownership Transformation

Let us now take a totally different view of politics and look at ownership transformation from the perspective of rent-seeking. We assume that the government is easy prey for the various lobbies. We assume here a much weaker government than in the preceding section, because it has no agenda-setting power.

At the beginning of transition, the view was expressed that the most important thing was to get the state out of the economy. Fast privatization was viewed as the instrument to achieve this objective. If we take the rent-seeking perspective seriously, we know that privatization will not prevent lobbies from intervening and constantly trying to influence the decisions of a weak government.

With respect to privatization and restructuring, it is also useful to make the distinction between *ex ante* and *ex post* rent-seeking activities.

Ex ante rent-seeking means that interest groups will devote effort and resources to influencing the privatization policies adopted so they can grab as much as possible in rents. The transfer of the bulk of government wealth to private hands is a unique historical opportunity for rent-seeking. One should thus not be astonished to observe large-scale rent-seeking activities in the context of privatization in Eastern Europe. How can we interpret actual privatization policies in this light?

First of all, one has observed that some restitution of assets to their former owners seems unavoidable in transition economies. In Hungary, for example, the Smallholders' Party was pivotal in forming the first noncommunist government coalition. Its only program was restitution of land to its former owners. In Czechoslovakia and East Germany, restitution has been prominent in privatization policy. In Poland there is also a restitution lobby trying to influence privatization policies in its favor. It is well known that privatization through restitution tends to create difficult legal battles (see, for example, Begg 1991; Sinn and Sinn 1993) and contributes to the confusion rather than the clarification of property rights. The observation of an irresistible trend toward restitution has thus more to do with rent-seeking activity than with the search for economic efficiency. Note, however, that in the Czech Republic, where restitution was restricted to objects such as housing, it has proceeded more smoothly than expected and has been evaluated positively by observers (see, for example, Kotrba and Svejnar 1994).

Rent-seeking may also mean that different groups try to influence the kind of free distribution program. If one compares, for example, the Polish and Russian plans of free distribution, they have very different redistributive implications. The Russian plan favors more insiders and workers, and the Polish plan includes more provisions benefiting the population at large. Comparing two mass privatization plans that are similar in design, but with one giving 15 percent of shares to workers and managers and the other 10 percent, may reveal great differences in rents. Various coalitions thus have a great incentive to fight each other to try to influence privatization policy in their favor. We may interpret the failure in Poland to get mass privatization adopted as a paralysis of decisionmaking because no coalition was strong enough to impose its own privatization plan over the preferences of opposing coalitions. Conversely, the Czech and Russian mass privatization plans could benefit from the support of sufficiently strong coalitions.

One should emphasize that the option for free distribution of assets rather than sales has negative effects in terms of rent-seeking. Once governments opt for free distribution, they open the gates for a big rent-seeking game. Conversely, policies of competitive sales would minimize rent dissipation in the privatization process. It is not clear, however, that the current weak governments in Eastern Europe are able to resist the lobbying activities of those who favor free distribution. If their resistance to lobbying from pressure groups is particularly weak, it is unclear why they should be more able to resist rent-seeking pressures in the domain of privatization than in other areas. Apart from Hungary and East Germany, most Eastern European countries have opted for forms of free distribution. There does not seem to be a foolproof method of avoiding rent-seeking and rent dissipation in privatization.

Another possible consequence of rent-seeking is the break-up of countries. To the extent that privatization is going to involve the redistribution of wealth, whether through a giveaway or through sales, regions that have a higher concentration of privatizable assets have an incentive to separate in order not to share the proceeds of privatization with the less well-endowed regions. Pressures for separatism observed in Eastern Europe and Russia are related partly to privatization (on separatism, see Bolton and Roland 1993).

Ex post rent-seeking means that enterprises or groups of enterprises will lobby for additional subsidies rather than engage in restructuring activities, leading to persistence of soft budget constraints. Let us just point out two problems related to *ex post* rent-seeking: the danger of too high an economic concentration, on the one hand, and the rent-seeking incentives of insider-controlled firms, on the other.

Concentrated ownership leads to more monitoring by shareholders and is thus preferable to dispersed ownership. There is, however, another dimension of concentration that must be considered—that of the size of the assets concentrated in single hands. Enterprises in Eastern Europe already tend to have a larger average size than that observed in developed market economies. Concentration of ownership over various firms, many of which are monopolies, may yield a high political leverage. Such a concentration of control is happening *de facto* through the mutual funds in the Czech Republic, and is a built-in feature in the Polish mass privatization plan. To the extent that there are returns of scale to rent-seeking (Murphy, Shleifer, and Vishny 1993), mutual funds may have a strong incentive to engage in rent-seeking activities to obtain subsidies and rents for their enterprises instead of engaging in restructuring activities. Economically weak enterprise groups facing high costs of restructuring may still be politically powerful enough to gain from substituting unproductive rent-seeking for restructuring.

A similar choice may be made by firms privatized to insiders, but for a different reason. To the extent that those firms may have very difficult access to private finance and face credit rationing or other liquidity constraints, they may have no other choice than to engage in rent-seeking to obtain the subsidies needed to survive. The larger the number of these firms, the more difficult it will be for government to resist.

Rent-seeking works in the opposite direction from privatization. Privatization tends to clarify property rights. Rent-seeking creates confusion over property rights by constantly trying to change their distribution through political means, implying the constant redefinition of the boundaries of existing laws.

Different interpretations of the same phenomena can be made, depending on whether one uses the agenda-setting or the rent-seeking perspective. For example, the failure to adopt mass privatization in

Poland was interpreted as a political feasibility problem in the agenda-setting framework and as the result of stalemate between interest groups in the rent-seeking framework.

The conclusions one may draw from the rent-seeking perspective are less positive than those drawn in the agenda-setting framework. If privatization must be interpreted as a huge rent-seeking game because of the ensuing confusion in property rights, the opposite of privatization tends to be achieved in the name of privatization. *Ex ante* rent-seeking may be difficult to avoid, but *ex post* rent-seeking could be partly avoided *ex ante* if governments are strong enough. Indeed, the analysis points to the risks of too much concentration and of mass giveaways to insiders. The general lesson is that governments should avoid favoring measures that may weaken them even more with given interest groups. In the agenda-setting framework, we also mentioned *ex post* risks associated to mass privatization policies, but the danger was related to the possibility of a political backlash.

In practice, neither the pure agenda-setting nor the pure rent-seeking framework applies to a given country. In a democracy, there always exist areas where amendment power is important. Similarly, a political system characterized only by rent-seeking of various groups reduces to the Hobbesian state of nature—that is, the absence of any state. In practice, political institutions combine elements of both. It is not always easy, however, to determine which of the models is more appropriate to understand reality. In the next two sections, we will test both approaches by focusing on two questions. How relevant is the Chinese experience for understanding political economy issues in Eastern Europe? What is the role of banks, against the background of political constraints to restructuring?

How Relevant Is the Chinese Experience?

The contrast between the Chinese and the Eastern European transition experiences is striking. The success of Chinese gradualism is generally praised, but the virtues of shock therapy are voiced very loudly in the context of Eastern Europe, despite massive falls in output and political instability. In the World Bank newsletter, *Transition*, I. J. Singh has even talked of "schizophrenia in socialist reform theory." Have the positive lessons from the Chinese experience been overlooked by analysts in Eastern Europe?

The argument is often made that the Chinese experience is not relevant for Eastern Europe because of the different initial conditions of transition. Sachs and Woo (1994) argue, for example, that a major difference between China and Eastern Europe is the difference in level of development. China is facing the "classical" development economy problem of rural populations migrating to the cities, whereas in Eastern Europe and the former Soviet Union, it is more painful to move from state-owned industry to the private sector because of the heavy subsidization of state-owned enterprises. Besides the differences in economic development, let us note that China is still a communist regime where democratic institutions are absent. For our purposes, this means that large-scale privatization is excluded for ideological reasons. There are also few signs of restructuring in large state-owned enterprises (SOEs), and structural change comes from the creation of new enterprises, especially in the countryside where township and village enterprises (TVEs) are booming.

Despite these differences, it would be a non sequitur to conclude that China and Eastern Europe do not face common problems in the transition from socialism to capitalism. At a more abstract level, the Chinese experience shows the political advantages of gradualism when the government has enough agenda-setting power. Reform started in the countryside first, while SOEs remained unaffected by large-scale decollectivization. The latter is comparable to privatization because peasant families were offered long-term leases (fifteen years). This change in incentives led to a doubling of agricultural output within less than ten years after decollectivization. This positive outcome of cleverly chosen initial reforms considerably increased the support for further reforms. Reform has led to industrialization in TVEs operating under hard budget constraints with high growth. At the same time, the development of coastal zones has been a success, attracting foreign investment and generating high growth and employment. These massive changes make it politically easier to address privatization and restructuring in the state sector.

The success in Chinese decollectivization does not mean that the pattern of Chinese reform should have been copied in Eastern Europe.

Whether intended or unintended, however, the Chinese reform strategy shows the advantages of gradualism with correct sequencing.

Hoshi's chapter in this volume shows that the Japanese postwar experience can also be interpreted as a case of successful sequencing under gradualism. Indeed, the restructuring of enterprises and layoffs of redundant workers only started around 1950, after a first period (1947–48) in which the focus was on writing off the bad loans, cleaning the balance sheets of banks, and rehabilitating production linkages between enterprises.

Returning to our political economy framework, it seems that the Chinese experience can be better understood through the agenda-setting framework despite the considerable rent-seeking activities at various levels of the economy. It would be difficult to interpret decollectivization in the rent-seeking framework. At a more general level, looking at Chinese reforms, it is important to note that the successful lobbying on the reform side was not directed toward restricting competition or extra subsidies to particular groups, but rather aimed at giving more economic freedom to agents. Rents obtained from such lobbying derive from the productive activity generated by more economic freedom and increased competition. Lobbying has taken place on the conservative side, but it was more defensive, with a goal of protecting given sectors from reform.

An important dimension of Chinese reforms that can be interpreted with regard to rent-seeking is the important decentralization of fiscal authority that has taken place in the 1980s. This decentralization has given more power to regional authorities and they have certainly derived more rents from these new powers, which give them more control over the resources of their regions. Decentralization has also created forms of economic competition between regions that have had a positive effect on the pace of reforms and on economic efficiency (see Qian and Xu 1992; Montinola, Qian, and Weingast 1993; Qian and Roland 1994).

In China, the rent-seeking framework is probably less valid than the agenda-setting framework because, for whatever reasons, Deng Xiao Ping has always managed to keep relative control over the agenda. This has restricted the room for rent-seeking—for example, by restricting rent-seeking to issues of regional decentralization while excluding privatization from the agenda. In Eastern Europe, the implosion of central authority has led to an institutional vacuum that increased the set of possible political outcomes, making "anything possible." In the absence of institutional rigidities, interest groups can expect great gains, provided they do the necessary lobbying. This is socially very costly because of the waste of resources used for rent-seeking. The conflict between pressure groups with contradictory interests, however, may lead to paralysis in decisionmaking. This is the case with mass privatization in Poland. In Russia, stalemate in Parliament has also tended to lead to a certain paralysis in decisionmaking. In the meantime, spontaneous activity develops on the basis of the institutional vacuum. Surprisingly, despite paralysis in decisionmaking, Poland has started to recover and has experienced an impressive growth spurt since 1992. It is not impossible that the same result will be repeated in Russia. Growth in the context of a relative institutional vacuum, however, has problems of its own. The new private sector that develops spontaneously pays no taxes to government and is easy prey for the rackets of organized crime.

The Role of Banks

Banks are likely to play a crucial role in the corporate governance of firms undergoing privatization and restructuring and it has been argued that a bank-oriented system will develop rather than a market-oriented system (Aoki 1994; Berglöf, in this volume). In this section, we want to look at the role of banks in ownership transformation under our two political economy frameworks.

In the discussion of the agenda-setting framework, it was emphasized that because of political constraints, the process of restructuring would be gradual, implying a slow hardening of budget constraints. The essential implication of gradual restructuring for financial developments is that the state will be tempted to intervene if it feels that the level of enterprise closures, liquidations, and redundancies is higher than it can tolerate given the existing political constraints. What role are banks likely to play in this matter?

Banks play an important role in the *ex ante* screening of good and bad enterprise projects. Through the threat of bankruptcy, they exercise *ex post* contingent control over firms and may take tough actions and initiatives to restructure. The existence of this contingent control leads to hard budget constraints in firms (Aghion and Bolton 1992; Dewatripont and Tirole, forthcoming). Several conditions must be met, however, for the banking sector to play its role.

Banks are likely to play their part only if they have a sound loan portfolio. Otherwise, there is the danger of creditor passivity, since filing for bankruptcy may reveal the weak financial situation of the bank (Mitchell 1993).

Banks must also be independent from government intervention in their resource allocation decisions. It is crucial to avoid the government "forcing" banks to lend to bad enterprises. Many of the loans granted by banks in Eastern Europe in recent years were actually hidden subsidies. In order to meet IMF targets for budget deficits, governments cut the level of official subsidies but continued hidden subsidization through the banking system. By forcing banks to lend to bad firms, governments contributed to the deteriorating financial situation of banks, inducing creditor passivity. The incentives to screen are also reduced because banks know that they will be bailed out in case of bankruptcy.

In order to gain a proper functioning of the banking system, the following measures are necessary:

- Political intervention in the microeconomic credit allocation decisions made by banks must cease. An obvious way to achieve this goal is to privatize the banks. This may not be done quickly because of the caution or lack of interest of potential acquirers. Another way to achieve the same objective quickly is to cut government's incentive to intervene in banks' allocative decisions. This can be done by the next measure.
- Firms that the government wants to subsidize should be financed directly through the budget. This is also likely to lead to a better monitoring of the use made of these subsidies. By guaranteeing bank loans to these firms, an alternative way of subsidizing them, firms get unmonitored access to finance. Under the planning system at least, there was an important amount of *ex ante* monitoring by state agencies of enterprise budgets (see Qian and Xu 1991).
- Banks must be recapitalized and given incentives to act as profit-maximizing intermediaries. It is important to distinguish

> here between the stock of bad debts and the flow of new credits. Banks clearly have a stock of inherited bad debts. This problem is best solved by recapitalization. Begg and Portes (1993) suggest doing this by replacing bad loans in banks' portfolios by three-month Treasury bills. Van Wijnbergen (1993) proposes instead to replace bad loans by equity in the firms. It is, however, fundamental to leave to banks the *option* of debt-equity swaps and to avoid forcing them into such an arrangement. If banks are forced to take equity in bad firms where the prospects of survival are dim and where closure is avoided essentially for political reasons, then one creates conditions for a future bank bailout; the level of recapitalization will not be high enough because the assets of these firms will be without value and the flow of credits to these firms will have a low likelihood of being repaid.

If bank managers are independent from government and given a sufficient part of residual claims, they will tend to engage in profit-maximization behavior. Assume that the government guarantees no bank loans. Banks will then tend to be careful in their screening of projects and will have more incentive to induce the bankruptcy of firms not paying back their loans. That banks know they will be bailed out if they are in financial distress does not necessarily mean that they will tend to choose riskier projects with lower returns. They will only engage in such a behavior when they are gambling for resurrection and where the choice is between failing or giving risky loans that may either push them further into the red or avoid failure. Otherwise, their behavior will be closer to profit-maximization. As a result, many firms, even those with positive chances of restructuring, will face credit rationing.

Should all these firms depend on government subsidies? It would be dangerous to put them too quickly under the control of state-owned "hospital" agencies. A better solution would be to let banks play an active role in the privatization and restructuring of enterprises and give them an incentive to do so by appropriate risk-sharing between government and banks. This amounts to introducing partial government guarantees for those firms. This can be done when firms are privatized through noncash bid methods (see Bolton and Roland 1992).

Assume, for example, that a manager of an enterprise proposes a privatization deal where he buys 20 percent of his firms' shares, leaving 80 percent to the state. Of this 20 percent, 5 percent is paid up front and 15 percent financed by a bank loan. In order to transform it into a profitable enterprise, a restructuring investment is needed. The loan for realizing this investment could be guaranteed by less than 80 percent by government. Such a risk-sharing arrangement would encourage the bank to give the loan, especially in the absence of collateral. The bank would also be encouraged to screen the project because it is taking the risk of losing at least 20 percent of the loan plus the loan on 15 percent of the shares. The bank would also be encouraged to file for bankruptcy if necessary because it is a senior creditor. For that purpose, it is important, as emphasized by van Wijnbergen (1994), that the government relinquish its rights as senior creditor.

Banks can thus play a role in a process of gradual restructuring. How should we now evaluate the role of banks if we take a rent-seeking perspective?

We do not want to discuss extensively here the issue of rent-seeking by banks, but rather want to emphasize some of the most acute problems from a rent-seeking perspective.

The first, and probably greatest, danger is related to potential lobbying of banks to obtain exaggerated loan guarantees from government. Given the absence of experience of genuine intermediation and the risks related to this lack of experience, the new banking sector in Eastern Europe will be tempted to develop a form of parasitic behavior, living off riskless loans made to government. The success of banks in lobbying for such rents, however, depends on the degree to which government depends on the banking sector itself for financing its objectives. If the government delegates to the banks tasks that are necessary for the normal functioning of government—and we have in mind the task of keeping afloat loss-making firms that are "too big to fail"—then it will be more inclined to give in to the demands of banks because they may threaten to stop fulfilling these functions. This leads to a policy prescription that is parallel to the one we derived in the agenda-setting framework—the necessity of keeping bad enterprises outside the banking sector and to finance them directly through the budget. The general lesson is that the more the government depends on banks to fulfill specific government objectives that cannot be fulfilled through the private markets, the greater the danger of government capture by the banking sector.

Banks may also lobby, as they have done already in Eastern Europe, to restrict competition— for example, by prohibiting access to foreign banks or restricting market access to new private banks. The absence of competition in the banking sector may lead to a substantial difference between the lending and deposit rate. This problem, however, is probably less serious than the previous one. First, one should note that the banking sector is a special sector where regulation is needed and where spontaneous private initiative and competition do not necessarily lead to optimal welfare outcomes (see, for example, van Wijnbergen 1993). Second, the main objective in Eastern Europe is getting a private banking sector off the ground. Too low a level of competition in the banking sector may be of second-order importance compared with that objective. It may be that positive rents in the banking sector lead to improvements in monitoring technology and banking skills and allow acceleration of the development of the financial sector, so urgently needed in these economies. Rent-seeking to restrict competition could thus have positive effects on efficiency and growth.

Conclusions

Will governments in transition economies be closer in their behavior to agenda-setting governments or to weak governments prey to rent-seeking? This will depend on the kind of constitution prevailing in those countries and how credible the constitution is in defining the rights of the people. This is certainly a matter for future research. This chapter has, however, shown that more optimistic policy conclusions may be drawn from the agenda-setting framework than from the rent-seeking perspective. In particular, our discussion of the dangers of rent-seeking in privatization shows the danger associated with weak governments in economies in transition. This reinforces a conclusion already made in the literature on transition (see, for example, Roland 1994; Weingast 1993)—the need for prior institutional consolidation at early stages of transition in order to have a political decisionmaking mechanism that does not lead to chaos and paralysis.

Bibliography

Aghion, P., and P. Bolton. 1992. "An Incomplete Contract Approach to Bankruptcy and the Financial Structure of the Firm." *Review of Economic Studies* 59: 473–94.

Aoki, M. 1994. "The Contingent Governance of Team Production: Analysis of Institutional Complementarity." *International Economic Review* 35: 657–76.

Atkinson, A., and J. Micklewright. 1992. *Economic Transformation in Eastern Europe and the Distribution of Income.* Cambridge, U.K.: Cambridge University Press.

Begg, D. 1991. "Economic Reform in Czechoslovakia: Should We Believe in Santa Klaus?" *Economic Policy* 13: 243–86.

Begg, D., and R. Portes. 1993. "Enterprise Debt and Economic Transformation: Financial Restructuring in Central and Eastern Europe." In C. Mayer and X. Vives, eds., *Capital Markets and Financial Intermediation.* Cambridge, U.K.: Cambridge University Press.

Bolton, P., and G. Roland. 1992. "Privatization in Central and Eastern Europe." *Economic Policy* 15: 276–309.

———. 1993. "The Break-up of Nations: A Political Economy Analysis." European Centre for Advanced Research in Economics, Brussels. Mimeo.

Boycko, M., A. Shleifer, and R. Vishny. 1993. "Privatizing Russia." Harvard University. Mimeo.

Carlin, W., J. Van Reenen, and T. Wolfe. 1994. "Enterprise Restructuring in the Transition: An Analytical Survey of the Case Study Evidence from Central and Eastern Europe." European Bank for Reconstruction and Development Working Paper 14, London.

Dewatripont, M., and G. Roland. 1992a. "Economic Reform and Dynamic Political Constraints." *Review of Economic Studies* 59: 703–30.

———. 1992b. "The Virtues of Gradualism and Legitimacy in the Transition to a Market Economy." *Economic Journal* 102: 291–300.

———. 1993. "The Design of Reform Packages under Uncertainty." Center for Economic Policy Research Discussion Paper 862, Stanford, California.

Dewatripont, M., and J. Tirole. Forthcoming. "A Theory of Debt Equity: Diversity of Securities and Manager-Shareholder Congruence." *Quarterly Journal of Economics.*

Earle, J., R. Frydman, and A. Rapaczynski. 1993. "Transition Policies and the Establishment of a Private Property Regime." Paper presented at the *Economic Policy Panel*, Brussels, October.

Estrin, S., M. Schaffer, and I. Singh. 1992. "Enterprise Adjustment in Economics in Transition: Czechoslovakia, Hungary, and Poland." CEP Working Paper 334, London School of Economics.

Kahan, A., and B. A. Ruble. 1979. *Industrial Labour in the USSR*. New York: Pergamon.

Kornai, J. 1992. *The Socialist System: the Political Economy of Communism*. Oxford, U.K.: Oxford University Press.

———. 1993. "Transformational Recession. A General Phenomenon Examined through the Example of Hungary's Development." *Economie Appliquée* 46 (2): 181–228.

Kotrba, Josef, and Jan Svejnar. 1994. "Rapid and Multifaceted Privatization: Experience of Czech and Slovak Republics." *Economic Policy in Transitional Economies* 4 (2): 147–85.

Mitchell, J. 1993. "Creditor Passivity and Bankruptcy. Implications for Bankruptcy Reform." In C. Mayer and X. Vives, eds., *Capital Markets and Financial Intermediation.* Cambridge, U.K.: Cambridge University Press.

Montinola, G., Y. Qian, and B. Weingast. 1993. "Federalism Chinese Style: the Political Basis for Economic Success in China." Stanford University. Mimeo.

Murphy, K., A. Shleifer, and R. Vishny. 1993. "Why is Rent-Seeking so Costly to Growth?" *American Economic Review, Papers and Proceedings* 83 (2): 409–14.

Pinto, B., M. Belka, and S. Krajewski. 1993. "Transforming State Enterprises in Poland." *Brookings Papers on Economic Activity* 1: 213–70.

Qian, Y., and C. Xu. 1991. "Innovation and Financial Constraint in Centralized and Decentralized Economies." Stanford University and London School of Economies. Mimeo.

———. 1992. "Why China's Economic Reforms Differ: the M-From Hierarchy and Entry/Expansion of the Non-State Sector." *Economics of Transition* 1 (2): 135–70.

Qian, Y., and G. Roland. 1994. "Regional Decentralization and the Soft Budget Constraint: the Case of China." Stanford University and European Centre for Advanced Research in Economics, Brussels. Mimeo.

Roland, G. 1994. "The Role of Political Constraints in Transition Strategies." *Economics of Transition* 2 (1): 27–41.

Roland, G., and T. Verdier. Forthcoming. "Privatization in Eastern Europe: Irreversibility and Critical Mass Effects." *Journal of Public Economics.*

Sachs, J., and W. T. Woo. 1994 "Reform in China and Russia." *Economic Policy* 18: 101–46.

Sinn, G., and H.-W. Sinn. 1993. *Jumpstart.* Cambridge, Mass.: MIT Press.

van Wijnbergen, S. 1993. "Enterprise Reform in Eastern Europe." *Economics of Transition* 1 (1): 21–38.

———. 1994. "On the Role of Banks in Enterprise Restructuring: the Polish Example." Center for Economic Policy Research Discussion Paper 898, Stanford, California.

Weingast, B. 1993. "The Economic Role of Political Institutions." Hoover Institution, Stanford University. Mimeo.

3

Corporate Governance in Transition Economies: The Theory and Its Policy Implications

Erik Berglöf

There is general agreement that production in the transition economies of Eastern Europe and the former Soviet Union must be fundamentally reoriented and enterprises thoroughly restructured. After the demise and final collapse of central planning, control over most of these strategic decisions is effectively in the hands of managers of firms; privatization has done little to change this. The strong insider control is reinforced by the weakness of financial institutions and the poor enforcement of property rights. In the absence of strong outside investors and an institutional framework supporting corporate governance, managers are unable to raise the capital needed for investments in new technologies and capacity.

The central question addressed here is what kind of corporate governance institutions are best suited for the transition economies. Gov-

This paper was written for the World Bank project, "The Roles of Banks in Corporate Governance in Transition Economies." I am grateful for discussions with other project participants, in particular with Masahiko Aoki, Gérard Roland, Ernst-Ludwig von Thadden, and Yingji Qian. Mathias Dewatripont, Claudia Senik-Leygonie, Georges Siotis, and Sweder van Wijnbergen have also made valuable suggestions.

ernments in these countries have looked both east and west for advice and models to emulate. Even when they were not looking, outside consultants and academics alike have offered their own favorite recipes. Much of the debate has concerned the role of stock markets in corporate governance and the choice between mutual funds and commercial banks as instruments of such governance. What has been lacking is a basic conceptual framework in which to describe and analyze existing models and proposals. The purpose of this chapter is to suggest such a framework based on a survey of the recent theoretical literature on corporate governance. Although this literature is still in its infancy and policy implications must be treated with caution, it provides a much better guide to understanding corporate governance than the traditional finance literature. In particular, through its emphasis on the institutional aspects of finance, this framework is more helpful in analyzing the transition economies.

This chapter will briefly characterize the present situation in Russia and the four Visegrad countries—the Czech Republic, Hungary, Poland, and Slovakia. While there are important differences in degree and in nature, the basic problem of insider control is pervasive throughout most of the region. The problem of insider control has been at the heart of an active recent literature on corporate governance discussed in the third section of the chapter. This literature provides a number of concepts useful for describing and analyzing the choice among different forms of corporate governance and governance institutions. The fourth section makes use of the basic conceptual framework to draw a number of lessons for policymakers. The analysis strongly suggests that commercial banks will come to play an important role in corporate governance in transition economies. These conclusions are worrying given the present state of the banking sector in most countries. The fifth section asks what we can expect from banks in transition economies and discusses what has been and what can be done to improve how they function.

Corporate Governance in Transition

With the growing interest in the issue of corporate governance in transition economies, the empirical evidence is mounting. Case studies and, increasingly, systematic surveys have forced us to change many of our preconceptions about how firms are controlled and how managers behave during transition. To provide a basis for the discussion of the conceptual framework and its policy implications, this section identifies the basic corporate governance issues in Russia and the four Visegrad countries.

Insider Control and Credit Constraints

The predominant feature of corporate governance in large and medium-size enterprises throughout Eastern Europe and the former Soviet Union is the strong control exerted by insiders, primarily by managers (for a survey of the empirical studies, see Aghion and Carlin 1994). In Russia, the shift of bargaining power toward insiders started with the enterprise reforms during the late 1980s, but the trend was reinforced by the collapse of the Soviet state. The new government has been unable to reassert its nominal property rights over state-owned assets, which still represent the bulk of large enterprises. For the most part, the privatization program has merely legitimized the de facto distribution of control. Most large enterprises have been privatized by transferring ownership rights to incumbent managers and workers. Through lock-in arrangements workers are prevented from selling their equity-holdings. Insider control is mirrored in boards and shareholder meetings captured by management, and with few external directors.

The picture in the Visegrad countries is similar, with some variations. For historical reasons, workers in Poland, and probably in Hungary, seem to have more influence over strategic decisions than Russian workers (Fan and Schaffer 1994). In the Czech Republic and Slovakia, the state—before the separation—managed to reassert its property rights, at least to some extent. Consequently, insider control is less pronounced, especially in the Czech Republic, where voucher privatization and the subsequent emergence of the investment privatization funds have led to a strong concentration of nominal ownership rights with outside institutions. In the average firm, the leading investment fund holds 14 percent, and in 25 percent of the firms privatized in this fashion the largest funds own more than half of the investment points (Earle, Frydman, and Rapaczynski 1993). Even though no single fund or group of jointly managed funds is allowed to vote for more than 20 percent of the outstanding shares, there appear to be ample opportunities for funds to circumvent these rules. There are few signs, however, of these control blocks being translated into active corporate governance.

The strong position of enterprise managers in the transition economies is reinforced by the weakness of the financial systems. Reforms to separate central and commercial banking have been undertaken in all the countries, but financial institutions are still rudimentary and financial intermediation is limited. The degree of intermediation and decentralization of credit allocation also vary substantially across countries. In Russia, where reforms are relatively recent, decisionmaking is still more centralized (Belyanova and Rozinsky, in this volume; Pohl and Claessen 1994). Money creation is dominated by outside money, with the central bank channeling considerable funds to state enterprises through the largest commercial banks. These so-called direct credit programs account for the bulk of loans from the banking sector. Under these programs finance is essentially passive, although banks have exercised some monitoring since the last years of the Soviet period.

Much of the Russian banking sector has effectively been captured by enterprises. Most of the large number of new banks have been created by enterprises or former ministries. In essence these institutions are little more than corporate treasuries that handle the cash flows of individual enterprises and to some extent reshuffle liquidity among affiliated firms; most credits are short term, typically two to three months. Enterprise ownership of banks has perpetuated connected and inside lending; enterprise deposits are, after central bank contributions, the most important source of funds for commercial banks. To an increasing extent banks also hold equity in borrowing firms and in voucher investment funds.

The financial systems in the four Visegrad countries have evolved further and decisionmaking has been decentralized (Dittus 1994). Banks are more independent from both the central banks and firms, and they play a more active role in managing their portfolios. Consequently, bank incentives matter more than in Russia. This is significant because most banks have been saddled with bad loans from prereform years, rendering the average quality of loan portfolios very poor. A number of recapitalizations have been undertaken with varying results, but most banks still suffer from low capital adequacy ratios. Commercial banks have become important owners in many enterprises, particularly in the Czech Republic and Hungary. Czech banks directly control more than 40 percent of the investment points in the first wave of privatization, and estimates suggest that the figure would rise to 60 percent if indirect holdings were included (Stern 1993). Three of the top four investment funds are controlled by banks. In Hungary, bank ownership is largely a result of conversion of old loans into equityholdings.

Enterprises in the transition economies are establishing links among themselves through the widespread use of trade credits and, to an increasing extent, crossholdings of equity. The widely reported rise in enterprise credits in Russia followed attempts by the government to cut subsidies. In the absence of alternative external sources of finance, trade credits may offer temporary relief from the effects of fiscal tightening. Initially the expansion of interenterprise lending and the potential consequences of accumulating arrears on these credits put strong pressure on the central bank, forcing it to bail out firms on several occasions. The growth in trade credits in Russian enterprises now seems to have leveled off, because many firms only accept cash payments (Fan and Schaffer 1994). Interenterprise credits have not been as important in the Visegrad countries, and they appear to have stabilized at a reasonable level. In Hungary, however, crossholding of equity has spread quickly and resulted in a complicated and nontransparent web of ownership that largely serves to protect insiders against outside intervention.

The strong insider control in the transition economies of Eastern Europe and Russia also stems from the poor enforcement of property rights. While the role of formal legal codes in economic transition probably should not be overemphasized, the general ambiguity about existing property rights is harmful. This ambiguity arises partly from weaknesses in the legal environment, but more important is the volatile macroeconomic situation and the fragility of the political system. The problem is particularly severe in the emerging private sector and recently privatized firms that want to raise external funds. The high uncertainty also increases the option value of waiting to invest and reinforces the corporate governance problem by contaminating the signals generated by increasing market competition.

The strong insider control, the ambiguity about property rights, and the high general uncertainty have made the legal buying and selling of corporate assets more difficult. The illiquidity of assets is particularly severe for real estate, where the details of the legal framework often have not been worked out yet through legislation and case law. The absence of a market for corporate assets severely impedes the possibilities of enterprises to raise outside funds.

What Do Insiders Do?

What kind of behavior should we expect from enterprises controlled by managers in what is, in effect, a corporate governance vacuum? First, while there are some spectacular examples to the contrary, widespread asset stripping in unlikely. Managers are de facto, and in Russia and Poland increasingly de jure, owners of the enterprises, and thus we should expect them to maximize the surplus generated by corporate assets. In highly liquid asset markets, liquidated assets sell at a large discount, and managers consequently prefer to keep the firm as a going concern. Furthermore, as managerial labor markets develop, short-term behavior is increasingly likely to be penalized. Scant empirical evidence also suggests that asset stripping has been less widespread than often is believed (see, for example, Pinto, Belka, and Krajewki 1993; Estrin, Schaffer, and Singh 1993; Fan and Schaffer 1994).

Second, it is not clear that firms controlled by managers will completely abstain from labor shedding and liquidation of unprofitable production units. Without access to external finance, cutting costs may be the only way to increase the surplus generated internally. While there undoubtedly are a number enterprises where management and labor have joined forces, surveys indicate that such collusion is not the general picture (Estrin, Schaffer, and Singh 1993; Fan and Schaffer 1994). On the contrary, insider-controlled enterprises have reduced their work force substantially and closed down loss-making activities. Even in Poland, where worker control plays an important role, firms fire employees and liquidate inefficient units.

Third, while Russian managers do seem to cut costs, they are not investing sufficiently in new technology and capacity. The level of investments in Russia has fallen more than production since the dissolution of the Soviet state; the current level is only 50 percent of that in 1990. At least to some extent, the disproportionate fall in investment activity can be explained by the lack of external funds. The fundamental dilemma of insiders is that their strong control over assets makes them unable to convince outsiders to contribute capital. In the Visegrad countries external finance does seem to play a larger role, and investment has not fallen as much as production.

The picture of corporate governance that emerges in the transition economies is a scattered one; in Russia many enterprises still have direct channels to the central bank or the state budget, but the bulk of industry is severely constrained by lack of corporate governance and subsequent problems in obtaining outside finance. If macrostabilization is to be successful, the budget constraint for the first group must harden, and viable firms need to find new sources of funds. For the second group, the external finance constraint will become increasingly severe as competition increases and internally generated funds decrease further. In the Visegrad countries the budget constraints have hardened significantly following stricter banking regulation and increasing competition among banks, but strong insider control and a weak legal framework still limit the possibilities of many firms to obtain outside finance (Dittus 1994). Mounting evidence also suggests that many of the soft financing practices of the prereform period persist (for a study of credit flows in Poland, see Anderson 1994).

Corporate Governance and Finance: A Conceptual Framework

To many observers the significance of corporate governance to the transformation process is of fairly recent origin; privatization and market liberalization were supposed to be sufficient. As the need for governance has become increasingly urgent, a heated discussion has evolved around the choice among institutional arrangements. To make this choice we need a conceptual framework that allows us to describe and analyze different kinds of corporate governance institutions and different forms of corporate governance. Furthermore, in order for us to evaluate the feasibility of particular governance arrangements in the transition economies, such a framework should say something about the conditions under which particular arrangements will emerge. A framework must therefore show how the different aspects of a corporate governance arrangement relate to each other, to other aspects of the financial system, and to the rest of the economy.

This section briefly surveys the recent literature on corporate governance and extracts some basic concepts that can provide building blocks in such a framework. These concepts distinguish the basic forms of external finance, and they allow us to classify existing and potential financial institutions and financial systems. This article certainly is not the first to present such a framework (see, for example, Rybczinski 1984; Zysman 1985; Mayer 1993). What distinguishes the framework advanced here is that it that is derived directly from an explicit theory of corporate finance. Thus, the first step is to understand the basic problems facing a firm seeking to raise external finance.

The Basic Finance Problem: The Insiders' Dilemma

While it may be expressed to extremes in the transition economies, the insiders' dilemma, in essence, is nothing but the agency problem at the core of recent literature on corporate governance in finance. An entrepreneur, or the management of a firm, has ideas but insufficient internal funds to realize these ideas. The firm must then ask investors to contribute capital against promises of being paid back out of future revenues. To reduce the costs of external finance, or sometimes to obtain funds at all, promises to use invested capital in particular ways and to pay investors back must be made credible. The insiders' dilemma is that to improve credibility they must either issue contingent ownership rights to assets and cash flows of the firm (for example, by providing collateral) or give up some control over investment decisions. These options—here called arm's-length and control-oriented finance—represent two generic solutions to the basic problem of corporate finance.

The choice of terminology is somewhat arbitrary. Holmström (1992) and Holmström and Tirole (1993) use the terms "intermediated," "monitored," and "informed" interchangeably for what is here called control-oriented finance, and "uninformed" and "unmonitored" for arm's-length finance. None of these terms is ideal. Monitoring is just one form of financial intermediation. The dichotomy "uninformed-informed" highlights the information available to investors, whereas the crucial distinction here is whether or not investors influence investment decisions; "monitoring" is also often used to denote the collection of information. Furthermore, "uninformed" and "unmonitored" suggest that assessing collateral requires no information. On the contrary, arm's-length finance requires information verifiable by courts; under control-oriented finance only the information of controlling investors matters.

Before discussing these generic forms of external finance, two points should be made. First, the relative importance of external finance, and consequently of corporate governance, depend on a firm's ability to generate funds internally. As this ability varies across firms and industries and over the business cycle, so does the role of external finance. Second, the finance decision—that is, the choice between internal and external finance and among sources of external finance—may itself be subject to agency problems. For example, even though a firm has profitable investment opportunities, a manager may decide not to raise funds externally, because he would have to give up some control rights. This seems to be the prevailing attitude among many managers in the transition economies at the moment.

Arm's-Length Finance: "Governance by Objective"

The literature on arm's-length finance has focused on the problem of getting the firm to pay out at all. Loosely speaking, arm's-length finance is "corporate governance by objective"; investors do not interfere directly in strategic decisions as long as they are paid according to contract. This, in a sense, is the extreme case of insider control. Arm's-length finance does not rule out intervention. Nevertheless, the initial investors rely on the external mechanisms such as the market for corporate control or bankruptcy courts to achieve such intervention.

While investors do not intervene in the investment decision itself, they can, when the firm fails to pay out, foreclose, or at least threaten to foreclose, on assets or cash flows specified in the financial contract. The scope for external finance is here limited by what is credibly contractable—that is, what can be enforced in court. Whereas cash flows in a firm may be difficult to use as the basis for a contract, physical assets, in particular buildings and land, but also machines, may be more easily valued. The use of such collateral reduces the downside risk for the investor, but it also affects the ex post bargaining situation between the firm and its investors (Hart and Moore 1989, 1991). If the collateralized assets are important to the future earnings capacity of the firm, a threat to take possession can be used to extract funds when the firm refuses to pay out. Giving an outside investor such liquidation rights ex post can make a commitment to pay out credible ex ante.

The problem with the threat to liquidate is that this also hurts investors if they have long-term interests, such as equity or long-term debt, in the firm. To make the threat more effective, and thus strengthen commitment ex ante, investors can separate their claims over time (Berglöf and von Thadden, forthcoming). When an investor with collateral only holds short-term claims, the liquidation threat becomes more credible. Thus, arm's-length finance helps explain why firms often have both long-term and short-term investors, why their financial claims differ in security interests and priority, and why they specialize in particular claims. The relative bargaining power of the firm may also depend on the number of investors involved in bargaining and the allocation of security interests among them (Bolton and Scharfstein 1992); theoretical and empirical evidence suggests that more complicated capital structures with a large number of investors holding different kinds of claims may make the firm weaker in ex post bargaining. When investors are dispersed and have conflicting interests, it may be more difficult for them to agree to reschedule their claims.

It should be emphasized that a firm relying on arm's-length finance does not only raise external finance in the form of secured debt. In Berglöf and von Thadden (forthcoming), the firm issues both secured short-term debt and equity, and sometimes bonds. In most cases some of the firm's cash flows are also verifiable, that is, enforceable in court, and can thus be contracted credibly in the form of equity or unsecured debt. The extent of verifiability of assets and cash flows depends on a broad range of factors, such as the nature of the firm's business, auditing requirements, the sophistication of outside analysts, whether the firm is publicly listed or not, and the capability of the legal system.

Under arm's-length finance there is a strong connection between the nature of a firm's assets and its finance capacity—the more liquid its assets are, the more, or the cheaper, capital it can raise. This may help explain why small firms, medium-size firms, and new firms, for which less information is publicly available, are more dependent on expensive short-term bank finance than larger and older, relatively better-known, firms. By the logic of arm's-length finance it is in a firm's interest to seek secured short-term finance from "tough" bargainers, such as banks with large resources and a reputation at stake in other credit relationships; this further improves the commitment power of security interests.

The scope for arm's-length finance is strongly affected by the general state of the economy. The threat to liquidate is more effective, and arm's-length finance consequently more attractive, when liquidation values are high—that is, when asset markets are liquid and assets are not specialized (Shleifer and Vishny 1992). When asset values are depressed—for example, in a recession or after demand has fallen in an industry—investors will demand more collateral and previously unconstrained firms may have problems raising funds. The need for collateralizable assets—and cash flows—can thus also help explain why the effects of economic downturns on financing conditions differ across firms of different sizes and across industries, and why in a recovery credit constraints loosen faster for some firms than for others.

In the transition economies the illiquidity of asset markets is further reinforced by the ambiguity of property rights and the prohibitions against transfers of certain assets. The extreme situation of insider control studied in the literature on arm's-length finance is not extreme enough—in many enterprises in the transition economies there may be few, if any, assets that can be contracted. In such an environment, control-oriented finance may be the only option open to firms.

Control-Oriented Finance: "Governance by Intervention"

Under control-oriented finance investors take it upon themselves to reduce agency problems by monitoring the firm's investment decisions (Holmström and Tirole 1993). If arm's-length finance implies "governance by objective," then control-oriented finance is "governance by intervention." The exercise of control can take many forms, such as vetoing inefficient decisions or using control rights to force the implementation of efficient decisions. Replacing management when it undertakes certain actions, or fails to undertake others, is a similar way of affecting investment decisions.

As illustrated by figure 3-1, the nature of control is affected by the kind of claims held by the investor and by her capital structure. If the investor only holds debt in the firm, control rights are state-contingent in the sense that they are exercised primarily in bad states of nature

Figure 3-1. Different Forms of Control and the Balance Sheet of Controlling Investors

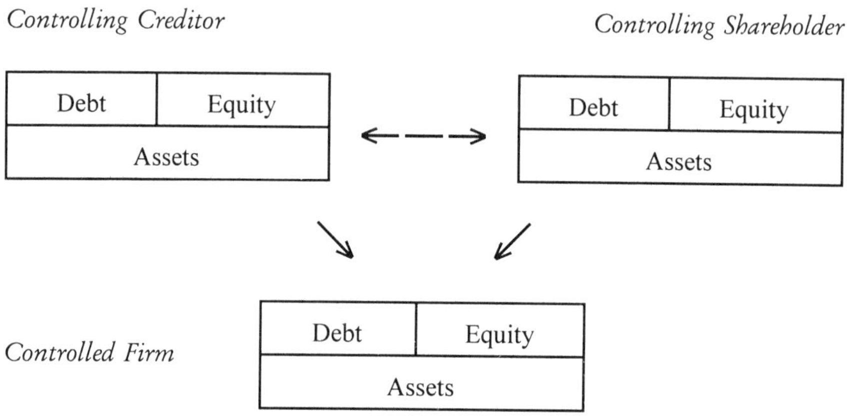

when the firm cannot meet its payment obligation (Aghion and Bolton 1992). If the intermediary only holds equity, control is confined to non-default states. In many firms debt and equity control are performed by different investors. In some cases the investor holds both debt and equity claims on the same firm, and the exercise of control could occur across all states, with the nature of intervention changing as the firm comes into financial difficulties.

Debt and equity control also differ because of the different return schedules associated with these instruments. The fixed payment with no share in upside returns makes the monitor tough—that is, more likely to favor less risky actions, such as a discontinuation of particular projects or of the entire firm (Dewatripont and Tirole, forthcoming). Equity, in contrast, is soft, with a bias in favor of incumbent management and continued operation of the firm. Thus, while debt and equity control complement each other, it is more doubtful whether they can serve as substitutes for one another.

The optimal form of control depends on the nature of the agency problem between the firm and its investor—that is, whether the firm is likely to underinvest or overinvest and whether conflicts are state-contingent or not. If the firm is inclined to excessively risky actions, the bias of debt could serve as a counterbalance to management. If potential underinvestment is the problem, debt may reinforce the agency problem. Similarly, if management is more likely to behave inefficiently when the firm is doing poorly—for example, by refraining from shedding labor or by gambling for resurrection—state-contingent, or debt, control may be preferable. If the main agency problem is to prevent managers from building empires in otherwise healthy companies, we should expect to observe equity control (under arm's-length finance the same objective would be achieved by issuing debt; see Jensen 1986). The difference in nature between debt and equity control suggests that a specialization among controlling entities may be preferable. Liquidation and restructuring in bad states of nature also require quite different skills from those needed to constrain a management inclined to empire building in a firm that is doing well.

Control can be exercised directly by an individual investor, but also by an intermediary with liquid claims (for example, short-term deposits and listed equity) on the liability side of the balance sheet and illiquid claims (such as debt and equity holdings in client firms) on the asset side; intermediation transforms illiquid claims into liquid ones. It is the combination of the information collected and the control rights exercised that allow such intermediation.

Thus, to understand the nature of monitoring we have to study not only the type of instruments held by the controlling entity but also the concentration of these holdings in its portfolio and the incentives provided by its balance sheet. Two useful distinctions can be made between portfolio-oriented and control-oriented investors, and between well-capitalized and heavily leveraged investors. A portfolio-oriented investor emphasizes diversification of risk and has little incentive to exercise control, and thus typically purchases arm's-length instruments. A control-oriented investor foregoes diversification opportunities to exercise control, or at least to have the potential of doing so. For a control-oriented investor the composition of the balance sheet may affect incentives to monitor. A poorly capitalized bank, or a bank that is explicitly or implicitly insured against downside risks, may support riskier investments than desirable, or it may shirk in the exercise of control. High leverage where default leads to dire consequences for management may also provide incentives for monitoring.

The control-oriented investor's costs of monitoring are the diversification opportunities foregone and the expenses in collecting information and influencing strategic decisions. Because holding large control blocks involves fixed costs, control-oriented financial arrangements are typically long term, and control blocks of equity and bank debt tend to be less liquid than minority equity and bonds. In addition, when resources available for the exercise of control are scarce (for example, in an economy undergoing transition and where existing institutions are still in embryonic form), state-contingent debt control may economize on controlling costs by allowing financial distress to serve as a screening device—as long as the firm is doing fine the intermediary basically remains passive, and its control is only activated when a firm enters into distress. Debt control thus offers a screening device that allows investors to identify the firms most in need of monitoring.

A wide range of institutions—not only banks, but also investment companies, mutual funds, and even other enterprises—may exercise control. Figure 3-2 classifies existing and potential control-oriented investors according to capitalization and kind of control. These basic concepts clarify the debate concerning the choice between different control-oriented intermediaries, such as mutual funds as opposed to commercial banks. In the terminology used here, the mutual funds put forth in the debate are well-capitalized (basically all-equity) intermediaries exercising governance through controlling blocks of equity. Commercial banks are less well-capitalized, particularly in the transition economies, and control is primarily based on large debt holdings, but possibly on holdings of equity as well. In the popular debate the two kinds of intermediaries are often treated as mutually exclusive. The corporate governance literature suggests, however, that mutual funds and commercial banks complement each other not only in the financial system as a whole, but also in the individual firm.

The conceptual framework also throws some light on the emerging intermediaries in the transition economies. Figure 3-1 suggests that the juxtaposition of mutual funds and commercial banks is misleading. Calling the Czech investment privatization funds "mutual" is a misnomer. These intermediaries have complex capital structures, with equity hold-

Figure 3-2. Control-Oriented Investors by Capitalization and Kind of Control

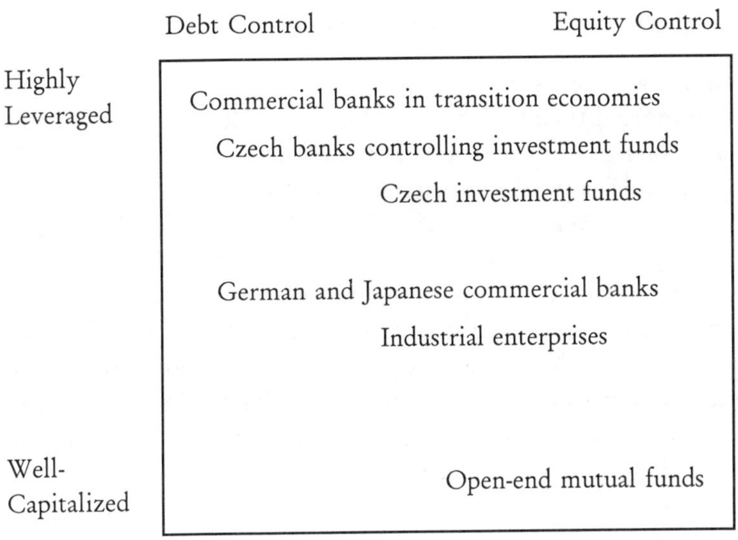

ings by banks and private individuals, and debt claims held by the original voucher holders. Viewed in this way, many of the funds are heavily leveraged and vulnerable to systemic shocks in much the same way as banks. Many of the so-called investment funds emerging from voucher privatization in the Czech Republic and Russia are strongly affiliated with commercial banks. Thus, for the purposes of governance, the two intermediaries form part of a single state-contingent corporate governance arrangement where control shifts from equity to debt when firms come into financial distress.

Intermediaries can also control each other through mutual arrangements, and one intermediary can specialize in controlling other intermediaries. Ultimately, however, the question of intermediary incentives raises the perennial issue of "who controls the controllers," and the credibility of the government in disciplining failing institutions—an issue of acute importance in the transition economies addressed in the final section of the chapter.

The Firm's Capital Structure and the Financial System

Whereas these two forms of finance are distinct in theory, in reality they may be more difficult to discern. For example, claims originally issued as arm's-length finance can later turn into control-oriented finance. For example, a portfolio-oriented investor may change strategy and decide to take over control of the firm by increasing her stake. Similarly, it is not uncommon for a bank, even though it was not control-oriented initially, to purchase the claims of other creditors when a debtor firm enters into financial distress. In their ambition to hold the market portfolio, certain large, portfolio-oriented investors—for example, some pension funds in the United States—also have come to hold such large stakes in individual firms that they are more or less forced to exercise control. Of course, a control-oriented investor may later divest his controlling share, as is common in venture capital finance, for example.

Arm's-length and control-oriented finance may also be difficult to distinguish because many, if not most, firms raise funds through both arm's-length and control-oriented finance; the two forms of finance complement rather than substitute for each other. For example, the contingent liquidation rights associated with secured debt may serve to increase the effectiveness of monitoring. Effective monitoring may also reduce the uncertainty about underlying assets, thus increasing the firm's capacity to raise arm's-length finance. Similarly, the guarantees implied by the presence of a main bank may make other investors more willing to commit to arm's-length finance. Indeed, the importance of commercial banks in most countries derives to some extent from the ability of these institutions to provide both kinds of finance. The combination of seats on the board, votes in the general shareholders' meetings, and security interests in crucial buildings or machinery should increase the likelihood of monitoring being effective.

The two forms of finance also complement each other because they are influenced by different factors. For arm's-length finance, the nature of a firm's assets plays an important role. This form of finance also strongly relies on the liquidity of markets for corporate assets, and consequently on the extent of enforcement of property rights and general business conditions. The conditions for control-oriented finance are less well understood, but establishing and maintaining monitoring relationships is costly; control-oriented finance should be expected to be more long term and less vulnerable to short-term fluctuations. In addition, while the exercise of control requires sophisticated institutions, control-oriented finance may be less dependent on the formal legal framework.

The relative importance of arm's-length and control-oriented finance should vary not only across firms and industries, but also across countries. Unfortunately, traditional financial statistics do not distinguish between arm's-length and control-oriented finance; equity finance can be both arm's-length and control-oriented, as can bank debt. In addition, differences in accounting and statistical methods make reliable international comparisons of patterns of finance across countries difficult. The evidence suggests, however, that internal finance is by far the most important source of finance, and debt finance the most important external source, in all the major industrialized countries (Mayer 1990). There appear to be significant international variations in the degree and nature of intermediation within economies, across industries, and across firms of different sizes, as well as across countries, depending on level of development and institutional arrangements.

While the dominance of internal funds in total finance and bank loans in external finance is virtually universal, there appear to be significant international variations in the degree and nature of control orientation within economies, across industries, across firms of different sizes, and across countries, depending on level of development and institutional arrangements. The clustering of these arrangements suggests a strong interconnectedness among different aspects of the financial systems. For example, countries with strong commercial banks tend to have a higher share of control-oriented finance, more concentrated ownership of debt and equity, less turnover in control positions, and less liquid markets for equity and debt. Attempts have been made to understand these patterns by classifying financial systems into broad categories such as bank-oriented and market-oriented, or market-based and credit-based. Table 3-1 shows one, necessarily simplistic, classification. To make clear the link between the basic form of finance and the financial system, and avoid some of the misleading associations of

Table 3-1. Financial Systems and Capital Structure

	Type of financial system	
Item	*Control-oriented*	*Arm's-length*
General characteristic		
Share of control-oriented finance	High	Low
Depth and width of financial markets	Low	High
Bank assets as a share of total financial assets held by financial institutions	High	Low
Control-oriented intermediaries	High	Low
Likelihood of going public	Low	High
Importance of market for corporate control	Low	High
Creditor structure		
Degree of concentration	High	Low
Bank credits to total liabilities	High	Low
Bonds to total liabilities	Low	High
Turnover of holdings	Low	High
Shareholder structure		
Degree of concentration	High	Low
Bank shareholdings	High	Low
Interfirm shareholdings	High	Low
Turnover of control blocks	Low	High

the previous typologies, the terms arm's-length and control-oriented financial systems are used here.

Some of the interdependencies in table 3-1 are self-explanatory, even tautological. It is obvious, at least given the argument pursued here, that a financial system dependent on control-oriented finance requires more control-oriented intermediaries, more concentrated capital structures, and will have lower turnover of large blocks of debt and equity. High ratios of bank credits to total liabilities and extensive interfirm shareholdings are also expressions of the significance of control-oriented finance. The existence of close control relationships may reduce the incentives to incur the costs of going public and prevent firms from going from closely held to widely held. When firms are not widely held, the market for corporate control can play little role in disciplining management; a hostile bid is only possible if the controlling owner has less than a majority of the outstanding shares.

The list of attributes of the financial systems in table 3-1 is by no means exhaustive, and there is reason to believe that there are more interesting interrelationships within the financial system, and between the financial system and the rest of the economic system. Aoki (1984, 1994), for example, in his discussion of the Japanese firm, notes a strong complementarity between external control systems and the internal organization and operation of firms. In particular, financial and employee interests complement each other in influencing managerial decisions. Given the tradition of worker influence in many of the transition economies, similar patterns are likely to emerge. Wymeersch (1994) argues convincingly for a relationship among the financial system, firm organization, and the legal framework. He distinguishes between company-based legal codes that focus on the contractual relationship between the firm and its investors and enterprise-based legal codes emphasizing the firm as a productive entity and the role of codetermination.

The distinction between arm's-length and control-oriented financial systems suggests two fundamentally different models of capitalism—one where ownership and control have become strongly separated and one where this separation is much less important. That ownership and control are more closely associated does not imply that this holds for the ultimate distribution of wealth and control over enterprises. While family ownership seems to play a more important role in large enterprises in control-oriented systems, indirect ownership through intermediary institutions also is more common; this helps explain the many layers of ownership observed in, for example, German enterprises by Franks and Mayer (1992). It is likely that we will see similar patterns emerging in the transition economies of Eastern Europe and the former Soviet Union.

The conceptual framework of table 3-1 places the corporate governance discussion in the larger context of the financial system. The classification is based on observations of developed capitalist economies, but it allows us to speculate about where the transition economies are heading. There are a number of signs that these systems, sometimes despite government policy, are becoming increasingly control-oriented. Even in countries that have followed equity-based voucher privatizations, such as the Czech Republic and Russia, banks seem to emerge as the most important outside investors, in some cases by investing directly in firms, but often indirectly by buying into investment funds. The observation that these financial systems are becoming control-oriented has implications not only for intermediation, but also for the evolution of equity and bond markets and financial regulation. Before suggesting the main lessons for policy, however, the framework is illustrated using a particular governance arrangement that combines different forms of finance and intermediation.

An Example: The Japanese Main Bank System and the Financial Keiretsu

A first indication of the usefulness of a conceptual framework is given by its ability to characterize existing governance arrangements. This section describes corporate governance in Japan, focusing on the main bank system and the closely associated financial *keiretsu*. These arrangements have been put forth as models for transition economies (for example, in Bardhan and Roemer 1992). Extensive research in recent years has provided detailed information on their structure and behavior (for a recent characterization, see Aoki, Patrick, and Sheard 1994). The example of corporate governance in Japan also yields further insights into how the different forms of finance complement each other and how the different aspects of governance arrangements are related.

The main bank system and the financial *keiretsu* are essentially two different, but overlapping and complementary, corporate governance arrangements. The main bank system combines relationships between banks and firms, among banks, and between banks and regulatory institutions. Almost all Japanese firms have close links to one particular bank. These relationships involve loans, but also assistance in bond issues, shareholdings, payment settlement accounts, and various informational and managerial services. Many, mostly larger, firms also have relationships among themselves, denoted financial *keiretsu*. These interfirm links include crossholdings of equity and debt (through trade credit), trade in goods and services, and, for core firms, membership in

Presidents' Clubs. The main bank can be viewed as the foundation, and the financial *keiretsu* reinforces this foundation. Core firms are more closely tied together, while peripheral firms form much looser relationships. There is also variation in the tightness of these linkages among the financial *keiretsu* (Hoshi and Ito 1991). For simplicity, this section focuses on the situation in firms that have both a main bank relationship and are affiliated with one of the large, more cohesive financial *keiretsu*.

The exercise of control in the financial *keiretsu* is state-contingent. As long as payment obligations are met, largely passive mutual equity monitoring among affiliated firms dominates. But when a firm gets into financial distress, the governance mode shifts to active intervention, generally led by the main bank. To obtain early warnings of potential problems and to facilitate coordination, the bank guarantees trade credits among *keiretsu* firms. If a firm defaults on one of its trade creditors, the claim is transferred to the bank, which then decides on the form of intervention. Such state-contingent control allows the bank to focus on restructuring in financial distress. Empirical evidence also shows that when profits fall in a member firm, both the main bank and the shareholders send directors to the ailing firm, but if there are liquidity problems, only the main bank sends directors (Kaplan and Minton, forthcoming).

Thus, the main bank arrangement with the associated financial *keiretsu* is a dynamic relationship that changes in response to the conditions of the individual firm and the general state of the economy. For firms that are doing well, the state-contingency feature plays little or no role, whereas in firms with liquidity problems the possibility of transferring control to the main bank is crucial. In the era of rapid growth in the Japanese economy, most firms relied heavily on the main bank relationship, but in the 1980s the importance of the bank lessened considerably.

An arrangement based on crossholdings of debt and equity could be used to entrench incumbent managers of banks and firms from the pressures of the marketplace. One reason that such "low-effort" equilibria are not observed may be found in the capital structure of the main bank. The bank is heavily leveraged, with most of its liabilities in short-term deposits. If the bank were to shirk in monitoring, it would be the first to suffer. Given the implicit and explicit government guarantees in case of bank failures, however, leverage may not provide sufficient incentives and may potentially make the bank take larger risks than desirable. Sheard (forthcoming) shows that these incentive problems can be mitigated through delegated monitoring among main banks. While the group bank is the largest lender in member firms, the lending relationship is not exclusive; a firm typically also borrows from main banks of other groups. These banks monitor each other and delegate to each group's main bank the responsibility of restructuring member firms in financial distress. The group bank's status as the largest lender, and in addition that it has guaranteed much of the outstanding trade credits, provides it with strong incentives to act on its promise.

The empirical evidence suggests that *keiretsu* firms, at least during certain periods, have been less profitable than independent firms (Nakatani 1984). The relatively high wage levels in *keiretsu* firms and the high interest rates paid to group banks indicate that this may reflect a distribution of output in favor of insiders at the expense of outside shareholders and creditors. More important, from an efficiency point of view, recent research by Hoshi, Kashyap, and Scharfstein (1990a, 1991a) shows that firms affiliated with a financial *keiretsu* and a main bank are less sensitive to liquidity fluctuations than independent firms. In other words, a *keiretsu* firm is less likely to have to reduce investments or shed labor in the event of a shortfall in liquidity; the main bank relationship provides insulation against the effects of cash shortages.

As evidenced by the pressure put on banks by the recent decline in real estate prices, arm's-length finance, although seldom mentioned, also plays an important role in main bank financing in Japan. The main bank usually has at least part of its debt collateralized in prime assets. While the bank appears willing to make concessions outside of formal bankruptcy, it seems to pursue its security interests vigorously once a firm has ended up in court (Packer and Ryzer 1992).

The financial *keiretsu* thus illustrates how arm's-length and control-oriented finance, along with debt and equity monitoring, can be combined into a state-contingent monitoring mechanism, with a critical role played by a heavily leveraged, control-oriented intermediary. The nature of the exercise of control changes from passive mutual monitoring based on equityholdings among firms to active intervention by a control-oriented intermediary holding debt claims. The example, however, also shows how the concepts provided by the framework only capture part of the complexity of the relationships between the bank and the firm and among firms. In particular, the analysis focuses only on the formal aspects of the relationships—the holdings of equity and debt—but does not include the informational and other services performed by the bank. The interfirm relationships within the financial *keiretsu* also involve the exchange of goods and services that are generally outside the analysis. Furthermore, the framework does not consider the role of the government in monitoring intermediaries. Finally, by focusing on the relationships between the firm and investors, this literature does not consider the interaction between these relationships and the internal organization of the firm. All these limitations should be kept in mind in considering the policy implications.

Some Lessons for Transition Economies

The research on corporate governance is still in its infancy, but the literature provides a basic framework for description and analysis. This framework suggests some preliminary lessons for corporate governance in transition economies.

- *Internally generated funds will be by far the most important source of finance.* This is true in all industrialized countries, but the costs of external finance are likely to be particularly high in the transition economies given the weak outside institutions and legal framework.
- *Most of the external funding will have to come from control-oriented finance.* The markets for real assets will remain illiquid, at least in the medium term, because of strong insider control and poor enforcement of property rights. Efforts to privatize and facilitate transfer of real estate are particularly important for arm's-length finance to develop.
- *Stock and bond markets are not going to play a major role in the provision of funds during early phases of economic transition.* Promoting the liquidity of stock and bond markets is of second order compared with the promotion of liquidity in markets for real assets. Raising funds through minority equity is likely to

be particularly difficult given the strong insider control and poor protection of minority interests. Nevertheless, equity markets may gradually come to play a role in facilitating ownership transfer, particularly if workers start to sell their shares, and ultimately also in generating information about the performance of companies. There may be a tradeoff, however, between the liquidity of stock markets and the incentives to take control positions and exercise control; investors may choose "exit" rather than "voice" as a means of expressing their dissatisfaction with incumbent management.

- *Holdings of debt and equity will be concentrated, with little turnover in control blocks.* The corollary of illiquid stock and bond markets is highly concentrated and stable ownership structures. Patterns of ownership and control established at early stages of transition are likely to persist over long periods of time. In general, intermediaries should be prone to control-orientation in transition economies given the limited diversification opportunities open to them.
- *Control-oriented intermediaries will use both debt and equity monitoring.* Debt and equity control complement each other; both are needed. Given the nature of the corporate governance problem, however, with severe agency problems in poorly performing firms and the need for drastic restructurings, the kind of control exercised through debt holdings is likely to be particularly important. The scarcity of monitoring resources also suggests some that state-contingent monitoring will dominate.
- *Both mutual funds and commercial banks will be needed, but banks are likely to be more important in corporate governance.* The two control-oriented intermediaries can complement, compete with, and monitor each other. Given the need for debt monitoring, however, commercial banks should play the most important role, and their ability to provide several kinds of finance may prove valuable.
- *The functional specialization associated with some Western financial systems may not be feasible in the transition economies.* The exercise of control typically implies functional overlap; control-oriented intermediaries are closely involved in all stages of financial relationships. Many of the countries in Eastern Europe

have already opted for legislation allowing banks to play such a role. Such broader banks may be the only feasible solution in situations where boundaries between different banking activities are by necessity going to be fluid. Allowing banks to hold equity and to take equity as collateral (debt is then transferred into equity in financial distress) may facilitate industrial restructuring.

- *The initial choice of a privatization scheme may not be decisive in determining the evolution of the financial system.* Whereas the initial distribution of property rights in privatization may affect which institutions come to exercise control, the choice of the basic form of finance and kind of control-oriented finance is determined by fundamental characteristics of the institutional environment and the governance problem at hand. In particular, "giveaway" schemes, as shown in the Czech Republic and Russia, do not guarantee that arm's-length systems will emerge. In the Czech case, the dispersed holdings of vouchers rapidly became concentrated with the emergence of the so-called mutual funds, and the strengthening of ties between these institutions and the commercial banks suggests that the financial system is becoming increasingly control-oriented. The equity purchases by Russian banks in investment funds indicate that this country is heading in a similar direction.

What Can We Expect from Banks?

The corporate governance literature emphasizes the need for strong, independent institutions capable of monitoring investment decisions in industrial enterprises. The discussion so far has suggested that commercial banks have an important role to play in the exercise of corporate governance in the transition economies. This section asks whether existing banks can be expected to play this role. The emphasis is on understanding the banks' incentives in monitoring firms in these countries.

Even someone sympathetic to the general approach of the corporate governance literature could question its applicability to the countries in transition. Bank monitoring may be desirable, the critic may argue, but the present state of the banking sector simply does not make this a feasible option. The large commercial banks in these countries are simply products of the old monobank system populated by thoroughly corrupt bureaucrats with limited understanding of finance in a market economy. Even if these banks and their staff were reformable, the analysis overlooks the fragility of the banking sector. Macroeconomic instability and the financial heritage from the old system is likely to give rise to repeated bank insolvencies, and subsequent bailouts by the government. Under such circumstances it is questionable whether banks have the right incentives to monitor firms.

Do Bank Incentives Matter, and What Are They?

A first question is, of course, whether incentives matter, or whether they are sufficient to change managerial behavior. In its extreme form, the corruption argument says that incentives will not make a difference when they are applied in the old institutional structures. When a group of managers decides to leave their old bank to set up shop next door, however, they will behave efficiently. At the other extreme, only incentives matter; with the appropriate reward and punishment structures, any manager can be expected to behave efficiently to the best of his ability. An intermediate view, and the one taken here, is that while institutions are important, much can be gained by getting incentives right. The skills and information necessary for effective monitoring are in short supply, and the problem is to determine where these resources are used most efficiently. In any case, from a policy point of view the debate over the choice between new and old banks appears to be dead; most countries have opted for policies that involve both new and old institutions. Early evidence suggests that competition in banking is increasing, and that new banks are gaining market shares (Dittus 1994). The issue addressed here is how these institutions—new or old—can be given the right incentives.

There is, however, a second reason why incentives, at least the incentives provided by the banks' balance sheets, would not matter: the banks may not be making the lending decisions. In the first phase of financial transition, at the stage of Russia at the moment, the banking system is still dominated by the large funds channeled from the Central Bank to state-owned enterprises. Most decisions in the financial systems remain centralized, and the incentives provided by the composition of bank portfolios, and potential future bailouts, thus play a limited role. In the second phase, where we find the most advanced transition economies of Poland, Hungary, and the Czech Republic, decisionmaking has become more decentralized. The incentives facing financial institutions, and commercial banks in particular, then become important. Banks that have inherited poor loan portfolios may not feel motivated to monitor clients, not even new customers. It is not until the financial system has entered into this second phase of transition that the fragility of the banking system has an important impact on banks' incentives.

How bad are existing bank portfolios? There is no easy answer to this question. A thorough study by Dittus (1994), however, suggests that the problem may have been exaggerated. Indeed, while the situation is still serious, and capital adequacy ratios low by Western standards, available evidence indicates that the problem is close to a solution in the Czech Republic and of manageable proportions in Hungary. In Poland, the poor quality of bank portfolios remains an important problem, and further recapitalizations will be needed. No reliable information is available for Slovakia after the separation, but earlier figures point to a situation somewhere in between those of the Czech Republic and Poland. In Russia the high inflation has drastically reduced the value of financial claims, eliminating the problem of bad loans, but leaving a very small and fragmented banking sector.

What, then, are the consequences of bad portfolios on the incentives of banks to take control positions and exercise control? The stance most often taken is that banks with poor portfolios will be soft in lending and negligent in monitoring enterprises; managers know that they are going to be bailed out, or that things are over no matter what. Surprisingly to many, recent survey evidence from Poland suggests that the effects of the poor quality of banks' loan portfolios on corporate governance are much weaker than expected (Estrin, Schaffer, and Singh 1993). Even banks with large amounts of bad loans seem to monitor new credits in a satisfactory way, and they do not throw good money after bad to the extent expected. The Dittus study reinforces this impression. In 1992 enterprises in the four Visegrad countries paid more in interest than they received in new loans. In Hungary, enterprises even paid back part of their loans. He also shows convincingly that the fall in bank lending does not reflect lower demand by enterprises. His findings raise the question of whether banking regulation may have become too strict too quickly; all the countries experienced a severe credit crunch in 1992, with potentially large costs in profitable investments foregone. Judging from the Dittus study, banks, if anything, seem to be too tough. A possible interpretation supported by other casual evidence is that while banks tend to be soft on old loans, they are hard on new lending.

One explanation for why the relationship between stocks and flows of loans may be weaker than previously thought is that the incentives facing a bank manager may have been conceived too narrowly. Managerial decision may, for example, also be influenced by an emerging market for bank managers and increasing competition in the banking sector. In addition, bank managers may take into account the expected consequences for management of government bailouts. A number of bailouts of banks have already taken place in Eastern Europe, and more must be expected. There is no question that across-the-board bailouts are bad for incentives; bad banks are rewarded whereas good banks are penalized. If bad banking can be distinguished from good ex post, however, at least to some extent, the government may be able to influence incentives ex ante. The experience from bank bailouts—for example, in Scandinavia—shows that the government, by default, has wide discretion after a bank failure has occurred. Regulators have used this discretion to, among other things, replace and fine managers and directors, force bank mergers, close unprofitable operations, undertake training programs, and alter lending routines. If bank managers know that, even though depositors are protected, they themselves are not, government guarantees may be less harmful to incentives. Indeed, bank bailouts, although costly and undesirable, have proven to be useful tools for restructuring the banking sector and correcting managerial failure.

Even if banks could be expected to monitor firms effectively in a fragile financial system, having banks heavily involved in the manufacturing sector could have negative consequences for the stability of banking and the entire financial system. The "corporate governance" view of banking does not address this second, systemic, effect of fragility. Mounting empirical evidence suggests that a collapse in the credit system, and ultimately in the payment system, can be very costly, in particular for small and medium-size firms. It seems to be these effects of fragility, rather than the weakened monitoring incentives, that have been on regulators' minds in many Western countries. Any discussion of the role of banks in corporate governance in transition economies must take these systemwide effects into account. The analysis thus suggests a tradeoff between gains from improved corporate governance and the costs of a more fragile financial system.

What Can Be Done to Reduce the Fragility of the Banking Sector?

Much of the fragility of the banking sector in the transition economies stems from bad loans incurred prior to or in early phases of economic reform. These bad loans represent claims on enterprises in need of restructuring, and sometimes complete liquidation. The corporate governance literature suggests that recapitalization and corporate restructuring must go hand in hand; the balance sheets of the banks should, as far as possible, be cleared up without destroying the incentives for firms to restructure and for banks to monitor such restructuring. A number of measures have been undertaken to improve banks' balance sheets, and others have been proposed. This section briefly describes the most important experiences and how they can be understood in the framework of this paper.

The Visegrad countries have tried several ways of recapitalizing banks. The choice of form has been motivated largely by whether loans were incurred before or after reforms started and whether problem loans were easily identifiable, but also by the preferences of the individual government (Dittus 1994). In former Czechoslovakia and in Hungary, where the stocks of old loans with low interest were reasonably well defined, the authorities chose to provide interest subsidies to make the loans yield market-related rates of return. When problem loans were clearly defined, these loans were transferred to special government agencies. In Poland old loans were generally wiped out by hyperinflation. When loans had been incurred after economic reforms, Czechoslovakia and Poland have chosen to recapitalize banks and leave them to reach workout agreements with debtor firms. Hungary initially preferred to transfer these loans as well to a government agency, but later decided to recapitalize. None of the countries, with the exception of a brief experiment in Hungary, has attempted to use government guarantees to clean up bank portfolios.

The Polish restructuring scheme illustrates well how incentives can be maintained throughout the process. After a major recapitalization early in 1993, the authorities deliberately involved the banks in the restructuring process; 3,000 enterprises with substandard loans have been allocated to special workout departments in nine "target" banks. The banks and the debtor firms were supposed to have struck agreements on their loans by March 31, 1994, or the firms would face liquidation. Some 200 enterprises were granted reprieves with gradually declining subsidies. The government could play an important role in restructuring (van Wijnbergen 1993). In most firms government is both the largest owner and the senior creditor because of tax liabilities. To achieve agreements among the involved parties, the government usually has to both extinguish its old equity and to give up its senior claim status. In addition, the government has matched debt reductions by other creditors and participated in the conversion of debt into new equity.

What Can We Expect from the Government?

A commercial banking sector involved in monitoring manufacturing firms clearly relies on the government playing an active role in maintaining the stability of the financial system. Is it realistic to expect the government to play this role in the transition economies? Without addressing this issue directly, we will indicate some factors that complicate state involvement in the financial system.

First, however, it may be useful to distinguish the role of the state in the two initial phases of transition of the financial system. In the first phase, the main preoccupation of the government is to resist the strong collusive pressure to continue its role as provider of outside money to enterprises through the banking system. The government has accumulated little credibility capital, and thus has little to lose from bailing out failing banks and continuing to subsidize ailing firms. This reinforces the weakness of the government in the bargaining process. As intermediation deepens and the linkages between firms and banks are weakened, conflicts are introduced into the system between different commercial banks and between banks and firms. In this phase, the emphasis should be on promoting competition among intermediaries and severing the ties between banks and enterprises. When banks are mere extensions of enterprises, intermediation will not develop.

Under these circumstances providing insurance to banks is not necessary—banks take deposits primarily from enterprises that can closely monitor their use. Indeed, insuring banks closely affiliated with a single firm could be particularly harmful for incentives.

With improved regulation and increasing competition the collusive pressure should subside. In this second phase, the government worries about the incentive distortions from poor banking portfolios and the risk of systemwide crises. As the government determination to resist outside money creation becomes more credible, however, the cost of bailouts in lost credibility increases. Under favorable circumstances the government may embark on a virtuous spiral of gradual credibility building, and a transition from a "weak" to a "strong" state. There is also, however, the nonnegligible risk of a relapse into the first phase, with increasing institutional pressures to refinance ailing firms. In this more pessimistic scenario, the strengthening of the state may never come about.

Ironically, the transition from "weak" to "strong" hinges on the ability of the government to withdraw from direct involvement in economic activities. Needless to say, this process will prove difficult. First, a sizable number of "basket cases" is likely to be impossible to privatize or to entice banks into restructuring. Second, the links between the government and firms seldom disappear completely with privatization. In many cases the government retains a minority position, and in an even larger number of enterprises state-owned banks remain important creditors. In addition, when privatization is financed through government loans, default is likely to send firms back into the state-controlled sector. Even completely privatized firms may be too many and too large to fail. Third, the government is unlikely to be able, or willing, to fully withdraw its ownership interest from the banking sector in most countries, and recurrent systemic shocks may force the government to take over privatized and new private banks. Recent recapitalizations have in some cases forced the government to increase its ownership stake. To expect the government to also play the role of restructuring the financial system may be expecting too much.

Ultimately, however, the commercial banking sector and other potentially control-oriented intermediaries must develop the capacities necessary to hold and exercise control. If they do not, the pressure will mount on the government to force the banks to extend arm's-length finance beyond the collateral base of debtor firms. Under these conditions the financial system may regress into the first phase, where the influence over credit allocation is centralized and budget constraints of firms are softened. This is one possible interpretation of recent developments in Hungary, where bank portfolios have worsened considerably in the last two years, and where the government has been forced into repeated bailouts of insolvent banks.

The discussion here has assumed that the government in a transition economy has at least some agenda-setting power. In a more pessimistic view, the state is inherently weak and merely the prey of different groups struggling over the appropriation of rents in society (Roland, in this volume). In such a world, few normative conclusions can be drawn. In a slightly more optimistic perspective, however, the government, or the original framers of the constitution, can influence where in society rents are appropriated. Under these conditions the discussion in this chapter suggests that these rents initially should be allowed to accumulate in the commercial banking sector to ensure effective corporate governance and reduce the fragility of the financial system.

Some Implications for Banking Reform

The basic conceptual framework suggests that reforming the banking system is necessary for effective corporate governance; banks with bad portfolios cannot be expected to exercise control effectively. Depending on the circumstances, banks will either be unwilling to provide finance without full collateral or too willing to extend credit, but lax in the exercise of control. This section summarizes the most important lessons for banking reform in the transition economies.

- *Corporate restructuring and the cleaning up of bank portfolios should actively involve the concerned parties.* Banks and debtor firms should be forced to renegotiate their relationships before banks are recapitalized. Bankruptcy courts should only be used as a last resort. Forcing firms into formal court proceedings according to some rigid criteria, as done in Hungary, only slows down the restructuring process.
- *The government has an important role to play in both corporate restructuring and banking reform.* Whether we like it or not,

and often by default, the government has to get involved, as an important owner of debtor firms and creditor banks, and as a senior creditor through its tax claims. To achieve restructuring, the government should be willing to concede its claims, but only conditional on restructuring. When banks fail, the government has no alternative but to intervene, either by recapitalizing the bank or by closing it down.

- *Financial regulation is crucial, but must be phased in with care.* Without regulation, abuse will be widespread, and corporate governance ineffective. When capital adequacy requirements are introduced too rapidly, however, credit crunches are likely; banks with bad portfolios will be too tough rather than too soft. Regulatory authorities will also be forced to exercise considerable discretion in the implementation of specific regulations. If used in a responsible way, this discretion can offset the distortions of financially weak banks.
- *Restricting competition in the banking sector may be necessary if banks are to play a constructive role in corporate governance.* This strategy has been followed by many governments in Western Europe since World War II. The rents accumulated in this way could help reduce the fragility of a banking system heavily involved corporate governance.

Bibliography

Aghion, Philippe, and Patrick Bolton. 1992. "An 'Incomplete Contract' Approach to Bankruptcy and the Financial Structure of the Firm." *Review of Economic Studies* 59: 473–94.

Aghion, Philippe, Oliver Hart, and John Moore. 1992. "The Economics of Bankruptcy Reform." *Journal of Law, Economics and Organization* 8: 523–46.

Aghion, Philippe, and Wendy Carlin. 1994. "The Economics of Enterprise Restructuring in Central and Eastern Europe." Oxford University. Mimeo.

Anderson, Ron. 1994. "Transition Banking: Poland 1989–94." Université Catholiqué de Louvain. Mimeo.

Aoki, Masahiko, ed. 1984. *The Economic Analysis of the Japanese Firm.* Amsterdam: North-Holland.

———— . 1988. *Information, Incentives and Bargaining in the Japanese Economy.* Oxford, U.K.: Oxford University Press.

———— . 1990. "Toward an Economic Model of the Japanese Firm." *Journal of Economic Literature* 28: 1–270.

———— . 1994. "Contingent Governance of Teams: Analysis of Institutional Complementarity." *International Economic Review* 35: 657–76.

Aoki, M., H. Patrick, and P. Sheard. 1994. "Monitoring Characteristics of the Main Bank System: An Analytical and Historical View." In M. Aoki and H. Patrick, eds., *The Japanese Main Bank System: Its Relevancy for Developing and Transforming Economies.* Oxford, U.K.: Oxford University Press.

Bardhan, Pranab, and John Roemer. 1992. "Market Socialism: A Case for Rejuvenation." *Journal of Economic Perspectives* 6: 101–16.

Begg, David, and Richard Portes. 1993. "Enterprise Debt and Economic Transformation: Financial Restructuring in Central and Eastern Europe." In C. Mayer and X. Vives, eds., *Capital Markets and Financial Intermediation.* Cambridge, U.K.: Cambridge University Press.

Berglöf, Erik, and Ernst-Ludwig von Thadden. Forthcoming. "Short-Term vs. Long-Term Interests: Capital Structures with Multiple Investors." *Quarterly Journal of Economics.*

Bolton, Patrick, and David Scharfstein. 1992. "A Theory of Secured Debt: Contracting with Multiple Creditors." Université Libre de Bruxelles. Mimeo.

Dewatripont, Mathias, and Jean Tirole. Forthcoming. "A Theory of Debt and Equity—Diversity of Securities and Management-Shareholder Congruence." *Quarterly Journal of Economics.*

Dittus, Peter. 1994. "Corporate Governance in Central Europe: The Role of Banks." Bank of International Settlements, Basle. Mimeo.

Earle, J., Roman Frydman, and Andrezj Rapaczynski. 1993. "Transition Policies and the Establishment of a Private Property Rights Regime in Eastern Europe." Central European University, Prague. Mimeo.

Estrin, Saul, Mark Schaffer, and Inderjit Singh. 1993. "Enterprise Adjustment in Transition Economies: Hungary, Poland and Czechoslovakia." *Moct-Most* 3, November.

Fan, Qimiao, and Mark Schaffer. 1994. "Government Financial Transfers and Enterprise Adjustments in Russia, with Comparisons to Central and Eastern Europe." London School of Economics. Mimeo.

Franks, Julian, and Colin Mayer. 1992. "Corporate Control: A Synthesis of International Evidence." London Business School. Mimeo.

Hart, Oliver, and John Moore. 1989. "Default and Renegotiation: A Dynamic Model of Debt." London School of Economics. Mimeo.

————. 1991. "A Theory of Debt Based on the Inalienability of Human Capital." London School of Economics. Mimeo.

Holmström, Bengt. 1992. "Financing Investment in Eastern Europe. A Theoretical Perspective." Yale University. Mimeo.

Holmström, Bengt, and Jean Tirole. 1993. "Financial Intermediation and the Real Sector." Centre for Economic Policy Research, London. Mimeo.

Hoshi, Takeo, and Takatoshi Ito. 1991. "Measuring Cohesion in Japanese Enterprise Groups." University of California, San Diego. Mimeo.

Hoshi, Takeo, Anil Kashyap, and David Scharfstein. 1990a. "Bank Monitoring and Investment: Evidence from the Changing Structure of Japanese Corporate Banking Relationships." In Glenn Hubbard, ed., *Asymmetric Information, Corporate Finance, and Investment.* Chicago, Ill.: University of Chicago Press.

———— . 1990b. "The Role of Banks in Reducing the Costs of Financial Distress in Japan." *Journal of Financial Economics* 27: 315–53.

———— . 1991a. "Corporate Structure, Liquidity, and Investment: Evidence from Japanese Industrial Groups." *Quarterly Journal of Economics* 106: 33–60.

———— . 1991b. "The Choice Between Public and Private Debt: An Examination of Post-Regulation Corporate Finance in Japan." University of California, San Diego. Mimeo.

Jensen, Michael. 1986. "Agency Costs of Free Cash Flow, Corporate Finance and Takeovers." *American Economic Review* 76: 671–94.

Kaplan, Steven N., and Bernadette A. Minton. Forthcoming. "Outside Activity in Japanese Companies: Determinants and Mangerial Implications." *Journal of Law, Economics and Organization.*

Mayer, Colin. 1990. "Financial Systems, Corporate Finance, and Economic Development." In Glenn Hubbard, ed., *Asymmetric Information, Corporate Finance, and Investment.* Chicago, Ill.: University of Chicago Press.

———— . 1993. "Ownership—An Inaugural Lecture." University of Warwick. Mimeo.

Nakatani, Iwao. 1984. "The Economic Role of the Financial Corporate Grouping." In M. Aoki, ed., *The Economic Analysis of the Japanese Firm.* Amsterdam: North-Holland.

OECD. 1994. "Transformation of the Banking System in Formerly Planned Systems." *Financial Market Trends* 57: 35–44.

Packer, Frank, and Mark Ryser. 1992. "The Governance of Failure: An Anatomy of Corporate Bankruptcy in Japan." Columbia University. Mimeo.

Pinto, Brian, Marek Belka, and Stefan Krajewski. 1993. "Transition State Enterprises in Poland: Microeconomic Evidence on Adjustment." Working Paper 1101. World Bank, Washington, D.C.

Pohl, Gerhard, and Stijn Claessens. 1994. "Bank, Capital Markets, and Corporate Governance: Lessons from Russia for Eastern Europe." Europe and Central Asia and Middle East and North Africa Regions Technical Department, Private Sector and Finance Team, World Bank Policy Research Working Paper 13-26. Washington, D.C.

Rybczinski, Tad. 1984. "Industrial Finance Systems in Europe, United States and Japan." *Journal of Economic Behaviour and Organizations* 5.

Sheard, Paul. 1992. "The Economics of Interlocking Shareholding in Japan." *Ricerche Economiche* 45: 2–3.

———. Forthcoming. "Delegated Monitoring among Delegated Monitors: Principal-Agent Aspects of the Japanese Main Bank System." *Journal of Japanese and International Economics*.

Shleifer, Andrew, and Robert Vishny. 1992. "Liquidation Values and Debt Capacity: A Market Equilibrium Approach." *Journal of Finance* 47: 1343–66.

Stern, Richard. 1993. "Fundamentals of the Financial Market in the Czech Republic and Its Implications for Corporate Governance." Rand Corporation, Santa Monica, California. Mimeo.

van Wijnbergen, Sweder. 1993. "On the Role of Banks in Enterprise Restructuring: The Polish Example." Centre for Economic Policy Research Discussion Paper 898. London.

Wymeersch, Eddy. 1994. "Corporate Governance in a Comparative Perspective." University of Gent. Mimeo.

Zysman, John. 1985. *Governments, Markets, and Growth*. Ithaca, N.Y.: Cornell University Press.

Part II

Country Studies in Comparative Perspectives

4

Corporate Governance, Banks, and Fiscal Reform in Russia

John M. Litwack

From the ashes of the Soviet political and economic system, the former U.S.S.R. and Eastern Europe are currently attempting an accelerated development of the institutions of capitalism. As existing capitalist economies demonstrate a wide range of institutional combinations, the government policies chosen today may have a permanent as well as a temporary impact on the nature of the emerging economic systems in Eastern Europe. The financial sector of the economy occupies a central position here. In the short run, the former Soviet and Eastern European countries face a common dilemma: the absence of developed institutions plagues capital markets precisely at a time when large investments are needed to create viable competitive industries. In the long run, the strong institutional variance among such countries as the United States, Japan, and Germany suggests that path dependence in the adoption of financial institutions may be quite significant.

I am thankful to Gerhard Pohl and Gerard Roland for helpful comments. This paper was written under exclusive contract with the World Bank. The first version of this paper, "Corporate Governance Issues in Russia," was presented at the World Bank Workshop on "The Corporate Governance Structure in Transforming Economies with Special References to the Role of Banks and Relevance of the Japanese Experience," Stanford University, April 22–23, 1994.

Several recent studies have been devoted to the question of the development of financial institutions in Eastern Europe and the former Soviet Union. Many of these studies suggest that a financial system of the Japanese or German pattern, based on bank finance and industrial-financial groups, may be the most appropriate model of success for economies in transition. Blinder (1992) proposes that the former Soviet and Eastern European economies are currently closer to a Japanese model than to a model of American capitalism. This includes the dominance of labor over capital, a smaller reliance on the price mechanism in wholesale markets, higher job security, the absence of a developed stock market for the transfer of corporate control, and active government industrial policies. Aoki (1988) illustrates the degree to which the financial system in Japan is intimately connected with, and complementary to, other Japanese institutions involving labor and interfirm industrial organization.

Many scholars also argue that the particular circumstances of economic transition make some aspects of a Japanese-style model more attractive. Tirole (1991) maintains that the degree of uncertainty and informational problems in the initial period of transition will make stock prices too noisy, and insider trading too great, for the stock market to facilitate effective monitoring and an efficient allocation of capital. He stresses the possible advantages of institutional investors. Similarly, Scarfstein (1992) argues that the Japanese financial model is a better fit for a capitalist economy at an earlier stage of development when information problems, including the lack of business reputations and sophisticated market analysis, make stock or bond-based finance exceedingly difficult. He points out that the American economy also relied heavily on bank finance and corporate control in an early period of its development. Hoshi, Kashyap, and Loveman (1994) point out the similarity of many of the features of the post–World War II Japanese construction and those of economic transition, and argue that an American-style system probably could not work well in such an environment.

Aoki (1993) also emphasizes the potential informational advantages of ex ante, concurrent, and ex post integrated monitoring by a main bank in an early stage of capitalist development. More recently, Aoki (in this volume) has suggested that the problem of insider control in the context of economic transition might be effectively addressed through a procedure of "contingent governance," in which a "lead bank" of a syndicate can obtain control rights over an enterprise in the event of default. As in the Japanese system, insider control essentially prevails in good states but is forfeited in bad states.

At the same time, some writers who are familiar with the prevailing conditions in the former U.S.S.R. and Eastern Europe express doubts about the potential role for banks and institutional investors in corporate governance in the near future. Kornai (1990) places faith only in individual private entrepreneurs, and argues that the particular circumstances of the former socialist economies are such that institutional investors will foster additional bureaucracy instead of the needed entrepreneurship. Phelps and colleagues (1993), while agreeing with the potential positive role of institutional investors in facilitating mass privatization, express great doubt that existing commercial banks could play a positive role. They point to the lack of experience and expertise of these banks with genuine market accounting and governance, the collusive relationships between many banks and the state enterprises that they are financing, and the intimate connection of the solvency of banks with them. They further argue that debt-equity swaps could strengthen the commitment of banks to keep bad firms alive and conclude that "unfortunately, the idea that the existing offshoots of the communist banking systems in Eastern Europe could be rapidly transformed into the future analogues of Deutsche Bank seems to slide over the tremendous obstacles that lie on the way of reforming the existing banking institutions" (Phelps and others 1993, p. 24).

This chapter addresses the question of corporate governance in the presence of strong insider control in Russia. It is argued first that, in addition to factors identified in the above-mentioned studies, there are social and economic traditions in Russia that also favor the development of a Japanese-style, bank-oriented financial system as opposed to an American-style model. Current problems and trends in the Russian economy are then discussed in the area of financial markets, investment, privatization, and fiscal reform. It is stressed that, in part because of agency problems that reflect a lack of effective corporate governance, capital markets in Russia are currently unable to substitute for declining state funds in the area of investment. Despite the arguments of Phelps and colleagues summarized above, Russian commercial banks possess many advantages as potential institutions for effective corporate governance and the financing of economic restructuring. The critical factor here concerns necessary changes in the fiscal and monetary spheres. In addition to other important changes in fiscal policy, this paper advocates a joint strategy of reconstructing the accounts of commercial banks along the lines of the Japanese experience after World War II (Hoshi, Kashyap, and Loveman 1994) and, at the same time, setting up large special subsidy funds in the state budget that would effectively eliminate the current practice of administering subsidies implicitly through the commercial bank system. The task of fiscal and monetary control, necessary for providing proper incentives to banks and firms, promises to be more difficult in Russia today than in Japan in the immediate post–World War II period.

The Russian Environment before 1992 and Insider Control

Industrial managers (directors) represented and continue to represent a special group in Russian-Soviet society. After some initial experimentation with workers' and collective employee control, the principle of one-man-rule was firmly established in Soviet enterprises by the end of the 1920s. Directors of industrial enterprises occupied highly prestigious and privileged positions in Soviet society. They were members of the Communist Party and belonged to the "nomenklatura" system of promotion and demotion in the party hierarchy. The prospect of such mobility in the party hierarchy was a central feature of the managerial incentive system in the Soviet period.

Most Soviet managers and directors are still occupying these positions today, and they have become more powerful as the control mechanisms of the planned economy have disintegrated. On the positive side, Soviet enterprise directors tend to be very ambitious and were often promoted because of special talents and expertise in industrial management. On the negative side, the Soviet system in the post-Stalin years tended to promote bureaucrats as opposed to innovators. The typical optimal strategy for an enterprise director in the Soviet period was to be reliable in fulfilling the (very similar) output plan year after year. Those who were inclined toward innovation usually were not rewarded or promoted (Berliner 1976). For this reason, many enterprise directors do not embody the entrepreneurial drive and capacity for risk that is necessary for massive restructuring and market competition. It is common knowledge that effective restructuring will require a high turnover of existing management. This makes the question of quickly developing outsider-influenced corporate governance for the monitoring of management critical for Russia, as well as other economies in transition.

Although enterprise directors were quite powerful in the Soviet period, their behavior was closely monitored from three directions. First, the local, district, and regional Communist Party committees represented an ultimate source of authority. A local party committee was always located in the enterprise itself for the purpose of continual monitoring. But even more important institutions for the day-to-day regulation and monitoring of the enterprise were the Industrial Ministry and the local branch of the government bank (Gosbank). The Industrial Ministry was responsible for input and output plans, as well as important decisions on changes in these plans, and for the regulation of tax rates and incentive and investment funds. The local branch of the government bank held the financial accounts of each enterprise in its jurisdiction and monitored all (official) transactions, a process known in the former U.S.S.R. as "control by the ruble." The bank also had some discretion in reallocating funds to facilitate plan fulfillment. In the post-Stalin period, the discretionary authority of local banks in the allocation of credit increased. In addition, it was common for bank representatives to carry out random spot checks of enterprises to uncover possibly illegally horded "reserves" of inputs or shirking among employees. Incentives for bank officials were generated largely through the Communist Party hierarchy and the nomenklatura system of promotion and demotion.

It should be noted that Russian (former Soviet) banks do have some important advantages over other Russian institutions in the area of corporate governance. They have both extensive experience in monitoring and a large amount of accumulated informational capital about the potential and reliability of enterprises. That these banks have worked for many years in close contact with certain industrial enterprises can be an asset as well as a liability. On the one hand, as pointed out by Phelps and colleagues (1993) and illustrated well in the long, disappointing experience of Yugoslavia, the collusion of banks and enterprises can be an effective means of pressuring the government and central bank to extend subsidies or special credits to loss-makers. On the other hand, the existing degree of trust and dependence between banks and enterprises is a potential help in facilitating the enforcement of loan contracts.

This latter point becomes particularly important in the light of the current legal vacuum in Russia, which makes such informal institutions essential for contracting in capital markets. The enforcement of commitment and trust in economic relationships through long-run personal and mutually beneficial ties has a long and rich tradition in Russia. In addition to official institutions of the planned economy, personal ties and repeated bilateral interactions were vital means of implicit contract enforcement in the Soviet Union (Grossman 1977; Shlapentokh 1989; Litwack 1991). In the presence of political instability and lacking a coherent system of contract law, this institution continues to be of fundamental importance. As in the Soviet period, every enterprise makes special efforts to develop long-run personal relationships with suppliers, customers, and potential sources of finance. This is a very important additional factor that favors a more Asian-style model for Russia. A primary motivating factor of the *keiretsu* is vertical relations between suppliers and consumers in the industrial sphere, as well as credit provision. It is still impossible to do business in Russia without such relations.

Although overall change in the Russian economy has been many times greater during the "shock therapy" period of 1992–94 than in the Perestroika years of 1985–91, the former period has so far featured more dramatic changes in the governance of individual enterprises. The power of the Communist Party, ministries, and banks over industrial enterprises decreased enormously, in most cases leaving complete de facto control to enterprise directors. The relationship between enterprises and banks changed in a somewhat different and more subtle way than did the relationship between enterprises and the Communist Party and industrial ministries. The power of the latter declined continuously, although a trend appeared in Russia in early 1994 to restore some of the ministries' power. Banks, however, were able to keep some control over the financial accounts of enterprises through legislation that required all enterprises to hold their accounts in a single bank and allowed banks to intervene in decisions on how to divide up enterprise profits between consumption and investment funds (Russia 1992). But the enforcement of such measures was haphazard.

That Russia begins its privatization process from a point at which enterprise directors are de facto owners presents particular problems for the development of corporate governance. It is sometimes recommended that the government use its coercive power through privatization programs to wrestle control from enterprise directors in favor of outside investors. These recommendations, however, often ignore the potentially disastrous short-run effects that such policies imply. If directors perceive themselves to be de facto complete owners today and expect a hostile takeover by the government in the future, they can be expected to strip their enterprises clean before such a date. This is a primary reason why preference may be given to a mechanism, such as that proposed by Aoki (in this volume), that allows directors to voluntarily relinquish some control for the possibility of investment finance.

The Period of "Shock Therapy": 1992–94

The years of 1992 and 1993 thoroughly transformed the Russian economy. This period featured very rapid price liberalization and the removal of most central price controls, an entirely new three-level tax system, and the beginnings of massive privatization. The latter includes the corporatization and privatization of a large share of state enterprises, the issue of vouchers to the population, and the emergence of many new private businesses, banks, and mutual funds.

Finance and Investment

This period has also been associated with a rapid fall in output. Industrial output is estimated to haven fallen roughly 27 percent between August 1991 and January 1993 (Bessonov and others 1993). Between January and September 1993, it fell another 14.5 percent (Institute of Economics 1993, p. 77). Although one might expect a significant output fall during a period of rapid restructuring, a more troublesome phenomenon concerns investment, which has been falling even more rapidly than output (50–55 percent in 1992 and roughly 15 percent in 1993; see Goskomstat, 1993a,b). Although the fall in investment appears to have at least stabilized relative to the fall in output in 1993, this statistic is suspect. Major new investment tax credits that gave enterprises an incentive to categorize more of their expenses as "investments" were a feature of 1993. Through numerous loopholes, enterprises could write off labor compensation as a form of investment (Economic-Finance Center 1993). Goskomstat, the official statistical agency of Russia, estimates investment to be 8 percent of gross national product (GNP) in 1993 (Goskomstat 1993b). There is reason to believe, however, that aggregate statistics underestimate the fall in productive investment. There has also been a dramatic change in kinds of investments. If the relative weight of investment in new capital to repairs was 5 to 1 in 1990, it fell to 2 to 1 in 1992. The relative share of investment that was classified as being for the "development and improvement of production" was 23 percent and 19 percent in 1992 and the first half of 1993, respectively (Institute of Economics 1993).

The catastrophic fall in investment, coming precisely at the unfortunate time when significant investments are needed for restructuring, has a variety of causes, many of which are related to problems of insider control and corporate governance. Lower profitability, inflation, pessimistic future expectations, and the absence of institutions for monitoring enterprise management have reduced funds and lowered the incentive to use retained earnings for investment. In addition, because the government has drastically reduced the direct financing of investment from the central budget, neither commercial banks nor stock or bond issues have been able to replace these funds. Over 90 percent of all credit in the Russian economy is very short term, with an average duration that has fallen from three-to-four months in 1992 to two months in 1993. This reflects the decline of direct finance from the central budget (Institute of Economics 1993, p. 57). Virtually all credit of longer than six months duration is backed by substantial collateral and almost half (46.2 percent) of this credit is going toward the construction of individual private houses (Institute of Economics 1993, p. 57). It is true that a large amount of short-run credit is rolled over continuously, but virtually all of this credit is used to cover operating costs and wage bills of loss-making enterprises and should not be considered as investment funds. Given the infancy of financial markets in Russia and the large number of poor enterprises and swindlers that are struggling to survive and obtain financing, banks possess too little information to effectively ration investment credits for restructuring or starting up new enterprises. In addition, rapid inflation and the significant decline in real wages in the last two years have reduced savings and the supply of loanable funds.

Given the situation described above, most Russian commercial banks fall into one of two categories. The first includes commercial banks with assets that are tied to bad loans to state enterprises (the intermediation of implicit subsidies from the central bank). These banks have an incentive to keep themselves alive by both keeping these enterprises going and lobbying the central bank. The second category includes commercial banks that avoid investment projects entirely and finance quick operations, usually with either intermediate trade or currency. The orientation of these banks can be understood through the knowledge that the relative weight of credits going to middleman activities in Russia increased by nine times and reached 45 percent of all credit in 1993 (Institute of Economics 1993, p. 58). The first group of banks contains a relatively large share of state and former state banks, and the second group includes a large share of new private banks. A detailed description of the kinds of banks functioning in Russia today can be found elsewhere in this volume (see the contribution of Belyanova and Rozinsky).

Only in very special cases has private stock or bond finance worked for purposes of investment in Russia. The most well-known such case concerns the firm Avtobaz, which possesses a monopoly on the very active Russian car market and has financed major investment projects through stock issues on two occasions (Institute of Economics 1993, p. 104). On the basis of a recent extensive survey of industrial enterprises throughout Russia, the Institute of Economics (Institut Ekonomicheskoi Politiki) concludes that the vast majority of stock issues by privatized enterprises are not investment-related, but are simply attempts to cover current operating costs (1993, p. 104). Given the presence of insider-controlled firms, a huge variance in their quality and reliability, and very poor information in financial markets, the stock of relatively "bad" firms is weeding out that of the "good" firms. A relatively good firm with competent management and real investment opportunities cannot usually receive a price on the market that is anywhere close to the value of its stock.

This financial dilemma has oriented the industrialist lobby toward pressuring the state to play an active role in investment policy and to grant special investment credits. Although such credits have been drastically reduced in the last few years, they still represent a primary source of investment finance for state and private firms alike, as confirmed by the survey of the Institute of Economics.

As can be seen from box 4-1, government long-run credits, provided at special interest rates, were at least as important, or more important, for state and private (joint-stock) firms alike in mid-1993.

Privatization and Financial Intermediation

The period of 1992–94 also witnessed the beginnings of the massive privatization of state firms, the emergence of a large number of new private firms, a program of voucher distribution to the population, and, beginning in 1993, the appearance of thousands of mutual (voucher) funds, which represent financial intermediaries between the vouchers of the population of purchases of stock. Vouchers themselves are returned to the central government. Therefore, sales of stock for vouchers do not represent a source of finance for firms. In September 1993, 77,810 enterprises were listed as privatized (Institute of Economics 1993, p. 95), although such numbers are difficult to interpret because of the confusing cross-shareholding between firms. In light industry and trade, the majority of all enterprises are now private. Between January and September 1993, 515 mutual funds were founded and their numbers continue to grow (Institute of Economics 1993, p. 100), although there is a vastly disproportionate concentration of these funds in the oblasts of Moscow, Leningrad (Petersburg), and Sverdlov (Ekaterinburg).

Privatization has been a particularly politically charged issue in Russia and the speed, mood, and nature of privatization has changed with the political climate. Original plans for privatization of the Yeltsin-Gaidar government stressed the desirability of transferring control to a number of groups, including outside investors. Actual privatization legislation and practice, however, reflected a political compromise in which firms could choose between different privatization programs, one of which (type II) transfers a controlling block (51 percent) of stock to management and employees. Although a number of benefits (such as free stock and stock at special low prices) were offered

Box 4-1. August 1993 Survey of Directors of a Representative Sample of Industrial Enterprises in Russia

Question: What sources of finance are you using for the development of your enterprise (investment)?
(Answers are recorded in percentages)

Answer	*All enterprise*	*State enterprise*	*Joint-stock firms*
I am not currently not putting anything in the enterprise	10	13.3	8
I am using internal sources only (excluding worker savings)	51.3	46.7	54
I am using loans from state enterprises	2.5	0	4
I am using savings of workers	7.5	0	12
I am using long-run credit from banks at market rates	20	23.3	18
I am using special state credits at artificially low rates	35	43.3	30
Banks are directly involved in supervising investment projects	1.3	0	2
I am using commercial loans from private (nonbank) sources	8.8	3.3	12

Source: Institute of Economics 1993, p. 114.

to management and workers in an attempt to entice them to select a privatization program that features outside control (type I), these incentives did not amount to much in practice. For any kind of privatization, workers were essentially given an option of a leveraged buyout through a no-interest, long-run state loan. In a time of 20 percent monthly inflation, that amounts to a giveaway. Not surprisingly, virtually all privatization has been of the type II variety, which has cemented and formalized the insider control that came about during the period of Perestroika. At the same time, workers have been granted the right to sell their stock to outsiders, which is a potential threat to such control.

Much attention has recently focused on the newly formed mutual funds. To what degree will these funds attempt to control firms and monitor management as opposed to profiting through speculation or the diversification of risk? Preliminary survey research indicates that existing mutual funds represent a very diverse group with differing objectives (Foundation for Privatization and the Development of Financial Markets 1994). Although the vast majority of funds mention no intentions of active management and monitoring, a few important examples do exist. Fund Alfa-Kapital has succeeded in buying up a controlling interest in several oil-fat processing and cement factories, and it is intent on active management. Fund Partnerstvo has bought a controlling interest in a number of metal extraction and lumber processing plants. (Privalov and others 1994, p. 44). Although mutual funds had been restricted by law from purchasing more than 10 percent of the stock of any one enterprise, there appear to be either numerous loopholes in this law or, as is often the case in Russia, the law was simply not being enforced. This limit has recently been extended to 20 percent.

The status of commercial banks in the current privatization process is both very important and confusing. The confusion derives from a lack of coherent legislation in this area in the Russian Federation. This lack of legislation, in turn, reflects a recent dramatic change in the privatization strategy of the government. Until 1993 banks were essentially prohibited from participating in the privatization of other economic organizations. But in the summer of 1993, banks suddenly were granted the right to purchase stock and to participate directly in the formation of mutual funds to accumulate vouchers from the population. Although these rights were granted only to banks with less than 25 percent state-owned capital, it is unclear to the author how this provision is being implemented. A large percentage of the stock of commercial banks is generally held by joint-stock companies that may be state owned. In 1993 banks purchased stocks under virtually no restrictions at all, but new legislation in 1994 limits banks to holding 10 percent of the stock of a single enterprise. In addition, the stock of a single firm must account for less than 5 percent of a bank's assets.

As a result of the emergence of mutual funds and the active role for banks in privatization, institutional investors have become the most important outside investors in the current Russian privatization process. The restrictions imposed by new legislation might be circumvented through cooperation among a number of banks and mutual funds. In this way a controlling block of stock could fall into the hands of a relatively small number of institutional investors.

Fiscal Reform and Prospects for Corporate Governance in Russia

On the basis of the above discussion, we can conclude that financial markets, which have the ability to supply investment capital, have yet to emerge in Russia. A primary obstacle to this development is the presence of insider-controlled state enterprises that embody a high variance of quality in both physical and human capital. In addition to many existing studies that suggest the relative advantages of adopting a Japanese-style bank model of industrial and financial group orientation for transition economies, there are several social, political, and economic factors associated with Russia that make this case even stronger. These factors can be summarized as follows:

- There is a political imperative to limit reliance on foreign investment, which makes imperative the internal development of institutions.
- Russia has a strong tradition and necessity of repeated interactions and personal ties for enforcing contracts.
- Russian banks have already accumulated significant knowledge (informational capital) about industrial enterprises in their regions and have experience in day-to-day monitoring. Although these banks must adapt new accounting and monitoring practices in accordance with market and profit motives, they are at no disadvantage in relation to other domestic organizations that are equally inexperienced.

- In most cases, directors of Russian enterprises have already seized control and become de facto, if not legal, owners. Any privatization scheme that attempts to wrest control from management in a hostile manner will lead to extensive stripping and pilferage of state assets.

The appropriateness of a model based on the institutional investor is also born out by Russian practice, where mutual funds and banks have become the main outside players in the privatization process. It could be argued that a spontaneous evolution to an institutional investor model is already occurring. Cross-shareholding between banks and enterprises, together with group formation, has become widespread. Recent surveys document a strong preference of banks to finance enterprises that are holding their shares. In some cases, these enterprises account for 90 percent of all credits (Institute of Economics 1993, p. 58).

But the success of current trends in creating an effective financial and corporate governance mechanism in Russia is currently being threatened in the fiscal and monetary arenas. Here, two primary problems can be identified. First, there is the direct effect of fiscal and monetary policies on profit incentives. Without strong profit incentives, neither outside investors nor insiders will be willing to pay the expenses associated with monitoring and governing enterprises effectively. Second, as a means of reducing state budget deficits on paper, central bank credit, intermediated by commercial banks, has become the primary medium for administering state subsidies in Russia. This has the effect of tying banks with poorly performing enterprises and—particularly in periods of relatively low inflation— saddling the balance sheets of commercial banks with bad loans. The solvency of these banks then becomes tied to the solvency of the enterprises for whom they are administering the subsidies. This gives rise to a strong incentive to keep these enterprises alive through refinancing and influencing the central bank to continue its refinancing policies.

Profit incentives have certainly become stronger in Russia in the last two years. Both implicit and explicit subsidies exhibited a strong downward trend between 1991 and 1994. This has occurred as inflation continually outpaced regular discrete upward adjustments in nominal state wages and transfers. Surveys of enterprise management over the past two years have consistently pointed to a growing concern about profitability and an increasing awareness that the state cannot be depended upon to bail out failing enterprises indefinitely. At the same time, it would be a mistake to conclude that hard market incentives, particularly in the industrial sphere of the economy, have already been established. It should be emphasized that the establishment of institutions of outside corporate control requires large fixed investment costs, particularly in setting up monitoring structures. An individual bank or investment fund that is contemplating shifting its activity from speculation and currency (voucher) operations to active management and investment will consider these costs carefully. Strong profit incentives are a prerequisite to bringing expected gains in line with such costs.

Furthermore, there is reason to believe that the current strong incentives for tax evasion at the enterprise level could also adversely affect the development of outside corporate governance. Tax evasion typically takes the form of minimizing legal profits, writing off various "costs," and diverting "productive" resources to hidden consumption for management and workers. Because of the natural complementarities in Russia, such activities are likely to be at the expense of outside stockholders and debtholders as well as the state. This situation poses the dual problem that (a) monitoring of management may be more costly to outsiders (a greater divergence will exist in the objectives of management and outside owners or debtholders) and (b) if legal profitability is discouraged by high and unstable taxes, such monitoring (and outside governance) may have less than the expected value.

In the area of subsidies and special credits to loss-making enterprises, the last few years have witnessed a continual cyclical pattern (Litwack 1994). In the first stage, subsidies, in the form of government credits, are drastically restricted, customarily as part of a plan to implement an ambitious deficit-reduction target. This is followed by a period of escalating interenterprise debt, reduced economic activity, and unpaid wages to a large number of workers. Social and political pressures then mount and force a government capitulation, featuring a massive increase in refinancing credits from the central bank. Furthermore, more generous credits are usually channeled toward regions and organizations that have engaged in the most effective lobbying and rent-seeking activities. In this scenario, a certain coordination failure can occur: the expectation that the government will eventually capitulate weakens profit incentives at the microlevel, lessens the concern of enterprises about holding each others' debts, and creates a high failure rate among good as well as bad enterprises. This forces the state into a position of refinancing to prevent massive bankruptcies that would claim good as well as bad enterprises. In this environment, commercial banks, whose assets are generally tied to failing enterprises, cannot be expected to behave in an economically responsible way.

The Russian government has made a more serious explicit effort in tax than in subsidy reform. There is now a new three-tier tax system in the Russian Republic that authorizes taxation at three levels: central, regional, and local. The design of the tax system reflected the practice and experience of existing market economies. The important taxes at the federal level were limited to value added, profits, social security (pension fund), luxury, and import duties (Foundation for Privatization and Development of Financial Markets 1992).

But the implementation of the new tax system in the last few years has saddled firms with a combination of very high taxes and the continued practice of discretionary adjustment in taxes and tax rates. These discretionary adjustments have taken many forms. There have been continual redefinitions of how profits and value added should be calculated and paid. Special new federal "funds" for social and economic development have been introduced, and each generally is supported by a new special tax. The year of 1993 witnessed a much more severe tax on wages. Other taxes, such as the enterprise property tax, have been changed retroactively. In an environment in which the government often goes into debt and owes significant back wages to workers, banks have sometimes implicitly implemented a redistribution policy that transfers funds from more to less profitable enterprises. This is achieved through making basic wages a priority for cash withdrawals and either withholding additional payments to successful enterprises as implicit low-interest loans or charging high fees (official or unofficial) for turning these funds into cash (Litwack 1994).

Given the instability and severity of taxation, very strong incentives for tax evasion have been maintained at the enterprise level, despite an effort by the government to crack down on this practice through a well-staffed internal revenue service and "tax police." In a large survey of June 1992, directors of enterprises responded quite openly that they are, on average, (illegally) evading 40 percent of all taxes

(Bessonov and others 1993, p. 16). The perception at the enterprise level that tax evasion is essential for survival makes random crackdowns by the government appear as a form of discretionary expropriation.

Therefore, for the reasons described above, the current fiscal situation in Russia offers serious reason for concern for the creation of effective outside corporate governance. In the current Russian environment, it is not surprising that commercial banks do not generally appear to be actively seeking profitable investments and involvement in corporate governance. But given their human capital and experience, their close relationships to enterprises, and their current active role in the privatization process, Russian banks have genuine potential for becoming critical players in creating institutions of corporate governance.

A first step toward this goal should involve a major change in the administration of explicit and implicit subsidies in the Russian economy. The current practice of using the commercial bank system for the administration of implicit subsidies naturally distorts the incentives of commercial banks and orients their competition to the acquisition of special state funding. This practice also naturally ties the assets and solvency of commercial banks to firms that are functioning through nonperforming loans. As long as this practice continues, commercial banks may never have proper incentives for effective finance, credit rationing, or monitoring and corporate governance. Phelps and colleagues (1993) are also correct in questioning the efficacy of a debt for equity swap in this environment, which would only solidify the problematic dependency.

While the experience of Japan after World War II in cleaning up the accounts of banks may provide some important lessons for Russia, implementation of such policies must be accompanied by other long-run measures. Hoshi, Kashyap, and Loveman (1994) argue that the decision to remove a large share of bad loans from the banks' current accounts was an essential ingredient in the revitalization of the Japanese financial sector after World War II. While this is true, a no less essential ingredient was the Dodge Line policy of 1949, which placed and enforced very strong restrictions on credit and introduced rigidity in the tax system (Hamada and Kasuya 1993). This succeeded in preventing today's "new accounts" from again becoming tomorrow's "old accounts." At the same time, a very active government investment policy in the priority sectors of iron and steel helped to jump-start the economy and quickly recover prewar industrial levels (Okazaki and Okuno-Fujiwara 1993).

There are several factors associated with the Russian situation today that make such a strategy of harsh fiscal and monetary restrictions after the reconsolidation of accounts more difficult to realize. First, the extent of necessary structural adjustment in Russia is much greater than in Japan after World War II. The majority of Russians are still employed in firms that probably could not survive without some form of state help. The task of restructuring is not so much the reactivation of already existing enterprises and human capital, but a complete structural shift from one kind of production and capital to another. Given the inability of capital markets to supply finance, a strong immediate restriction of credit is likely to bring down firms with potential, as well as those without it. Although concentrated strategic government investments may indeed play a positive role in this period of weak financial markets (Litwack and Qian 1993), the generation of these funds and the search for appropriate places for investment are more complicated than in Japan after World War II.

Perhaps most important, the volatile political situation in Russia and the significant power of industrial interest groups puts constraints on government policies, particularly on the restriction of subsidies, that were not as pronounced in Japan. The West cannot simply impose its will upon Russia and force compliance with a policy similar to the Dodge Line. Therefore, the interests of the various political groups and the constraints that they impose must be accounted for in any solution to this problem.

Although the situation in Russia is sufficiently complicated to threaten the success of any potential strategy, we believe in adhering to two central principles. First, in the interests of social, political, economic, and welfare concerns, subsidies should not be reduced too quickly. Given the need in almost every industrial enterprise for significant investments to become competitive, a drastic reduction in subsidies is a sure method of bringing down virtually all industrial firms, good or bad. Furthermore, social and political variables dictate, and the past record demonstrates, that the central government will not be able to credibly maintain such a policy. The reduction in state subsidies should therefore be gradual and, optimally, be based on an explicit dynamic plan that involves the agreement of the interest groups in the country.

Second, to provide appropriate incentives for banks during the period of large-scale subsidization, the administration of subsidies should not occur through the commercial bank network. After the accounts of commercial banks are cleaned up, the refinancing of loss-making firms should be shifted to special funds associated with the state budget. Although this will create larger state budget deficits on paper, it will not be more inflationary than the creation of bad credit.

This separation of state subsidy funds from commercial credit will also facilitate a strengthening of the incentive effects of privatization. So far, according to survey data, privatized and nonprivatized firms do not notice a difference in their access to state funds and credit (Institute of Economics 1993, p. 110). As box 4-1 illustrates, special state credits at low interest rates were a major source of finance for private and state firms alike. Although it was a slightly more important source in state firms, this is probably because privatized firms, on average, are more independently profitable than nonprivatized firms.

Under the policy discussed above, state subsidy funds could specifically target state firms and thereby tighten the budget constraints of privatized firms. Privatization could then become a self-selection mechanism that would allow firms with potential to signal to financial institutions. Because of the current lack of a perceived difference at the microlevel between the financial constraints imposed on state or privatized firms, virtually all enterprise directors are jumping on the privatization bandwagon (Institute of Economics 1993, p. 110).

It is our opinion that such a mechanism, together with commercial banks with reconstructed accounts, provides the best hope for the development of effective corporate governance in the near future in Russia.

Bibliography

Aoki, M. 1988. *Information, Incentives, and Bargaining in the Japanese Economy*. Cambridge, U.K.: Cambridge University Press.

———. 1993. "Monitoring Characteristics of the Main Bank System: An Analytical and Historical View." Center for Economic Policy Research Publication no. 352, Stanford, California.

Berliner, J. 1976. *The Innovation Decision in Soviet Industry*. Cambridge, Mass.: MIT Press.

Bessonov, V., L. Bogdanov, T. Gurova, N. Kirichenko, A. Malov, A. Privalov, M. Rubchenko, A. Tolkushkin, D. Tushunov, V. Fadeev, and A. Shmarov. 1993. "Obzor makroekonomiki." *Kommersant* 28: 13–18.

Blinder, A. 1992. "Should the Former Socialist Economies Look East or West for a Model?" Princeton University. Mimeo.

Economic-Finance Center. 1993. *Vse nalogi rossii 1993 g.* (Collection of tax documents relevant for 1993). Ekonomiko-finansovyi tsentr. Moscow.

Foundation for Privatization and Development of Financial Markets. 1992. *Nalogovaia sistema rossii*. Moscow: I. Ts. Garant.

————. 1993. "Izuchenie opyta a analiz problem funksionirovaniia investitsionnykh fondov (I and II)." Fond podderzhki privatizatsii i razvitiia finansovogo rynka. Moscow.

Goskomstat. 1993a. "Sotsial'no-ekonomicheskoe polozhenie i razvitie ekonomicheskikh reform v rossiiskoi federatsii v pervom polugode 1993 goda" (Goskomstat summary of the Russian Economy in the First Half of 1993). *Ekonomicheskai Gazeta* 31: 21–23.

————. 1993b. "Sotsial'no-ekonomicheskoe polozhenie i razvitie ekonomicheskikh reform v rossiiskoi federatsii v 1992 godu" (Goskomstat summary of the Russian Economy for 1992). *Ekonomicheskai Gazeta* 4: 13–15.

Grossman, G. 1977. "The Second Economy of the U.S.S.R." *Problems of Communism* 26: 26.

Hamada, K., and M. Kasuya. 1993. "Reconstruction and Stabilization of the Japanese Economy." In Dornbusch and others, eds., *Postwar Economic Reconstruction and Lessons for the East Today*. Cambridge, Mass.: MIT Press.

Hoshi, T., A. Kashyap, and G. Loveman. 1994. "Lessons from the Japanese Main Bank System for Financial System Reform in

Poland." In M. Aoki and H. Patrick, eds., *Japanese Finance and the Main Bank System*. Oxford, U.K.: Oxford University Press.

Institute of Economics. 1993. *Rossiiskaia ekonomika: Oseniu 1993 goda*. Institut ekonomichekskoi politiki. Moscow.

Kornai, J. 1990. *The Road to a Free Economy*. New York: W. Norton.

Litwack, J. 1991. "Legality and Market Reform in Soviet-type Economies." *Journal of Economic Perspectives* 5 (4): 77–89.

———. 1994. "The Trap of Fiscal Instability: The Case of Russian Economic Transition: 1992–mid-1993." Stanford University. Mimeo.

Litwack, J., and Y. Qian. 1993. "Economic Transition Strategies: Imperfect Fiscal Commitment Can Favor Unbalanced Investment." Stanford University.

Okazaki, T., and M. Okuno-Fujiwara. 1993. "Historical Origins of the Contemporary Japanese Economic System." Tokyo University. Mimeo.

Phelps, E. S., R. Frydman, A. Rapaczynski, and A. Sheifer. 1993. "Needed Mechanisms of Corporate Governance and Finance in Eastern Europe." European Bank for Reconstruction and Development, Working Paper 1, London.

Privalov, A., I. Nikolaev, N. Kalininchenko, and V. Fadeev. 1994. "Privatizatsiia v zerkale chekovykh fondov. Glavnoe–ne pobeda, a uchastie." *Kommersant* 5: 43–51.

Russia, Supreme Soviet. 1992. "O bezotlagatel'nykh merakh po normalizatsii nalichno-denezhnogo obrashcheniia v Rossiiskoi Federatsii." Decree of the Presidium of the Supreme Soviet of the Russian Federation of January 13, 1992. *Finansovaia Gazeta* 7: 1.

Scarfstein, David. 1992. "Japanese Corporate Finance and Governance: Implications for the Privatization of Eastern European Enterprises." Mimeo.

Shlapentokh, V. 1989. *Public and Private Life of the Soviet People.* New York: Oxford University Press.

State Committee on Property of the Russian Federation. 1993. "Gosudarstvennaia programma privatizatsii gosudarstvennykh i munitsipal'nykh predpriiatii v Rossiskoi Federatsii na 1993 god" (Privatization program of the Russian Republic for 1993). Moscow. Mimeo.

Tirole, J. 1991. "Ownership and Incentives in a Transition Economy." Institute for Policy Studies Working Paper. Washington, D.C.

5

Enterprise Governance and Investment Funds in Russian Privatization

Noritaka Akamatsu

The structure of Russia's industrial sector at the start of reform reflected the most extreme scenario of a planned economy. Production enterprises specialized in production of only a few lines of products, and often in only one line. Trading enterprises carried out only the distribution of merchandise. So-called "research institutes" had the sole task of developing new products (R&D). At the same time, an "enterprise" consisted of everything necessary for people working in the enterprise, including housing, schools, sports facilities, hospitals, and so forth. In other words, an enterprise in a Russian context made up an entire community. In addition to such functional segmentation and communal integration, many enterprises had monopolistic positions either in their products or services or in the regional market (or in both) in order

This paper is a preliminary draft for the joint research project, "Corporate Governance in Transition Economies: Insider Control and Role of Banks," undertaken under the auspices of the World Bank EDI Program for the Study of Japan's Development Management Experience and the Economy of Japan Program at the Center for Economic Policy Research of Stanford University.

to take maximum advantage of scale economy in the absence of competition. The monopolistic structure also means that Russian industrial enterprises tend to be huge, and ignore managerial efficiency. Clearly, Russian enterprises require a great deal of restructuring to become efficient and competitive with their Western counterparts.

Considering the historical monopolistic position of enterprises, however, competition in the product market will take some time to emerge. The market for skilled managers will not be liquid any time soon because of the scarcity of skilled managers. Although many gigantic enterprises will need to downsize, it does not mean that managers' positions (rather than workers') will become contested. The stock market is unlikely to gain significant liquidity in the near future because investment demand for shares is driven by desire to gain control rather than return, and because an efficient payments system and centralized securities depositories and share registrars will take some time to develop. Takeover threats will not be a function of underpricing in the market because there are no meaningful market prices of shares without active share trading and sufficient disclosure of reliable business information. Enterprises do not have a sense of the cost of equity capital because the primary market of shares is not functioning. It will not function properly unless the secondary market gains significant liquidity. All in all, competition in the factor markets will likely be the result of further reform, and control and monitoring by owners and creditors thus seem to be the only sensible means of managerial discipline for the majority of Russian enterprises today.

The driving force behind the design of Russia's privatization scheme is the scarcity of two critical resources: financial means and skilled management. A system of postprivatization governance must make optimal use of the limited resources available. This need is quietly overriding the political and social factors in determining the course of Russia's economic reform. Russia's privatization scheme can be characterized as a combination of management-employee buyouts (MEBOs) and voucher-based mass privatization. The MEBO aspect of the scheme has made the incumbent work force (both managers and employees) the largest group of shareholders. Incumbent managers have gained strong control over their enterprises as "owner-managers." At the same time, the voucher-based mass privatization scheme, which was adopted after the Czech model, enabled voucher investment funds (VIFs) to become another group of significant shareholders. Commercial banks are also placed to exercise significant influence on enterprise governance and management. With their universal status, not only can they monitor operations of the borrower enterprises, but also, as owners or agents of owners, have direct "say" about management of the enterprises. Further, as creditors, they have the power to determine the fate of enterprises at risk of bankruptcy. Foreign strategic investors are also emerging as a potential major player in this game.

Construction of a legal and regulatory framework is under way. It represents rules of the game among the potential "governors" of enterprises, and consists of human resources (software) such as corporate lawyers, prosecutors, and judges, and of infrastructure (hardware) such as written law and regulations and court systems. Russia's Company Law specifies a two-tier structure of enterprise governance board, as does the German law. Power of external shareholders, however, is significantly limited in comparison with the German case, not to mention the Czech arrangement. Central European experiences would be a good reference for Russia in her effort to press forward with the economic reform. The Czech Republic, where voucher investment funds have become a superpower in governing enterprises, created a situation in which all leading voucher investment funds are controlled by major commercial banks. Russia's legal framework needs to structure ownership relationships among potential governors of enterprises with care in order to avoid an excessive agency problem and conflict of interest.

Development of a corporate governance structure in a transition economy is a dynamic process that must respond to the needs of different stages of the transition. Russia has gone through the stages of corporatization and privatization of state enterprises, and is now faced with a need to press forward the postprivatization restructuring of the enterprises. The crucial questions are who has the ability to: (a) restructure the enterprises; (b) finance the restructuring; and (c) run the restructured companies. The party that restructures and runs a company should have: (a) strong incentives; (b) the necessary skills; (c) the necessary resources; and (d) access to relevant information. Major investors and creditors would satisfy these criteria. Traditionally minded incumbent management groups with vested interests often have not proved to possess these requirements. It is hoped that foreign strategic investors, who can bring in both financial and managerial resources, will play a direct and important role in restructuring the enterprises. The New Privatization Program reflects that the rule of the governance game among domestic institutions is shifting toward mobilization of the power of the voucher investment funds as major outside shareholders in disciplining incumbent managers. At the same time, the program tries to restrict emerging anticompetitive powers—such as commercial banks with universal status, holding companies, and emerging "financial-industrial groups"—although they now have stronger control over enterprises.

This chapter analyzes the dynamic emergence of a corporate governance structure in Russia's privatization and postprivatization restructuring process. The key players of the game are the incumbent work force of the enterprises, commercial banks, institutional investors, and strategic investors. This chapter pays particular attention to one group of institutional investors—voucher investment funds (VIFs)—and to the dynamic interaction among the key players in response to the emerging legal and regulatory structure and the underlying politics. Should voucher investment funds be involved in restructuring? How capable are the voucher investment funds of restructuring enterprises, or how can they be made capable? In what areas could they be more effective than incumbent management, creditor banks, or even potential strategic investors? Russian reformers need to keep asking these questions in order to press forward with their reform efforts.

Russia's Privatization Scheme and the Power of Incumbent Management

From the initiation of Russia's First Privatization Program in the beginning of 1992 to the completion of the program on June 31, 1994, 70 percent of Russia's industrial sector had been transferred into private hands. This impressive speed was achieved through the following steps: initiation of privatization, development of a privatization plan, and implementation of the privatization plan. Each step deserves further attention in order to analyze the way this speed was achieved and its implication for governance of privatized enterprises.

Initiation of Privatization

First, incumbent management, incumbent employees with no less than 50 percent endorsement, and potential strategic investors (including related enterprises such as banks and suppliers) could all submit an application for privatization of a particular enterprise to GKI (or a local KI). Upon approval of GKI (or a local KI), the application was passed on to a privatization commission established by GKI (or a local KI) within the enterprise, made up of representatives of the GKI, the local Council of Peoples' Deputies, financial institutions, incumbent management, the work collective, and outside private consultants.

Development of a Privatization Plan

A privatization commission was to develop a privatization plan for a particular enterprise in which the commission was to specify the method of privatization (that is, a choice among the three options), the starting price (to be sold through an auction or tender), the size of the authorized capital (in case of a joint-stock company), and the recommended form of payments. The plan was then submitted to the local Council of People's Deputies and to the employees of the enterprise for approval. Upon nonrejection of the two bodies, the plan was submitted to the GKI for final approval. The requirement to specify the starting price and the authorized capital necessitated valuation of the enterprise. The valuation was based on the book value of assets, including fixed assets, accounting for depreciation, inventory, work in process, and intangibles. Deduction was made for debts—any monetary resources held in the economic incentive, including the privatization fund that was funded out of profits of the enterprise in order for the incumbent work force to acquire shares of the enterprise.[1]

Implementation of the Privatization Plan

Once a privatization plan was approved by the commission, GKI transferred ownership rights to the Russian Federal Property Fund. At this

---

1. The hyperinflation necessitated periodic revaluation of the book-value-based value with a coefficient set by the government.

point, an enterprise was made independent from the state or a municipality, and corporatized to form a joint-stock company. The Property Fund was then charged with implementing the privatization plan (that is, divesting from the enterprise).

Three Privatization Options

In the process of developing a privatization plan, a privatization commission could choose one of three options for the privatization method, which allowed considerable flexibility (see box 5-1). All of the three options can be characterized by a combination of subsidized management-employee buyout (MEBO, that is, a closed sale to the incumbent work force) and public offering of shares, which was mainly done through voucher auctions. The extent of subsidization varied from one option to another.

CHOICE OF OPTIONS. All the options strongly favor the incumbent work force. Option 1 is the cheapest investment option for the incumbent work force, but it significantly limits their control of the enterprise.[2] In contrast, Option 2 ensures majority ownership for the work force, but at a much higher price. Although GKI openly promoted Option 1, about three-quarters of the enterprises have chosen Option 2 (and most of the rest have chosen Option 1). Only about 2 percent of the enterprises have selected Option 3, suggesting the scarcity of the entrepreneurial endeavor among the management (see table 5-1 for the allocation of shares by privatization option; table 5-2 for distribution of shares).[3]

LOVE FOR INSIDER CONTROL. The strong preference of the incumbent work force for Option 2 is a clear sign of their desire to retain

---

2. Option 1 was amended later, and now the nonvoting shares have been made convertible into voting shares at some cost.
3. But if there are entrepreneur-managers, they would have found it very difficult to run their enterprises in the new environment with the tied contract with the rest of the work force. In that sense, Option 3 seems to carry ill-structured incentives.

Table 5-1. Allocation of Shares under Privatization Options 1–3 *(percent)*

Description	*Option 1*	*Option 2*	*Option 3*
Free to employees	25		
Sold to employees at a 30% discount (cash or vouchers)	10		20
Sold to employees at 1.7 index of nominal value (cash or vouchers)		51	
Sold to management at nominal value (cash or vouchers)	5		
Sold to employee group committed to fulfilling the privatization plan and managing the enterprise at nominal value after one year (cash only)			30
Sold to Enterprise Employees' Shareholder Fund (EESF) with 2-year right to purchase (cash only)	10	5	10
Subtotal retained by enterprise	50	56	60
Voucher auction (minimum percent by law)	29	29	29
Investment tender/retained by government/other	21	15	11
Subtotal available to investors/ government	50	44	40
Total	100	100	100

Source: Price Waterhouse 1994.

control of their enterprises rather than to seek a return from the advantageous share investment of Option 1. A determinant in the choice of Option 1 over Option 2 was not the low cost, but the insufficiency of a privatization fund in a particular enterprise. The incumbent work

Box 5-1. Three Options of the Russian Privatization Scheme

Option 1

Work force. The work force will receive nonvoting shares up to 25 percent of the capital of the enterprises for free (each employee can receive a maximum of twenty times the minimum salary, and the work collectives decide the distribution of the shares among employees). Workers can purchase up to 10 percent of voting shares at 30 percent of the book value (workers are entitled to receive 10 percent of proceeds from the sale of the enterprise into a privatization fund; the sum is set aside from the enterprise's profit to purchase shares in the enterprise for the work force). Employees cannot resell these shares for three years. Also, some restrictions apply to the methods of payment while vouchers can be used. Acquisition of shares in the open market is not restricted for employees.

Managers (part of work force). Managers can purchase an additional 5 percent of the shares at par value. Furthermore, 10 percent of shares are deposited in a development fund (FARP), which is established by enterprises to retain part of their earnings for investment in restructuring.

The remainder. The remaining shares, 50 percent, are held in the property funds and can be sold through auction and competitive tender.

Option 2

Work force. The work force can purchase 51 percent through a closed subscription at 170 percent of the 1992 book value on the approval of

force, which was the largest faction in a privatization commission, generally favored privatization, and thus the privatization could proceed smoothly. The reason for their preference for privatization was not that they wished to commercialize themselves to adapt to the new environment, however, but because they could become independent from state or municipal control. The choice of Option 2 clearly showed that they did not favor any outsider control of their enterprises. The inten-

two-thirds of the work force. Vouchers can be used to pay up to 50 percent of the purchase, but some restrictions apply to the methods of installment payment. An additional 5 percent can be deposited in FARP.

The remainder. The 44–49 percent remaining is sold through voucher auctions or competitive tender.

Option 3

Option 3 is a rather pure case of MEBO, applicable only for enterprises with more than 200 employees and assets valued at 1–50 million rubles at 1991 prices.

Work force. By the approval of a general meeting of two-thirds of the workers, a group of workers is given the power to purchase 20 percent of shares at par value on the condition that the group accept responsibility for implementing the privatization plan and for the solvency of the enterprise, and signs a one-year contract specifying the obligations of the group. The group must make a security deposit of 200 monthly minimum wages for each member of the group. In addition, workers can purchase 20 percent of shares at 70 percent of book value (up to a maximum of twenty times the minimum wage of each employee). Some restrictions apply to the methods of installment payment, although full payment can be made in vouchers. FARP retains 10 percent of shares, but those can be bought by employees after auctioning/tendering the remaining 50 percent of shares.

The remainder. The remaining 50 percent of shares is to be sold through voucher auctions/competitive tenders.

tion of incumbent managers was to maintain the status quo rather than to restructure the enterprises into more efficient forms.

TIE BETWEEN MANAGEMENT AND EMPLOYEES. Within the incumbent work force, management, rather than employees, was the group that wished to retain the control. In order for the management to make insider control effective, they needed to collude with the employees.

Table 5-2. Distribution of Shares for Selected Russian Enterprises *(percent)*

Item	*ZIL (automobiles)*	*Saransk Factory Orbita (semi-conductor devices)*	*Amurenergo (electric utilities and thermal power)*
Privatization option	1	1	1
Internal placement			
Preferred stock placement for employees (Option 1 only)	25.00	25.00	18.53
Closed subscription of common stock for employees	10.00	10.00	5.56
Common stock placement for managers (Option 1 only)	5.00	3.60	5.00
Enterprise employees' share-holding fund	10.00	10.00	10.00
Total internal placement	50.00	48.60	39.09
External placement			
Voucher auctions	35.00	29.00	11.91
Retained by government or holding company	13.00	20.00	49.00
Distribution to the Far North Population and employees of the oil transportation companies and/or subcontractors	0.00	0.00	0.00
Investment tenders	0.00	0.00	0.00
Cash sale	2.00	2.40	0.00
Total external placement	50.00	51.40	60.91
Total shares	100.00	100.00	100.00

Source: Price Waterhouse 1994.

Lukoil-Kogalim-neftegas (oil drilling and gas extraction)	*Krasnoyarsk Tire Factory (tires)*	*Krasnoyarsk TsBK (cellulose, paper and cardboard)*	*Tekstilmash Tekstilmash (textile looms)*	*Tomsk Neftekhimichesky Factory (oil-based chemicals)*
1	2	2	2	2
18.60	0.00	0.00	0.00	0.00
10.00	51.00	51.00	51.00	51.00
5.00	0.00	0.00	0.00	0.00
0.00	5.00	0.50	0.00	5.00
33.60	56.00	51.50	51.00	56.00
17.30	29.00	29.00	29.00	44.00
38.00	15.00	19.50	20.00	0.00
9.70	0.00	0.00	0.00	0.00
0.00	0.00	0.00	0.00	0.00
1.40	0.00	0.00	0.00	0.00
66.40	44.00	48.50	49.00	44.00
100.00	100.00	100.00	100.00	100.00

The majority of employees also preferred control by the incumbent management over that by Russian outsiders and foreigners, at least initially. In some cases, management established an ESOP-like structure, as a legal entity controlled by the management. By having employees participate in the structure, the management can control participating employees' voting rights. The nature of the tie between management and employees was generally a function of the size of the enterprise—the larger the enterprise, the weaker the tie. The government prohibits imposition of any limits preventing employees from selling their shares freely to outsiders.[4] Nevertheless, management has come up with direct and indirect ways to prevent or control employees' sale of shares to outsiders.

SWIFT PRIVATIZATION. With a privatization scheme that strongly favored the insider, the Russian reformers cunningly depoliticized the reform process. This "success" significantly contributed to speeding-up the privatization process, and thus to cost reduction, making the reform process irreversible. Although this allowed a priority objective to be achieved at an early stage of the reform, it also created the unavoidable problem of excessive insider domination in governing the privatized enterprises. The voucher-based mass privatization scheme was designed to counter-balance the power of the incumbent work force.

Voucher-Based Mass Privatization and the Emergence of Voucher Investment Funds

Russia employed vouchers as a means of mass privatization, as did the Czech Republic.[5] A voucher with a par value of 10,000 rubles was distributed to every one of Russia's 150 million citizens. A presidential

4. Not only employees, but any shareholder should not be restricted from selling their shares freely under Russia's privatization program.

5. An important difference is that the Czech privatization program weighed the mass privatization much more heavily than the Russian program did. As a result, VIFs in the Czech Republic hold a very large portion of enterprise shares and, generally speaking, are much more powerful than their Russian counterpart.

decree, "On The Creation and Regulation of Specialized Voucher Funds" (hereafter the Investment Company Law) was signed on October 7, 1992, and voucher investment funds (VIFs) were initiated in the beginning of 1993.[6] Since then VIFs have mushroomed to number over 650. Individuals could invest their vouchers directly into shares of enterprises at voucher auctions or into those of VIFs that would invest the collected vouchers in enterprise shares on behalf of their investors. VIFs have proven to be effective "privatization intermediaries" that facilitate individual participation in the mass privatization. Without them, most individual investors would possess neither sufficient information to choose appropriate enterprise shares nor enough resources to diversify the risk widely. At the same time, the reputation of VIFs has hit a low point because of fraud and an inability to pay the high dividends they promised to their investors. (See table 5-3 for VIF statistics.)

Voucher Auction and Valuation of a Voucher

Voucher auctions against shares of privatizing enterprises were completed on June 30, 1994.[7] Every month, 400 to 500 voucher auctions were held across the country. Because Russia's privatization scheme auctions enterprises one by one, 400 to 500 enterprises were privatized every month.[8] Out of approximately 150 million vouchers distributed to the Russian citizenry, about 45 million vouchers have been collected by VIFs, and over 27 million of those have been invested into shares (as of April 30, 1994). It is estimated that over 60 million citizens out of a total population of 150 million had participated in the mass privatization by the end of the program, and that there are about 30 million individual Russian shareholders through VIFs.

---

6. A few VIFs existed in 1992, even before the decree was issued.
7. The city of Moscow will continue to allow use of vouchers to participate in the privatization of the city's assets until the end of 1994.
8. Compared with the collective auction systems found in the Central and Eastern European countries, this system makes it very difficult, often impossible, for investors to make cross-enterprise comparisons of value in making investment decisions.

Table 5-3. Statistics on Voucher Investment Funds in Russia

Category	*Date*			
	28.05.93	*30.06.93*	*31.07.93*	*31.08.93*
Funds				
Regions polled	5	26	69	52
Percentage of all regions	5.6	29.2	77.5	58.4
Funds licensed by KIs	85	211	370	435
Funds licensed by GKI	42	62	77	80
Total number of licensed VIFs in FMU database	127	273	447	515
Percentage increasing	NA	115.0	63.7	15.2
Vouchers				
Number of funds polled	50	87	145	256
Percentage of total number of funds	39.4	31.9	32.4	49.7
Number of vouchers accumulated	2,619,381	5,819,874	8,598,714	12,224,618
Number of vouchers accumulated per fund	52,388	66,895	59,301	47,752
Total number of vouchers[a]	6,653,228	18,262,363	26,507,760	24,592,493
Number of vouchers invested	842,467	1,612,420	2,886,178	4,808,718
Number of vouchers invested per fund	16,849	18,534	19,905	18,784
Total number of vouchers invested[a]	2,139,866	5,059,663	8,897,390	9,673,788
Percentage of vouchers invested	32.2	27.7	33.6	39.3
Shareholders				
Number of funds with shareholder data	NA	NA	76	181
Percentage of total number of funds	NA	NA	17.0	35.1
Number of shareholders	NA	NA	3,400,950	5,387,116
Number of shareholders per fund	NA	NA	44,749	29,763
Number of vouchers	NA	NA	5,992,588	10,355,267
Number of vouchers per shareholder	NA	NA	1.76	1.92
Total number of shareholders in Russia[a]	NA	8,000,000	15,000,000	15,327,982
Percentage of the total population[a]	NA	5.4	10.1	10.3

a. FMU estimations.

Source: Capital Market Surveillance Unit (formerly, Fund Monitoring Unit) of GKI.

Date							
30.09.93	*30.10.93*	*30.11.93*	*15.12.93*	*31.01.94*	*28.02.94*	*31.03.94*	*30.04.94*
57	63	71	71	71	72	75	75
64.0	70.8	79.8	79.8	79.8	80.9	84.3	84.3
482	498	514	515	518	521	535	538
84	102	117	117	117	119	121	121
566	600	631	632	637	640	656	659
9.9	6.0	5.2	0.2	0.8	0.5	2.5	0.5
307	370	421	428	450	466	492	505
54.2	61.7	66.7	67.7	70.6	72.8	75.0	76.6
18,196,624	23,022,418	26,158,309	27,839,694	29,625,642	30,317,824	31,961,326	34,678,461
59,272	62,223	62,134	65,046	65,835	65,060	64,962	68,670
33,548,173	37,333,651	39,206,397	41,109,081	41,936,742	41,638,213	42,615,101	45,253,675
8,425,031	12,404,011	15,182,382	15,714,755	18,231,302	19,212,205	20,600,187	21,135,704
27,443	33,524	36,063	36,717	40,514	41,228	41,870	41,853
15,532,793	20,114,612	22,755,542	23,204,965	25,807,421	26,385,861	27,466,916	27,581,047
46.3	53.9	58.0	56.4	61.5	63.4	64.5	60.9
223	290	371	378	406	420	445	457
39.4	48.3	58.8	59.8	63.7	65.6	67.8	69.3
8,937,555	11,852,655	14,384,240	14,784,086	14,100,959	14,502,364	14,796,164	14,352,798
40,079	40,871	38,772	39,111	34,731	34,529	33,250	31,407
15,120,334	20,437,761	24,140,393	25,816,640	28,336,330	28,829,243	30,302,664	33,093,186
1.69	1.72	1.68	1.75	2.01	1.99	2.05	2.31
22,684,557	24,522,734	24,464,839	24,718,366	22,123,918	22,098,840	21,811,873	20,696,923
15.3	16.5	16.5	16.6	14.9	14.9	14.7	13.9

Vouchers were exchanged for shares according to a price determined in each auction. The initial value of an enterprise (shares) in auction was evaluated based on book value of its assets in rubles. A sale price of an enterprise, however, was determined by the number of vouchers successfully bid.[9] Therefore, the initial value was nothing more than a reference price to start an auction.[10] At a voucher auction, investors could acquire shares only with vouchers, but not with cash.[11] Prior to the summer of 1993, lack of an interregional network of voucher depositories required VIF managers or their agent broker-dealers to carry a large number of voucher documents to an auction center. They had to do so without knowing whether their bids would be successful,[12] which was a costly and risky thing to do, especially in the case of interregional investment. As a result, each voucher auction was initially regionalized by participating investors, and so were the portfolios of many VIFs. Establishment of an interregional network of voucher depositories in the summer of 1993 enabled VIF managers to bid without physically presenting voucher documents.[13] This substan-

---

9. There are two ways to bid with vouchers: a noncompetitive bid (Type 1) and a competitive bid (Type 2). A noncompetitive bid assures success of the bid, while the bidder has to be a "price taker." Competitive bids specify a price (in number of vouchers) the bidder is willing to pay to obtain a share. If a clearing price of an auction turns out to be higher than the price specified, then the bid is considered "unsuccessful," and the competitive bidder will receive no shares.

10. A consequence is that the market price of a voucher at a given time reflected the demand for shares of a particular enterprise that was coming into auction soon. Therefore, a market price of a voucher has been volatile, although it proved to be an inflation and ruble devaluation hedge, showing a general upward trend in dollars.

11. Investors can buy vouchers in commodity exchanges and then participate in voucher auctions with the vouchers.

12. That is, if they are not determined to make a noncompetitive bid. See footnote 9 for "noncompetitive bids."

13. With financial and technical assistance from USAID and Deloitte & Touche, the Cash Union, a Moscow-based depository, was established and linked with other regional depositories.

tially facilitated interregional investment of vouchers, although VIF managers or their agents still had to visit local auction centers to participate in auctions.[14]

Classification of VIFs by Size and Regional Coverage

As of April 30, 1994, there were 659 licensed VIFs.[15] They can be classified by size and area of geographic coverage as listed in table 5-4. The top fifty own about 50 percent of the industry's assets.

Legal Form of VIFs

Although investment funds in Russia include both VIFs and cash investment funds (CIFs), almost all investment funds are VIFs.[16] The majority of Russian citizens, with limited savings, were unable or unwilling to invest rubles on a long-term basis, especially in the presence of vouchers. A distinction between VIFs and CIFs remains in licensing bodies and regulatory matters, even though VIFs completed

---

14. The network of depositories also facilitated interregional voucher trading, although settlement of payments was still a major obstacle, and therefore terms of the voucher delivery and the payment settlement have influenced the price of a voucher in a particular voucher trading deal. VIFs could trade vouchers they bought with cash while they were prohibited from trading vouchers they collected in exchange for VIF shares because of their special role in privatization. Many VIF managers seem to have been engaged in trading of collected vouchers anyway, because voucher trading has been an important source of income for VIFs. Some anecdotal evidence also shows that short sale of vouchers was common, despite the illegality of short-sale of securities in Russia. The network of depositories is a key infrastructure to support the practice of short sale. Vouchers were easy to trade because they were homogeneous, bearer securities.

15. Of the 659 VIFs, over 130 are in Moscow, and about 45 in St. Petersburg. Major VIFs include First Voucher Privatization Fund, Alfa Capital, Privatization Program, Moscow Real Estate Fund (MN), and so forth.

16. There was only one CIF licensed by the Ministry of Finance, but it has gone under, unable to attract enough funds to be economically feasible. VIFs in aggregate have received less than 1 percent of their assets in cash.

Table 5-4. VIFs by Size and Regional Coverage

Type of VIF	*Number of VIFs*	*Regional coverage*	*Number of shareholders*	*Asset size*
Large, nationwide	5	Nationwide	1–3 million	$25–50 million
Interregional	50	5–30 regions	40,000–250,000	$1–10 million
Regional	50	One	50,000–300,000	$1.5–12 million
Small, regional	500	One	1,000–10,000	$20,000–300,000

the conversion of vouchers into enterprise shares. VIFs have been licensed and regulated by GKI.[17] They took a form of "open joint-stock company" defined under the Company Law.[18] Since a VIF was a "company," investment certificates issued by a VIF are "equity shares," and investors of those shares are "owners" of a VIF.[19] In that sense, they

17. CIFs are licensed and regulated by the Ministry of Finance.
18. An "open joint-stock company" means a "public" company in Western terms. It should not be confused with an "open-end fund." A public company is a company with shares widely held among the public. A company may be legally considered as a public company if it has more than 50 shareholders, for example. Of significance in being a public company in the West is that it is subject to disclosure requirements set up by appropriate authorities.
19. General characteristics of an investment fund: An investment fund usually has no employees of its own and is operated by external agents such as fund managers, broker/dealers, principal underwriters, transfer agents, and custodians. It is governed by its board of directors, who are to be "independent" (particularly its fund manager and underwriter) and "prudent." A fund management company establishes investment funds and contracts with them for managing the funds. A fund manager, as fiduciary of the investors, selects a portfolio in accordance with the objectives and policies specified in each fund's registration statement (for example, trust deed), places orders with broker/dealers, and makes sure that transactions are executed at the best price and cost. A bank normally acts as a custodian to safekeep the securities of the fund and makes sure that delivery of cash or securities is done only for specified transactions and according to proper instructions received from officers of the fund. Banks, brokers, and/or nominees having shares of the fund registered in their names normally act as proxy of the shareholders in voting at shareholders' meetings of the fund.

are similar to mutual funds in the United States or investment funds in the United Kingdom.[20] Unlike mutual funds, however, the Russian VIFs are required to be "closed-end" funds by the Investment Company Law.[21] This requirement reflects the GKI's commitment to press forward with privatization by making the investment with vouchers irreversible. At the same time, open-end funds would be impossible in the illiquid Russian stock market of today.

Aggressive Advertisement

VIFs have grown in number through aggressive advertisement promising unrealistically high return or dividends on their shares, as happened in the Czech Republic. Unfortunately, most VIFs could not pay enough dividends in spring 1994, if they paid dividends at all, which disappointed their investors. As a result, public confidence in the VIFs is now at a low ebb. Promising return is illegal in the West, and it has been made illegal under the Investment Company Law in Russia as well. Advertising is also restricted financially by the law.[22] Nevertheless, one VIF "promised" up to 700 percent in dividends, and while it actually paid this amount, it went to only a select few. A weakness of the present legislation is a lack of effective punitive actions and enforcement. It cannot be denied, however, that the mass privatization

---

20. "Unit trusts" were not suitable for the lengthy privatization process, and thus do not exist in Russia today.
21. A closed-end fund does not redeem its shares at investors' requests. Closed-end funds are, therefore, traded in the market. Russia's CIFs can be either open-end or closed-end funds. Open-end funds must stand ready to redeem their shares for the net asset value of the share at the request of their investors.
22. Annual management expenses of an IF, including the cost of advertising, is restricted to a maximum of 10 percent of the VIF's net assets. This seems completely out of the Western standard, which is normally around 1 percent for a closed-end fund. The hyperinflation, lack of an appropriate NAV accounting, and the costly operational environment, however, seem to make this level of management expenses inevitable.

might not have been launched successfully if such aggressive advertisement were strictly prohibited.[23]

Capital Income Taxation

Although VIFs have mushroomed to number over 600, one-third of them were said to not be in operating condition. The most serious obstacle for the growth of the VIFs was Russia's system of capital income taxation. Return on investment in investment funds was taxed three times: first as a corporate income, second as dividend income to the VIFs, and third as personal income to the VIF investors. The triple taxation seriously discouraged investment in VIFs, and small VIFs were unable to collect vouchers.[24] Two-thirds of the existing VIFs are expected to go under if the triple taxation remains. This means that one-third of the VIFs that are actually functioning would go under.[25]

GKI has so far come up with three solutions to this problem. First, GKI promoted consolidation of the VIFs by allowing them to purchase one another's shares,[26] an action that was previously prohibited. As a result, there have recently been a growing number of M&As among the

---

23. Lack of liquidity in the stock market is a major impediment for VIFs to grow into professional mutual funds. Regional share depositories and registrars will be in operation by early autumn 1994 to enable speedy and reliable trading of shares, at least on an intraregional basis. Voucher auctions were completed on June 30, however, and this improvement of market infrastructure has proven to come a little too late.

24. As described in footnote 9, setting up and operating a fund is a complex and costly process involving a number of external agents for which fees must be paid. Therefore, a fund must attain a certain asset size in a relatively short period of time to be economically viable. In the United States, for example, the size required is said to be $50 to $100 million.

25. In addition, interest expense on long-term debt is not deductible from taxable income. The heavy turnover tax on enterprises also encourages cash payments, tax evasion, and vertical integration of industry to create industrial-financial groups. Russia's capital income taxation system discourages long-term financing and investment and promotes speculative trade practices and inflation.

26. Article 9.4, the New Privatization Program.

VIFs. The number of VIFs increased toward the end of voucher privatization on June 30, 1994, which was due to the second solution. In January 1994, a VIF tax privilege was made effective, allowing them to be exempted from tax on dividends received during the first two years of their establishment. A number of industrial enterprises established new VIFs to take advantage of this new privilege. The irony is that this privilege does not apply to the dividend income received prior to January 1994; the better-established VIFs were created around the end of 1992 and will celebrate their second anniversary by the end of 1994. Therefore, the established VIFs will not benefit very much from the privilege, and it contributed much more to the creation of new VIFs, mainly for the purpose of tax avoidance.

The other solution is creation of a contractual form of funds (trust funds) that is not subject to corporate income tax, thus eliminating an effect of the triple taxation.[27] A concept of "trust" was introduced in December 1993 by the presidential decree on trust. Investors in an existing VIF would not have to pay extra tax if the VIF transforms itself into a "trust fund." Such a transformation, however, requires the following steps: (a) establishment of trust funds as new organizations, (b) transfer of the VIF's assets into the trust funds, and (c) dissolution of the old VIF structure. At this moment, the VIFs cannot carry out this transformation because the Investment Company Law prohibits the voluntary liquidation of VIFs for three years from their establishment. According to the regulation, their reorganization within the three years also requires approval of GKI.[28]

If the triple taxation should remain after the first three years, there will be a massive transformation of VIFs from a company form into a trust form, which would be socially costly, with little benefit. More

---

27. In the past, commercial banks seem to have acted not only as custodians, but also as share trusts for investors without having separate trust accounts. Depositors in the banks and investors in relevant VIFs could have fallen into conflict with each other in case of bank failure unless the Banking Law and the Investment Company Law were mutually consistent in protecting the interest of depositors and investors.

28. CIFs are subject to such a restriction neither for liquidation nor for reorganization.

generally, the triple taxation would distort the financing patterns of enterprises in favor of short-term debt financing, leaving enterprises in a weak capital structure. Enterprises would tend to rely on bank financing,[29] and capital market development would be hindered. Such a lack of "neutrality" in the tax regime would also entail effectiveness of taxation and the government's fiscal financing. Therefore, amendment of the triple taxation is necessary.[30]

Valuation of Shares and Research Capacity of VIFs

Disclosure of financial information by enterprises has not been effectively enforced. Accounting based on Western financial accounting principles is little practiced, although the new form of Russia's financial statements and the underlying accounting principles required by law do resemble a Western form.[31] There are no regulations (including the Company Law) that specify disclosure requirements in detail.[32] Out of the 5,000 enterprises privatized, about 100 publish financial statements. Their balance sheets, however, consist of three lines on the assets and two lines on the liabilities, without footnotes, which is just nonsense. Enterprise managers do not wish to go public, and therefore there is no incentive for the managers to disclose.

---

29. Original regulations in the Investment Company Law prohibit VIFs' investment in nongovernmental debt securities. VIFs should also not acquire more than 15 percent of the debt of the single issuer.
30. The neutrality in the regime of capital income taxation is such that the tax system does not favor a particular means of investment financing, especially among the following three options: borrowing, new share issues, and reinvestment of retained earnings. This means that a neutral system of capital income taxation should provide the same effective net tax burden on interest income, dividend income, and capital gains.
31. A critical remaining difference is that the income statement is based on cash accounting and the balance sheet is based on accrual accounting. Because of the use of cash accounting for the income statement, there is no statement of cash flow in the present set of the Russian financial statements.
32. There is no securities law or securities exchange law, which often specify disclosure requirements in detail, especially in civil law regime countries.

In the current environment, where valuation based on income or cash flow is ineffective,[33] VIFs are concentrating on asset valuation techniques. Major VIFs also carry out intraindustry analysis. Their industry analysts look at the relevant industry branch and make intraindustry comparisons. There tends to be a wide range of differences among enterprises in a single industry branch. Some enterprises are clearly better than others, and good ones often have equipment that can be valued in hard currency. Accounting for depreciation with age, the analysts estimate replacement value of major equipment. Marketing research is also carried out by the analysts. They analyze an enterprise's relations with suppliers and their reliability, superiority of products, and sales network relative to those of other enterprises, and estimate resulting market share, growth potential, and cost structure. They also try to analyze the experience and ability of management.[34]

These analyses and judgments are largely based on the analysts' experience, on-site observation, and interviews with management, and are age-old practices performed by the Western securities analysts as well. Taking this into account, the valuation efforts made by leading Russian VIFs seem reasonable, given the current circumstances. In any case, well-established methods of valuation certainly do not seem to exist, and even a naive method such as the above is limited to some leading VIFs. Macroeconomic analysis[35] in the present environment is not useful because the problems that many enterprises are faced with seem to come much more from the payment system failure than the apparent macroeconomic slump. The evaluation of an enterprise hinges on the ability of the management and their success in collecting payments.

Popular shares have been in oil, gas and minerals, construction, tourism and hotels, and consumer products. Generally speaking, enter-

---

33. Inflation and the inefficient payment system make those techniques ineffective.

34. Information sources are: a) VIF's broker/dealers; b) State Property Funds; c) State Committee on Statistics of Russia and other statistical organizations; d) research institutes; e) commercial information sources; f) data banks; and g) personal connections.

35. That is, stock picking and portfolio management based on recognition of an economic cycle (boom and recession) and a pattern of industrial linkage.

prises with a monopolistic position in a regional market and with producers of finished goods are considered attractive, and industrial giants (probably with the exception of oil, gas, and minerals) and Moscow-based enterprises are found unattractive by some fund managers. Oil, gas, and minerals generally have a good export market. Local monopolists tend to have stable demand and revenue, and producers of finished goods (or consumer goods) usually have few payment collection problems. At the same time, gigantic industrial enterprises, particularly producers of intermediate products, tend to bear high bankruptcy risks and are difficult targets for the acquisition of controlling stakes for VIFs, even through collusion. Moscow-based enterprises (hotels, department stores, and the like) can be expensive because they are well known, and therefore are popular investment targets.[36] Share prices have also been pushed up after public exposure of some major VIFs' plans to place bids on particular enterprises (signaling effect of credible bidders). It was, therefore, critically important for major VIFs to disguise their participation in an auction.

VIF Associations and Self-Regulation

Leading VIFs try to promote as well as govern themselves through participation in industry associations. There are three major associations of VIFs—the Association of Investment Funds,[37] the League of Assistance to Investment Funds,[38] and the Moscow Public Shareholders' Rights Committee.[39] The League is acting as a self-regulatory organiza-

---

36. In Moscow oblast, the number of vouchers invested in shares has exceeded the number of vouchers issued there. This means that there has been a considerable net inflow of vouchers from outer regions into Moscow oblast. Moscow-based leading VIFs have a substantial brokerage network either through their own network or through affiliated brokers or bank branches.
37. The members include medium-size VIFs, other financial and investment service companies, and some production and trading companies.
38. The members include fifty-three major VIFs (but not Alfa Capital), which hold 50 percent of the VIF industry's assets.
39. Established by Mr. Andrei Vogin, President of Adamant Financial Corporation, a fund management company for Derzhava Investment Fund, a Moscow-based, major VIF.

tion (SRO)[40] of the VIF industry, although SRO status is not yet official and will be defined in the securities law now being drafted. Jointly with the Committee, the League has recently produced a code of conduct and fiduciary duties of investment fund managers. Three of them also publicize good and bad practices of managers of VIFs as well as enterprises.

VIFs' Sources of Income

VIFs' sources of income have been dividends from enterprises,[41] voucher trading, and enterprise share trading.[42] Because of the recent poor business performance, however, most enterprises are unable to pay significant dividends, if they can pay dividends at all.[43] In addition, VIFs have been prohibited from trading vouchers collected in exchange for their shares. Besides, most vouchers disappeared as the voucher privatization was completed on June 30, 1994. Therefore, trading of enterprise shares has become the only source of immediate income. OTC share trading has been active, particularly after a voucher auction. VIFs acquired as many shares as possible at each voucher auction and sold the shares as a bloc at a higher price.[44] Broker/dealers (B/Ds) also

---

40. It was modeled after ASD of the United States and CIDA of Canada.
41. Interest income would also be earned if a VIF manages its liquid assets in T-bills or bank deposits.
42. IF management companies also have fee business, such as brokerage and management consulting. The consulting department of the management companies handles the restructuring of enterprises.
43. The poor business performance is largely the result of the payment of enterprises.
44. If a VIF honors regulations by GKI, it had to sell excess holdings to meet the portfolio diversification requirement of the Investment Company Law at the time of quarterly reporting to GKI. VIFs must meet two portfolio diversification tests. One is that a VIF should not hold more than 10 percent of outstanding shares of an enterprise, and the other is that a VIF should not invest more than 5 percent of its assets into shares of one enterprise. The first of these was relaxed from 10 percent to 25 percent in December 1994, which has a significant implication for enterprise governance structure.

have been buying up shares (dealership operation) from individuals and selling those as blocs.[45] Such bloc sales by VIFs and B/Ds have been made to strategic investors who sought control of the enterprise.

Nature of the Present Stock Market

The Russian stock market has been predominantly a market for "control" rather than return, although some sign of change is slowly emerging. The motive behind most investment has been to gain or retain control of the enterprises. Except for the case of dealership operation of B/Ds, therefore, block trading is very common.[46] Certain groups of sellers and buyers of shares can be clearly identified. A major group of sellers includes employees of privatized enterprises who obtained shares cheaply through the work force allocation part of the privatization program. B/Ds acquire shares from such individuals, bundle them in blocs, and sell the blocs to control-seeking buyers. A major group of domestic buyers is incumbent managers of the enterprises and their potential group companies, which are in many cases purchasers of the products sold by the target enterprises. Foreign strategic investors are another group of buyers that is steadily increasing its importance. Exchange trading is limited, and OTC trading accounts for over 90 percent. The market is segmented and illiquid because of the atomized asset registrars and lack of depositories while shares are dematerialized.[47]

---

45. Sales of VIF holdings are carried out by fund managers. Fund management companies in Russia often have their own broker/dealer functions, although they also worked with independent broker/dealers as necessary. B/Ds are licensed by the Ministry of Finance, and there are over 2,000 of them in the country today.
46. Between 2 and 3 percent of shares outstanding are commonly traded as a block.
47. A combination of dematerialized shares, an atomized registrar system, and lack of central depositories makes each registrar function as if it is also a depository, a situation that makes the market highly segmented.

Structure of VIF Groups and Their Involvement in Enterprise Governance

Because the Russian privatization has so far taken the form of subsidized MEBOs, almost all enterprises are controlled by the incumbent management. Management generally tries to buy back shares from their own employees and VIFs through direct and indirect means, attempting to assure their controlling power. VIFs often have no choice but to accept these deals (if management offers a good price) because of their need to realize a return on the investment in the illiquid stock market in order to pay dividends and to meet the portfolio diversification requirement of the Investment Company Law. Therefore, the illiquidity in the secondary market is not only a result of the control-oriented market, but also made control-driven investment inevitable for VIFs.[48] Employee share-ownership is not proving to be an effective control mechanism because employees of smaller enterprises, where the relationship between management and the employees is close, almost always vote for incumbent management. Employees of a large enterprise compete to cash out their holdings.

Problems with Manager Ownership

The enterprise managers' love of control stems from their desire to maintain their position and vested interest. Many managers appear to think that the enterprises are theirs and that using assets of the enterprises for their personal interest is justified. Many do not recognize the difference between debt and equity capital and, therefore, do not honor shareholders' rights. More serious is their intentional theft of enterprise assets. Some managers have established and become the owners of a new company (or joint venture), transferred quality assets from their former enterprise into the new company, and let the old enterprise go bankrupt. This suggests that there is a good potential for quick-and-easy efficiency gains in enterprises without a sophisticated

---

48. In this sense, an appropriate name for the Russian VIFs may be "voucher buy-out" (VBO) funds.

and expensive restructuring workout if the excessive controlling power of the incumbent management is challenged by outsiders.

Role of VIFs in Enterprise Governance

The role of VIFs in privatized enterprises is primarily to "contest" the positions of incumbent managers. VIFs can also cooperate with the managers to enhance efficiency of the enterprises. Recognizing the potential role of VIFs in counterbalancing the power of incumbent managers, the New Privatization Program has lifted the portfolio diversification requirement of VIFs from 10 percent to 25 percent. The 25 percent represents a critical level of share ownership that gives the VIFs veto power over major corporate decisions, including liquidation and restructuring. The deregulation was packaged with tighter regulation on shareholding by commercial banks, to a maximum of 10 percent, and on formation of holding companies and financial-industrial groups. The tighter regulation indicates GKI's cautious attitude toward emergence of anticompetitive power, while the deregulation promotes governance by independent outside shareholders.

Classification of VIFs by Founder

VIFs are managed by 538 fund managers, including 346 individuals and 192 legal entities (see table 5-5).[49] A founder of a VIF first establishes a fund manager/management company, which in turn organizes a VIF(s). When a VIF is invested sufficiently by voucher holders, the voucher investors become the new owners of the VIF. VIFs are

---

49. The 192 fund managing companies include: 1) Pure managing companies (33), 2) Investment companies (55), and 3) Broker/dealers, consulting firms, insurance companies, banks, law firms, individual private firms, trade houses, and production firms (25), and so forth. In addition, 79 (40 percent) do not have a clear profile. The 33 pure fund management companies can further break down as follows: a) companies that have been established only for managing a particular fund; b) companies managing more than one fund; and c) enterprises that concentrate on managing financial assets of companies including VIFs.

founded by several different kinds of institutions and individuals as listed below.

- 1. *Broker/dealers and financial consulting firms* are involved in professional funds with a variety of investment strategies. Most of the leading VIFs belong to this category.
- 2. *Major banks* (only a few) collected vouchers of the banks' individual clients and employees of institutional clients, and made conservative, long-term investment in the banks' client enterprises for control. They initiated no aggressive marketing and advertising.
- 3. *Industrial enterprises* collected vouchers of their employees or employees of their group enterprises to buy their own shares and shares of the same or a related industrial sector for control (that is, sector VIFs).
- 4. *Local authorities/associated entities* collected vouchers of regional residents and invested in shares of regional businesses for control (that is, regional VIFs).
- 5. *Individuals and nonfinancial private companies* generally included small regional VIFs, most of which did or will not survive (amateur VIFs). Some disappeared with collected vouchers (fraud VIFs).

In a Western context, the new owners should be empowered to choose any new fund manager/management company to separate the founder's interest from the VIF. In Russia today, however, structures of the VIFs' business and the nature of their investment strategies differs distinctively depending on the category of founder. That is because voucher investors themselves are often closely associated with the founders. Such VIFs would inevitably be subject to a serious agency problem in governing VIF investment activities.

Investment Strategies of VIFs

Few VIFs specified their investment strategies in the beginning and consistently followed them, as is commonly done in the West. Most VIFs changed strategies in response to the changing environment. Nevertheless, several characteristic strategies can be found in the extent of the diversification of portfolios and the investment time horizon. VIFs founded by enterprises of a particular industry often first invested

Table 5-5. Groups of Interests with VIF Participation

Region	*Fund*	*Manager*	*Participants and activities*
Archangelsk	Fund Severa	Andrey Butakov	SR
Bashkortostan	Vostok	Rafis Kadyrov	Bank "Vostok," depository
Vladimir	PIK-Invest	Sergey Konin	Concern PIK, depository "Deposit-reserve," insurance company "Unico," trade house "Trans-market," activities in transport, informational systems, and poligraphia
Volgograd	Tsaritsa	Alexey Morozov	Holding: commodity trade, brokerage, investment company, industrial production
Vologda	Vologda–Agro-prominvest	Commercial bank Vaskbank	Bank, agriculture machine-building, technical service
Ivanovo	Activ-center Shiit	Investment company	Bank "Ivanovskiye sitsy,"Trust company "Trust-TK," trust company "Kon-Trust"
	Garant	Fondovy center	
	Investor	Boris Zalutovsky	Depository Promyshlenny, SR, bank license exists
Kaliningrad	Zapadny	Anatoly Sablin	Bank, brokerage firm, insurance company, depository
Kirov	Lepse-check	Stanislav Gorokhov	Depository, brokerage firm, plant
Krasnodar	Invest-servise-1	Klimenty Kotov	Bank Kubinbank, depository, brokerage firm; Mr. Kotov is the president of an investment company connected with the bank
Marij-El	Zemlya-Invest	Vitaliy Kuznetsov	SR, commodity trade
Nizhny Novgorod	Pervy Obraztsovy Nizhegorods-kaya Yarmarka	Nizhegorodskaya Fondovaya Company	Pension fund, brokerage, commodity trade, construction

Novosibirsk	Ermak	Company Ermak	Depository, bank, industrial production
Omsk	Vysokii Tech-nologii Sibirsky Capital Khiminvest	Sibirsky Capital-Manager	Depository, brokerage firm, commodity trade
Perm	Narodny	Investment company BIS	Bank BIS-Credit, pension fund BIS-Garant, trust and intermediary service by the company BIS
Primorsky	Pasific-Invest	IPK Fedgi	Brokerage firm, commodity Kraj trade, technological investment, realty
Rostov	ROSIF	Company PIF	Brokerage firm, depository
Tyumen	Sodeystviye	Investment company Olimp	Realty, brokerage firm, commodity trade
Udmurtia	Certralny	Company Upravlya-yushaya Gruppa	Depository, investment in technologies
Khabarovsk	Kholder	Petr Sukhanosov	Brokerage firm, consulting, commodity trade
Moscow	Alpha-Capital	Company Apha-Capital	Bank, enterprise Bolshevichka, a number of food enterprises in Nizhny Novgorod
	MMM-Invest	Alexander Bychkov	Bank, commodity trade, realty
	Eximer	Constantin Korenevsky	Consulting, trade, service, technical equipment
	Germes	Yury Anisov	Oil trade, commodity trade, securitites operations, bank, exchanges, service, leather production, money market operations
	LLD-fund	Self-managed	Bank, insurance, brokerage, SR, realty, commodity trade
	Fintrust 100 + 1	Company Marion-Invest	Credobank, audit, consulting, insurance, industrial production

(continued on following page)

Table 5-5 *(continued)*

Region	*Fund*	*Manager*	*Participants and activities*
Moscow *(cont.)*	Equipage		Realty, trust, banks, brokerage, commodity trade
	Yamal	Center Moscovs-kiye Finansy	Relations with Gasprom
	RPB	Company Fondoby Dom	Russian food exchange, bank, insurance, commodity trade, Agroprom structure, brokerage
	MN-fund	Trade House Simpex	Bank, realty, brokerage
	Incomfund	Nataly Roslyakova	INCOMBANK group
	Pervy Voucherny	Mikhail Chebotarev	Pension fund
	Grant-Invest Kapsula Shahtyor (Rostovsky region)	Company INIT	SR
	Neft-Almaz-Invest	Company Delta	Margo-bank
	VPK (??)	Self-managed	VPIK-military production and service
	MIF (??)	MIF-LTD	Banks, Moscow governmental structure, gold production

Note: Information as of March 30, 1994.
Source: Capital Market Surveillance Unit (formerly, Fund Monitoring Unit) of GKI.

heavily in the founders' industrial branch. This group mainly includes 1 and 3 of the founders listed above. Their portfolios now consist of healthy enterprises thanks to the industry knowledge from the founder enterprises. These VIFs, however, will face tough competition from more professional VIFs in the future, constrained by an agency problem. Most regional VIFs diversified their portfolios widely by investing in a large number (70–240) of smaller enterprises. A main component of this group is founder 4 in the above listing. These VIFs are now burdened by the need to monitor closely the management of many enterprises because the smaller the enterprises are, the more easily their performance is damaged by management misbehavior.

Speculative VIFs

Among the more independent VIFs, some concentrated on voucher trading and speculation on the immediate resale opportunities of acquired shares. This kind of VIF includes many of the amateur VIFs of 5 in the listing and part of the professional VIFs of category 1. They acquired vouchers from the public and shares from voucher auctions and employees of the enterprises in the hope of selling them in a bloc to incumbent managers of the enterprises or their groups, or to external strategic investors. Incumbent managers often used money of the enterprises to acquire the shares. Although the speculation was profitable, the speculators did not always successfully unload the shares because the opportunities to resell were not sure ones. As a result, some VIFs, particularly amateurs in category 5, are now loaded with illiquid shares of poor performance. In addition, their asset size is usually too small to survive as collective investment vehicles that have to pay fees to their funds managers, custodian banks, transfer agents, lawyers, and the like. Amateur VIFs are now in the process of consolidation. They are merging among themselves, being acquired by larger VIFs, or disappearing.

Speculation Plus Venture Capital VIFs

Many smaller speculators have been engaged in venture capital business in addition to participating in the privatization. Venture capital business, however, required a significantly larger amount of funds than the

VIFs of moderate size with illiquid assets could generate. This led such VIFs and fund managers to establish new financial institutions to form financial groups. Thirty to forty pension funds were established as a part of such groups to raise capital for the venture business. This implies that the pension funds are actually venture capital and engaged in quite risky investment. These pension funds should be distinguished from more professional pension funds designed to serve employees of large enterprises, their groups, and other social organs.

Long-Term Portfolio Plus Venture Capital VIFs

The most successful kind of VIF combined long-term portfolio investment and venture capital business. Their portfolios consist of shares of following three kinds of enterprises: strategic enterprises that the VIFs try to participate in restructuring, nonstrategic enterprises that they hold for income gain and liquidity,[50] and venture businesses. Managers of these VIFs try to participate in restructuring of strategic enterprises in their portfolios, while also developing venture investment projects. This form of VIF also closely monitors behavior of managers of nonstrategic enterprises. Managers of these VIFs carefully selected shares based on investment quality rather than short-term speculative potential. They avoided explicitly promising unrealistically high returns in a short period of time. This kind of VIF has the healthiest financial position among all categories of VIFs and are involved actively in restructuring and governance of enterprises.

Governing Power of Long-Term Portfolio VIFs

Poorly performing amateur VIFs are going bankrupt because they are unable to cover their costs, while less poorly performing groups are merging among themselves or being acquired by major VIFs.[51] The

---

50. Many VIFs also hold T-bills for liquidity management.

51. Recently, however, the number of VIFs has not decreased because many industrial firms established VIFs for control in the last minute of voucher privatization to take advantage of the newly introduced tax privilege mentioned above.

long-term portfolio VIFs will grow further through acquisition of some or part of the amateur VIFs. In addition, they are acquiring a number of smaller banks that are losing in the recent environment of positive real interest rates. VIFs with a long-term orientation try to acquire controlling shares of privatized enterprises. Although they often own more than the stipulated maximum of 25 percent of an enterprise, they can obtain the controlling share in two principal ways. One is through their group structure, and the other is by colluding among VIFs. Their group structure generally includes a private founder company (or a holding company), a fund management company, a broker/dealer, and a bank.[52] When they collude, a VIF that holds the largest share tends to assume leadership in syndicating the stake and pressuring the enterprise managers by their collective voting power. Such VIFs often send their managers to the board of directors of enterprises.

Resistance by Enterprise Managers

Many enterprises do not appreciate managerial intervention of this kind. Enterprise managers think that VIFs have served as intermediaries of privatization, simply reallocating ownership of the existing assets, and have not brought any financial or managerial resources into the enterprises. Therefore, they believe that VIFs' intervention is irresponsible, without necessary capacity, and thus unacceptable. Some VIFs are using "a carrot and a stick" approach in dealing with enterprise managers. For the carrot, for example, VIFs usually try to convince enterprise managers that they can offer quality service (for example, attract good foreign investors, arrange competitive loans, underwrite new share issues and marketing, and so forth). For a stick,

---

52. A share depository also exists and contracts with the VIF for share custody. They all exist under the umbrella of a founder (holding) company, and tend to be located on the same premises. "Fire walls" are, therefore, not at all strict. In addition, VIF management companies have a brokerage function within. There is no "Chinese wall" between the underwriting (or investment) operation and the trading operation of an IF management company. Therefore, the current structure of the IF management companies appears to be a perfect source of conflict of interest and agency problems.

as a major shareholder some VIFs have taken an enterprise to court for their violation of shareholders' rights.[53]

Governance by Sector VIFs

Sector VIFs do not actively manage their portfolios, but act more like holding companies. This kind of VIF is often considered a group company by the enterprises, and their intervention is more accepted. Thanks to the industry knowledge from their founder companies, they are often capable of providing managerial resources and control over the companies in the portfolio. Because they were founded by an enterprise in a given industry in which they have invested, however, they are subject to an agency problem. Founder enterprises created such VIFs to control the invested enterprises in the particular manner the founder desired. Shareholders' interest to maximize the value of the portfolio does not necessarily coincide with the objective of managers of the VIFs. This kind of VIF may well become subject to close monitoring by the State Anti-Monopoly Committee.

Governance by Regional VIFs

Many regional VIFs, which hold diversified portfolios of many small, regional enterprises, are bound to monitor closely the behavior of the enterprises' managers. This is because the smaller an enterprise is, the more severely the company's performance will be affected by the misbehavior of its managers. In outer regions, the domination of the commercial banks is much less strong than it is in Moscow or St. Petersburg. Some leading regional VIFs that invested vouchers of regional residents into many regional companies are often considered

---

53. Alfa Capital bought 25 percent of Bolshevid Biscuit Co. in December 1992. Bolshevik Biscuit, however, did not permit Alfa in their shareholders' meeting. Alfa then took the company to arbitration court for violation of shareholders' rights, but the court had no capacity to judge, lacking experience in this kind of case. Only after Alfa promised foreign money to modernize the factory did the managers allow Alfa in the meeting.

as representatives of the regions' residents. Managers of such VIFs are respected and viewed as if they were "mayors" of the regions. Invested enterprises often invite managers of such VIFs to their board as directors. Monitoring closely many small companies is a costly process for VIFs of this category.

It needs to be emphasized that, except for the holding company form of VIF, an ultimate objective of VIFs is not to manage the enterprises but to maximize the value of their portfolios. Many VIFs would happily remain "silent" investors if some other outside strategic investors (likely to be foreigners) invest in the enterprises and improve their profitability. Incumbent enterprise managers initially tried to keep the control of their enterprises in their own hands. Having succeeded, largely because of the subsidized MEBO part of the privatization scheme, they are now at sea, loaded with poorly performing enterprises. Most of the managers are now quite willing to give up the control if capable strategic investors approach them with investment proposals and some acceptable conditions, such as security of the managers' employment and the like.

Structure of the Enterprise Governance Board and the Power of Outside Owners

The governing power of a particular interest group over an enterprise is determined by two factors. One is a legal structure of enterprise governance defined in the company law, provided that the law is honored. The other is an actual shareholding structure of the company in question. Chapter XVIII of the Regulations Governing the Activity of Joint-Stock Companies[54] (the Company Law hereafter) defines the legal governance structure of a Russian company.

Russia's Company Law

1: SHAREHOLDERS' MEETING. According to the law, the general meeting of shareholders, which is to be held annually, is the highest

54. Decision of the RSFSR Council of Ministers No. 601 of December 25, 1990.

governing body. In particular, election of directors and reorganization or liquidation of the company are within its jurisdiction. The meeting is deemed valid if attended by shareholders or their legal representatives who represent at least half of the total number of the company's outstanding shares. Any decisions at a meeting are to be made by voting (one share, one vote).[55] A resolution about the reorganization or liquidation of the company must be passed by 75 percent of the total votes cast by the shareholders present at the meeting. All other matters, including approval of the appointment of directors, is decided by a simple majority of the attending shareholders.

2: BOARD OF DIRECTORS. In the intervals between general shareholders' meetings, the highest governing body of the company is its board of directors.[56] The number of directors is to be determined by a shareholders' meeting, but should be an uneven number and no fewer than five in an open company.[57] *Only a shareholder or a representative of a shareholder who has the number of shares specified in the charter has the right to become a director.* Directors are to be elected for a two-year term, and may be re-elected an unlimited number of times. A shareholders' meeting can increase the number of directors and elect additional directors to fulfill certain functions. Nevertheless, a shareholders' meeting cannot remove a director before the expiration of his term of office. Directors are to elect a chairperson and deputy chairpersons of the board for a period of two years. A quorum requires the presence of two-thirds of the members of the board, and the board is to meet at least once a month.

---

55. If a shareholder fails to attend the meeting, he/she is obliged to delegate his/her vote to the board of directors or his/her proxy, and if no power of attorney is presented, the shareholder is to be deemed not to have participated in the voting.
56. Extraordinary meetings of shareholders to discuss special issues can also be called by the board of directors, the auditing commission, or by the holders of at least 10 percent of the company's shares.
57. No fewer than three in a close company unless the number of founders-shareholders is smaller than that.

3: PRESIDENT AND THE MANAGEMENT. A shareholders' meeting directly appoints a president out of the members of the board of directors. The president submits the composition of the management of the company, and the board of directors approves it. In the intervals between board and shareholders' meetings, the management directs all the company's activities, and meetings of management are to be held as required. The president presides over the meetings of management and organizes the keeping of minutes at the meetings, which are to be open for inspection by shareholders at any time.

4: AUDITING COMMISSION. The general shareholders' meeting elects an auditing commission among shareholders who are not directors. The commission is to oversee the financial and economic activities of the company by carrying out audits: (a) on instructions from a general shareholders' meeting, (b) on its own initiative, or (c) on the demand of the shareholders with more than a 10 percent holding. It can demand production and submission of all required documents and personal explanations by company officers. The results of the audits are to be presented to a shareholders' meeting. In the absence of auditors, the auditing commission draws up balance sheets and income statements and submits these to a shareholders' meeting for approval. Members of the auditing commission can call an extraordinary meeting of the shareholders should they believe that the shareholders' interest may be jeopardized.

The U.S. and the German Models

Governance structures of U.S. and the German companies contrast well with the Russian structure, and one another. A U.S. company has only one governance board, which is a board of directors, and the members are elected at the annual shareholders' meeting. The highly dispersed ownership structure of a large U.S. corporation, however, limits the power of each shareholder. Generally, 50 percent of a big U.S. company is owned by a large number of individuals, and a good part of the rest is owned by institutional investors, each of whom owns a maximum of a few percent and tends to be a "silent" shareholder.[58] Man-

58. Some U.S. institutional investors do participate in corporate governance (for example, public employee pension funds such as the State of Wisconsin Investment Board, California Public Employees' Retirements System, and so forth).

agement plays a major role in selecting members of the board through its control over the voting process at the annual shareholders' meeting. Naturally, management elects itself to the board, and also nominates outside directors to the shareholders for their approval. Employees do not have an automatic right to be represented on the board unless they are significant shareholders. As a result, the board is dominated and controlled by the incumbent managers, who often put their self-interest ahead of the shareholders', creating an agency problem.

In contrast, a German company has a two-tier governance system. Shareholders are represented on the supervisory board, while management is represented on the management board. Banks and other companies often own and/or represent significant shares in a large German company and elect their representatives, as well as outside members who represent minority shareholders, to the supervisory board. Employees are entitled to elect one-half of the members of the supervisory board, which in turn appoints senior managers to a management board. The supervisory board sets broad corporate policy, while the management board is in charge of the day-to-day implementation of that policy. The German system of corporate governance, therefore, mobilizes participation of a wider range of parties in governing the company and reduces an agency problem.

Power of Major Shareholders in a Russian Company

Russia's Company Law defines a two-tier structure of a corporate governance board, as is the case in the German company. Russia's Company Law, however, does not allow outsiders who do not represent the interests of major shareholders into the board of directors. Neither does it automatically allow representatives of insiders, such as managers or workers, into the board unless they are at the same time significant shareholders or their legal representatives. A shareholders' meeting directly appoints a president,[59] a head of the management board, out of the members of a board of directors and elects members of an auditing

---

59. This potentially weakens the power of the board of directors to exercise control over the president and the management board.

commission from among nondirector shareholders. The auditing committee, as a supervisory body, is also appointed directly by shareholders. The governance structure of a Russian company is, therefore, to be strongly dominated by major shareholders. This is one reason the Russian stock market has so far been strongly driven by the desire to gain controlling shares.

Actual Shareholding Structure and Dominance of Owner-Managers

When a Russian enterprise was registered as a joint-stock company, the first board of directors consisted of the president, a representative of the labor collective, a representative of either the Property Fund or GKI (or an appointed representative), and a representative of the local Soviet. This assured the majority voting shares of the incumbent work force, and it dominated the governance structure until the first shareholders' meeting. A president was simultaneously a chairperson of a board of directors, almost without exception. Members of an auditing commission were often part of the incumbent work force, middle-managers reporting to senior managers who are members of the board of directors. Furthermore, employees, an important group of the owner work force, tended to limit voluntarily their participation in managerial issues to only the smallest, least significant range of decisions in running the enterprises, while the manager would undertake to keep as many people employed as possible.[60] In this situation, there has been little managerial discipline imposed on the incumbent management.

Potential for Changes in Power Balance

For management ownership to act as an effective governance device in the large and medium-size enterprises, managers must have a reasonably high ownership stake, and yet not be completely entrenched, so that

60. There is anecdotal evidence that the work force has voluntarily restricted (or agreed with the management to restrict) their wages to a low level in order to secure employment.

outsider investors can force them out when they fail to maximize profits. The New Privatization Program stipulated a limitation on the absolute control of the management over the privatized enterprises. In particular, incumbent work force (including management) participation in the board of directors has been limited to one-third of the board members. Deregulation of VIF shareholding in one enterprise from 10 percent to 25 percent is a significant move to mobilize outside shareholders' control, because with a 25 percent shareholding, one VIF can have veto power over decisions related to reorganization and liquidation of an enterprise.

In addition to the regulatory factor, there are two other principal ways that incumbent management's dominance may be challenged. One is an emergence of outsider shareholders, either by acquisition of existing shares or by making a fresh strategic investment, and the other is a control by creditors over enterprises in financial distress. Both of these possibilities are now materializing in Russia. The tie between management and employees is weaker in large enterprises. It is also being weakened in many medium-size enterprises whose profit performances have been poor and whose wages have been kept low. Few managers view employee shareholding as an impediment to laying off the workers, although a labor collective is often a major shareholder and represented on the board of directors. Employees are now selling out their holding of shares, as happened in postwar Japan. Broker-dealers offer attractive prices for shares in which they expect foreign investment. Bankruptcy is now to be enforced with state-owned enterprises. As inflation is coming down and the real interest rate has become positive, some privatized enterprises are also exposed to considerable bankruptcy risk.

Enforcement of Shareholders' Rights

The first shareholders' meeting is required to be held within twelve months after registration of the company as a joint-stock company. Many were held toward the beginning of 1994, but with some irregularities to obstruct participation of outside shareholders. In some cases, management required shareholders' representatives to have authorized certificates to participate in the meetings as an excuse to exclude sham shareholders, and to have those certificates validated by notaries. In other cases, the voting at the meeting was counted on the basis of "one person one vote" rather than "one share one vote."[61] To begin with, over 10,000 enterprises issuing shares planned to have annual shareholders' meetings at about the same time, making it impossible for multiple shareholders such as VIFs to attend most of the meetings.[62]

The Company Law defines rights of shareholders, but their enforcement is another issue. An effective way to enhance enterprise governance is to promote awareness of public shareholders about their rights to the profit of the enterprises they own. The Moscow Public Shareholders' Rights Committee was established by an initiative from the VIF industry to promote public awareness.[63] The committee publishes periodicals and publicizes practices in violation of shareholders' rights, as well as good practices by managers of enterprises and VIFs. As shareholders become educated about their rights (and the procedures for claiming them), enforcing the law will become less of a problem. Now the inadequacy of the court system itself is being highlighted in the fight to enforce laws and regulations.[64]

Power of Commercial Banks and Foreign Investors and Their Relationship with VIFs

Russia's private commercial banking sector started in 1989, while VIFs emerged at the end of 1992. Although many purely private banks started from nothing, they have shown an impressive growth in the past

---

61. There is an ongoing discussion in academia as to whether "one share, one vote" is the optimal rule of corporate governance. In the Russian system, they have both voting and nonvoting shares. The issue here is not the voting rule itself, however, but the universal enforcement of whatever rule exists.

62. The accounting year ends December 31, and dividends must be paid within sixty days. This means that all the privatized enterprises try to pay out dividends at almost the same time. It may be imagined what a mess this can cause in present-day Russia, with its inefficient payment system.

63. It was established by an initiative of Mr. Andrei Volgin, President of Adamant Financial Corporation, a fund management company for Derzhava Investment Fund, a Moscow-based, major VIF.

64. A bottom line is that the Russian judges, juries, and lawyers do not have any experience in handling private commercial lawsuits and are unable to function effectively in those capacities.

five years, and commercial banks number about 2,000 in Russia today. Moscow has attracted nearly 600 bank headquarters, which include most of Russia's leading commercial banks.

Commercial Banking Sector

Major commercial banks are currently better placed to influence corporate control than any other financial and investment institutions, including VIFs. First, banks have been able to provide financial resources to enterprises, which VIFs have not. Second, former state banks (for example, Promstroibank) have traditionally strong ties with former state enterprises, and purely private banks have worked together with private enterprises from the beginning of their establishment. Third, the universal banking status gives a capacity to the Russian banks to control enterprises.[65]

SOURCE OF BANKS' GOVERNING POWER

Medium-term loans and loan provisions. Leading banks are trying to strengthen their relationships with client enterprises and recently started medium-term (1–3 year) hard currency lending.[66] In the current inflationary environment, hard-currency credit is the only way to provide medium-term financing, while such credit can only be provided to reliable hard-currency earners. Furthermore, medium-term credit can only be given to a borrower who has a stable, long-term revenue base. As a result, long-term credit has been concentrated in resource-based, export-oriented project financing. The banks' loan provisions when granting such credit include imposition of ceilings on additional borrowing and dividend payments of the borrowers, and a requirement to channel set minimum amounts of the export revenues through them. If a borrower

---

65. In asset size, banks are significantly larger than VIFs, and therefore claimed to be more powerful. A comparison of asset value between banks and VIFs under the present illiquid stock market with inflation is not very meaningful in the long run, because net asset values of VIFs are greatly undervalued relative to those of banks under a circumstance that is unlikely to persist in the long run.
66. International Moscow Bank, Tokobank, and Mosbizinesbank are among such banks (see Elena Belyanova and Ivan Rozinsky in this volume).

fails to meet such provisions, the bank may undertake a wide range of possible actions. Today, Moscow-based major banks claim to have about 20 percent of their assets in this kind of lending. As an enterprise becomes dependent on a particular bank, a threat to withdraw credit becomes a powerful tool.

Share custody and registrar. Russia's commercial banks are considered as universal banks because they are allowed to engage in securities business. Commercial banks' direct investment in equity, however, is generally not a very significant source of corporate control because of bank regulations such as capital adequacy requirements and the single-risk exposure restriction. Nevertheless, banks' share custody business, which often gives proxy voting rights to the banks, is another potential source of governance power. A number of banks playing the role of custodian are affiliated to major VIFs, however, and do not play an independent role as proxy voters. VIF managers vote by themselves most of the time. More independent custodians are major banks with trust, brokerage, and/or registrar operations but without affiliation with major VIFs. Aiming to be a full-scale universal bank, Inkombank, for example, is said to control 20 percent of the shares of all the enterprises in St. Petersburg. It achieves that level of control by the proxy voting power gained through its custodial business. Inkombank operates a leading independent registrar in St. Petersburg, and the registrar can assure proper registration of shareholders and hence their rights, such as the right to receive dividends, to vote at the shareholders' meetings, and the like.[67] Because Inkombank also offers custody service, investors of companies registered at the bank's registrar tend to prefer to use the bank's custody service.

ENTERPRISE GOVERNANCE BY BANKS. Whether or not the Russian banks will play a significant role in corporate governance—as their German or Japanese counterparts do—remains to be seen. The strong ties between major commercial banks and enterprises raised a concern in GKI about their potentially anticompetitive nature and led to tight-

67. When GKI started promoting establishment of independent registrars, half of individual Russian shareholders were said not to be registered properly and, therefore, often failed to exercise their rights.

ening of the regulation on the banks' enterprise shareholding. The New Privatization Program announced by GKI in December 1993 stipulates that commercial banks are limited to a holding of a 10 percent of equity share in each enterprise.[68,69]

So far, banks' involvement in privatization and governance of privatized enterprises has been limited.[70] One reason is that the controlling power of the incumbent work force was much greater than expected in the beginning of the privatization. Except for the hard-currency project lending, banks are not providing long-term credit to enterprises. Even in the case of the hard-currency project lending, foreign investors and financial institutions tend to take a major stake. In such a case, the governing power of the Russian banks would be limited. In addition, major banks have recently become increasingly conservative and lost interest in equity investment and trading as the real interest rate has become positive. In the recent environment of positive real interest rates, with inflation and nominal interest rates falling steadily, the most sensible way to manage bank assets is to invest in fixed income instruments of longer duration and high creditworthiness.[71] T-bills are an

---

68. Prior to the new program, there was no automatic restriction on banks' shareholdings, unless a banking law regulation on single-risk exposure also applies to equity shareholdings. The only explicit restriction was that banks' acquisition of beyond 35 percent of shares required approval of the State Anti-Competition Committee. More general rules of significant share acquisitions are: 1) a purchase on the market of over 15 percent of a company's shares by one party requires the consent of the Ministry of Finance (this provision does not apply to the company's founders) and 2) a purchase of over 50 percent requires consent from the Anti-Competition Committee.
69. Total value of equity shareholding by a bank was also restricted to a maximum of 5 percent of the banks' assets. This, however, is rather a matter of prudential operation of banks and, therefore, a concern of the Banking Law rather than the Anti-Competition Law.
70. Only 3 percent of enterprises surveyed by *The Russian Economic Barometer* in November 1993 indicated that the banks' representatives became members of the board of directors (see Elena Belyanova and Ivan Rozinsky in this volume).
71. T-bills are discount instruments; therefore, their duration is as long as their maturity. There are three- and six-month bills being issued today, and an issue of one-year bills is planned to start in late 1994.

ideal instrument for this purpose and, therefore, have recently been increasingly popular among major banks.

In contrast, smaller commercial banks were engaged in risky investment.[72] Small banks have tried to attract deposits by offering high rates because they needed to have greater liabilities to take advantage of scale economy in financial intermediation. On the asset side, however, this forced them to be engaged in high-risk, high-return business (moral hazard). Small banks continued to speculate in foreign exchange and interest rates and to be engaged in equity investment and trading. However, the ruble did not depreciate much more as inflation cooled, and interest rates in hard-currency deposits have come down with competition. Property and equity do not appreciate as real interest rates become positive with falling inflation. It is speculated that a large number of smaller commercial banks will go under by the end of 1994.[73] Such smaller banks are now trying to sell themselves to leading VIFs.

SIZE OF COMMERCIAL BANKS AND BANKING SECTOR STRUCTURE. In order for Russian banks to play an active role in enterprise governance, they would have to be able to contribute significantly to financing the enterprises. While provision of short-term working capital serves to monitor the activities of the client enterprises, banks should also be able to provide longer-term financing in order to participate in the enterprises' strategic business planning. The requirement of a significant financial contribution means that the banks have to be large enough relative to the size of a client enterprise.[74] At present, even

---

72. In 1993, banks were said to be responsible for half of trading turnover.

73. Article 11 of Russia's Bankruptcy Law stipulates that a petition for insolvency (bankruptcy) of a licensed bank cannot be filed by its creditor and/or a public prosecutor until the Central Bank of Russia suspends the banking license. This is an exception of the enterprise bankruptcy rule applied only to licensed banks. The Central Bank of Russia and commercial banks are now also working on introduction of a deposit insurance scheme and a bank rating system to increase the transparency of the banking system.

74. Prudent management of a bank should require diversification of the loan portfolio. This normally materializes in the form of a regulation to limit a bank's lending exposure to a single risk source.

leading Russian banks are still small if compared with the gigantic Russian industrial enterprises, such as the oil and gas. Commercial banks will have to syndicate loans among themselves to meet the financing needs of such industrial giants.[75]

In order for individual Russian banks to be larger, the banking system would have to be relatively concentrated. The banking sector would need to have a two-tier structure, with a limited number of large commercial banks with extensive, nationwide branch networks in the first tier, and a large number of smaller regional banks in the second tier. Although Moscow-based leading banks are significantly larger and more sophisticated than other regional banks, emergence of such a banking system is still at a beginning stage.[76] Major banks have expanded their branch networks to gain a competitive position in correspondent banking to consummate interregional payments.[77] They did so both by establishing new branches and by acquiring small local banks.

VIF-BANK RELATIONSHIP. As of July 1993, about 16 percent of the banks had VIFs managed by their affiliated fund management companies.[78] The relationships between leading VIFs and major commercial banks, however, appear to be quite independent from each other. In general, it is much more likely that a group involving a major VIF has a commercial bank as a member than that a major commercial bank

---

75. Although some major industrial groups have commercial banks as their members, such a "house bank" tends to be too small to satisfy the investment needs of its group enterprises and to specialize in working capital financing and payment services.
76. The World Bank announced loans to strengthen banking institutions on May 19, 1994, which will permit thirty to forty "core banks" to be upgraded to an international standard.
77. Because the payment system of the Central Bank of Russia takes at least two weeks to consummate interregional payments in the inflationary environment, demand for a swift payment service has been very strong. A bank with a nationwide branch network could offer an interregional payment service by correspondent banking, which allows the bank to internalize the payments as its free liquidity and, therefore, has been a very profitable business.
78. *The Russian Economic Barometer*, July 1993. Also, see Elena Belyanova and Ivan Rozinsky in this volume.

controls a VIF through its affiliated fund management company. When a leading VIF has a commercial bank in its group, the bank's core activity tends to assist the operation of the VIF, especially in the provision of services of share custody and payment for dividends and settlement of share trading. In other words, financial groups involving leading VIFs often have VIF business in their core, and commercial banking operations as a supplement. In contrast, VIFs controlled by leading commercial banks collected vouchers from the bank's depositors and employees of the bank's client enterprises and invested in the client enterprises for control. Such VIFs act more like holding companies, and their marketing strategies have been conservative.[79] There are only a few VIFs of this kind, and they are likely to be subject to close monitoring by the Anti-Competition Committee.

Commercial banks are not necessarily the dominant financial institutions in the outer regions of Russia. There are a number of regions where only a few VIFs exist and banks are small. Some VIFs in such regions collected vouchers from the majority of the residents of the regions and are viewed as "representatives" of the citizens who are workers in the region's enterprises. The president of such a VIF resembles a regional mayor. Enterprises in such a region often invite representatives from the VIF to be members of their boards of directors. Such VIFs claim no difficulty in competing with the commercial banks of their regions. In general, Russian banks and VIFs maintain a rather competitive relationship with each other, although a competitive advantage clearly lies with commercial banks at the moment.[80]

---

79. They do not aggressively advertise their investment performance and dividends to attract individual voucher investors.

80. This contrasts with the situation in the Czech Republic, where the banking system is dominated by a limited number of former state banks. All the major banks own leading fund management companies that manage the ten largest VIFs. As a result, the Czech banks have a strong influence on the management of VIFs. Through the VIFs, Czech banks exercise significant governance over enterprises, which creates an agency problem and conflict of interest with investors of such VIFs.

Subsidiaries of Foreign Banks

Several foreign investment banks and commercial banks have established subsidiaries or joint ventures in Russia. They are serving as the catalyst for foreign investment in three different ways. First, they are the agents for foreign strategic investors in cross-border acquisitions.[81] The foreign banks then work with VIFs and B/Ds in the acquisition of shares of target enterprises. With their "well-capitalized position" with vouchers, VIFs acquired shares of a target enterprise and sold them as a bloc to a foreign investor through a foreign investment bank.[82] Some VIFs profited significantly from this operation. Second, they served as advisors for joint ventures between foreign investors and privatized Russian enterprises. Third, they have been custodians for foreign portfolio investors. Naturally, the investment banks are stronger in the first two areas,[83] and the commercial banks are stronger in the last.

Role of Foreign Investment

A common perception of foreign investment in Russia is that it would be insignificant compared with the resources needed to restructure the huge Russian industrial sector. Contrary to this perception, the impor-

---

81. The foreign banks take either buy-side or sell-side, depending on the case. In some cases, they seem to have acted as middleman on behalf of both sides, which is unconventional, and often unacceptable, in the Western investment banking practice.

82. If a foreign bank tries to take a sell-side, they visit Russian enterprises individually and identify potentially marketable enterprises. If an identified enterprise seeks foreign investment, the bank arranges for lawyers and accountants to carry out Western-standard due diligence and advise on the minimum restructuring acceptable for foreign investment. At the same time, the bank markets such Russian enterprises and brings in the best Western partner through their international network. They commonly charge the seller a fixed fee plus a success fee as a portion of the capital they successfully solicited from a foreign investor.

83. Among them, a subsidiary of Credit Swiss First Boston (CSFB) is the most well-established, active, and successful in Russia.

tance of the role of foreign investment has received increasing recognition. Foreign strategic (that is, direct) investment provides confidence to the target Russian enterprise, and thus helps mobilize domestic investment and financing as well. Foreign portfolio investment, which has recently become noticeable, accelerated the increasing trend of foreign investment,[84] a response to the undervaluing of Russian enterprise shares relative to the value of their assets.[85] Long-term investment, whether strategic or portfolio, is quite limited in Russia today, and within that limited investment, foreign investment comprises a substantial part. It is generally the foreign investor with a large amount of long-term funds who has the capacity to take short-term risks for long-term strategy and return in the present risky business environment of Russia.

Bankruptcy, the Power of Creditors, and the Role of VIFs

Bankruptcy and the Power of Creditor Banks

As a debtor falls into financial distress, the voices of creditors become louder. Enforcement of bankruptcy law strengthens the governing power of creditor banks, which comes to supersede that of shareholders. The governing power of commercial banks over a debtor in financial distress would be determined by two principal factors. One

---

84. Foreign portfolio investors are particularly concerned about the Russian market's capacity to ensure ownership rights and their sure transfer on a nationwide basis. The system of share custody and company registrar, particularly to ensure swift and sure interregional share trading, needs to be upgraded as soon as possible to give confidence to the domestic as well as the foreign investors. As for an organized trading system, a centralized exchange or a NASDAQ-like networking OTC market needs to be established. To generate liquidity, listing of blue chip enterprises needs to be promoted simultaneously with upgrading of the market infrastructure.

85. In terms of Western securities analysis, price-to-book-value ratio (PBR) of Russian shares, if the book value is adjusted for inflation, tends to be far below 1.

is the legal power given to creditors in bankruptcy law,[86] and the other is the extent to which the commercial banks are creditors of the enterprises. If the commercial banks were not lending extensively to enterprises, the banks would not be in a position to command strong legal power over the debtor. If the banks were financing enterprises extensively, their voice would be stronger. At the same time, however, a large-scale bankruptcy of enterprises would seriously hurt the soundness of the banks and the banking system.

Russia's Bankruptcy Law

Russia's Bankruptcy Law was revised in December 1993, and the Federal Agency of Bankruptcy was established simultaneously to administer enforcement of the law.[87] In May 1994, a presidential decree set up specific criteria for recognition of bankruptcy. Further, on June 2, 1994, President Yeltsin signed a decree "On the Sale of Debt-Owing State Enterprises." This decree established a normative base for bringing insolvent enterprises out of crisis. The general structure of the law is similar to those of most Western bankruptcy laws, and it describes court and out-of-court procedures, reorganization, and voluntary and involuntary liquidation. Russia's bankruptcy law is designed with greater similarity to the U.K. or the German law than to the U.S. law, in that its reorganization procedures are not as permissive with the debtor as is Chapter 11 of the U.S. law (see table 5-6).[88] Liquidation of a debtor under the Russian law would leave nothing to govern afterward, although it gives foremost power to the creditors in the recovery

---

86. Assuming that the law can be enforced, which seems a reasonable assumption in the long run.
87. The agency can also initiate bankruptcy procedures for unprivatized state enterprises.
88. The 1978 U.S. Bankruptcy Law was revised in 1989 as a cautious response to the rise of LBO (leveraged buyout) transactions in 1980s. The revised law has been criticized by academia for giving too much chance to the debtor to reorganize itself, which tends to be a lengthy and costly process, and gives less incentive to restructure (see Jensen 1991).

Table 5-6. Bankruptcy Reorganization: The United States and the United Kingdom

United States Chapter 11	*United Kingdom Administrative receivership[a]/ administration*
Debtor in possession	Debtor loses control
Process dominated by management	Process dominated by (secured) creditors
Easier to raise finance[b] creditors	Finance usually from secured creditors
More costly because it takes longer	Lower costs
Deferred liquidation	Premature liquidation

a. Appointed by the court.
b. Any new loans given to the firm for reorganization are considered "preferred credit," which is higher in seniority than existing debt.
Source: Atiyas 1994.

of the credit. Reorganization is, therefore, the matter of more relevance in considering the issue of enterprise governance in Russia.

Opening Bankruptcy Cases

According to Russia's Bankruptcy Law, a creditor (as well as the debtor, the owner, or a public prosecutor) can file a petition to open a bankruptcy case to the Court of Arbitration, with a prior notice to the debtor, if a payment becomes overdue by more than three months.[89] The petition can include a request for reorganization. With

89. The debtor's petition must be filed by decision by the owner or board of directors of the enterprise, signed by its manager, and accompanied by the debtor's financial information. The debtor must also send a copy of the petition and the financial information to each of its creditors. The financial information must include a list of its creditors and debtors, a breakdown of payables and receivables, and a balance sheet or substitute financial documents.

the attendance of representatives of the debtor, the owner,[90] the creditor, the local financial agencies, and the work collective, the Court of Arbitration is responsible for reviewing the case and deciding whether to accept the petitions. The court first considers whether to recognize the debtor as bankrupt and institute bankruptcy proceedings (liquidation). If it decides not to recognize bankruptcy, and the petition includes a request for reorganization, the court also reviews that possibility and decides on an appropriate action to be taken.

Reorganization and the Power of Creditors

The legal concept of enterprise reorganization consists of two principal components—outside management of a debtor's property and rehabilitation. Outside management of a debtor's property includes the organizational procedures ordered by the court upon receiving a petition and is designed to sustain an enterprise's activities by transferring the functions of managing the debtor enterprise to the arbitration manager. An arbitration manager works out a restructuring plan that is to be effected through merger, division, detachment, takeover, or transformation.[91] Rehabilitation aims at recovery of a debtor enterprise and consists of financial aid administered to the debtor enterprise by the owner, creditors, or third parties.

Outside Management of a Debtor's Property

To institute outside management of a debtor's property, the debtor and creditors can nominate candidates for arbitration manager, and the

---

90. Including appropriate authorities if the enterprise is still owned by the state or other public bodies.
91. A merger is to be effected by combining controlling interests with subsequent conversion of shares or by the replacement of the shares of one company with the equivalent value of the shares of the other company and by consolidation of balance sheets. A takeover is to be effected by purchasing 100 percent of the company's shares.

court endorses the nomination, or tenders the position on a competitive basis if more than one candidate is nominated. The law requires that an arbitration manager not be a staff member of the debtor or the creditors.[92] A meeting of creditors has numerous powers, including: 1) establishment of a creditors' committee, which is entitled to request information and explanations from the arbitration manager; 2) endorsement or amendment of an outside management plan made by the arbitration manager; and 3) establishment of the amount of remuneration the arbitration manager will receive, which is to be approved by the court. Within three months of appointment, the arbitration manager must obtain an endorsement from a creditors' meeting for a plan for outside management. If an outside management plan is not endorsed by representation of two-thirds of all creditors' claims, the court may revoke its judgment on outside management of the debtor's property, or leave the decision in force but replace the arbitration manager. Any creditor (or owner) can also file a petition with the court for a review of the outside management plan by an arbitration manager if it finds the plan to be detrimental to its interest. If the outside management should be terminated for reasons of its ineffectiveness or incompletion within eighteen months, the court may declare the debtor bankrupt and begin bankruptcy proceedings.[93]

Rehabilitation

The priority right to participate in rehabilitation belongs to the creditor, the owner, and members of the work force.[94] If the owner and the creditors agree, however, the court may call an open tender for participation in the rehabilitation. If no one wishes to participate, the

---

92. An arbitration manager must also be either a lawyer or an economist with practical experience and must disclose his/her income and property.

93. As a disincentive against an unelaborated rehabilitation attempt for an unviable enterprise by the owner or creditors, the remuneration for the arbitration manager is to be charged to the requester if the court decides to terminate the outside management.

94. If the owner and/or the work force are to participate, the work force must participate in an independent capacity.

court may revoke its rehabilitation decision. The participants in rehabilitation must perform their assumed obligations to creditors in full and are collectively liable for their fulfillment. The creditors (as well as the owner or the work force) can complain to the court about the ineffectiveness of the reorganization, and the court may then take an appropriate action, including termination of the rehabilitation. At least 40 percent of the combined amount of creditors' claims must be met in order of seniority within twelve months, and the duration of rehabilitation should not exceed eighteen months.[95] There are several other restrictions on the duration of procedures to carry out rehabilitation in order to ensure swift and cost-effective actions. If rehabilitation is terminated for reasons of its ineffectiveness, incompletion, or failure to satisfy requirements, the court declares the debtor bankrupt and begins bankruptcy proceedings. The court may not decide on rehabilitation if the case of bankruptcy is to be reopened within three years.

Russian Banks' Exposure to Enterprise Financing

In light of Russia's Bankruptcy Law, creditors are given considerable power and control to protect their interest in the process of enterprise reorganization. Russian banks' enterprise financing, however, has so far been limited. Unlike many of the Central European countries, Russia has employed a decentralized approach to promote development of a competitive banking sector.[96] The commercially minded Russian banks of today do not easily lend to risky Russian enterprises, except for companies in their groups. In addition, long-term investment credit was traditionally provided directly by the government, and therefore traditional business ties between banks and enterprises are generally not strong compared with those in many Central European countries. Furthermore, inflation has wiped out past debt of the enterprises. Therefore, it seems unlikely that the Russian banks will be faced with a phe-

95. The court may extend the duration by a maximum of six months upon a request from the participants.

96. The physical size of the country and other political factors necessitated such an approach.

nomenal nonperforming loan problem, which has been a common problem in formerly planned economies that employed a centralized approach to develop their banking sector. At the same time, it is also unlikely that banks will develop a widely encompassing governing power over the enterprise sector through the process of enterprise bankruptcy.

Status of Enterprise Bankruptcy

According to the Federal Agency of Bankruptcy, there are said to be over 1,000 state-owned enterprises that have filed for bankruptcy either voluntarily or involuntarily. They comprise a third of enterprises in which the government still owns over 25 percent of the shares, and 250 have already been recognized formally as bankrupt. Some of those enterprises are now being sold into private hands. In addition, inter-enterprise arrears have shown phenomenal growth, to amount to over 70 trillion rubles,[97] suggesting a possible domino bankruptcy of enterprises. Many enterprises seem to have continued to produce and deliver products as has been done in the past, but without the assurance of payments. Inflation is now being cooled off steadily, and the real interest rate has become positive in the gradually tighter monetary environment, while the payments system remains inefficient. All this implies that more bankruptcy may be realized with private or privatized enterprises, which now comprise about 70 percent of all the Russian enterprises. It is beyond the scope of this chapter to forecast whether the seemingly bottomed-out recession will help enterprises escape from a grand-scale bankruptcy.[98]

It needs to be mentioned, however, that an incentive to evade tax is generating a lot of sham insolvency. Enterprises can easily hide transactions and profit in reality by barter, by cash payments with no transaction records, and by manipulating transfer pricing, particularly within

97. The total is 112 trillion rubles, according to the State Statistics Office.

98. In Hungary, strict enforcement of the Bankruptcy Law in a tight monetary environment resulted in the ballooning of nonperforming loans in the banking system for which neither the authority nor the banks were prepared.

their corporate groups. By hiding transactions, an enterprise can disguise revenues and manipulate taxable profit while evading turnover tax.[99] In particular, the incentive to evade turnover tax encourages barter transactions and growth of interenterprise arrears.[100] In these circumstances, some credible threat to enforce the bankruptcy law may be effective in forcing enterprises to disclose their real performance and pay taxes. Asset registrars are now developing, and private land ownership is now legally defined. Nevertheless, the authorities and the legal system have so far not been very successful in enforcing the law because they lack understanding of enterprise valuation and restructuring.

Potential Role of VIFs in Debt Restructuring

One way for VIFs to deal with creditor banks and enterprises is to buy nonperforming loans from banks at discount and engage in debt-equity swaps with the debtor enterprises. This can be a mutually beneficial business among VIFs, banks, and potentially viable enterprises. In addition, it will reduce the government's fiscal burden by having the private sector shoulder the cost of restructuring. This will also help avoid development of excessive cross-shareholding relationships between banks and enterprises through direct debt-equity swaps.[101] Bills of exchange have been introduced to carve out the uncontrolled growth of interenterprise arrears. The introduction of bills of exchange is expected to accelerate growth of a secondary market for enterprise debt, which will be a good foundation for VIFs to acquire those debt instruments and engage in debt-equity swap transactions.

---

99. Russia employs a turnover tax, which is different from the value-added tax (VAT), although both are indirect taxes. Turnover tax is similar to consumption tax and is levied thinly on the gross transaction amount, while VAT is levied on value newly added by the enterprise. Therefore, there is a strong incentive to hide transactions, which also often leads to vertical integration of industry.

100. By postponing payments, revenue and profit would not be recognized under Russia's cash accounting of profit and loss. Therefore, enterprises do not have to pay income and turnover taxes for such unpaid transactions.

101. This will help banks meet the maximum of 10 percent corporate shareholding restriction on banks.

Currently there is said to be an obstacle against debt-equity swap transactions. The current Russian law seems to stipulate that the par value of shares be written against the value of fixed assets on the book. Under the current law, debt equity swaps are considered as issues of new equity shares with par value against nothing tangible and, therefore, not permissible. The authorities, however, recognize such regulation to be an obstacle to promoting restructuring of enterprises. VIFs are lobbying for revision of this regulation in order to be able to engage in debt-equity swaps, particularly in the capacity of distressed restructuring.

Concluding Summary

Russian enterprises currently are controlled by incumbent management. The strength of insider control stems not from the legal structure of the enterprise governance but from the actual shareholding structure of the enterprises. A majority of the management, however, has not been successful in restructuring and improving the enterprises to adjust to the new market environment. Positions in enterprise management need to be made competitive so that incumbent management is pressured to do a better job, or to leave the position in one way or another. The role of outside shareholders, creditors, and potential investors is thus critically important in Russia today.

Commercial banks have some governance power as creditors, especially over enterprises of moderate size with a close business or group relationship. Nevertheless, their governing power does not reach widely over the huge Russian industrial sector. Operation of leading banks is becoming increasingly conservative as they become established and the real interest rate becomes positive with cooling inflation. Public trust in VIFs is generally low following several examples of fraud, nonpayment of promised dividends, and the failure of VIFs to provide financial resources for enterprises.

Nevertheless, the importance and capacity of VIFs should not be underestimated, for four reasons.

- They were intermediaries in privatization and, therefore, are politically supported by the powerful GKI. The failure of VIFs would mean failure of privatization, which GKI would try to avoid as much as possible.

- Leading VIFs have become a group of significant enterprise shareholders, and thus have a significant governing power over enterprises. Currently, privatized enterprises are controlled by incumbent owner-managers who are in many cases unwilling or unable to restructure their enterprises to adjust to the new environment. Governance by outside owners such as VIFs is an important source of managerial discipline for the enterprises.
- Because they are completely new entities without any roots in a communist organization of the past, many VIFs and fund management companies are run by an innovative new generation of Russians. The managerial capacity and entrepreneurship of the management of leading fund management companies is particularly noteworthy.
- If the liquidity of the stock market increases, and stock prices start reflecting the true value of the enterprises, the net asset value of leading VIFs will likely increase dramatically to a level beyond that of commercial banks. Infrastructure to support generation of liquidity is now being worked out.

Some long-term-oriented VIFs are involved directly in the governance of invested enterprises. Their ultimate objective, however, is not to manage the enterprises, but to earn a higher return. They would be happy to remain silent investors if strategic investors come in and restructure the enterprises. Leading Russian banks, VIFs, and B/Ds cooperate with foreign investment and commercial banks with operations in Russia. These foreign banks are acting as a catalyst for foreign strategic and portfolio investment. By using well-capitalized positions with vouchers, some VIFs are playing the role of subagent for the foreign banks. Foreign investment is increasing its importance, and it also encourages domestic investment by giving confidence to the domestic investors. VIFs' role in enterprise governance seems to lie in intermediation of strategic investment, through which they solicit managerial resources while, in the interim period, keeping the management position contested. As they go through that process, they are expected to become long-term portfolio investors, much like mutual funds in the United States.

VIFs also have the potential to play a role in restructuring of distressed enterprises and assisting banks and creditor enterprises in dealing with nonperforming credits. If VIFs buy the bad credit and carry out debt-equity swaps with the issuing enterprises, they may gain substantial influence over enterprise governance. So far, the relationship between major VIFs and major banks in Russia is rather independent, especially compared with that in the Czech Republic, and thus it is unlikely that an agency problem will be a serious impediment in coordinating among VIFs, banks, and enterprises. Development of a secondary market of bad credit with an introduction of a bill of exchange is an encouraging sign that such debt-equity swap deals will be possible, although an obstacle seems to be Russia's accounting regulation. While the banking system has been playing a leading role in enterprise financing and governance, the capital markets also have the potential to grow into large-scale markets because of the massive privatization of industrial assets.

The mixture of a German-style banking system and an Anglo-American model for capital markets may well result in the Japanese model. The Japanese financial system is characterized by the following three factors: 1) Article 65 of Securities and Exchange Law (equivalent to the Glass-Steagall Act of the United States), prohibiting securities business by the banking institutions; 2) the Banking Law, allowing banks' corporate equity holding in their investment accounts; and 3) a relatively concentrated financial sector. A compromise between 1) and 2) is made through the Anti-Trust Law, which limits the banks' corporate equity holding to 5 percent in any company. Some Central European countries have also been driven to a system similar to the Japanese model as a result of the tug-of-war between the German-style banking system and the Anglo-American model of capital markets. In the New Privatization Program, the GKI restricted banks' enterprise shareholding to 10 percent, which is similar to Japan's antimonopoly regulation on banks.

Bibliography

Akamatsu, Noritaka. 1993. "Privatization and the Role of Investment Funds." World Bank, Economic Development Institute, Washington, D.C.

Anderson, Robert E. 1994. "Voucher Funds in the Transition Economies: The Czech and Slovak Experience." Europe and Central Asia, and Middle East and North Africa Regions Technical

Department, Private Sector and Finance Team, World Bank Policy Research Working Paper 13-24. Washington, D.C.

Atiyas, Izak. 1994. *Bankruptcy Policies.* Washington, D.C.: World Bank.

Boycho, Maxim, Andrei Shleifer, and Robert W. Vishny. 1993. "Privatizing Russia." Paper presented at the Brookings Institution Panel on Economic Activity, Washington, D.C., September 9–10.

Jensen, Michael C. 1991. "Corporate Control and the Politics of Finance." *Journal of Applied Corporate Finance*, summer.

Klebnikov, Paul. 1994. "Russia—The Ultimate Emerging Market." *Forbes*, February 14.

KPMG Management Consulting and the Centre for Economic Reform and Transformation, Heriot-Watt University and SovEcon. 1993. "A Study of the Russian Privatization Process—Changing Enterprise Behaviour." London.

Price Waterhouse. 1994. "Techniques of Mass Privatization—Russia's Voucher Auction Program, October 1992 to June 1994." Working Paper, International Privatization Group. New York, New York.

Russia. 1992. The RSFSR Law on Insolvency (Bankruptcy) of Enterprises. Moscow.

———. 1993a. Presidential Decree No. 2284. December 24. "On the State Program of Privatization of State and Municipal Enterprises in the Russian Federation" (The Second Privatization Program). Moscow.

———. 1993b. Presidential Decree No. 2296. December 24. "On Trust." Moscow.

U.S.S.R. 1990a. The RSFSR Law On Enterprises and Entrepreneurship. Moscow.

———. 1990b. Regulations Governing the Activity of Joint-Stock Companies (RSFSR). Moscow.

Vasiliev, Dimitry, John Erickson, and Mark St. Giles. 1992. "The Progress of the Privatization Programme (The First Privatization

Program)." Codogan Management Ltd., Credit Commercial de France, and White and Case. London.

Volgin, Andrei. 1994. "Voucher Investment Funds in Russia." Paper presented at the World Bank Conference, "Privatization and the Emerging Private Sector in Russia," Washington, D.C., June 20–21.

6

Evolution of Commercial Banking in Russia and the Implications for Corporate Governance

Elena Belyanova and Ivan Rozinsky

The first stage of creating the commercial banking system in Russia has been completed. In the early 1990s, restructuring and corporatization of the state banking system were carried out. Hundreds of regional branches of three former specialized state banks that had serviced enterprises in different sectors of the economy—Promstroibank, Agroprombank, and Zhilsotzbank—were transformed into separate commercial joint-stock banks. The state savings bank (Sberbank), which had accumulated all the household savings, and later Vneshekonombank, which had monopolized hard currency transactions, were corporatized as well. At the same time, the highly intensive process of creating new commercial banks was being carried out.

The authors would like to thank Sergei Aukutsionek, the leader of the research program "The Russian Economic Barometer," who provided them with the results of the entrepreneurial surveys. Special thanks for their many helpful comments go to the participants of the CEPR conference, "Roles of Banks in Corporate Governance in Transitional Economies: Lessons from Postwar Japanese Experience," especially to Professor M. Aoki, John Litwack, and Noritaka Akamatsu.

Comprehensive descriptions of developments in the Russian banking system in 1989–92 have been given in a number of publications (IMF 1991; World Bank 1992, 1993). This chapter focuses on the recent changes in the banking sector's size and its updated structure; evidence of increasing competition in the banking sector as an effect of decentralization; and the relationships between the banks and the privatized enterprises, with primary concern being given to corporate governance problems in postprivatization Russia.

The analysis is based on two primary sources of information: (a) official statistics and (b) results of the regular panel surveys of commercial banks and industrial enterprises by *The Russian Economic Barometer*.[1] The surveys provide certain quantitative data that are still unavailable in Russian official statistics, as well as qualitative data that the traditional statistics fail to provide. Along with these, factual data from periodicals and interviews with bank management and customers are used in this chapter.

Commercial Banking Sector: 1993–1st Quarter of 1994

The period of extensive growth of the commercial banking sector in Russia—first through restructuring of the state banking system and then by establishment of the new commercial banks—is likely to be coming to an end. At the beginning of 1994 the number of banks exceeded 2,000 (see table 6-1). As early as 1993, the number of banks increased by 306 (while the corresponding average figure for the previous four

1. *The Russian Economic Barometer* (a quarterly bulletin published in Moscow in English) has carried out regular (bimonthly for commercial banks and monthly for industrial and agricultural enterprises) entrepreneurial panel surveys by the standard procedures since December 1991. The surveyed executive managers fill in questionnaires concerning operations of their enterprises, as well as most urgent aspects of their activities, strategy in the changing economic environment, response to CBR and/or government policy, and the like. The sample includes about 150 commercial banks and 600 industrial enterprises located all over Russia. The response rate for 1993 amounted to 33 percent. Distribution of surveyed enterprises in the sample roughly corresponds to that of Russia as a whole.

Table 6-1. Number of Banks and Branches, 1993–94

Date	*Banks* (1)	*Branches*[a] (2)	2/1
January 1, 1993	1,713	3,135	1.8
January 1, 1994	2,019	4,539	2.2

a. The Sberbank's branches are not included.
Source: Central Bank of Russia.

years exceeds 400). In the future, the banking network will enlarge chiefly through an increase in the number of branches. Acceleration of growth already can be observed. Thus, in 1993 alone, the number of branches increased by 1,404 (during the previous four years, its average annual increase was less than 800).

In addition to purely economic factors, the growth in the number of banks will be encumbered by institutional constraints. Beginning on March 1, 1994, the minimum size of initial statutory capital of newly registered banks was sharply (by a factor of 20) raised by the Central Bank of Russia (CBR). From now on, it will be equivalent to 1 billion ECU in rubles. At the same time, the supervisory and regulatory functions of CBR and its control over banks' soundness are being gradually supplemented. From the beginning of the third quarter of 1993 to the end of the first quarter of 1994, the licenses of more than twenty banks were repealed.

Exhaustion of the sources of extensive growth is also supported by changes in the overall volume of banks' assets (see table 6-2). In 1993 they increased by a factor of 5.7, whereas in 1992 they grew by a factor of 27.5. Moreover, in 1993 their volume in real terms shrank by two-fifths, whereas over the whole of 1992 their growth roughly corresponded to inflation, and throughout the last three quarters of 1992 the assets increased far more rapidly than prices (in nominal terms the former rose by 13.1 times, and the latter by 4.3).

Structure Updated

Moscow Banks and Regional Banks

It is not in the least surprising that Moscow has become the heart of the Russian banking sector. The number of banks in Moscow is still

Table 6-2. Banks' Assets, 1991–94

Year	*Date*	*Billion rubles (1)*	*Ratio over previous year (2)*	*Inflation rate (3)*[a]	*2/3*
1992	01/01	703.7	27.5	26	1.1
1993	01/01	19,343.2	5.7	9.4	0.6
1994	01/01	110,466.8			

a. Consumer price index, December to December.
Source: Central Bank of Russia; Goskomstat of Russia.

exceedingly great considering the immensity of the rest of the country, the small size of banks' branch networks, and the poor state of communications. In number of banks and bank branches, Moscow by far surpasses the rest of Russia. According to the CBR data,[2] as of October 1, 1993, there were about 24.3 commercial banks for every 100,000 inhabitants of Moscow, and 10 times fewer—2.43 for every 100,000—in the rest of Russia (excluding about 40,000 branches and offices of Sberbank, situated in virtually every small locality and every district of the cities).

Moscow outnumbers the regions not only in the banking network size, but also in the rapidity of its extension. Among banks newly founded in 1993, more than two-thirds are in Moscow. According to the data of the Moscow head department of the Central Bank, 576 banks were operating in the capital of Russia by the beginning of 1994 (122 of which have in sum 672 branches inside and outside Moscow), along with 90 branches of regional banks. Only one of the top ten banks of Russia—tenth in size—is located outside Moscow, in St. Petersburg.

In the list of the 100 largest banks of Russia, published by the Rating Information Center, 40 are in Moscow. According to the data of the Rating Center on the top banks' assets, between January 1, 1993, and January 1, 1994, the share of Moscow banks' assets in the overall

2. *Economica'i zhizn*, Vash partner, No. 5, March 1993.

assets of the 100 top banks increased from one-half to two-thirds.[3] Although these should be treated as approximate figures (the list includes only banks that agree to report, and the data they provide may be biased), they reflect a tendency toward further concentration of banking capital in Moscow.

Thus, while Moscow is oversaturated with banks, the rest of Russia (with the possible exception for St. Petersburg, where several dozen commercial banks are operating) is far from being amply provided with them. This should be considered when enforcing new standards on all Russian banks.

Former State Banks and New Banks

When characterizing the types of commercial banks in transitional economies, the two major categories are usually distinguished by origin—the former state banks and the new ones (Thorne 1992; World Bank 1992; Johnson, Kroll, and Horton 1993; Aukutsionek and Belyanova 1993). In Russia, as of the beginning of 1994, the ratio between them was approximately 1:2. The starting conditions of development for commercial banks in these two main categories differed greatly. While the former "inherited" everything that is needed to start business (offices, facilities, personnel, clients), the latter had to begin virtually from scratch.

Initial ownership capital of the former state banks was formed by distribution of shares among state-owned enterprises (SOEs) that had been served by the regional branches of specialized banks. Many banks count several hundred such founders. The new banks were founded at the initiative of the so-called "new commercial structures" as well as SOEs and public organizations, the former prevailing in most new banks. As a rule, the number of founders was not large.

Gradually, old and new banks are becoming similar. Nevertheless, the process cannot be treated straightforwardly: along with commercialization and privatization of the former state banks through privatization of their main shareholders (SOEs), new banks were partially

3. *Finansovye izvestiya*, February 4–10, 1993; February 17, 1994.

"etatized" by integration into the system of centralized distribution of loans.

Still, it would be preposterous to speak about complete removal of distinctions between the former state banks and the new ones. They differ both in the composition of their shareholders and main customers and in their chief sources of funds. A survey of commercial banks from all over Russia by *The Russian Economic Barometer* (table 6-3) demonstrates that by the beginning of 1994 the state share in the former state banks' capital had been significantly reduced by massive privatization of Russian industrial enterprises, but it is still more than twice that of new banks (one-fourth against one-tenth). The overall share of the former state banks in present and former SOEs is also twice as great as that of the new banks (one-half against one-fourth), whereas the share of the former state banks in new private companies is only about 40 percent of the new banks'.

Among the customers of the former state banks, the present and former SOEs prevail, while the new banks prefer to service the new commercial sector. This division was not only determined by starting conditions, but also continued after the banks were established. The data of the January 1994 survey support the view that discrepancies in priorities of former state and new banks in providing loans remain substantial.

Table 6-3. Bank Ownership Structure, January 1994
(percent of share capital)

Type of shareholder	*Former state banks*	*New banks*
SOE and other state institutions	24	11
Privatized enterprises	25	14
New private companies	26	65
Individuals	19	5
Others	6	5
Total	100	100

Source: The Russian Economic Barometer, 1994 bank survey.

The survey reveals that about one-quarter of the former state banks prefer new private companies, which might indicate that the strategies of assets management of the two kinds of banks are becoming more alike (table 6-4). The greater number of the former state banks still gives preference to SOEs, while the majority of new banks selects clients of the new type.

Appreciable differences between the banks of the two categories are observed in their sources of borrowed funds (table 6-5). For the

Table 6-4. Bank Preferences in Selecting Borrowers, Second Half of 1993
(percentage of total respondents)

Preferred borrowers	*Former state banks*	*New banks*
SOEs	60	8
Privatized enterprises	40	15
New private companies	27	85

Note: The totals do not make 100 percent, since some respondents marked two variants of an answer.

Source: *The Russian Economic Barometer*, January 1994 bank survey.

Table 6-5. Main Sources of Banks' Borrowed Funds, Second Half of 1993
(percentage of respondents)

Main source of funds	*Former state banks*	*New banks*
Enterprises' current accounts	80	54
Directed centralized loans	73	38
Enterprises' deposits	47	92
Households' accounts and deposits	40	31
Interbank loans	33	69
Other	0	0

Note: The totals of the lines exceed 100 percent because the respondents were asked to mark up to three variants of answers.

Source: *The Russian Economic Barometer*, January 1994 bank survey.

majority of former state banks, the most important source in the second half of 1993 was enterprises' current accounts and directed centralized credits. This signifies that their functions under the centrally planned system—running the SOE accounts and channeling resources to them from the state—are still crucial.

Although two-fifths of those responding for the new banks reported that directed centralized credits were one of the three main sources of their funds, the majority listed main sources that differed from those of most former state banks—enterprises' deposits and interbank loans—implying more active liabilities management.

Competition

One of the essential results of dismantling the former state banking system and replacing it with hundreds of commercial banks is the gradual sharpening of competition in the banking sector, followed by its partial transfer from the lobby to the marketplace.

EVIDENCE OF DIRECT COMPETITION. According to the survey data, by now the overwhelming majority of banks have recognized their mutual interdependence. This has created changes in their behavior patterns, leading to a consideration of rivals when making decisions and taking actions. To the question "Do you perceive any competition on the part of other banks?" in July 1993, more then four-fifths of the interviewees answered in the positive, and in January 1994 all the banks' respondents, without exception, did the same (table 6-6). Nevertheless, at the same time only slightly more than one-tenth of the banks called competition "intense"; for the rest it is "weak."

RIVALRY FOR ALLOCATION OF CENTRALIZED CREDITS. Until recently it has been access to centralized credits that determined—to a great extent—the viability of many of the Russian banks. With a deep economic recession accompanied by the fall of the savings rate and accelerating inflation, banks found it increasingly difficult to attract funds. Lobbying for allocation of centralized loans seemed to be less costly than promarket competition for depositors, not only for the former state banks, but for the new banks as well.

The situation was greatly aggravated in the beginning of 1993, when the largest of the commercial banks that formerly had isolated

Table 6-6. Banks' Assessments of Competition with Other Banks, January 1994
(percentage of total respondents)

Variants of answer	*July 1993*	*January 1994*
Competition is		
Intense	14	14
Weak	70	86
Zero	12	0
No idea	4	0

Source: The Russian Economic Barometer, July 1993 and January 1994 bank survey.

themselves from this activity entered the competition for centralized credits. The newly established state and semistate financial institutions (the Russian Industrial and Investment Fund, State Investment Corporation, Russian Bank of Reconstruction and Development, Russian Bank of Project Financing, and the Russian Financial Corporation) also claimed preferential rights in this field.

As regards the Joint Stock Investment Commercial Promstroibank (a legal and actual successor of one of the three state specialized banks, previously servicing the bulk of industrial SOEs), for the first time since it was founded it perceived a serious threat to its monopolistic position. To prevent the entrance of potential competitors, the Promstroibank succeeded in gaining a decree from the government of the Russian Federation (RF) acknowledging its special status and gaining additional privileges.[4]

Since the summer of 1993, there has emerged a weakening of the banks' interest in allocating the directed centralized credits, essentially because of the tightening of CBR and RF government credit policy. The spread between interest rates on directed credits and market rates was reduced appreciably, and unconditional extension of the bad credits to SOEs and automatic covering of the banks' debit balances (even when brought about by nonredemption of directed loans by its recipients) ceased. This enhanced the bank's responsibility for the credit-

4. For details see "Participation of Russian Commercial Banks in the State Investment Programs." *The Russian Economic Barometer* 2(3), 1993.

worthiness of government-selected borrowers. The March 1994 survey of banks shows that throughout the half-year preceding to the survey, an average of more than two-fifths of the directed credits were not repaid by the borrowing enterprises in time. It goes without saying that under the circumstances, the banks are increasingly intent on treating the allocation of those credits as a trouble or duty rather than a profitable business (see table 6-7).

In the beginning of 1994, competition for depositors and the most reliable borrowers was stated to be the main line of competition by the majority of the surveyed banks (see table 6-8).

SEEKING FUNDS. Banks' interests come into conflict more and more frequently when they seek funds from business, households, public institutions, and so forth. Banks compete for running the current accounts and to attract time deposits, for both clients' rubles and dol-

Table 6-7. Answers to the Question: "Is It Profitable for Your Bank to Allocate Directed Credits?" September 1993, March 1994
(percentage of respondents)

Variants of answer	*September 1993*	*March 1994*
Yes	14	0
No	59	100
Difficult to answer	27	0

Source: The Russian Economic Barometer, September 1993, March 1994 bank survey.

Table 6-8. Lines of Competition

Target groups	*Percentage of respondents*
Depositors	80
Reliable borrowers	72
Centralized loans	20
Interbank loans	20
Other lines	12

Note: Respondents were allowed to mark all the suitable answers.
Source: The Russian Economic Barometer, January 1994 bank survey.

lars (DM, and so forth). In this connection, a number of peculiarities in the current situation should be mentioned.

Prior to the banking system reform, neither enterprises nor individuals had the opportunity to choose a bank. Currency accounts were concentrated in Vneshekonombank; household ruble accounts in Sberbank; and those of enterprises and public institutions in one of the three other state specialized banks—Promstroibank, Zhilsotzbank, and Agroprombank—in compliance with their branch affiliation. Following the banking system decentralization, the relationships between the customers and the banks were liberalized, and "attachment" strictly to a single bank was no longer the rule.

Depositors of every category take advantage of their right of choice. As a rule, the flow of funds is directed from the former state banks to the new banks. Enterprises change their bank at their own initiative and at the request of new banks, in case the latter become their creditors. Instances of governmental bodies changing banks are also not isolated. One of the recent and quite specific cases is the refusal of the Moscow government to be serviced by one of the former state banks and the transfer of its current accounts to the five advanced new banks.[5]

As for raising the household deposits, recently both new and former state banks succeeded in crowding their main and—as it seemed not long ago—invincible rival, Sberbank. Thus, according to CBR data at the beginning of 1993, the proportion between the household ruble deposits in Sberbank and in the rest of the commercial banks was 10:1, whereas at the beginning of 1994 was 6:4.[6]

In the bankers' opinions, the main current hindrance to the banks' activity in the area is not rivalry on the part of Sberbank, but the lack of proper facilities to deal with large numbers of depositors (see table 6-9).

Elimination of the state monopoly and establishment of a competitive environment within the financial sector is one of the most significant results of institutional reforms implemented in Russia during the past five years. The strengthening of competition, however, does

5. For details of this transaction see "New Banks Win the Competition, the Central Bank Materials." *Economika i zhizn* 11, March 1994.

6. *Finansovye izvestiya*, February 4–10, 1993; February 17, 1994.

Table 6-9. Factors Constraining Household Deposits in Banks, March 1994

Variant of answer	*Percentage of respondents*
Lack of proper facilities	43
High costs of servicing small depositors	43
Household unwillingness to deposit	36
Rivalry on the part of Sberbank	7
Other	14

Note: Respondents were allowed to mark all the suitable answers.
Source: The Russian Economic Barometer, March 1994 bank survey.

not lead automatically to the pro-market slant of the backgrounds of Russian bankers' behavior. Rivalry among banks encourages not only profit-seeking, but also rent-seeking—investment resources in lobbying the state, selective law enforcement, and the like. The example of Promstroibank activities in this field is neither the least nor the last. One of the more recent examples of successful efforts of Russian banks to set legislative barriers to foreign banks' entry is the Presidential Decree prohibiting the foreign banks to service residents up to January 1, 1996. This decree applies even to banks that received the general license but have not started operations. Thus, only three foreign banks were allowed to service the residents—Credit Lyonnais/St. Petersburg, BNP-Dresdner Bank, and Citibank.

The profit-seeking strategy, in its turn, does not lead automatically to improvements in the banks' services. Improvement of service quality has not become the banks' major weapon in the competitive struggle, particularly in the struggle for household deposits. In order to attract more funds from small depositors, many of the Russian commercial banks offer high interest rates on deposits; consequently, they have to accept higher levels of risk to meet the interest payment obligation. Given the essential instability of such a deposit base and absence of deposit insurance in Russia, aggressive price competition of this sort creates a real danger of bank runs.

Whether the society will in the end gain or lose from the increasing competition in the commercial banking sector of Russia depends on how soon the state begins to perform the conventional regulating role instead of a paternalistic one toward both the production and financial sectors.

Banks and Corporate Governance in the Postprivatization Period

Russian Privatization—Outcome

The corporate governance system emerging in Russia is to a great extent the result of massive privatization of SOEs. Some features of this process are worth considering because they provide necessary background for the analysis of the corporate governance in Russia in general, and the prospects for the banks' role in particular.

MANAGEMENT'S VICTORY. According to the Russian privatization program, employees (including management) could elect Variant 1, which gives the employees 25 percent of nonvoting shares free of charge, or Variant 2, a closed subscription to insiders, in which employees are able to buy up to 51 percent of shares at a low multiple of preinflation book value (we omit considering Variant 3, for its role was negligible). The state officials in charge of privatization openly expressed their support for Variant 1, limiting the employees' control over enterprises. The results, however, revealed a strong unwillingness on the part of management and employees to give up control over "their" enterprise and to tolerate a significant role being played by outsiders. Industrial management unequivocally preferred Variant 2.

The leading position of enterprise management during privatization came about because its support, or at least a lack of opposition, is the essential precondition for the whole process to start up. There are a number of perfectly legitimate ways open to management to block the process—the simplest one is just to refrain from enterprise privatization plan preparation. Without management involvement, a plan cannot be prepared because management is the sole holder of the relevant information.

Another privatization process feature that enabled management to hold control is the lack of privatization experts. Given that local authorities in charge of privatization rarely have enough specialists at their disposal, all the privatization documents are normally elaborated by the managers themselves, or by the consultants hired by the enterprise (in other words, hired by the enterprise management). Evidently, in both cases the resulting privatization plan ensures the interests of the management. As one should expect, most favor is given to Variant 2.

The conclusion of the Russian experience is that the privatization process will be either management-controlled or it will not proceed at all (Rozinsky 1993).

As the leading force of the privatization process, Russian managers do not act as textbook investors searching to maximize profit on their investments. Their motivation is related to the preservation and strengthening of control over the enterprise.

Management preferences are reflected in the results of privatization as of 1992–93. The vast majority of enterprises (according to *Goskomimushchestvo*, three-fourths) have chosen Variant 2. The survey conducted by *The Russian Economic Barometer* in November 1993 (enterprises from different industries have been involved) yields the following data: 91 percent of privatized enterprises that participated in the survey used Variant 2; after privatization the management team remained the same in 72 percent of the enterprises, less than half were changed in 25 percent, and more than half were changed in 3 percent only.

Variant 2, giving employees the majority of votes, provides a solid base for management control. As in other countries (Frydman and others 1993; Hannsman 1990), employee ownership may well be viewed as a mechanism for entrenching the control rights of the managers against those of outside shareholders. According to the poll data published by CBR, 52 percent of the employees classified their enterprises as either director- or management-controlled, compared with those claiming that their enterprise was controlled by employees (15 percent) or by shareholders (5 percent).[7]

Management positions are particularly strong in large enterprises. First, managers of such enterprises have traditional links with government bodies, which makes it possible to influence political decision-

7. Two thousand employees of industrial enterprises were polled by the *Economic and Social Changes: Monitoring the Public Opinion* bulletin in April, 1993. See: *Monitoring the Lines of Banks' Policy*, No. 1, 1993, Central Bank of Russia, Moscow.

making. Second, obtaining large blocks of shares of such an enterprise obviously is a more difficult task for the outsider, both financially and technically.

The question arises of whether the employees are willing to sell their shares to outsiders. Although legally the shares are alienable, managers usually succeed in preventing the vote outflow. Although the government explicitly prohibits the imposition of any limits on the shareholders' free disposition of shares gained under privatization, such a practice remains common in Russia. One of the legitimate ways to create obstacles to free disposition of shares and thereby prevent a voting power shift to outsiders is the management-led establishment of ESOP-like structures. In this way, employees become the shareholders, with their shares in the enterprise serving as a contribution to the share capital of the structure. This swap-like operation leads to concentration of the initially dispersed enterprise shares in the management-controlled legal entity.

The employees may quite reasonably be regarded as very conservative shareholders, because they are reluctant to sell their shares to outsiders. Their reluctance has two major explanations: first, selling the shares to outsiders will be considered an opportunistic behavior by their colleagues, and second, holding shares of the enterprise is widely regarded as a device diminishing the possibility of dismissal. It should be stressed that the most important reason for the employees to acquire the shares of their enterprises is their desire to preserve the existing employment level and social comfort (as put by Russian trade union leaders, "We do not want somebody to buy us"). The poll results published by CBR indicate that only 7.3 percent of the employees want their enterprise to be owned by Russian outsiders; 5.2 percent would prefer foreign ownership; and 55 percent voted for employee ownership. Such an attitude provides fertile ground for establishing unquestionable management control over the enterprise.

The provisions established by the State Privatization Program for 1994 supposedly limit the absolute control of the management over the privatized corporation. It is stipulated that employee participation (including managers) in the board of directors shall not exceed one-third of the board members. Nevertheless, no mechanism exists to enforce this provision. In addition, the well-known ways to avoid this restriction (election of the representatives of the management-controlled investment funds, retired managers, and the like) make it very unlikely to be effective.

LACK OF EXTERNAL CONTROL. The privatization process in Russia has thus resulted in a system of management-controlled corporations. The likely implications follow.

Low propensity to pay dividends. Prevalence of Variant 2 makes it unprofitable to insiders to vote for large, if any, dividends. With the insiders' majority guaranteed, dividend payments become unlikely, because every hundred rubles paid in dividends results in forty-nine given to outsiders. The evidently more attractive alternative is to distribute the whole amount available for dividends among insiders (the simplest way to do this is through bonuses to employees). The interest in paying dividends is further reduced by double taxation.

Outsiders face prohibitions against entry and there is no mechanism ensuring outside control of corporations. One of the privatization outcomes is the "entry prohibited" situation facing the outsiders. Variant 2 and the corresponding measures to prevent vote outflow push outsiders into a permanent minority position. Changing the situation through a takeover is an extremely costly device and very difficult to implement without a liquid capital market (one should also once again take into consideration the hostility toward outsiders). Therefore, being a shareholder, the outsider has virtually no access to inside information and control.

One of the most promising features of the privatization process, and definitely one of those most utilized by the government, is the role and potential of "privatization intermediaries"—the voucher investment funds. Sometimes it is claimed (Stiglitz 1992) that these intermediaries, if permitted to engage in brokerage, commercial, and investment bank operations, may come to resemble the German universal banks and play a decisive role in imposing outside control over industrial management. Up to now the Russian experience has given little if any support to this proposition. Facing the extremely low propensity to pay dividends demonstrated by the newly privatized enterprises, and at the same time being under heavy pressure from dividend-seeking shareholders, the investment funds devote themselves to trading in vouchers (privatization checks) and, to a much lesser extent, to the acquisition of securities of enterprises.

The available data on dividends announced by the investment funds in 1993 shows that (a) in all the cases the dividend rate achieved by the investment funds falls short of the rate of inflation, and (b) average interest rates quoted by banks on deposits tended to be higher than the dividend rate paid by the investment funds. The vast majority of investment funds is expected to announce zero or insignificant (inflation given) dividends. This is very likely to affect the broad public confidence in these intermediaries, in spite of massive advertising campaigns (under most favorable conditions, their profit, if consisting of dividends paid by industrial enterprises, will not make it possible to pay dividends comparable to rates on deposits actually offered by the Russian banks). In addition, the investment funds are subject to several legal constraints that limit the scope of their operations and prevent them from becoming "bank-like" institutions. Although the new State Privatization Program for 1994 has raised limits on the investment funds' holding of one enterprise's shares and on the value of such shares in the investment fund's assets, emergence of the "new banking sector" on the basis of the "privatization intermediaries," as well as their important role in promoting outside control, is very unlikely.

In our opinion, the attention normally paid to the Russian voucher investment funds exceeds their real economic role and prospects. The same may be said about the partnerships between banks and investment funds, sometimes regarded as the force capable of providing a foundation for outsider control. Not excluding such a possibility in principle, it should be noted that up to now the partnerships of this sort have not played a significant role in the Russian economy. Typical is the situation where there is either a pocket bank controlled by an investment fund or a pocket investment fund created by a bank (in the latter case the investment fund creation is generally initiated by managers of the enterprise/shareholders of the bank). In both cases the establishment of relationships between banks and investment funds does not add much to the stronger party's capability to exercise outsider control over corporations. What really matters is the strength of the participant that initiates the partnership, not the partnership itself.

Theoretically outsider control may be imposed through, for example, pressing the management to issue additional shares, thus eroding the management-controlled stock majority. Russian privatization explicitly favors this approach. In practice, however, it is hardly possible, taking into consideration the political and economic power of Russian industrial management. Even if pressed hard to issue additional shares, management is very likely to do so through private placement—that is, through direct distribution of shares between the known-in-advance investors, presumably between the enterprise's suppliers and buyers (in other words, other management groups). The resulting corporate structures would thus remain closed, although perhaps they would be slightly more effective than the existing arrangements.

Rudimentary equity market. The implications of the privatization process in Russia virtually block equity market development. On the one hand, managers and employees are expected to be very conservative shareholders, reluctant to sell their shares. On the other, the industrial shares are not attractive to potential buyers because of low dividends and the virtual impossibility of obtaining large blocks of shares. One may thus predict that the demand for such shares will only be expressed by takeover practitioners, constituting a small portion of the potential equity market participants. The equity market therefore tends to be thin and incapable of providing adequate control mechanisms.

INVESTMENT HUNGER. When assessing the corporate system likely to be established in Russia, one should bear in mind certain essential features of the current economic situation, which determines the problems facing the management-controlled enterprises. Having inherited obsolete production capacities, most newly privatized enterprises badly need modernization. Obtaining investment funds for modernization is widely regarded as the core problem, the one that will determine the survival of the enterprise under emerging market economy conditions. Huge investment amounts are also needed for restructuring the enterprises to adjust to the new economic environment. "Investment hunger" would be a proper term to describe the attitude of the industrial management toward investments.

Seeking to finance its investment program, the enterprise may rely on (a) stock issuance; (b) bond financing; (c) government support; (d) retained earnings; and (e) borrowing from the banks.

The large-scale issuance of stock may result in an erosion of the existing management control, the possibility Russian industrial management does its best to avoid. In addition, the Russian equity market is thin and definitely not prepared to raise funds sufficient for modernization.

The enterprises cannot rely on bond financing in modern Russia until the pace of inflation slows. In addition, lack of an adequate legal environment leaves the bondholders' rights unprotected: the Russian bondholder is unlikely to rely on courts, even in an attempt to force the borrower to meet his obligations to the bond issue, to say nothing about the relevant disclosures. Russian law on bankruptcy remains dormant. Therefore, a high default risk combined with high and unpredictable inflation makes Russian investors—private persons as well as institutions—reluctant to buy industrial bonds in sufficient amounts. This is particularly true for private persons lacking the information needed to assess the relative attractiveness of different securities.

Direct governmental transfers and subsidized loans may quite reasonably be regarded as important sources of the funds needed to modernize the obsolete production facilities. Several factors tend to diminish the importance of this source. First, the government support programs are likely to be concentrated in the so-called target industries. Second, their amount is limited by the anti-inflation policy targets. Third, direct government support implies additional costs for the management of newly privatized Russian enterprises in the form of tightening state control.

The retained earnings of a vast majority of Russian enterprises, being permanently depleted by inflation, are simply not sufficient to finance the huge investment programs.

To summarize: (a) huge investments are badly needed by the Russian economy to renovate its obsolete production facilities; (b) heavy reliance on stock or bond financing is unlikely because of the institutional characteristics of Russian securities markets and galloping inflation; and (c) possible government support and the enterprises' retained earnings are insufficient. It follows, then, that about the only way open to the newly privatized Russian enterprises searching for large-scale financing for investment purposes is to rely on bank loans.

Russian banks look strong and relatively stable in comparison with other Russian financial institutions. Their assets many times exceed those of other financial intermediaries, such as insurance companies or investment funds. In addition to size, the most important feature is the existence of links between the largest Russian banks and foreign financial institutions. Given that the amounts needed for the large-scale Russian modernization cannot be raised in the domestic market only, channeling funds from abroad becomes crucial. The banks are clearly the financial institutions best prepared to assume such a role. These features of the banks—relative financial strength and the existing international links—make it likely that bank loans will become the main external source of financing modernization in Russia, with other sources of less importance.

Thus the banks possess "an asset"—funds potentially available for investment needs—which puts them in a much stronger position regarding corporate governance than that of the other outsiders. The banks may bargain on equal grounds with the industrial management. "A money-for-power swap," that is, granting large credits for investment purposes in exchange for at least partial control over an enterprise, becomes quite possible.

Banks and Enterprises: Current Relationships

GENERAL SITUATION. In spite of the banks' great potential for involvement in corporate governance, data reveals that the vast majority of the Russian banks are still standing aside from the productive sector of the economy (World Bank 1993; Belyanova, Aukutsionek, and Gracheva 1993). Inflation leads to the prevalence of short-term lending, making unnecessary and cost-ineffective any monitoring of the borrower's performance.

At the same time, there exists a basic understanding by the banks of the need to become more deeply involved in relationships with industrial enterprises. The survey results show that the banks themselves were ready to participate in the process rather actively. Nevertheless, results show considerable divergence between the expected and real figures of Russian banks' participation in privatization (table 6-10).

In virtually every sphere the actual participation of the banks in privatization appeared to be less than expected. Moreover, the number of respondents not participating in privatization at all is significantly greater than the number of banks that did not intend to participate (16 percent against 5 percent).

Table 6-10. Bank Participation in Enterprise Privatization, October 1992, July 1993
(percentage of respondents)

Item	*Anticipated*[a] *(October 1992)*	*Actual*[a] *(July 1993)*
1. Lending for privatization	67	32
2. Buying vouchers	48	40
3. Securities transactions (at least one of 3.1–3.3)	62	36
3.1. Acquisition of shares of the enterprises	38	24
3.2. Placing of shares of the enterprises	38	16
3.3. Establishment of an investment fund	24	16
4. Other	19	20
5. No participation at all	5	16

a. Respondents were asked to mark all the intended and actual steps of importance for them.

Source: The Russian Economic Barometer, October 1992, July 1993 bank survey.

The significant gap between the banks' realized and intended degree of involvement in the privatization process reveals their (as well as officials') initial underestimation of the role to be played by industrial management in the privatization process.

Minor participation in enterprise privatization is followed by the banks' minor involvement in corporate governance. Only 3 percent of enterprises surveyed by *The Russian Economic Barometer* in November, 1993, indicated that the banks' representatives became members of the board of directors. If compared with the already cited poll figures concerning management participation in the boards of directors of the newly privatized corporations, the conclusion is justified that industrial management control remained unchallenged by the banks.

"HARD CURRENCY ISLANDS" IN THE RUSSIAN BANKING SYSTEM. Although up to now there has been little evidence of Russian banks' visible role in corporate governance, the picture is not the same in all segments of the commercial banking system. One may notice the emergence of the so-called "hard currency islands"—banks specializing in hard currency operations (including hard-currency-denominated loans), with Russian exporters their main customers. This small group of "the export-sector banks" (ESBs) tends to overcome the Russian banks' general inability to interfere in corporate governance. Russian experts' estimates vary concerning the number of the Russian banks in this group, but three of them—International Moscow Bank, Tokobank, and Mosbizinesbank—are definitely to be included.

Specialization of these banks in hard currency operations, supported by their larger-than-average size and lending capacity, determines their potential capability to exercise control over the industrial enterprises.[8] The three-digit annual inflation rate in Russia makes hard-currency-denominated loans the only possible instrument of middle-term bank lending. Given that financing for enterprise modernization necessarily requires at least middle-term (one-to-five year) credit facilities, and that modernization by itself is very likely to require huge hard currency amounts to pay for the new equipment and technologies produced abroad, the banks comprising this group may well be expected to become the very important providers of funds for the enterprises' renovation. As far as large enterprise renovation is concerned, this group of banks may be regarded as the only channel of providing sufficient private financing.

Therefore, even taking into consideration the reluctance of the Russian enterprises' management to tolerate outsiders' participation in corporate decisionmaking, these banks may well become influential enough to be allowed to enter. If compared with other groups of potential "outsiders seeking to enter," the ESBs are the ones capable of paying the highest entrance fee.

Two features of ESBs make it likely that they will monitor the borrowers. First, these banks grant middle-term loans on a commercial, not government-directed, basis, and thus face the need to enforce contracts. Second, they can afford to pay salaries sufficient to attract the best experts in monitoring the enterprises.

Close links between these banks and Russian export industries are currently emerging and are very likely to develop further. In order to avoid the exchange rate risk when granting hard-currency-denominated

8. It should also be mentioned that the ESBs are not normally involved in operations with small depositors such as households, and their deposit base is therefore considerably more stable.

middle-term loans, the banks tend to push the potential borrowers toward export orientation. The newly adopted legal requirement to register every contract with a foreign counterparty in the authorized bank (that is, in the bank authorized to conduct international transactions) will undoubtedly facilitate the bank's monitoring of the enterprise's export amount. In its turn, the larger the portion of an enterprise's production volume that is exported, and the deeper its involvement in international trade, the more sensitive it is to the international reputation of its bank. Given that the vast majority of other Russian banks lack this reputation, as well as appropriate experience, the enterprise's opportunity to choose among banks lessens. Thus, demand for middle-term loans requires heavier reliance on export; the latter limits the choice faced by the enterprise to a very small number of banks. Establishing a reputation acts as a barrier to entry (Stiglitz 1989).

Presumably it is too early to speak about these banks as being engaged in control of corporate governance as is seen in the German model. Nevertheless, first steps have already been made. In addition to pushing the prospective borrowers toward export orientation, there are examples of banks' representatives sitting in the borrower's board of directors.

When granting medium-term credit facilities, the banks are imposing ceilings on additional borrowing and dividend payments of the borrowers or setting required minimum amounts of the export revenues to be channeled through them. It should be stressed that such provisions, quite common in Western banking practice, are entirely new for Russia, and their implementation is therefore an event for the Russian banking system. A borrower's failure to meet the mentioned requirements may result in a wide range of actions by the bank, from expressing concern and asking for explanations to declaring default, leading to acceleration of repayment.

There thus exists the potential capability of the ESBs to overcome the "closed-door" policy of the enterprises' management, and steps in this direction have already been made. Moreover, several factors of the Russian economic life provide evidence of the largest ESB's increasing involvement in corporate governance.

On the one hand, there are reasons why the enterprises' management is likely to tolerate the increasing interference of the banks in corporate control and decisionmaking. First, the threat to withdraw credit becomes an increasingly powerful weapon in the bank's hands as the role of direct government support diminishes, and Russian stock and bond markets cannot be relied upon. Second, some large-scale modernization programs (for example, the modernization program of the Angarsk Petrochemical Plant in Eastern Siberia, requiring approximately $0.5 billion) are feasible only if they are supported by international financial institutions such as the World Bank or the International Finance Corporation or foreign-export-promoting agencies such as the U.S. Eximbank. In such a case the ESB's role in channeling funds to Russia (through funding lines or cofinancing agreements) is essential because their international reputation makes them the only local banks whose risk may be acceptable to international bankers. Thus, the position of the ESBs looks strong enough for them to insist on access to corporate control mechanisms if they consider it necessary.

Another aspect worth mentioning here arises when comparing the control by the bank and that of other outsider shareholders. The difference between them matters for the management's choice between financing through the stock market and bank lending (bond financing is not considered for the reasons mentioned above). This difference stems from the realization that when the bank is exercising control, its behavior is generally predictable, whereas the behavior of outside shareholders is not. In other words, when comparing the possible sources of financing and their relative costs, corporate managers, holding other things equal, will prefer control by the bank as a well-known institution to that of an unknown one. Also important in this connection is the social factor: top industrial management's social position (at least at present) is closer to that of the largest banks' management than to the social position of other outsiders. For all these reasons, it is easier for the industrial management to tolerate control by the banks.

At the same time, there are some arguments backing the thesis that large Russian banks are increasingly interested in obtaining access to corporate governance. The prime argument arises because Russian banks' collateral-based lending is a highly unsuitable alternative.[9] Lack

9. For the distinction between collateral and monitored finance, see the chapter by E. Berglöf in this volume.

of a pledge contract enforcement mechanism prevents the banks from wide reliance on collateral when granting loans. The excessive registration fee (3 percent of the pledged property value payable upfront) also impedes the use of pledge contracts. Determination of the real value of the asset to be pledged is an extremely difficult task in modern Russia, because the asset markets either do not exist or are extremely thin. Under these circumstances, the banks' switching to monitored finance may well be expected.

Other arguments backing the thesis are as follows. First, given the large size of the modernization projects to be financed and the corresponding exposures, substantial costs of monitoring and control are justified. Second, lack of legal mechanisms capable of forcing the borrower to repay gives the banks another incentive to exercise close control over its operations. Third, obtaining control becomes essential for banks, because under the "closed" system of shareholding, there is no other outside control over the corporation. The risk-averse bank is unlikely to lend sufficient money to a Russian company controlled entirely and exclusively by its management. To summarize: elaboration of the workable mechanism of the bank's control over enterprises is an essential precondition to the bank's participation in the large-scale financing needed for modernization of the Russian economy.

DESIGN OF BANKING IN THE GERMAN STYLE. The large ESBs seem to be the only visible economic agents prepared to get access to control over strategic decisionmaking in the newly privatized Russian corporations. These banks are able to "pay the entrance fee" in the form of investment loans high enough to overcome corporate managers' unwillingness to give up absolute control over "their" enterprises. The system of bank-enterprise relationships likely to emerge is thus closer to the German model, with the banks' substantial involvement in production firms, as opposed to the Anglo-Saxon model of arm's-length bank-industry relations.

It should be mentioned that certain historical parallels also indicate that the emerging Russian financial system is likely to follow the German style of development (Belyanova 1992; Gracheva 1993). Analysis of the history of Russian banking before the Bolshevik Revolution reveals great similarity with German bank-industrial enterprise relations.

The situation in modern Russia is also more similar to the German than to the Anglo-Saxon pattern. The formation period of the British banking system was the period of their worldwide textile industry leadership. Since this industry was characterized by a relatively high ratio of working capital to total assets, short-term credit was of most importance. In contrast, the German banks' formation was greatly influenced by the demand for long-term investment loans by heavy industries, primarily by the metallurgical complex. In Russia as well, the need of enterprises to modernize obsolete production capacities makes the availability of long-term financing crucial, along with all the implications for banks' incentives to exercise control.

The need to provide the banks with adequate control mechanisms does not necessarily require that Russia follow the German pattern. Apart from German example, the Japanese model is also available for consideration. With the general idea of both models much the same (close involvement of the banks with production firms), they differ in the means normally employed. While the Japanese model rests mostly on the existing personal links between management of the banks and industrial enterprises, whether or not the bank is a substantial shareholder, the German model relies on substantial stock ownership (normally 25 percent plus one share), giving the bank veto rights when crucial problems of corporate life are considered. In addition, a very important role is played in the German system by the supervisory boards participating in major financial and investment decisions concerning the industrial enterprise.

One of the arguments for the advent of the Japanese system in Russia is the important role played by implicit as opposed to explicit contracts in Russia as well as in Japan. It may be claimed that by providing training to the smaller Russian banks' personnel and by arranging syndicated loans to their large corporate customers, the ESBs tend to approach the "main bank" position in relation to both corporate clients and smaller correspondent banks.

Current economic and institutional conditions in Russia, however, may not favor the establishment of a Japanese-style system of bank-industrial enterprise relations. There are no tradition-based links between managers of the banks and corporations as there are in Japan, although, as mentioned earlier, the managers belong to social strata that are relatively close to each other. Typical careers of banking and industrial managers are segregated, as opposed to the practice prevalent in Japan, where horizontal movements of managers from the banks to their client corporations are rather common. There are no historical traditions of large, family-based, financial-industrial groups with a bank at the center. Consequently, although the possibility of following the Japanese pattern does exist, Russian bankers are likely to need some formal instruments ensuring control, instruments normally attributable to the German model.

Among such instruments, those normally proposed are setting legislative provisions to promote banks' control (apart from that provided through shareholding) and the banks' holding of corporate shares.

The provisions likely to promote banks' control over industrial enterprises include establishing industrial supervisory boards empowered to make strategic decisions, especially regarding the enterprise investment projects. Banks are assumed to play the leading role in these bodies.

Another proposal concerns the privatization procedure. It is a normal practice in Russia that the regional Funds of Federal Property (government bodies in charge of selling the privatized companies' shares) retain the ownership of an essential block of shares (usually about 20 percent of the share capital) for a given period of time. This time period varies from industry to industry and from region to region, reflecting the strategic importance of the enterprise as perceived by the government. According to the legislation, this block of shares may be given in a trust; normally the trustee is the top management of the enterprise. Changing this practice and promoting bank trustholding may significantly increase the banks' means of control over enterprises.

One more proposal relates to setting of the special default provision. Creditor influence over enterprises depends on legal provisions for bankruptcy. This maxim, although evident as such, requires caution when applied to the current situation in Russia, and presumably in other postcommunist countries. Here the enterprises may not be allowed by the state to go bankrupt because of unbearable social costs inherent in their bankruptcy (for example, if the large enterprise is the only possible workplace in the town, a situation rather common in eastern Russia). Under such circumstances, the opportunity for the creditors to initiate the bankruptcy procedure is limited.

One way of solving this problem is simply to prohibit bank lending to such enterprises. Less radical and seemingly more realistic proposals include setting bankruptcy provisions whereby creditors can change the manager in case of default. Fear of being dismissed may be relied upon as a force motivating management to consider the bank's interests. In addition, the spillover effect of such a provision will be a tendency to lower the interest charged by the banks, providing debt financing badly needed by the Russian economy.

Until recently the Russian legislation on the banks' holding of industrial shares could be considered rather liberal.[10] If granted the "general license" by the Central Bank of Russia, a Russian commercial bank felt free to buy, to sell, or to hold the shares of industrial enterprises. Even the acquisition of more than 35 percent of voting shares was not prohibited, subject to the approval of the State Antitrust Policy Committee.

The newly adopted State Privatization Program for 1994 tends to restrict banks' purchases of corporate stock. The program imposes limits on bank ownership of corporate shares (not more than 10 percent of an enterprise's share capital) and on total value of stock as a portion of the bank's assets (maximum, 5 percent). The banks are now prohibited from buying shares of the enterprises under privatization.

* * *

Thus, initially being very close to the German pattern, the legal framework of interrelations between banks and enterprises is likely to drift toward the Anglo-Saxon model. This trend could considerably hinder the shaping of the efficient market mechanisms of financial control over the Russian productive sector, as well as prevent the banking sector from extending long-term financing for modernization purposes. Restrictions on banks' holdings of industrial shares will bound both incentives and opportunities to exercise effective control over nonfinancial corporations. An alternative to control by the banks requires highly developed financial markets, primarily the secondary stock mar-

10. "Banks and Privatization: Legal Framework." *The Russian Economic Barometer* 2 (4) 1993; 3 (1) 1994.

ket, which may take decades to achieve in Russia. Therefore, given the stock market's failure to provide adequate outsider control, it is very likely that the real choice is between banks' control over industrial enterprises and no external control at all (or reimposing control by the state).

Promoting banks' control over industrial enterprises undeniably leads to concentration of economic as well as political power in the hands of a small number of financial groups. The degree to which competition between such groups can be relied upon to deal with such a concentration remains an open question. Presumably, some additional elements of the economic check-and-balance system are to be elaborated.

Bibliography

Aukutsionek, S., and E. Belyanova. 1993. "Russian Credit Market Remains Distorted." *RFE/RL Research Report* 2(4): 37–40.

Belyanova, E., ed. 1992. *The Problems of Transition to the Market Economy and the World Experience*, issue II, *The Banking Sector*. Moscow: IMEMO.

Belyanova, E., S. Aukutsionek, and M. Gracheva. 1993. "Surveys of Russian Industrial Enterprises and Commercial Banks: Application for Research into Transition to the Market." Report to the 21st CIRET Conference, Somerset West, October.

Central Bank of Russia. 1993. *Monitoring Lines of Banks' Policy*. Moscow.

———. 1994. *Current Tendencies in the Monetary Credit Sector*, No. 10. Moscow.

———. Various years. *Bulletin of Banking Statistics*.

Economica i zhizn, Vash partner 5. 1993.

Finansovye izvestiya. February 4–10, 1993; February 17, 1994.

Frydman, R., E. Phelps, A. Rapaczynsky, and A. Shleifer. 1993. "Needed Mechanisms of Corporate Governance and Finance in Eastern Europe." *Economics of Transition* 1(2).

Gracheva, M. 1993. "The Russian Banks in Transition: Financial System Model Approach." Report to the Scientific Board of IMEMO, Moscow, November.

Hannsman, H. 1990. "When Does Worker Ownership Work? ESOPs, Law Firms, Codetermination, and Economic Democracy." *Yale Law Journal* 99(8).

IMF. 1991. *A Study of the Soviet Economy*. Paris.

Johnson, Simon, Heidi Kroll, and Mark Horton. 1993. "New Banks in the Former Soviet Union: How Do They Operate?" In Anders Aslund and P. Richard Layard, eds., *Changing Economic System in Russia*. London: Pinter.

Rozinsky, I. 1993. "Privatization, Stock Market, and 'Director's Model' Perspectives." *The Russian Economic Journal*, April.

The Russian Economic Barometer. Various years. Moscow.

Stiglitz, J. E. 1989. "Using Tax Policy to Curb Speculative Short-Term Trading." *Journal of Financial Services Research* 3.

———. 1992. "The Design of Financial Systems for the Newly Emerging Democracies of Eastern Europe." In C. Claug and G. Rosser, eds., *The Emergence of Market Economics in Eastern Europe*. London: Basil Blackwell.

Thorne, Alfredo E. 1992. "The Role of Banks in Transition: Lessons from Eastern European Countries' Experience." World Bank, Europe and Central Asia, and Middle East and North Africa Regions Technical Department, Private Sector and Finance Team. Washington, D.C.

World Bank. 1992. *Russian Economic Reform: Crossing the Threshold of Structural Change*. Washington, D.C.

———. 1993. "The Banking System in Transition—Russia." Europe and Central Asia Department Report 12763. Washington, D.C.

7

Reforming Corporate Governance and Finance in China

Yingyi Qian

Reform of corporate governance and finance is the central issue in the next stage of enterprise reform in China. Although small-scale privatization is under way and spontaneous privatization is not uncommon, for political reasons mass privatization as seen in Eastern Europe and Russia is unlikely to occur in China, at least for the next several years. Nevertheless, a great deal could and should be done in reforming corporate governance and finance in China to improve the performance of its enterprises.

In addressing governance and finance reform, or enterprise reform in general, the first thing to note is the great variety of ownership and property rights arrangements in China. Until recently, Chinese statistics classified enterprise ownership into four general categories: state-owned, collectives, individuals (private firms with fewer than eight employees), and "others," the last including private enterprises with more than eight employees, joint ventures, wholly owned foreign ventures, limited liability companies, joint-stock companies, and so forth. We actually find even more variety within each category (see table 7-1).

I am grateful to Masahiko Aoki, John Earle, Lawrence Lau, John McMillan, Juro Teranishi, and Ernst-Ludwig von Thadden for helpful discussions and comments.

Table 7-1. China: Types of Enterprise Ownership

Area	*State-owned enterprises*	*Non-state-owned enterprises*			
		Collectives	*Individual*		*Others*
	Public enterprises		*Private enterprises*		
Urban	Controlled by central, provincial, city, and county governments	District and neighborhood enterprises	Urban cooperatives	Urban individual	Private; joint-stock; joint-ventures
Rural	n/a	Township and village enterprises (TVEs)	Rural cooperatives	Rural individual	

First of all, the state sector is far from homogeneous. Unlike Eastern Europe and the former Soviet Union, where most state-owned enterprises were controlled by the *central* government, most state-owned enterprises in China are controlled by governments at the provincial, city, and county levels. According to the 1985 industry census of China, the shares of industrial output of the national total (at or above township level) produced by state-owned enterprises under the control of central, provincial/city, and county governments were 20 percent, 45 percent, and 9 percent respectively (see also Granick 1990).

Second, the fast-growing "nonstate sector" has a mix of private and public enterprises, the latter including "collectively owned" enterprises that are controlled by governments at the township or village levels, known as "township-village enterprises" (TVEs). The main difference, in property rights, between a state-owned enterprise and a collectively owned enterprise is this: because state ownership means ownership by all the people, the central government reserves the ultimate rights of reallocation of residual cash flow and assets in state-owned enterprises (SOEs), even if the control rights have been delegated and residual income has been assigned to local governments. But the central government (and any government except those of the townships and villages) has no such rights over the assets of collectively owned enterprises.

Third, there is a growing number of enterprises that fall into the category of "others"; the state or collectives still control more than 50 percent of their shares. At the moment, they are classified as the "nonstate sector" and are often regarded as "private enterprises" because they are neither SOEs nor collectives. But this could be misleading. The misclassification problem will become worse when more and more public enterprises are incorporated in the near future. This is not simply a statistical problem; rather, it is a problem concerning property rights and corporate governance.

In this chapter, I will restrict myself to SOEs and "other" types of enterprises, such as limited liability and joint-stock companies, in which the state controls more than 50 percent of interests.[1] After all, in most cases, limited liability and joint-stock companies evolved from the former SOEs.

I will focus on four major issues concerning current reforms of corporate governance and finance in China. First, it will be shown that the gradual process of the reform emphasizing an "expansion of enterprise autonomy" and "increase in retained profits" has led to a significant reallocation of control rights (mainly the use of assets) and cash flows from government to enterprises, especially to managers. At the same time, the Communist Party still firmly controls personnel appointments and dismissals. These dual features make China's case in part similar to that of Eastern Europe and Russia, and in part different.

Second, evidence will be presented to demonstrate that the past fifteen years of economic reform in China have also been associated with two major shifts in savings and finance: a shift of the savings source from the government to households, and a shift of the financing source of enterprises from the government budget to the financial system, especially the state banking system. The shifts are so dramatic that the savings and financing patterns in China are moving closer to those of other East Asian countries, including Japan.

Third, different views in the current debate over corporate governance reform in China will be considered. In particular, the benefits and costs of alternative governance structure in the political and eco-

---

1. Governance and finance issues in TVEs are studied in Che and Qian 1994.

nomic environment of China will be analyzed, especially the role of financial intermediaries such as holding companies, investment companies, and pension funds, as well as commercial banks.

In order for the banks to play useful roles in corporate governance, the incentives for banks must first be addressed. Finally, issues related to reforming the existing banks and creation of new commercial banks in China will be discussed.

The chapter is organized as follows. The first section summarizes briefly the government policy of enterprise reform in the past fifteen years (1979–93). The second section reviews the enterprise reform experience, focusing on the dual features of managers' control over use of assets and the Party's control over managerial appointment and dismissal. The third section demonstrates how the patterns of savings and finance have been changing toward the banking system. Corporate governance reforms will be discussed in the fourth section, and the needed banking reforms in the fifth section. The final section offers conclusions.

Enterprise Reform Policies of the Government

The governance of SOEs in China before the economic reform was similar to that in Eastern Europe and the former Soviet Union, except that in China, the local governments played more prominent roles in planning. Under the classical planning system, enterprises had little autonomy, and their incentives from retained profits and bonuses were low; this was known as overcentralization in the relationship between government and enterprises. The profit incentives were even lower in China than in Eastern Europe and the former Soviet Union because of Mao's preference for political and spiritual incentives over material incentives.

The main theme of the enterprise reform policies between 1979 and 1993 was decentralization from government to enterprises under "expanding enterprise autonomy" and "increasing retained profits" for the purpose of improving incentives. This strategy was prompted to a large extent by the overcentralization of the authority in the past; the successful experience of the contracting system in agriculture; the slowness in progress of fiscal, financial, and price reforms; and the political constraint on privatization.

Experiments with expanding enterprise autonomy and providing enterprises with profit incentives started as early as 1978, at the same time as the agricultural reforms. The major effort of enterprise reform by the government in this period was the introduction and promotion of the "contract responsibility system," started in early 1987. By the end of 1987, about 80 percent of large and medium-size SOEs had adopted some form of the contracting system. By 1989 almost all SOEs had adopted a contract responsibility system that continues today. Under the contract responsibility system, enterprise autonomy was expanded, and retained profits were also increased. Contracts typically last for a period of three to five years, and are designed to provide incentives for enterprises by giving them shares of profits or the residual profits after fixed remittance. The government promoted the contract responsibility system because of political and economic constraints and the ease and intuitiveness of the concept. Some economists advocated it because they believed that a thorough contract responsibility system is a *de facto* privatization, and they regarded the contract responsibility system as a substitute for privatization.

The contract responsibility system was not interrupted by the Tiananmen Square incident. The system was enhanced by the Regulations on Transforming the Management Mechanism of State-Owned Industrial Enterprises issued in July 1992 by the central government. The specific purpose of this new regulation was to further expand enterprise autonomy, which officially granted enterprise managers the "14 rights" of control in: production, pricing, sales, procurement, foreign trade, investment, use of retained funds, disposal of assets, merger and acquisition, labor, personnel management, wages and bonuses, internal organization, and refusal to pay unauthorized charges by the government. In practice, enterprises gained full control in some areas, but only limited or no control in areas such as disposal of assets and the right of refusal to pay unauthorized charges.[2]

2. Several empirical works have shown that the policies of enterprise reforms in the past have improved SOEs' incentives and increased productivity to some extent. For incentive effects, see Groves, Hong, McMillan, and Naughton, forthcoming; for productivity, see Jefferson and Rawski 1994.

The second approach to enterprise reform was the experimental use of other organizational forms, such as joint ventures, limited liability companies, and joint-stock companies. By mid-1993, of 3,800 limited liability companies, unlisted joint-stock companies, and listed joint-stock companies, 62 percent were limited liability companies, 34 percent were unlisted joint-stock companies, and 4 percent were listed joint-stock companies. In addition to securing greater enterprise autonomy, another reason for setting up joint ventures was to attract foreign capital. It was also hoped that setting up experimental joint-stock companies would raise funds to circumvent credit quota regulations imposed on banks. In all cases of limited liability companies and in the majority of cases of joint-stock companies, new funds were raised by private placement, often through closed subscription by employees and institutional investors. In many cases, with guaranteed dividends and no voting rights, the shares were more like bonds or preferred stocks.

As a consequence of the focus on fundraising, as well as the lack of reform in government functions, the issues of ownership and governance reforms were overshadowed in the process of organizational transformation. In almost all joint-stock companies, the state continues to own controlling interests. Although joint-stock companies enjoy greater autonomy than ordinary SOEs—in investment decisions and disposal of assets, for instance—it is still the government, rather than the board of directors, that appoints top managers, as is the case in ordinary SOEs.

Enterprise grouping was another attempt at enterprise reform, which usually did not involve raising new funds. This industrial reorganization was a response to the segmentation of industrial structures inherited from the planning system, especially after regional decentralization. In most cases, industrial grouping explored vertical and horizontal linkages without formal control rights shifts. These linkages were established to explore economy of scale and to obtain supply assurance without the involvement of financial and control issues.

Changing Patterns of Governance

It is generally agreed that ownership and enterprise reforms in the industrial sector are not as successful as the reforms in the agricultural sector. There are two basic reasons why industrial reforms are much more difficult than agricultural reforms in China. First, unlike the technology in family farming in China, technology in industry determines that enterprises have both complex internal organizational structural and external interrelationship (in that sense, Soviet agriculture has different technology than the Chinese). Second, unlike the simple institutional environment of agricultural organization, enterprise reforms depend on other complementary reforms in the tax and fiscal system, financial and banking system, investment system, social safety net, government bureaucracy, and so forth. Without those complementary reforms, enterprise reform alone cannot be successful. Hence, even though reforms in agriculture and industry face similar incentive, ownership, and governance problems, simple (for example, family-based) incentive schemes would work in agriculture, but would be unlikely to work in industry.

The central dilemma of enterprise reform in China has been this: either the enterprise complains of *lack of autonomy*, or the government as an owner loses control and suffers from *lack of accountability*. The economic reform has granted managers increasing control rights over the use of assets, which leads to a mixed outcome. On the one hand, giving control to managers has a potential efficiency gain because managers, unlike bureaucrats or politicians, have the skill and information to run the enterprises. On the other hand, because managers do not own the assets of enterprises, misgovernance of SOEs caused by the agency problem remains and has even worsened in some cases.

Control and Benefits for Managers and Workers

Even without formal privatization in China, significant control rights and incomes have been transferred to managers through "expanding enterprise autonomy." The evolutionary process toward managerial control is similar to that of Hungary both before and after its political change in 1989 (Voszka 1993). The trend in China is reinforced because most managers are promoted from within the enterprises during the reform.

Like managers in publicly held corporations in the West, today's managers of SOEs in China exercise great discretion over the use of assets and maintain considerable on-the-job consumption and other rents. The formal rights of managers include the "14 rights" stipulated in the 1992 regulations. The *de facto* rights vary; in some cases they are less and in other cases more than the formal ones. There are some common features concerning managerial control rights over assets. First, enterprise managers typically have rights to use state assets and to enjoy incomes so generated, but they have no formal rights to dispose of assets. Second, the allocation of control rights and cash flow are not entirely clear, which often leads to conflicting claims. And third, there is no formal legal recognition and protection of the effective property rights.

Although a top manager's salary and bonuses are only about three times the compensation of an average worker, their benefits depend much more on on-the-job consumption or perks, including assignment of better and larger apartments, private use of cars, availability of "corporate accounts" for business lunches and dinners, entertainment, domestic touring, traveling abroad, and the like. To appreciate the relative magnitude of perks compared with salary and bonuses, one needs to consider the following: one average business dinner in a decent restaurant could cost about an average worker's monthly salary. While all of the above consumptions are perfectly legal, some others are not. As a result of fast development of the nonstate sector, managers, or their relatives and friends, often have their own businesses, which provide opportunities for diverting state assets to private benefits.

Managerial autonomy is greatly enhanced through a common practice in China—a series of organizational transformations effected by breaking up existing enterprises to form "secondary legal entities" (that is, subsidiaries), joint ventures with foreign and/or domestic partners, limited liability companies, and joint-stock companies. This practice in China is again very similar to that in Hungary, where it is known as "transformation" or "partial transformation."[3] The motivations of managers in the two countries for such a reorganization are also similar: desire for independence from the government, for shifts of bad debts and overemployment burdens onto parent companies, and for under-

3. In the past few years, transformation without formal privatization has been typical in Hungary (Voszka 1993), and it is also called "decentralized reorganization" (Stark 1993).

taking new business opportunities without losing existing connections to and benefits from the state.

But this process in China is more often associated with new business projects, especially new ventures set up in special economic zones and development zones. The following scenario is hypothetical, but highly suggestive: a state-owned enterprise (say, of Beijing) first sets up a wholly owned subsidiary in a special economic zone (say, in Guangdong); then the subsidiary enters into a joint venture with several domestic and foreign partners; later the joint venture sets up another subsidiary in another development zone (say, in Shanghai); and finally the last subsidiary forms another joint venture with a TVE (say, of Jiangsu). After several rounds of transformation, the managers obtain a great degree of autonomy. The key to this process is the relatively little start-up capital required, which is used as collateral for securing large bank loans at a very low interest rate.

Qian and Stiglitz (forthcoming) report several cases of such organizational transformation. For example, a joint venture in Guangdong was formed by a Hong Kong partner and three Chinese partners (each with a one-quarter share). Of the Chinese partners, one is a company affiliated with the central government, another with the provincial government, and yet another with the municipal government. The Hong Kong partner contributed some initial capital and technology and is managed by a Chinese manager from an SOE. In another almost identical case in the same area, the Hong Kong investor is in fact a Hong Kong company wholly owned by one branch of the Chinese government.[4] In the latter case, the "Sino-foreign" joint venture is actually 100 percent state-owned, but both companies would fall into the category of the nonstate sector. The managers claim that they have greater autonomy because of the new ownership and organizational structure.

With the expanded enterprise autonomy, the agency problem of managers in China is much more serious than it is in the West because

---

4. This is called "fake foreign capital" in China. The incentive of doing so is twofold: to be qualified for tax benefits and to gain greater autonomy from the government.

of property rights and other institutional reasons. First, managers generally are not given shares or stock options that link the net worth of the enterprise with their efforts. Second, although product market competition is getting tough because of the entry of the nonstate sector, there is a lack of capital and managerial labor market competition. Third, and most serious, there is no clearly accountable representative of the state with supporting institutions that has both the information and profit incentives to monitor the performance of managers. The monitoring roles of both banks and branch ministries/bureaus are diminishing quickly in the reform of expanding enterprise autonomy, and no replacement has been formed.

All these factors contribute to the phenomenon of coalition between managers and workers in state-owned enterprises, as opposed to conflicting interests between the two in a typical capitalist firm, where the managers represent the owners' interest. The collusion between managers and workers is better sustained because most managers were promoted from within the enterprise. As returns to capital in the state sector steadily declined from 25 percent in the early 1980s to less than 10 percent in 1992, wages and bonuses per worker in the state sector increased (table 7-2). The workers in SOEs benefited from expanding enterprise autonomy in several ways: increased wages and bonuses (both pecuniary and in-kind); expanded residential housing; job opportunities for employees' children in collective enterprises sponsored by SOEs; and so forth. But in many enterprises, the greatest benefit for workers is the opportunity to purchase "internal shares," which are sold to them at discount prices (or options to buy the shares in the future). These shares often have guaranteed dividends and command a premium that could double the interest rates of bank deposits. If the enterprise goes public, capital gains can be as high as five to ten times the face value, a windfall gain.

Unlike Poland, however, workers' control of enterprises in China was never significant because the trade unions and workers' congresses in enterprises have been, and still are, under strict control by the Party. The Party and the government continue to view an independent trade union as one of the most serious threats against its leadership and social stability. Not surprisingly, the role of workers within the enterprise is mostly consultative.

Table 7-2. China: Returns to Capital and Labor in the State Sector, 1981–92

Category and year	*Percentage*
Profits and taxes per value of net fixed assets and working capital in industry	
1981	23.8
1986	20.7
1991	11.8
1992	9.7
Increases of real wages and bonuses per worker over the previous year	
1981–85	4.3[a]
1986–90	2.6[a]
1991	3.2
1992	7.0

a. Average figures in five years.
Source: *Statistical Yearbook of China*, 1993.

Spontaneous or Informal Privatization

This practice in China, which has become more common recently, refers to the process of unauthorized transfers of assets from either the state or collectives to formal or de facto private ownership. The phenomenon is similar to that in the Eastern European countries and Russia, but to a lesser extent (see, for example, Stark 1993; Voszka 1993; Shleifer and Boycko 1993). Typically, managers and employees of the enterprise are the main beneficiaries, but local government officials also become beneficiaries, because managers often bribe them to let the deal go through.

Spontaneous privatization often occurred following the introduction of the contract responsibility system and during a series of organizational transformations as described above. Nee and Su (1993) report several interesting cases of informal privatization in China. One case concerns informal privatization of a part of an SOE. The Xiamen Food Company, an SOE, converted a department into a subsidiary, the Food

Trading Company. According to the profit-sharing contract, the parent SOE claimed 90 percent of earned profits. The subsidiary was then contracted out to three employees of the original department. The subsidiary expanded quickly, and the three employees wished to purchase the assets of the subsidiary. They lobbied to have their contract lapsed on the ground that their business changed and the original terms no longer applied. Eventually the parent company agreed to sell the assets used to start up the subsidiary. These original assets were worth considerably less than the business that the three former employees developed themselves.

In this case, informal privatization started with the contract responsibility system. The contractors then were able to secure loans to expand the business. Subsequently they acquired complete control rights over the expanded and successful business, and eventually the contractors obtained ownership rights of the entire business. But what happens if the business goes under? Of course, the state absorbs any financial losses—it is the owner in that event. Because of this feature of transfer of property rights, I call it "contingent privatization," which means that the government does not give away assets in the usual sense; rather, it gives away an opportunity in exchange for an informal, noncash "bid." If the business grows, the contractee pays back the debt and becomes the owner of the new business, and the share of the state is reduced in the economy. If the business goes under, the government takes back control.

This process has some interesting features. First, this is not, strictly speaking, privatization, because the old stock is not sold. Second, the scheme by its nature focuses on new business (rather than old), on flow (rather than stock), and on growth. Third, the share of the state sector is gradually reduced as that of the private sector is increased. And fourth, because of the personal efforts involved, the process likely favors entrepreneurs who take big risks (that is, the screening effect). Regardless of the distributional issues, the contingent privatization is not always efficient.

Not surprisingly, the government seriously worries about "state assets stripping" from such spontaneous privatization. According to the National Administrative Bureau of State-Owned Property, any transfer at below fair market prices of state assets to nonstate entities—such as individuals, collectives, and joint ventures—is considered state assets stripping. There is no precise figure on the magnitude of this practice, but some estimate that about 100–300 million yuan worth of state assets flow out of the state coffers each day, or around 30–100 billion yuan every year.[5]

State assets flow out in two main channels. The first channel is during and after formal property rights transformation. For example, it is estimated that in Guangdong Province, which has the most joint ventures of any province in China, about 90 percent of Sino-foreign joint ventures were formed without assets appraisal from the Chinese partner. Also, during the formation of a joint-stock company, undervaluing the present value of state assets is a common practice. A recently emerging method uses the chance of bankruptcy to liquidate state assets at low prices and divert them for private uses, which explains why some enterprises are very enthusiastic about bankruptcy, and some even made a fortune from it.[6]

The second channel of state assets stripping is through control rights transfers under the contract responsibility system of 1987 and the new operating mechanism of 1992. For instance, in order to fulfill the contract obligation of current profit remittance to the government and to please workers by maintaining high welfare, managers often sacrifice the future of the enterprise by reducing assets-enhancing activities—for example, by using up depreciation funds ("eating up the equipment") and by overborrowing.

The biggest social problem with the ongoing state assets stripping and spontaneous privatization (and associated corruption) is the discontent of the public. Fairness is an issue, both because it avoids social unrest that would destroy stability and because it has its own value. One of the purposes of the Russian voucher program is to address the needs of the public when state assets are quickly stripped away through spontaneous privatization (Shleifer and Boycko 1993). China does not have a similar means to please the public. State assets stripping and spontaneous privatization offer tremendous benefits to some segments

---

5. *Guangming Daily*, October 5, 1993.
6. *China Business Times*, June 29, 1994. This type of "bankruptcy" is given the nickname "fake death" (*jiasi*) in China.

of the population, such as some workers, managers, local government officials, and perhaps foreign investors too. Some economists regard this as a more effective and less costly means of transition to capitalism for China. Others disagree, and they argue that not only is the public interest not served, but continuing the practice of state assets stripping and spontaneous privatization would only promote corruption and would not lead to a stable and well-functioning market economy.

Party Control of Personnel Appointments and Dismissals

As described above, managers in enterprises have been able to secure substantial control rights in the use of assets. One important dimension of the control rights concerning an enterprise, however, is the right to appoint and to dismiss top managers of the enterprise, which is still firmly controlled by the Communist Party. This is an important difference between China and the Eastern European countries and Russia. Because of that, despite the similarity of the manager's discretion on the use of assets in the two cases, China is still one step short of the "insider control" regime observed in the latter. The roles of the Party in China's economic reform could be better understood through a comparison with Eastern European countries and Russia.

The Party Organization Department, although not visible, is the most important agency that has the ultimate control over personnel above a certain rank (including top managers of large and medium-size SOEs); this is the principle known as "the Party controlling personnel."[7] For example, the legal representative of an enterprise (that is, the top manager) must be appointed and certified by the Party Organization Department when it registers with the National Administrative Bureau of Industry and Commerce, and joint-stock companies must do this as well (even in special economic zones such as Shenzhen). The Party Organization Department can arbitrate when different government agencies have conflicting interests and claims.

---

7. The supervising branch ministry or bureau of an enterprise makes nominal appointments after approval from the Party Organization Department or makes low-level appointments.

In 1988 there was a plan by the Party to reform this system by shifting the authority to the government's newly established Ministry of Personnel, but it was aborted because of the Tiananmen Square incident. There were also experiments in the mid-1980s in which managerial positions in some SOEs were auctioned off (see Groves, Hong, McMillan, and Naughton, forthcoming), but these experiments have never become a mainstream mechanism. To the contrary, after the Tiananmen Square incident, the Party reasserted its control over personnel to a greater degree. Overall, the authority of the Party Organization Department has not been seriously challenged by the previous economic reforms because it has always been regarded as the domain of political reform. As political stability and control are given first priority, political reforms are indefinitely postponed.

The authority of the Party in appointment—and especially in dismissal—of managers serves as an important counterbalance against managerial discretion. Although the appointment does not carry an explicit compensation package as typically observed in a capitalist firm, each managerial position is automatically associated with a huge amount of control rents from managerial discretion, especially in the fast-growing areas and in the newly emerged business lines such as real estate, security brokerage, futures trading, financial intermediaries, and the like. Therefore, although promotion within the bureaucratic hierarchy becomes less attractive than before, disciplinary dismissal by the Party severely damages managers because of the removal of the rents associated with their position. Even though some people do not want to be promoted, they still have strong incentives to *maintain* their positions for obtaining such rents. If managers succeed in capitalizing the rents, however, they may quit the job at some point to start their own business. By that time, the personnel control of the Party will be less effective.

The continuity of the Party's control in personnel decisions has important implications. On the one hand, this clearly does not represent a very efficient governance structure, because the selection criteria of the Party are not entirely based on economic performance, and the evaluation methods are largely primitive.[8] But reforming the system of

---

8. The criteria are not entirely political either. The managers generally may pass the political screening as long as they are not involved in political incidents such as the Tiananmen Square incident.

the Party's control, although necessary, will not be easy for obvious political reasons, especially at the present time. On the other hand, the willingness of the central government and the Party to decentralize (delegate) control rights to managers without fear of a complete loss of control is perhaps the result of the continuing Party centralization of appointments and dismissals of managers and control of their incentives. This is somewhat similar in spirit to the Japanese organizational features of the firm, where most decisions are decentralized, but personnel decisions are all centralized. This "Duality Principle," as termed by Aoki (1990), may also operate in China. Indeed, the power balance between the Party/government and the enterprise has to some extent prevented state assets from being stripped away at a faster pace, as seen in Eastern Europe and Russia.

Relationships between Enterprises and Local Governments

Often there is a conflict of interest between the central and local governments, and local governments *collude* with enterprises against the central government. This is more evident in fast-growing areas such as Guangdong. Collusion between local government and SOEs can be explained by the competition pressure among different jurisdictions and by the insecure property rights of local governments. Although the local government has the control rights of SOEs, those rights are not completely secure for two reasons. First, the local government worries about possible future reallocation of assets by the central government, and it often encourages the enterprise to pursue short-term goals of profit maximization, rather than increasing the net worth of the assets. The local government may also want to privatize SOEs under its control, or tacitly consent to or even encourage the spontaneous privatization described above, which explains why spontaneous privatization is under way despite prohibition from the central government. Second, the local government also worries about the ratchet effect, so it often helps the enterprise to hide profits. The pattern is the following: the local government allows profits to go untaxed, and the enterprise picks up the bill for some government expenditures, such as dining and traveling expenses.

Needless to say, conflict between local government and enterprises exists. Managers continue to complain about the lack of full autonomy and government interference in such areas as appointments and the imposition of unauthorized fees. Again, situations vary. In poor areas, where the industrial base is small, but fixed government expenditure is large, the local government tends to impose more fees on enterprises. But competition among jurisdictions to get rich first is one check on the local government's predatory behavior, especially in the fast-growing areas where potentially large gains prevent the local governments from becoming predatory. Local governments in advanced areas may even make preemptive moves through reform to attract capital and skilled labor from other regions in order to better compete.

Changing Patterns of Savings and Finance

In contrast to Eastern Europe and Russia, China's economic reform has been associated with high and stable national savings, which increased from 30 percent of gross domestic product (GDP) in the early 1980s to about 35 percent in the 1990s. More significantly, major saving sources have shifted from the government and enterprises to households. In 1978 household savings accounted for only 23 percent, enterprises for 34 percent, and government for 43 percent of total saving. In 1991 household savings increased to 71 percent, enterprise savings decreased to 25 percent, and government savings fell to a mere 4 percent of the total (table 7-3).

Not only household savings increased dramatically; the increase is closely associated with financial deepening, that is, the process of rapid increase of household financial assets. Total household bank deposits reached 1.5 trillion yuan in 1993, or about 50 percent of GDP, from merely 6 percent in 1978. Total household financial assets increased from about 19 percent of GDP in 1980 to about 70 percent of GDP in 1991. For broader measures, in 1991 the M2 to GDP ratio reached about 100 percent and total the financial assets to GDP ratio topped 232 percent (table 7-4).

In contrast, the past fifteen years witnessed a steady decline of (consolidated) government budgetary revenue as a share of GDP, down from 35 percent in 1978 to about 16 percent in 1993. Much of the budgetary revenue decline can be attributed to the decrease of enterprise

Table 7-3. China: Changing Pattern of Savings, 1978–91
(percent)

Share of national savings	*1978*	*1991*
Government	43	4
Enterprises	34	25
Households	23	71

Source: Xie 1992, table 3-13.

Table 7-4. China: Financial Deepening, 1978–91
(percent)

Item	*1978*	*1991*
Household bank deposits/GDP[a]	6	46
Household financial assets/GDP[b]	19	70
M2/GDP[c]		99
Total financial assets/GDP[c]	95	232

Source: (a) *Statistical Yearbook of China*, 1992; (b) Xie 1992, table 3-8; (c) Xie 1992, tables 3-2 and 3-3.

income tax and profit remittance, which fell from 21 percent of GDP in 1978 to about 5 percent in 1992. Some of the reduction of profit remittance, however, reappeared as the so-called "extra-budgetary" revenues. The extra-budgetary revenue, most of which is retained profits of enterprises, expanded moderately. Before the reform, the extra-budgetary revenue was relatively small, 9 percent of GDP in 1978 compared with the budgetary revenue of 35 percent of GDP. By 1991 the extra-budgetary revenue was up to 15 percent of GDP, while the budgetary revenue was down to 18 percent of GDP. Still, the combined budgetary and extra-budgetary revenues have declined significantly during the reform period (table 7-5).

The natural consequence of the decline of government revenue and savings and the increase of household financial savings through bank deposits is the changing sources of financing by enterprises. Budgetary

Table 7-5. China: Changing Pattern of Government Revenue, 1978–91 *(percent)*

Item	*1978*	*1991*
Consolidated budgetary revenue/GDP	35	18
Enterprise revenue/GDP	21	6
Extra-budgetary revenue/GDP	9	15
Combined revenue/GDP	44	33

Source: *Statistical Yearbook of China*, 1992.

financing of capital expenditure as a percent of GDP fell dramatically, from 15 percent of GDP in 1978 to less than 5 percent in 1992. Although some of the financing comes from extra-budgetary revenue (another 5 percent of GDP), the major source of financing comes from the banking sector. The share of bank loans in total budget and bank loans financing in fixed assets and working capital increased from 39 percent in 1978 to 73 percent in 1991 (table 7-6). Between 1981 and 1990, domestic bank loans for fixed investment financing increased from 13 percent to about 20 percent, and in working capital, bank loans accounted for more than 80 percent (at or above township level enterprises) (Xie 1992, p. 87).

During this period, the government ran a moderate open or official budget deficit (around 1–3 percent of GDP), of which about one-third was financed by bonds. Hidden or quasi budget deficits under the name of "policy loans" (that is, loans not on commercial terms), however, may actually equal or surpass the figure on the open budget deficit. Total seigniorage (including both inflation tax and an increase in real money balance) could be as high as 8–9 percent of GDP in some years (for example, 1990 and 1991). Very fortunately for China, much of the seigniorage in the past fifteen years has taken the form of an increase in the demand for real money balance; therefore, the government was able to keep inflation at a moderate level, although official and quasi budget deficits ("policy loans") were high.

These stylized facts highlight the following points. First, bank loans are becoming the main external source of enterprise financing, while the government budget and direct financing are relatively small.

Table 7-6. China: Changing Pattern of Financing, 1978–91
(percent)

Item	*1978*	*1991*
Budgetary capital expenditure/GDP[a]	15	5
Shares of fiscal budget and bank loans in fixed assets and working capital financing		
Fiscal budget	61[b]	27[c]
Bank loans	39[b]	73[c]

Source: (a) *Statistical Yearbook of China*, 1992; (b) 1980 figures, Xie 1992, table 3-11; (c) 1990 figures, Xie 1992, table 3-11.

Second, many enterprise problems are caused by, or are shown as, the problem of "policy loans," or bad debts in the financial system, rather than the open budget deficits in the fiscal system. And third, the interrelationship between enterprise reform and banking reform is closer than ever.

Current Issues in Governance Reform

Reforming governance of SOEs in China can be viewed as a three-step process: corporatization, rearrangements of corporate control, and privatization. At the present time, the first two steps are feasible, but privatization is restricted to small-scale firms. In Eastern Europe, corporatization was carried out only as a quick prelude to privatization, and rearrangement of corporate control was carried out either during or after privatization. In China, the particular political condition dictates that the period of corporatization and rearrangements of corporate control without privatization will last longer. Privatization is not impossible, however, as we see from the recent flexibility regarding sales of small SOEs. It is also possible to privatize part of some of the large-scale enterprises in the near future as political constraints are relaxed or the performance of these enterprises becomes worse. In any event, privatization will be much slower in China than in Eastern Europe and Russia.

From the perspective of political economy, the mechanisms of corporate governance currently needed in China should satisfy three basic requirements: first, they should be politically feasible without too much resistance from the government bureaucracy; second, they should improve managerial accountability and limit bureaucratic interference; and third, they should facilitate the eventual diminution of state shares either through dilution by issuing new shares to the private sector, or by privatization. Of course, there is no one model of corporate governance for SOEs. But the common problems need to be addressed in a systematic way.

In the view of economists, corporate governance is a set of institutional arrangements governing the relationship among several groups of stakeholders (investors, both shareholder and creditor; managers; and workers) in order to realize economic gains from such a coalition. The structure of corporate governance concerns (a) how control rights are allocated and exercised; (b) how boards of directors, managers, and workers are monitored and evaluated; and (c) how incentives are designed and enforced. Generally, good corporate governance recognizes the complementarity of these institutional arrangements and selects a structure to limit total agency costs. The research has generally focused on the issue of how managers (insiders) are monitored and/or disciplined by investors (outsiders).[9]

All transition economies are constrained by the scarcity of financial and skilled management resources. Hence, the desired corporate governance structure should be able to make optimal use of the available resources. From an economic perspective, an appropriate governance in a transition economy must be able to deal with two special problems associated with the transition. First, it should provide managers with incentives to restructure the enterprises, prevent them from further thefts of enterprise assets, and be able to replace them quickly when they are found incapable. Second, it should also be able to facilitate raising badly needed external capital to finance restructuring and technology upgrades.

Even with private ownership, property rights allocation among many stakeholders and forms of corporate governance in a publicly

---

9. Much of the principal-agent theory developed in the past twenty years addresses this issue. See Hart and Holmstrom 1987 for a survey of that literature.

held corporation are much more complicated than they are in a small, family-owned and operated business (Milgrom and Roberts 1992). Because property rights consist of rights of control in many dimensions, and most modern business organizations involve many stakeholders, it is important to know how and why control rights along different dimensions are allocated and incomes shared among these stakeholders. Therefore, in studying the issues of reforming governance of large and medium-size SOEs, it is more relevant to make use of the studies of corporate governance and finance in modern corporations in the West, because the potential agency problem is more pervasive than it would be in a simple case of an owner-managed private firm.

Corporatization and Corporate Control

Corporatization in China is first associated with defining property rights of legal entities, that is, corporate property rights. After corporatization, an enterprise, as a legal entity, has property rights over its assets. According to the Chinese company law passed in December 1993, three major forms of companies will be identified: joint-stock companies (including a small number of enterprises to be publicly traded), limited liability companies, and wholly state-owned companies. In the future, boards of directors will be established to represent the interests of shareholders. The boards will make major and strategic decisions, including appointments and dismissals of top managers. Generally, board members and managers will not be government officials from the civil service.

Economists agree that corporatization is a useful step of enterprise reform even without privatization. Corporatization helps to hold directors responsible for the assets of the company, prevent further asset thefts, provide a mechanism for information exchanges, set a stage for selling shares, and separate the state from enterprises (Lipton and Sachs 1990; Shleifer and Boycko 1993). That is why corporatization was carried out before privatization in Eastern Europe and Russia. The idea of corporatization only started to gain more and more approval in China from the government, enterprises, and economists in 1993.

A more complicated and controversial issue regards rearrangement of corporate control. The experience in the West shows that governance structure can take a variety of forms. In many corporations, outsiders such as block shareholders (core investors), investment funds, strategic investors, or banks are active in corporate governance through their representations on the board, in particular in decisions leading to the dismissal of top managers. In the case of Japan, a typical large corporation is actually controlled by insiders, because all board members are managers, but managers can be replaced by the main bank when the corporation is in financial trouble.

Experience in Eastern Europe and Russia has shown that during transition, insiders obtain substantial control of enterprises. In the cases of Hungary and Russia, insiders are managers, and in the case of Poland, they are workers. This could have happened because of privatization schemes (as in Russia) or because of weak government supervision and spontaneous privatization (as in Hungary, Poland, and Russia, as well). Economists are in agreement that such governance by insiders without the possibility of outsider intervention is generally not good for the health of the economy. Distortions arise from insiders' control because they may act out of self-interest rather than in the interest of the owners (that is, value maximization), and there is often a short-term bias toward managers' preferences compared with those of the owners. Insider control often implies that (a) managers may refuse to restructure; (b) bad managers cannot be replaced without incurring substantial costs (because they are bad, they are also unlikely to find good replacements for themselves); and, especially, (c) no new capital can be raised at a low cost. All of these are important considerations for transition. One of the themes of reforming corporate governance in Eastern Europe and Russia is how to institutionalize corporate control by outsiders in the process of privatization (Phelps, Frydman, Rapaczynski, and Shleifer 1993).

The case of China is similar, but differs from those in Eastern Europe and Russia as discussed earlier. Complications in China arise because of the majority of public ownership of enterprises, the unwillingness of the government to privatize, and the continuity of the Party's role in personnel decisions. Although corporatization has already become an official reform policy in China, the role of the Party after corporatization it is still not clear. Will the Party send its representatives to the board, will the board be required to get approval from the Party for personnel decisions, or will the Party stop making personnel decisions below a certain rank altogether?

Economists in China hold different views regarding the current trend toward managerial control in enterprises and advocate different approaches in reforming corporate governance as well. In one view, shared by those described above concerning insider control, the tendency toward managerial control of enterprises is regarded as bad and requiring balance. Because of political constraints in China, according to this view, state-sponsored financial intermediaries such as investment companies or commercial banks can be used to minimize such a problem. In another view, shared by those who support privatization, spontaneous privatization and insider control by managers and workers is the (second) best choice for China, because formal privatization is impossible. The needed strategy for reforming corporate governance, according to this view, is not to reassert ownership rights by the state, but rather to continue the trend of giving managers more control and eventually making them *de facto* owners. In this view, spontaneous privatization is good and should continue.

Alternative Governance Structures

In reforming corporate governance, China needs diversity. This is not just because China is a large country and variations are huge across different regions and industries. Diversity also has value because the kind of enterprise reforms to be carried out in China are unprecedented and must encompass a wide range of experiments. Even in the capitalist economies, one observes that organization of firms varies greatly both across countries (for example, the United States, Japan, and Germany) and within each country. The most dangerous policy in enterprise reform in China is perhaps the insistence on one particular model.

One possible governance structure is through a management and employee buyout (MEBO), which enables managers and employees to obtain control by buying up the majority interests, as seen in some cases in Russia and Eastern Europe. This could be a good solution for small-scale SOEs or collectives, but it would not be formally feasible for large and medium-size enterprises in China.[10]

---

10. Frydman, Rapaczynski, Earle, and Turkewitz (1994) examine the experiences of the Czech Republic, Poland, and Hungary on the privatization of small, nonmanufacturing business units. It contains practical lessons and operational recommendations for implementing small-scale privatization programs that might be useful for China.

The second promising governance structure in China is through joint ventures with foreigners. China attracted more than US$20 billion annually in foreign direct investment (FDI) in 1992 and 1993. This provided a rare opportunity to utilize foreign physical and human resources for enterprise reforms. The practice of taking a part of an SOE and forming a joint venture with foreigners has become more and more popular in recent years and has received the nickname of "grafting" (*jiajie*) in China. In addition to the tax benefits, availability of cheap labor, and the huge potential market in China, the incentives for foreign investors to invest and form joint ventures with Chinese SOEs also come from the weak ownership claims of the state. Very often, managers from SOEs collude with foreigners in underestimating the value of assets contributed by the Chinese partners. A similar pattern is also observed in Hungary.[11]

The third alternative comes from transformation of current enterprise groupings. There were fifty-five large enterprise groups in China approved by the State Council by the end of 1993. Some Chinese economists and government officials believe that these groups have a bright future in corporate restructuring because they have advantages of linkages in production, supply, and marketing. After restructuring, the parent company will be transformed into an assets management company (still to be owned by the state) when it stops the production supervision it now performs.

The most difficult part of reform concerns large and medium-size SOEs that cannot find foreign partners and are in no particular grouping. The same is true for Eastern Europe and Russia, where, after privatization, the large and medium-size enterprises have many dispersed investors. The problem with ownership and corporate control of these enterprises in China differs from that in Eastern Europe and Russia (because of no privatization); the central issue is how the state shares should be represented in a less harmful way. A more specific question in this regard concerns whether state-owned (or sponsored) financial intermediaries should be established between incorporated SOEs and the State Assets Management Committee (SAMC). If these intermedi-

11. Hungary attracted about US$2 billion foreign investment in 1991, much more than China on a per capita basis.

aries need to be established, then in what forms? And who will play the prominent role in corporate governance: holding companies, investment companies, assets management companies, commercial banks, or a combination of these?

Opponents of using state-owned financial intermediaries argue that this will result in the same bureaucracy as before, and maybe worse, particularly if the intermediaries are based on existing branch ministries or bureaus (however, private financial intermediaries would be acceptable). It is very likely that these future holding companies or assets management firms might want to take back decisionmaking authority from the enterprises, becoming a "mother-in-law cum boss." Because the intermediaries like to hold power, this could also be bad for future privatization.

Without intermediaries, the SAMC would appoint directors of the boards of corporations directly, which would eliminate one layer of bureaucracy. Obviously the SAMC must employ an internal hierarchy (again, perhaps organized by industry) to make appointments of directors, collect information, evaluate their performance, and so forth. As the capacity of the state to monitor lessens, managers of enterprises will continue to enjoy the control rights they currently hold, and more and more will become *de facto* owners, which will naturally lead to future privatization. This approach is consistent with the view that state ownership is totally hopeless, no matter what form it takes. Therefore, the purpose of the current enterprise reform is to make *de facto* privatization easier.

Proponents of using financial intermediaries argue their case on several grounds. First, if spontaneous privatization and state assets stripping are serious political issues to be dealt with to avoid political backlash, then the best chance for the state to reclaim ownership rights is to use financial institutions, rather than ministries or bureaus as in the past. Second, with transforming government functions, many branch ministries and bureaus will be eliminated, and the organizational facilities and human knowledge could be useful (after some retraining) in these intermediaries. Third, from an international perspective, institutional ownership in corporations (such as financial intermediaries) is a common feature of all mature market economies, particularly those associated with large corporations, and especially in Japan. And finally, holding companies and other financial intermediaries were also used in the public sector in other market economies; although they did not work very well, they were better than the existing Chinese system. Given the political constraints in China, this is worth trying.

The Role of Nonbank Financial Intermediaries

Most economists from the West agree that the stock market will play a limited role in corporate control through takeovers or proxy fights in the transition economies in the near future; this role tends to be overestimated, however, by people inside the transition economies. The experience of continental Europe and Japan shows that the block investors (or core investors) and banks have played an important role in outsider control. Given the wealth distribution in transition economies, the core investors are more likely to be institutional investors of a variety of financial intermediaries (except for possible foreign investors). In Eastern Europe and Russia, these intermediaries are known as "privatization intermediaries." Examples include private investment funds in the Czech Republic and Russia and state-sponsored mutual funds in Poland.[12]

There are two basic problems concerning the role of financial intermediaries in corporate governance. The first is that these intermediaries may play too small a role, which leads to *de facto* insider control. Experience in the West has shown that pension funds and mutual funds have never been active in corporate control, even when they hold substantial shares in a company (and in most cases, they do not—for example, if they follow the index investment strategy). The same problems appeared in investment funds and mutual funds in Eastern Europe and Russia. One possible remedy, in the context of Eastern Europe, requires government regulation to restrict the extent of diversification of these intermediaries and make the "exit option" more costly to exercise. Of course, there is the usual tradeoff between risk diversification and incentives to monitor.

---

12. Proposals were also made to transform these intermediaries into a kind of universal bank by extending their activities to a wide range of financial services (see Phelps, Frydman, Rapaczynski, and Shleifer 1993).

The other problem more relevant for China is that these intermediaries may become "too active" in corporate governance. This is more relevant in China precisely because these intermediaries are likely to be state-owned holding companies or assets management companies and to be established based on the existing institutional facilities and personnel from places such as branch ministries. In these cases there is a real danger that these intermediaries will become active interventionists—bureaucratic and political.

Several steps could be taken to limit such a problem. First, it is well known that politicians and bureaucrats often have objectives other than profits and economic efficiency, which is believed by many economists to be the major deficiency of public ownership and the fatal factor of socialist economies.[13] To address this issue, the state financial intermediaries together with the SAMC could be strictly separated from the ordinary government bureaucracy for social regulation and administration ("government A"). To this end, a separate "government B," which consists of the SAMC and the state financial intermediaries, could be set up under the supervision of the People's Congress and given the mission or objective of value maximization of the state assets. Evaluation and rewards for people working in "government B" would be based exclusively on their financial performance, as in the private sector.

Second, although separation of the assets management function of government B from the regulation function of government A is crucial, it is hardly sufficient to achieve economic efficiency. The government regulations could be designed to force financial intermediaries to sufficiently diversify their portfolios to prevent them from establishing monopolies in product market. Financial intermediaries in market economies serve the purpose of coordination, control, and commitment, and they do so in an environment of competition. One crucial difference between the proposed financial intermediaries and the former ministerial system of planning is the possibility of competition among financial intermediaries when they have diversified and the potential for overlapping portfolios, even though they are still state-sponsored. It is

---

13. See, for example, Kornai 1992 and Shleifer and Vishny 1994.

hoped that capital market competition will not only better discipline managers of firms, but also provide better information for the evaluation of managers of these intermediaries.

Finally, it should be noted that these proposals are, at best, social experiments that have no precedent. Although no theory proves they are doomed to fail, there is also no theory to guarantee their success. Therefore, steps should be taken to prepare for dilution of state ownership in these financial intermediaries either by selling shares to domestic nonstate investors (private or collective), or in the case of investment funds such as pension funds, by spinning off the funds management company to private firms. In the latter case, although shares of the investment funds are still owned by the state, the funds could be managed by, for instance, Fidelity Management Company.

The Role of Banks in Corporate Governance

As discussed earlier, the banking system in China has become the most important external source of financing of enterprises, and therefore the relationships between banks and enterprises are naturally close. China's reform is entering a stage in which the enterprise and banking reforms intertwine and become the major bottleneck. In relation to enterprise reform, the role of banks is instrumental to solving the massive bad debt problems of enterprises and to satisfying the demand for new capital. In addition, because of their abilities in financing and monitoring, banks also have *potential* special leverages in corporate governance.

Banks have financial resources as well as monitoring capacity, and banks do not interfere with enterprises on a daily basis. As creditors, banks' decisions generally are important only at the time loans are to be approved and when things go wrong; in between, banks accumulate information (that is, *selective intervention*). In comparison, the equity financial intermediaries discussed above usually have limited capacity to mobilize financial resources, and at the same time they may not refrain from *constant intervention* on a daily basis, which is likely if they are transformed from the former industrial ministries. Perhaps no single group will become the dominant institution in corporate governance in China; instead, some kind of "shared governance" may arise in which banks play an important role as the counterbalance to the inside-managers in enterprises on the one hand, and as the check on a possible abuse of power by holding companies on the other.

The postwar Japanese experience with corporate governance led by main banks illustrates such a possibility (Aoki 1994). Unlike corporate governance with only equity investors or diffused creditors, such as bondholders or arm's-length commercial banks, the Japanese main banks play an active role in corporate governance. First, the syndicated monitoring led by main banks at the times of *ex ante*, *interim*, and *ex post* is more effective in disciplining enterprise managers. Second, the syndicated monitoring also saves scarce monitoring resources. Third, the "contingent control" mechanism underlying bank loans features no external intervention from the bank during the normal states of enterprise operation (the insider control) and an automatic shift of control rights to the main bank during the bad states (the outsider control). This mechanism provides incentives for enterprise managers in normal times and facilitates restructuring by banks in bad times.

The process of enterprise financial restructuring usually provides a good opportunity for banks to engage in close relationships with the enterprises. In Japan, one historical reason for the rise of close bank-firm relationships has been the banks' active participation in the postwar reorganization of firms (see Hoshi, in this volume). Similarly, the development of a close relationship between banks and enterprises in China will likely depend on the following factors: the extent of banks' involvement in the process of dealing with bad debts; the way bad debts are absorbed by the banks; regulations on equity holdings by banks; the political power of the banks compared with the holding companies; and so forth.

Some Chinese economists are in favor of a Chinese-style main-bank system in which banks are allowed to hold some equity shares in enterprises and play major roles in corporate governance (Wu 1993). Because the adoption of a universal banking system in China is currently out of the question, the state banks in China opt for separating commercial and investment departments inside the banks, with the latter holding equity shares.

Nevertheless, a precondition for the banks to take major roles in corporate governance in China is that they must have the capability—and especially the incentives—to do so. This requires some fundamental reforms in the banking sector, the issue I will turn to next.

Needed Banking Reforms

Banking reform is complementary to enterprise reform, especially so in China's reform at this stage. Most people blame bad debts on SOEs. Of course, if enterprises perform well, there should be no bad debt problem in the first place. The causality could also be in the other direction, however: because the banking system fails in its role as an efficient allocator of financial resources and as the monitor of enterprises, the enterprises perform badly. This is a plausible linkage because the banking sector is far less market-oriented than all the other nonfinancial sectors. It is well known that the specialized banks are more subject to political control than industrial enterprises. Despite the diminishing role of planning in all other sectors amid the deepening of reforms, the central government recently increased administrative control over specialized banks, which in turn rely more on administrative means for allocating credits. This is partly the result of a general lack of economic instruments to achieve macroeconomic stability, but the recent tendency is also reinforced by two interrelated phenomena: interest rates fell far below the market equilibrium because of inflation and large financial resources flows outside state regulation were encouraged by the local governments, known as "raising capital in an unorganized way" (*luanjizi*). Clearly, the existing banking system in China is unable to perform the needed tasks in enterprise restructuring and to play a role in corporate governance. Banking reforms are especially needed in two areas: reforming incentives for the existing banks and the creation of new commercial banks.

Reforming Incentives for the Existing Banks

The recent experience in Eastern European countries has shown that privatization of state banks is much slower than privatization of nonfinancial firms. But even without privatization, state banks, after some restructuring, have shown some changed behavior—they have become more prudent in lending and have more incentives in monitoring restructuring of firms (Dittus 1993). This suggests that reforming incentives of the existing state banks without privatization offers promising possibilities.

After all, state banks are SOEs in the financial sector. Because of the special importance of the banking sector to the economy, banks in

China are generally placed outside the coverage of reform policies applied to nonfinancial enterprises, such as anti-trust regulation, entry of nonstate enterprises, and corporatization, to name but a few important ones. Lack of these reforms is certainly responsible for the failure in the banking sector. There are three immediate tasks needed in the reform of the existing state banks in order to improve banks' incentives: (a) removing all the policy loan obligations; (b) cleaning up the balance sheets; and (c) corporatizing state banks into joint-stock companies. Full commercialization of specialized banks can only be achieved after stopping policy loans, cleaning up the balance sheets, and corporatization.

First, removing policy loans from the portfolio of state banks addresses the flow problem that directly affects banks' current and future behavior and incentives. The problems with the policy loans have been long recognized. Since January 1994, three policy banks have been established that are supposed to take the responsibility for policy loans. Because each of the three policy banks has specific development missions, they are really development banks in infrastructure, export-import, and agriculture. Therefore they started to take away only loans for development purposes from the specialized banks and they are unable to remove *all* policy loans from the specialized banks. As a result, the remaining part of the policy loans (the hardcore of the problem) is still the responsibility of specialized banks—the flow problem continues.

Policy loans are really disguised fiscal subsidies to loss-making enterprises. These subsidies cannot be terminated immediately without mass layoffs and should be continued for some time. The key is to terminate them with a fixed timetable. State banks should not continue to assume fiscal responsibility. Hence, there is a need to let some other nonbank government agency deal with the problem and turn "policy loans" into explicit fiscal subsidies, as in some Eastern European countries.

Second, the scale of nonperforming debts in China is massive. If 20 to 30 percent of total outstanding loans are regarded as nonperforming, which is a reasonable estimate, bad debts would amount to 17 to 25 percent of GDP by the end of 1993, as the total outstanding loan to GDP ratio is 84 percent. This would translate into about 530–800 billion yuan (*A Statistical Survey of China*, 1994). Although this stock problem is, by-and-large, a result of the past problem, it nevertheless affects current incentives. On the one hand, with debt-overhang, banks have no incentives to restructure enterprises. On the other hand, unconditional and complete recapitalization of banks is also not desirable because burdens of the bad debts are completely removed from the enterprises and banks, and banks are underutilized in restructuring enterprises.

Therefore, a good method of recapitalization of banks should provide banks with incentives to restructure firms and should also be feasible in financial terms. Many Eastern European countries have opted to use government bonds to recapitalize banks; some of the recapitalizations are unconditional and others are conditional (Dittus 1993). In comparison, postwar Japan mainly relied on the stock market before it collapsed for the recapitalization of banks (Hoshi, in this volume). Given the scale of the problem, the nascent stock market, as well as the limited capacity of issuing government bonds, China can adopt a partial recapitalization scheme that combines government bonds with the stocks.

Third, in conjunction with removing policy loans and cleaning up the balance sheets, a critical step in the conversion of specialized banks into commercial banks is corporatization. Corporatization is important even without privatization, as we have argued in the context of enterprise reform. After corporatization, the bank can still be initially fully state-owned, with several different state agencies holding shares. In Shenzhen Special Economic Zones, some joint-stock banks (with all shares held by the state agencies) have much a lower incidence of nonperforming loans compared with state specialized banks. This provides some evidence of the benefits of corporatization. Corporatization of banks also enables the banks to issue new shares in the stock market for recapitalization purposes.

Creation of New Commercial Banks

Reforming existing specialized banks is certainly important, but it is likely to be very difficult. Therefore, the banking reform should include a concurrent plan for allowing entry of new commercial banks.[14] There are several advantages to creating new commercial banks. New banks have fresh ownership and governance structures to start with; they have no bad debt problems, which plague the existing banks; they will not have policy loan obligations; and they have to compete with the existing banks for growth. The reform experience of the past fifteen years in the industrial sector has provided relevant lessons in this regard: how difficult it is to reform the existing enterprises, and how important and valuable it is for the new entry of the nonstate enterprises in both outputs produced and competition pressure so generated for the state sector. The value of the new commercial banks will be similar, coming also from competition pressure on the existing banks. Competition is crucial for providing banks with incentives for monitoring enterprise performance and playing an active role in corporate governance.

To date, China has four specialized banks that dominate the market. Although there were encouraging signs recently for allowing foreign banks to open their branches in China or form joint ventures with the Chinese, the process is likely to be slow and restricted. The process of entry of new banks could be vastly improved if China created new regional commercial banks sponsored mainly by provincial governments. These banks are not private banks to start with, so there should be no political difficulties. Local governments should also be enthusiastic.

One practical method to establish new regional-based commercial banks is to convert the existing branch facilities of the central bank at the county and municipal levels (Qian, forthcoming). China's central bank has branches all the way down to the county level and employs more than 170,000. When the central bank is downsized, the lower-level branches at the city and county levels will be abolished and the personnel and branch facilities will be released. Then transprovince regional commercial banks could be created, each encompassing three to four provinces. These regional commercial banks will be joint-stock companies with shares held by the concerned provinces (with no single province having a controlling share to prevent a single province from

14. Creation of new private banks is emphasized in Eastern Europe and Russia (Phelps, Frydman, Rapaczynski, and Shleifer 1993).

monopolizing the market), and possibly with minority shares held by the central government. Of course the ownership structure will evolve, possibly involving foreign or private partners in the future.

In addition to the advantage of making the best use of the existing branches and personnel, which could reduce the cost of reemployment of the redundant central bank employees, another important advantage of the scheme is to gain political support from local governments for reorganization of the central bank. China's past experience has shown that local government's influence on the central bank branches is the major reason for monetary instability. The proposed transprovince central bank reorganization (Qian, forthcoming) intends to centralize monetary policy and to dramatically reduce local influence by eliminating province-based branches. Obviously, this reorganization will meet with strong local resistance. If the central government implements the central bank reorganization plan together with creation of new regional commercial banks, the local resistance will diminish substantially.

The third advantage is that the new banks will serve to channel local financial resources in a more organized way. One problem with the current banking system is that local enterprises are reluctant to use state banks for fear of state credit quotas and administrative controls from the central government. Regional commercial banks, when properly regulated, will be more effective in mobilizing financial resources, in part because they are supported by local governments and in part because they are legal entities.

Finally, with the establishment of a dozen or so new commercial banks at one stroke, a competitive banking environment could be formed quickly. The national commercial banks have to face competition from regional commercial banks, and vice versa. Of course, we can foresee possible protectionism arising—for example, local governments may use administrative means to force local enterprises to deposit in their banks and to restrict lending activities. These are natural incentives from the local governments; the role of central government is to prevent such practices on the one hand and to encourage competition by allowing entry on the other. Realization of the advantages of competition depends on proper regulations. Overregulation, however, may become self-defeating if the regulation prevents healthy competition between national and regional commercial banks, and between state banks and nonstate banks. Therefore, the design of regulation in areas such as branch opening, bond issuing capacity, and lending restrictions should be carefully studied.

Concluding Remarks

Since January 1994, China has proceeded successfully in tax, fiscal, and foreign exchange reforms in its second stage of economic reforms. It is now time for China to concentrate on the most difficult part of all: enterprise reform and financial and banking reform. In this respect, reforming corporate governance and finance forms the key linkage between the two reforms.

Given the huge size of the country and the varying institutional and political constraints facing different sectors of China, reforming corporate governance and finance should not follow a single model. Even within the state sector, there could be a variety of approaches. Unlike some other reforms in aspects of macroeconomic management control (such as the fiscal and financial control) where externality is strong, enterprise reforms are necessary for a wide range of experiments. In property rights and enterprise reforms, China needs *diversity*. In this sense, the most dangerous reform strategy is to insist on a single organizational model for all enterprises in the country.

Bibliography

Aoki, Masahiko. 1990. "Toward an Economic Model of the Japanese Firm." *Journal of Economic Literature* 28:1–27.

———. 1994. "Monitoring Characteristics of the Main Bank System." In Masahiko Aoki and Hugh Patrick, eds., *The Japanese Main Bank System: Its Relevance for Developing and Transforming Economies*. New York: Oxford University Press.

Che, Jiahua, and Yingyi Qian. 1994. "Understanding China's Township-Village Enterprises." Stanford University. Mimeo.

China, State Statistical Bureau. 1994. *A Statistical Survey of China 1994*. Beijing: China Statistical Press.

———— . Various years. *Statistical Yearbook of China*. Beijing: China Statistical Press.

Dittus, Peter. 1993. "Corporate Governance in Central Europe: The Role of Banks." Monetary and Economic Department, Bank for International Settlements, Basle.

Frydman, Roman, Andrzej Rapaczynski, John Earle, and Joel Turkewitz. 1994. "Eastern European Experience with Small-Scale Privatization." CFS Discussion Paper Series 104, World Bank, Washington, D.C.

Granick, David. 1990. *Chinese State Enterprises: A Regional Property Rights Analysis*. Chicago, Ill.: University of Chicago Press.

Groves, Theodore, Yongmiao Hong, John McMillan, and Barry Naughton. Forthcoming. "Autonomy and Incentives in China's State Enterprises." *Quarterly Journal of Economics*.

Hart, Oliver, and Bengt Holmstrom. 1987. "The Theory of Contract." In Truman Bewley, ed., *Advances in Economic Theory—Fifth World Congress*. Cambridge, U.K.: Cambridge University Press.

Jefferson, Gary, and Thomas Rawski. 1994. "Enterprise Reform in China's Industry." *Journal of Economic Perspectives*, Spring.

Kornai, Janos. 1992. *The Socialist System*. New York: Oxford University Press and Princeton University Press.

Lipton, David, and Jeffery Sachs. 1990. "Privatization in Eastern Europe: The Case of Poland." *Brookings Papers on Economic Activity* 2: 293–341.

Milgrom, Paul, and John Roberts. 1992. *Economics, Organization and Management*. Englewood Cliffs, N.J.: Prentice-Hall.

Nee, Victor, and Sijin Su. 1993. "Local Corporatism and Informal Privatization in China's Market Transition." Cornell University. Mimeo.

Phelps, Edmund S., Roman Frydman, Andrzej Rapaczynski, and Andrei Shleifer. 1993. "Needed Mechanisms of Corporate Governance and Finance in Eastern Europe." Working Paper No. 1, European Bank for Reconstruction and Development, London.

Qian, Yingyi. 1994. "Financial System Reform in China: Lessons from Japan's Main Bank System." In Masahiko Aoki and Hugh Patrick, eds., *The Japanese Main Bank System: Its Relevance for Developing and Transforming Economies*. New York: Oxford University Press.

Qian, Yingyi, and Joseph Stiglitz. Forthcoming. "Institutional Innovations and the Role of Local Government in Transition Economies: The Case of Guangdong Province of China." In John McMillan and Barry Naughton, eds., *Reforming Asian Socialism: Evolving Market Institutions*. Ann Arbor: University of Michigan Press.

Shleifer, Andrei, and Maxim Boycko. 1993. "The Politics of Russian Privatization." In Olivier Blanchard and others, eds., *Post Communist Reform: Pain and Progress*. Cambridge, Mass.: MIT Press.

Shleifer, Andrei, and Robert Vishny. 1994. "Politicians and Firms." Harvard University. Mimeo.

Stark, David. 1993. "Recombinant Property in East European Capitalism." Cornell University. Mimeo.

Voszka, Eva. 1993. "Spontaneous Privatization in Hungary." In John Earle, Roman Frydman, and Andrzej Rapaczynski, eds., *Privatization in the Transition to Market Economies*. New York: St. Martins.

Wu, Jinglian, and others. 1993. "Qiye yu Yinhang Guanxi de Chongjian" (Reconstruction of the Relationship between Banks and Enterprises). *Reform* 6.

Xie, Ping, and others. 1992. *Zhongguo de Jinrong Shenhua yu Jinrong Gaige* (Financial Deepening and Financial Reform in China). Tianjin: Tianjin People's Press.

8

Centralized Decentralization: Corporate Governance in the German Economic Transition

Ernst-Ludwig von Thadden

Following its integration into the political and economic system of the former Federal Republic of Germany (West Germany), the transition of the former German Democratic Republic (East Germany) to a private-ownership economy has been markedly different from the transition experiences of other economies. Therefore, most comparative studies of monetary, fiscal, or trade policy in economic transition do not include East Germany. The same is true with respect to enterprise reform and corporate governance,[1] although it is repeatedly emphasized that, as far as established corporate governance structures are concerned,"German and Japanese models may offer some clues" (Gray and Hanson 1993). Yet, although the corporate governance structures in the East German transition have been quite different from the established

I am grateful to Christian Hoßbach of the Treuhandanstalt and Siegfried Hornich of Verlag Die Wirtschaft for support, and to Masahiko Aoki, Theodor Baums, Martin Hellwig, Hideaki Miyajima, Gerhard Pohl, Gérard Roland for helpful comments.

1. See, for example, Dittus 1994; Gray and Hanson 1993; Phelps, Frydman, Rapaczynski, and Shleifer 1993; or van Wijnbergen 1993. A notable exception is Carlin and Mayer 1992.

structures in West Germany, they offer some interesting insights into the problem of enterprise reform. This chapter describes and analyzes these transitional governance structures.

The transformation of the East German corporate sector started from conditions that differed in many respects from those in the rest of Eastern Europe. West Germany was ready to provide huge amounts of physical as well as human capital and a set of established and highly refined institutions and regulations. Furthermore, the corporate and financial structures to emerge from the transition process were to some extent predetermined by the existing West German models. Yet, the basic problems for the transition were the same as those faced throughout Eastern Europe and Russia: "enterprise reform, which requires the imposition of bottom-line discipline, definition and change of ownership, and reform of management" (Fischer and Gelb 1991). The experience in most Eastern European countries during economic liberalization, most notably in Russia and Poland, has shown that these problems are especially difficult for larger corporations,[2] where insider interest groups and the size of the firms have prevented the effective transfer of control and the implementation of a hard budget constraint (Kornai 1979).[3] For these larger firms, the problem of "controlling the insider control" (Aoki, in this volume) has become a crucial issue in the transformation process.

As analyzed in detail below, the East German transformation experience has been quite different in this respect. After an initial period of uncertainty and experimentation, accompanied also by attempts at asset stripping and "self-privatization" on the side of the firms, a strong, centralized public trust company was built up, which owned all formerly state-owned firms and over a period of four years restructured and sold them off. I will argue in more detail below that, taking into account the enormous amount of resources available from the West, privatization has been relatively slow in its early phase, and that after the

2. See, for example, Berg 1993; Litwack, in this volume; and Boycko, Shleifer, and Vishny 1993. An interesting review of empirical evidence and some recent theories is given by Aghion and Carlin 1994.
3. According to Berg 1993, Poland loses firms "in the 'Bermuda Triangle' of management, the Workers' Council and the unions."

initial investment in organizational structure, corporate control exercised by the trust company has been strong. The transformation process has produced a corporate structure in which almost all big firms have been broken up or liquidated, top managements exchanged, and large parts of the work force dismissed. Insider control has been largely dismantled, and the industrial structure has changed drastically. The privatization process has completely changed the problem of corporate control by virtually eliminating all large, independently owned companies (see section entitled "Decentralized Ownership: Postprivatization").

On a macroeconomic level, this transition is comparable to the workings of the takeover mechanism in the theory of the "market for corporate control," as developed by Manne (1965), Jensen and Ruback (1983), and others, where the individual firm is the focus. "When a breakdown of the internal control system imposes large costs on shareholders from incompetent, lazy, or dishonest managers, takeover bids in the market for corporate control provide a vehicle for replacing the entire internal control system" (Jensen and Ruback 1983, p. 44). During this process, a "raider" concentrates the shareholding of the company in one hand by buying out small shareholders, undertakes the restructuring deemed profitable, and sells out again to diversify his risk. Although in some respects this analogy is inappropriate for the observed macroeconomic process,[4] it correctly captures the feature of successive centralization and decentralization in the transformation of corporate East Germany.

In competitive capital markets, market conditions and the endowment and management abilities of the raider determine how long the raider will keep the acquired company under his control and what restructuring will be undertaken. In the transitional context, a government-owned trust company has different incentives. In particular, prof-

4. The process is described in more detail in the following two sections. Yet it is certainly true that the breakdown of the economic system of East Germany before November 1989 imposed high costs on the population, that the overthrow of the system was triggered by the population (through the mass exodus in September–October 1989 and the peaceful revolution in November 1989), and that the compensation was considerable (several hundred billion dollars within a decade—the estimates vary).

itability is not the sole criterion that determines how the trustee exercises control. Just as government regulatory agencies can be "captured" by the firms they are supposed to regulate (see Stigler 1971 and Laffont and Tirole 1993), a privatization agency is likely to be captured by the interest groups under its supervision.

The institutional development in the East German privatization process exhibits two highly complementary features, which, I will argue, can be interpreted as responses to this problem. First, the public trust company was designed to be in an institution with a fixed, finite lifetime, so that expected rents from long-term collusion between the agency and its environment were limited.[5] Second, the agency was given a high degree of independence from government and parliament, limiting the pressure from public interest groups. ("External Control of the THA," below, describes these features in some detail and provides a preliminary assessment.)

This chapter is organized as follows. The next section gives a brief survey of the evolution of the corporate sector in East Germany before 1989. The third section sketches the economic development after the fall of the Berlin Wall. The fourth section analyzes in detail corporate governance issues during the transformation process, and is followed by a description of the external control mechanisms of the privatization agency. The sixth section describes the pattern that emerges from the transition. The final section offers some interpretations and an assessment of the relevance of the East German experience for other transforming economies.

Some Determinants of Economic Structure before 1989

Soon after the four zones in occupied Germany had been established, large-scale nationalization of private property began in the Soviet Zone in 1945. In 1947, the land reform, which nationalized all land holdings

---

5. Historically, the original law enacting the institution did not set a time limit; the consensus emerged in the subsequent legislative process. See "External Control of the THA," below.

above 100 hectares, was largely completed. From 1946 on, all companies owned by former war and Nazi criminals and almost all larger companies were transformed into "people-owned businesses" (*volkseigene Betriebe*, VEBS). As a result, a three-tier pattern of state ownership of industry emerged: 1,631 firms with 580,000 employees came under the control of the "Deutsche Wirtschaftskommision" (central government control), 3,064 firms with 220,000 employees came under Länder (state) control, and 2,064 smaller firms were under community control.

On October 7, 1949, the constitution of the GDR (*Deutsche Demokratische Republik*) came into force, in 1950 the first five-year plan was adopted, and in 1951 the ruling Socialist Party declared the building of socialism the goal of the new state. Still, in 1955 more than 44 percent of the gross national product of the GDR was produced by small and medium-size private companies (THA 1993a).

From 1966 on, centralized planning and economic concentration were intensified through the creation of large conglomerates, the *Kombinate*. The largest *Kombinate* were directly subordinated to one of the planning ministries, and the smaller ones were usually overseen by local authorities, in particular the district governments (see figure 8-1). In 1972 the remaining private companies (approximately 11,000) were nationalized, and in 1986 the Eleventh Party Congress declared the *Kombinate* to be the backbone of the centrally planned economy.

Inside the *Kombinate*, the businesses were usually grouped around one core company that had economic and political control and whose top management was controlled by party officials. Among the *Kombinate*, by far most important were the 152 centrally controlled *Kombinate* of industry and construction. By June 30, 1990, there were approximately 2,450 VEBs employing a total of about 2.7 million people; only 17 of these *Kombinate* had less than 5,000 employees, and 48 had more than 20,000.[6] All 430 *Kombinate* taken together accounted for 90 percent of total employment in industry and 72 percent in construction.

6. The data are based on the *Statistical Register of Business of the GDR* as of June 30, 1990, provided by Die Wirtschaft 1993; 2.7 million represented approximately 30 percent of the total workforce of the GDR at that time.

Figure 8-1. Socialist Governance

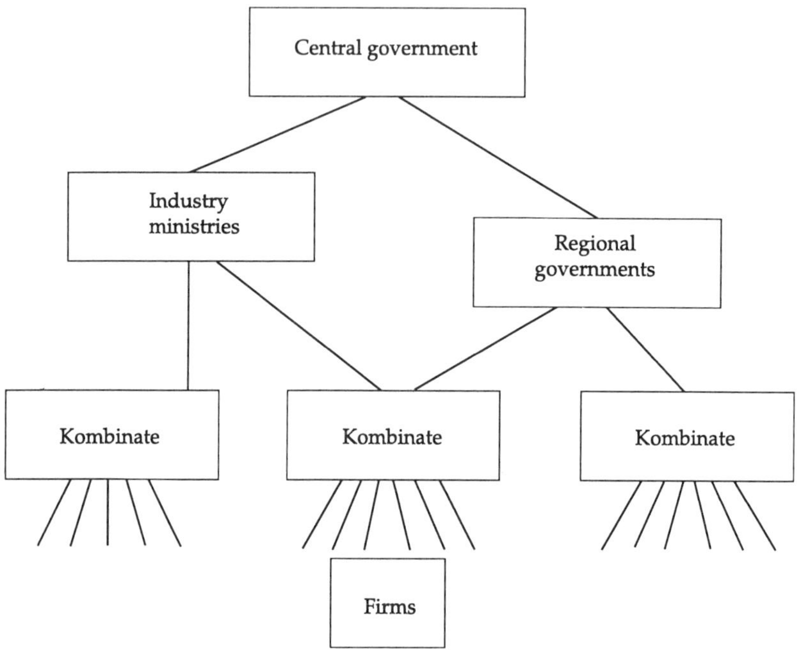

Historically the emergence of the *Kombinate* coincided with the wave of conglomerate mergers in the Western world, in particular the United States, at the end of the 1960s (cf., for example, Scherer 1988). Yet, while many of those mergers were subsequently undone, the trend in the GDR led to ever-increasing integration. The degree of vertical integration of the *Kombinate* was significantly higher than in Western companies. For example, the "IFA-Kombinat Pkw Karl-Marx-Stadt," responsible for the production of automobiles, produced about 80 percent of the value of their cars within the *Kombinat*, including machine tools and metals (von Schleinitz 1993); the corresponding value for Toyota in the late 1980s was 27 percent (Womack, Jones, and Roos 1991, p. 155).

The *Kombinate* were also usually excessively horizontally integrated. This was mainly because of politically motivated merger decisions, but also because of the desire to be autarkic within the *Kombinat* ("an economy within the economy") and government regulations that prescribed the provision of certain services by the *Kombinate*. Reflecting the excessive degree of horizontal integration, most *Kombinate* were also highly dispersed geographically.[7]

While excessive integration was a common phenomenon in all Eastern European economies, the emphasis on vertical integration was particularly strong in the GDR. Similarly problematic was the industry structure that had been developed under central planning. As documented by Sinn and Sinn (1993, pp. 52–53), 9.9 percent of the labor force of the GDR were employed in agriculture, compared with 4.2 percent in the West, and 34.1 percent in manufacturing (29.7 percent in the West). Trade and services employed only 19 percent of the Eastern work force, as compared with 37.4 percent in the West.

Political and Economic Development after 1989

On November 9, 1989, the Berlin Wall fell, and on October 3, 1990, the GDR ceased to exist, joining the Federal Republic of Germany in the form of five new states and East Berlin.[8] In the less than eleven months between these dates, the GDR had two governments—a reform-socialist one, trying to preserve as much of the old order as possible by modifying it, and, after March 18, 1990, a freely elected conservative government that paved the way for reunification as efficiently as possible.

By January 1990 it had become clear to most participants in the political decision process that drastic measures were necessary to pre-

7. For example, the "Kombinat Haushaltsgeräte Karl-Marx-Stadt" consisted of 29 businesses with 217 production units in 118 districts (Hornich 1993).

8. An excellent account of the economic and political development from 1989 to 1992 and its problems is given by Sinn and Sinn 1993. The standard reference on most legal, economic, and institutional aspects of the workings of the Treuhandanstalt is Fischer, Hax, and Schneider 1993.

vent the economic collapse of the GDR, and that in this process the traditional model of full state-ownership of the means of production was no longer tenable. On March 1, the government passed the "conversion decree," which stipulated that each business had to be converted into a joint stock company (*Aktiengesellschaft*) or limited liability company (*GmbH*) according to West German law. Furthermore, the foundation of a public "trust institution" (*Treuhandanstalt*) was announced, which was to take over all previously state-owned enterprises.

Although impeded by a plethora of technical and institutional problems, this decree triggered a wave of spontaneous corporate reorganizations. By the end of June, 3,605 former VEBs incorporated themselves, and more than 200 *Kombinate* were dissolved (von Gusinski 1993). The powerful need to break free of the old *Kombinate* was occasionally supplemented by strategies to create joint structures, born out of the hope of exploiting scale economies or obtaining greater bargaining power with potential investors or the government.

Parallel to this flurry of reorganizations, the law of March 7 concerning the reprivatization of companies that had been nationalized in 1972 initiated a first wave of reprivatizations. By the end of September, almost 3,000 small and medium-size companies were transferred back to their previous owners (THA 1993c).

After the elections of March 18, the movement toward a market economy, and finally toward economic unification with the West, became irresistible. On June 17, the government passed the "Treuhand Act," which stipulated that every VEB not yet incorporated was declared to be so by July 1. More important, the *Treuhandanstalt* (henceforth, THA) was given the explicit task of privatizing the people-owned property. The main purpose of the law was "to reduce, by means of privatization, the entrepreneurial activity of the state as fast and as far as possible."[9] The THA was to be incorporated as a public institution according to West German law and designed, in a decentralized fashion, as a holding company with several independent subsidiaries.

On July 1, the Treaty on Currency, Economic, and Social Union (CESU) between the two parts of Germany came into force. Under the

9. Gesetzblatt der DDR I, S. 300.

terms of the treaty, the GDR adopted most of the economic and social legislation of West Germany, as well as accepting the DM as its currency. Except for limited amounts of personal wealth, the exchange rate between the East German mark and the deutsche mark was set at 2:1. Because this rate also applied to corporate balance sheets, East German firms found themselves indebted by approximately DM 130 billion overnight.[10] From July to September alone, the THA guaranteed DM 25.4 billion of liquidity credits from Western banks to prevent the immediate bankruptcy of East German firms.

As of July 1, the THA owned approximately 8,500 firms with 4.1 million employees.[11] From September on, the new President, D. Rohwedder (formerly CEO of Hoesch AG, Dortmund), determinedly transformed the THA into a large organization with a hierarchical central structure and well-defined decentralized competencies. Under the new structure, the center in Berlin was to be directly in charge of all firms with more than 1,500 employees, and the 15 regional branches would oversee the remaining firms (see figure 8-2). On the day after German unification, on October 3, all 15 heads of the regional branches were replaced by Western managers, and in the following days the East German managers in the THA's supervisory board were dismissed.

The tightening of control allowed the THA to interfere effectively with early attempts at asset stripping and self-privatization, which plague the transition process in many other Eastern European countries (see, for example, Phelps and others 1993) and had begun to develop in 1990 in East Germany.[12]

---

10. Sinn and Sinn (1993, p. 276) report total debt of GDR firms with the central bank in 1989 of 260.4 billion East German marks. The opening balance sheet of the THA (THA 1992, p. 17) as of July 1, 1990, reports total liabilities of THA firms with credit institutions of DM 104 billion.

11. Some authors put the initial number of THA firms at 8,000. The figure here is from THA (1993a). To put the employment figure into perspective, total employment in East Germany in the third quarter of 1990, was 8.8 million (Statistiches Bundesamt 1991).

12. The most famous example is the attempted self-privatization of the former state monopoly hotel group, Interhotel. This case played an important part in the resignation of the first THA president. For other instances, see the case studies compiled by Die Wirtschaft (1993).

Figure 8-2. Treuhand Governance

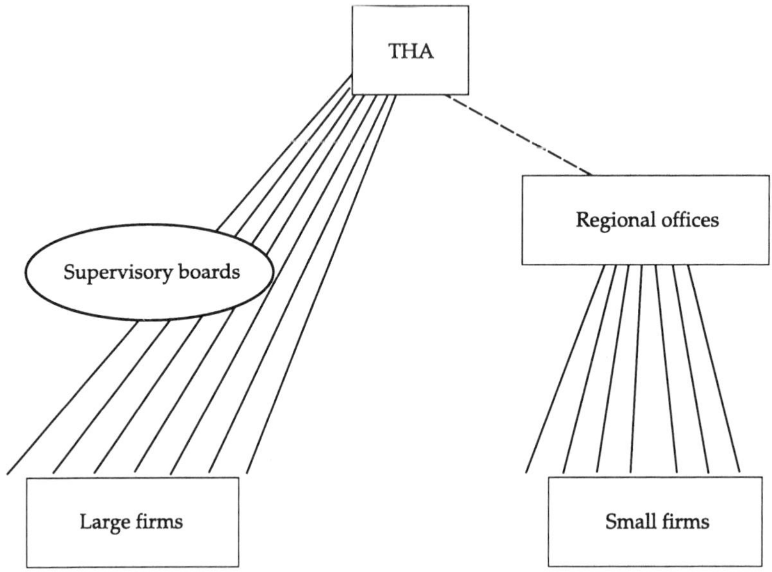

As a basis for its future operations, the THA requested its firms to provide opening balance sheets (*Eröffnungsbilanzen*) by October 30, 1990, a deadline that soon had to be extended to June 30, 1990, and to January 31, 1992, for conglomerates. The opening balance sheets had to be accompanied by a three-year corporate strategy and were evaluated by THA managers (volumes up to DM 10 million) and a "governance committee" (*Leitungsausschuß*), a group of up to eighty top West German managers assembled by the Ministry of Finance (see THA 1993a, p. 22). This evaluation determined which firms were to be liquidated if no buyers could be found, and which could be restructured.[13] During the subsequent process of breaking up the *Kombinate*, the THA was assigned far-reaching competencies by the so-called "Splitting Act" (*Spaltungsgesetz*) of May 4, 1991, a law that facilitated the split of Treuhand companies into marketable units.

13. In September 1991, a preliminary analysis of the available evaluations found approximately 70 percent of the THA firms to be viable (*Treuhand Informationen* 1991).

The consolidation of the THA's structure and the preparation of the opening balance sheets proved to be time-consuming. By March 31, 1991, the THA had sold or reduced its interest to a minority stake in 1,378 firms, about 15 percent of its total stock at the time. By May 1991, only 6 percent of all balance sheets had been evaluated (Sinn and Sinn 1993). Sales in this early phase were often impeded by organizational problems on the side of the THA and driven by the prospect of potential bargains for the buyers. This early stage of privatization certainly was considered to be a buyers' market.[14] The THA finalized its opening balance sheet—which valued its net corporate holdings as of July 1, 1990 at –DM 179 billion—only on September 29, 1992.[15]

By this time, the East German economy had experienced a depression "without precedence in modern economic history" (Sinn and Sinn 1993, p. 35). Between early 1990 and the end of 1991, gross domestic product (GDP) fell by 35 percent.[16] Employment fell on a similarly dramatic scale. Between the first half of 1990 and the second half of 1993, when the transitional depression seemed to have reached its bottom, employment in East Germany dropped from around 9.3 million to 6.3 million.[17]

By early summer of 1991, the THA had largely consolidated its structure. It had increased the number of its employees by more than 500 percent between June 1990 and June 1991 (see figure 8-3)—a num-

---

14. "Well-informed buyers, who were interested in specific parts of the Kombinate . . . could buy at favorable terms during this period" (Müller 1993). For a description of the state of East German firms and the difficulties faced by prospective investors, see also Albach 1992.

15. Carlin and Mayer (1992) rightly emphasize that most of this debt is completely unrelated to the THA's restructuring and privatization tasks—in particular, the large financial and environmental liabilities the THA had been forced to take on.

16. The measurement of GDP in the GDR is subject to well-known difficulties with data of Eastern Block countries. The figure reported here is the estimate by Sinn and Sinn (1993).

17. Officially, in the second half of 1993 unemployment in East Germany was 1.2 million. The difference is explained by the 0.6 million in publicly funded employment or qualification programs, 0.8 million in early retirement, and 0.35 million commuters to West Germany (Statistisches Bundesamt 1994).

Figure 8-3. Employment Treuhandanstalt

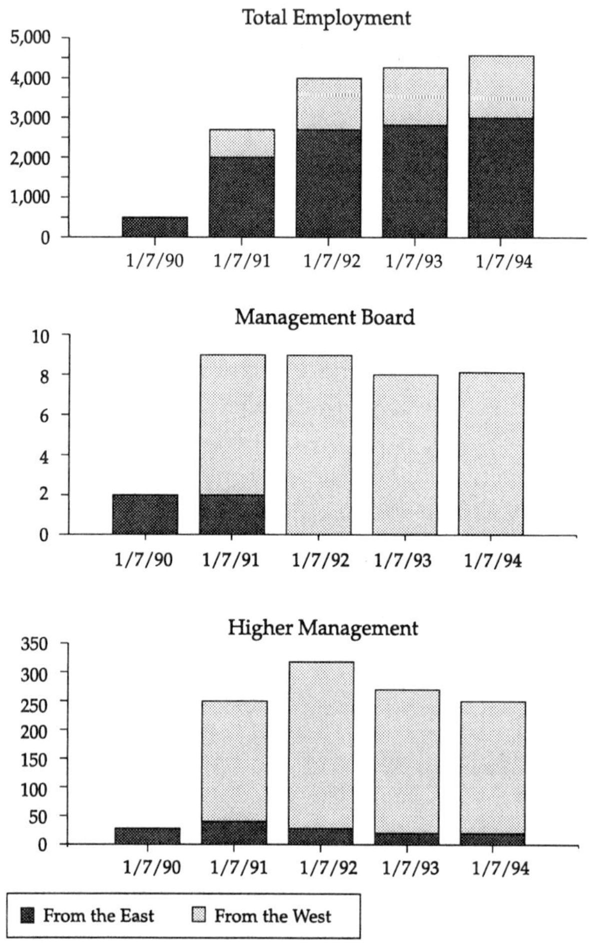

Note: East: Five new federal states plus East Berlin. West: Old federal states and abroad.

Source: Treuhandanstalt; Müller 1993; author's calculations.

ber that does not even count the replacements of East Germans by West Germans—it had created 455 supervisory boards for its larger firms, and it had completed large parts of the so-called "small privatization," that is, the sale of retail stores, pharmacies, and the like. The structure and activity of the THA will be analyzed in more detail in the following two sections.

By March 1993, the 232 *Kombinate* the Treuhand had owned in July 1990 were almost all split into smaller units, 44 of them were privatized and 72 were liquidated (see figure 8-4). As of March 31, 1994, the THA had sold or restituted to former owners 8,620 companies and 7,182 company parts, had liquidated or was in the process of liquidating 3,276 companies, and still owned 788 companies. By the end of 1994, the THA will cease to exist in its present form. It is estimated that approximately 100 of its firms will neither be sold nor liquidated by then. Too large to be liquidated, they will stay under public ownership, in the form of a limited liability holding company that will be 100 percent owned by the Ministry of Finance. The bulk of the THA's present administrative functions (contract monitoring, reprivatization, and so forth) will be continued until the end of 1996 by a federal agency under the authority of the Ministry of Finance. The THA's closing balance sheet, including provisions for future financial and environmental liabilities, is expected to show a deficit of –DM 275 billion.[18]

Centralized Ownership: The Treuhand

When the Treuhand Act assigned the THA the task of reducing the "entrepreneurial activity of the state as fast and as far as possible," it had approximately 440 employees; an improvised, mainly regional structure; no supervisory board; and a small management board, mainly staffed by government bureaucrats. Two weeks later, the supervisory board and the management board had been newly appointed.[19]

The THA's broad goals were defined by the Treuhand Act. Its two most important immediate strategic problems, however, were to re-

18. This figure includes provisions for future liabilities, for example, DM 20 billion for the cleanup and repair of nuclear sites and coal mines.
19. An excellent reference for the evolution of the THA's structure is Seibel 1993.

Figure 8-4. Breakup of the 232 Treuhand-*Kombinate*, March 1993

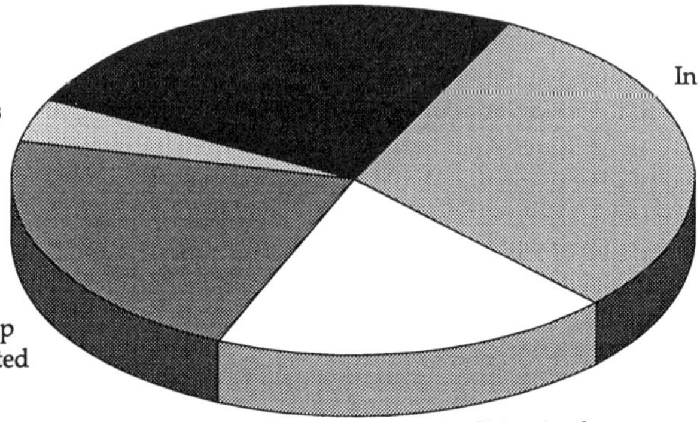

Source: Treuhandanstalt 1993b.

define its organizational form and the priorities in building up its new structure. On both issues, the management seemed to be indecisive, consumed by the magnitude of the daily problems. After five weeks in office, the new president had to step down and was replaced by the chairman of the supervisory board, D. Rohwedder, who subsequently implemented a structure that partly substantiated and partly contradicted the initial framework set by legislation.

The Treuhand Act had prescribed a decentralized structure, with several subholdings integrating the old industry ministries, next to regional agencies, all under the control of a weak center. Within days after taking office, Rohwedder announced that he would drop the concept of subholdings in favor of a more concentrated organizational form. Although formally in breach of the law,[20] the dynamics of the

20. The Treuhand Act stated: "The Treuhandanstalt realizes its tasks in a decentralized organisational structure through Treuhand sub-holdings" (Gesetzblatt der DDR I, S. 300). When asked about the legal implications of his concept, Rohwedder replied that "where there is no claimant there is no judge" (Handelsblatt August 27, 1990).

institutional development proved that, in this early phase of the transition, there was room for discretionary strategic choices.

The second important decision in the early phase of the THA was to place emphasis on the development of its internal organization. On the one hand, this emphasis is reflected in the enormous growth of the work force in the THA center (which grew from 123 to 1,564 within one year) and by the expansion of all levels of higher management, which grew from 24 in July 1990 to 250 in July 1991 (see figure 8-3). In contrast to the policy in its firms, where the THA used local management resources as much as possible,[21] the share of Westerners among higher-level managers in the THA increased from 0 to 91 percent between July 1990 and July 1991 (see figure 8-3), about three-quarters of whom came from the West German private sector.[22] Hence, a significant part of available human resources was invested in the THA rather than its firms.

On the other hand, at least as important in the structure were the considerable amount of time and resources invested in the search for the most appropriate organizational form of the THA center. While the center had initially—after the decision to drop the plans for decentralized organization—experimented with a strictly unitary organizational structure (see Williamson 1975), after several months it adopted a more sectoral structure that was reminiscent of the branch structure of the former industry ministries.[23]

In principle, the decision to invest heavily in the development of the center was contestable because the Treuhand Act had explicitly stated that privatization was to be undertaken as fast as possible. Yet, since the act had stated several potentially conflicting objectives, this choice of priorities was clearly defendable (for a discussion of legal issues, see Hommelhoff 1991). The relatively slow start of the privatization process, however, created another problem. The THA came

21. The share of Westerners on THA firm management boards rose from approximately 4 to 8 percent between July 1990 and July 1991 (Dyck 1992). See below.

22. Numbers are based on the preliminary evaluation of questionnaires reported in Czada 1993.

23. See Seibel 1993 for a more detailed account.

under increasing public pressure to undertake "regional structural policies" in spring 1991, when the East German economy began to collapse, and the overwhelming portion of the formerly state-owned firms were still under the control of the THA. Indeed, in March 1991, in a crisis consultation among the federal government, the heads of the new East German states, and the THA, the THA acknowledged its responsibility to cooperate in such policies.[24] It is difficult to speculate about possible THA policies in the absence of this agreement. But the division of roles between government and THA was so well defined by spring 1991, and privatization was pursued so energetically from spring onward, that it is unlikely that this agreement induced more than minor changes of THA strategy.

The THA's choice of its organizational strategy is quite clearly reflected in the time series of company sales, shown in figure 8-5. Within the first year of its existence, when it put emphasis on the development of its internal structure, the THA sold less than 20 percent of its firms. During the next eighteen months, using its increasing experience in marketing, information processing, and international relations, it sold another 38 percent of its stock at a relatively steady, fast pace. During the next year, when most of the obviously interesting companies had been sold, it still sold another 6.5 percent, and in its final year sold an estimated 4 percent.[25] The resulting graph has a slight *S*-form: relatively low sales initially; relatively high, steady sales in the middle period; and declining sales during an extended final period.

To put this graph into perspective, consider a hypothetical, alternative "fast" policy choice, under which the THA would have been smaller and less active.[26] Suppose that the THA had chosen to auction

---

24. "Principles of the Cooperation of Federal Government, New Federal States, and THA for the Recovery East" (Bundesregierung 1991).

25. These percentages refer to the number of businesses sold. Although "stock value" is difficult to define for East Germany, the number of transactions probably provides a better measure for the THA's activity than the value of transactions.

26. Some observers find that the THA accomplished most of its task "in the amazingly short span of four years" (*The Economist*, April 30, 1994). This cannot be debated. The question is whether, given the amazing amount of funds available, one could have amazed these observers even more.

Figure 8-5. Evolution of Treuhand Sales and Liquidations

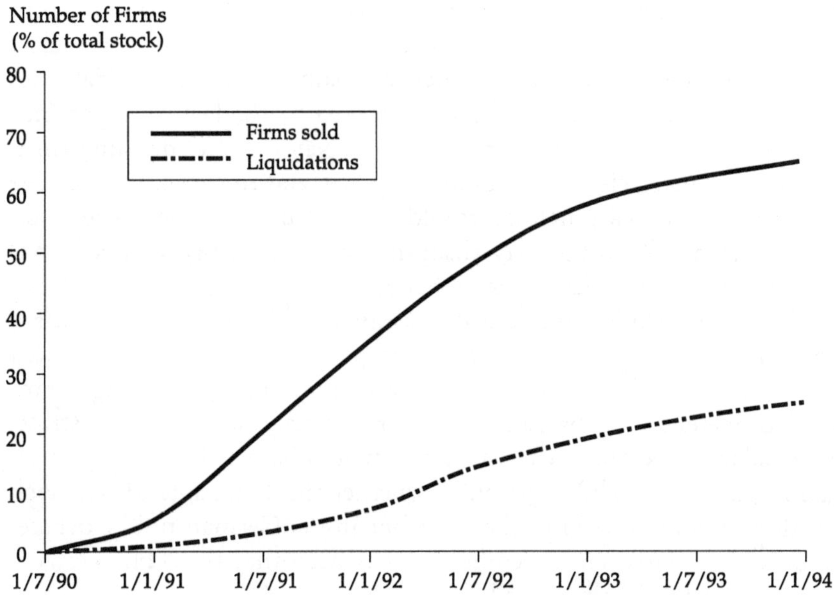

Note: "Firms sold": fully or majority privatized or transferred to local authorities; "liquidations": liquidation completed or in progress.
Source: Treuhandanstalt; author's calculations.

off its stock of firms rather than rely on extended bilateral negotiations,[27] break the stock-flow constraint of mass privatizations along the lines proposed by Sinn and Sinn (1993) and Bolton and Roland (1992), leave the restructuring of its firms entirely to their buyers, and establish its organizational structure with lower priority and on a lesser scale during the process.[28]

27. See Akerlof, Rose, Yellen, and Hessenius 1991 (section 5) for a discussion of possible employment consequences of such policies.
28. This policy would have been closer to the Czech and the attempted Polish mass privatization policies (Berg 1993; Carlin and Mayer 1992). Auctions, in particular, were used by the THA only twice and for a specific group of firms.

Such an approach, by all expectations, would have led to a much more strongly front-loaded evolution of sales. The most profitable purchases and the most favorable matches between buyers and sellers would have been undertaken quickly, resulting in high initial sales rates. This effect would have been reinforced by the lack of experience and internal control in the privatization agency.[29] At the same time, the exhaustion of clearly profitable matches and uncertainty over the value of the residual portfolio would have resulted in lower sales rates in the later phases of the privatization process, possibly with a higher overall share of liquidations at the end.

Whether such a front-loaded strategy would have been superior is a question beyond the scope of this chapter.[30] The point to be noted here is that the THA's actual strategy of building up a strong center with competence and bargaining power was only one of several strategies available, and that other strategies would have led to other privatization patterns.[31] The question of whether the THA sold off its stock too slowly has not been in the forefront in the German public debate. A more frequently voiced complaint has been that the THA restructured too little and privatized too fast.[32]

By all accounts, the THA was fully operative by the early summer of 1991. The remainder of this section will discuss in more detail the governance structure of the resulting organization. The question of

---

29. Even under the actual policy of the THA, these effects were quite visibly present in the time between July 1990 and summer 1991 (see the brief remarks in the section "Political and Economic Development after 1989," above). Some of the critical assessments of the THA's activity, such as Kampe 1993, emphasize such cases.

30. On the problem of the optimal speed of restructuring see Aghion and Carlin 1994.

31. One particular feature of the German privatization process, however, suggests that the THA's chosen strategy was superior in practice. The "Property Act" of September 23, 1990, imposed a general priority of restitution over compensation for most former owners of East German companies. In practice, this led to a significant delay in the privatization process, and this would have impeded any possible policy variant (see Bundeswirtschaftsministerium 1991; Sinn and Sinn 1993).

32. In view of the disastrous employment situation in East Germany, this is a predictable public reaction. For a more systematic argument, see Nolte 1993.

external control mechanisms of the THA will be taken up in the next section.

The organizational change initiated by the THA's president in August 1990 entailed a strengthening of central control, complemented by a well-defined element of regional decentralization. The resulting hierarchy was extremely flat (see figure 8-2). Treuhand firms with more than 1,500 employees (as of January 1, 1991) reported directly to the center, and most firms with fewer than 1,500 employees were administered by the THA's regional offices.[33] The regional offices had a high degree of autarky, with full financial responsibility for all decisions up to DM 30 million. Under this two-tier structure, full control over each firm generally rested either with the center or a regional office. In addition to this structure, the center established so-called task forces of outside consultants to provide the regional offices with expertise and regulatory know-how from the top and to facilitate the information flow from the regions back to the center.[34]

For firms controlled by the center, major questions concerning the survival and reorganization of the firm were decided directly by the THA's management board, and regular issues were dealt with by the "industry directorate" (*Branchendirektorat*) responsible for the respective firm. As of August 1991, there were twenty such directorates, designed along the standard industry classification standards, and three to five directorates reported to one member of the management board. As an additional layer of control below the center, larger firms were endowed with supervisory boards, which were usually grouped around a senior, sometimes retired, Western manager. Yet, in contrast to West German practice, supervisory boards of THA-owned firms often get actively involved in the restructuring process, contributing financial know-how, management experience, and contacts. Therefore, the controlling function of supervisory boards of THA firms is superseded, and to some extent reduced, by their consulting function.

It has been pointed out repeatedly by the THA, as well as by economic and political commentators, that the THA has neither the task

---

33. Of the total number of 10,344 THA firms of July 1, 1991, the center controlled 36 percent, and the regional offices 64 percent.

34. In practice, these flows were less than smooth because of agency problems in the relationship between task forces and regional offices.

nor the resources to restructure and run the operations of its firms.[35] It is clear, however, that because of the complexity of the firms' adjustment dynamics and the size of its holdings, efficiency considerations force any organization the size of the THA to limit the center's operational activities and to delegate authority down through the hierarchy.[36] The more interesting question is, given the THA's constraints and political task, to what extent its governance structure has been hierarchical and centralized.

In this respect, the principal yardstick to judge the THA's governance structure is the extent to which key decisions are taken by the center and how lower-level planning is controlled by the center. Here, I will use four criteria to evaluate this structure: the extent of company liquidations, the supervision of corporate planning, company breakups, and management turnover. According to these criteria, and given its socioeconomic environment, the THA's governance of larger firms[37] must be considered to be strongly centralized.

Under the THA's policy, the most important decision for each firm—liquidation or continuation—has rested with the center and has been reconsidered regularly. Figure 8-5 depicts the evolution of liquidations of THA firms through January 1, 1994. By summer 1994, one-quarter of all THA firms had been liquidated or were in liquidation. Compared with all other transitional economies, this is an extraordinarily large number.

Because the center judged less than 10 percent of its firms to be viable without much restructuring at the end of 1991,[38] the decision to

---

35. Many economic observers, free from political pressure, go even further. For example, Fischer, Hax, and Schneider (1993, p. 5) state that "the effective re-organization and rescue of thousands of companies cannot be initiated by a bureaucratic organization such as the Treuhandanstalt."

36. See Milgrom and Roberts 1992 for a detailed discussion of the principles of organization, and Aghion and Tirole 1994 for an analysis of different realizations of authority.

37. Recall the division of responsibilities between the center and regional offices described above.

38. As of December 31, 1991, for 1,536 center-controlled firms the evaluation of opening balance sheets found 9 percent to be viable without much restructuring and 18.2 percent to be absolutely unviable. The remaining 72.8 percent were judged to be more or less promising after restructuring (Gless and Schwalbach 1993).

continue usually implied the decision to restructure. The general stance of the THA toward restructuring firms has been described by the THA's vice president as follows: "We shall give the firms sufficient time, which we set individually. Firms that cannot be privatized for certain in the foreseeable future are looked after intensively . . . and controlled individually."[39] Accordingly, the THA's industry directorates are in regular contact with all firms under restructuring, control their quarterly reports, and evaluate their business concepts.[40] Although much of the operational part of the restructuring is delegated to external consultants, overall central planning and the threat of selective intervention impose tight restrictions on THA firms.[41]

Complementing the center's control of the operation of its companies, the 1991 Splitting Act facilitates the redesign of the corporate structure of the old state-owned firms. The act provides the THA with a relatively flexible and extensively used tool to split up companies and resize business structures according to its own or, prospective investors' concerns. As a result of this activity, the approximately 8,500 firms the THA owned on July 1, 1990, had become 23,188 units by March 1994, including reprivatized or spun-off business parts, but not counting formal dissolutions through mergers and splits. This figure actually underestimates the extent of corporate breakups under THA control, because it does not include the transfers of business parts with communal functions to local authorities. Conversely, an explicit aim of the THA's policy is to realize synergies between its firms, either by directly merging otherwise unviable units or by coordinating activities between firms (THA 1993a, p. 2).

Finally, consider the issue of management turnover. In the context of established stock market economies, corporate control has been defined as "the rights to hire, fire and set the compensation of top-level managers" (Jensen and Ruback 1983). While this is certainly too narrow

39. H. Brahms in *Treuhand Informationen* 17 (1992), p. 3.

40. For a more detailed description of the planning instruments used by the center, see THA 1993a (p. 2).

41. The following complaint by the head of the supervisory board of Takraf AG is typical for the control exercised by the THA: "We had to pre-plan the cost of material up to DM 5,000 for the next year. This makes entrepreneurial activity quite impossible" (*Wirtschaftswoche* 50, 1992, p. 198).

a definition for transitional economies, it still constitutes an important element of corporate control. Although the German Stock Company Act provides management of joint-stock companies—and hence many of the large THA firms—with a considerable degree of independence from their owners, the THA has used this control right very actively. Between September 1990 and July 1991 alone, the THA dismissed 1,400 top managers, 400 of them for political reasons (Fischer, Hax, and Schneider 1993, p. 554). Although many of the immediate problem cases were solved in this early phase, the THA maintained a policy of active managerial control. In 1992 the THA dismissed 500 top managers directly, and an additional 300 were replaced in companies with supervisory boards (THA 1993a, p. 24).

In the early period of management restructuring, a significant portion of managerial turnover was accomplished by internal succession. The longer the restructuring lasted, however, the greater became the need for Western management qualifications, particularly in strongly market-dependent areas such as finance and marketing. The THA's policy toward its management clearly reflects this need. While the share of Westerners on managing boards of THA firms—also because of the large number of firms—was still relatively low in July 1991 (8 percent), this share increased to approximately 30 percent by July 1992 (see Dyck 1992 for a comprehensive analysis).

External Control of the THA

From its creation under the socialist government of the GDR on, the THA had the legal status of a "federal agency" (*bundesunmittelbare—Anstalt des öffentlichen Rechts*). Although it was not entirely clear what this meant under the legal system of the GDR,[42] it gave the THA a high degree of formal independence in the administrative hierarchy of post-reunification Germany. It removed it from the direct control of the executive and put it in the same legal category as the Bundesbank and the Federal Employment Agency (*Bundesanstalt für Arbeit*). The THA operates largely independently of government orders, but is subject to legal supervision by the Ministry of Finance.[43] Schuppert (1992,

---

42. This kind of institution did not exist under East German law.

43. For details, see, for example, Kloepfer 1993.

p. 186) describes the THA as an "organization in the overlap of two legal domains" (that of public and private law). Therefore, control of the THA is effectively shared among the Ministry of Finance, the THA's supervisory board, the Federal Accounting Office (*Bundesrechnungshof*), and the Parliament, which I will briefly discuss in turn.

Until reunification, legal supervision of the THA was incumbent on the prime minister of the GDR. Since October 3, 1990, this task has resided with the Federal Ministry of Finance. As a consequence, the THA reports to the Ministry monthly and needs the Ministry's approval for its yearly budget. The Ministry's approval is also required if the THA wants to exceed its yearly credit limit of DM 30 billion (this figure has been increased from DM 25 billion in 1990 and 1991). Within this limit, the THA has direct and virtually unrestricted access to the credit market: the "Treuhand Credit Act" of July 1992 permits the THA to issue government-backed bonds up to this amount without the disclosure requirements imposed on other issuers.[44]

On the operational level, the Ministry must approve of all restructuring decisions involving volumes above DM 100 million.[45] In practice, the Ministry's role in controlling the THA can be considered to have been largely passive. A perceived lack of control of the THA led to the appointment of a special investigatory committee of Parliament in 1993. Here, for example, the vice president of the Federal Accounting Office accused the Ministry of "shortcomings" in its supervision of the THA.[46]

Reflecting the THA's hybrid legal status between public and private law, Ministry supervision is complemented by that of a supervisory board (*Verwaltungsrat*) modeled along the lines of corporation law.[47] The supervisory board appoints and dismisses the management board, must approve major management decisions, and advises the man-

---

44. In practice, the placement of THA bonds is undertaken in close cooperation with the Ministry of Finance and the Budesbank (THA 1993a, p. 28).
45. This is according to THA guidelines of August 1991. The figures have changed slightly since then (see Gless and Schwalbach 1993).
46. *Frankfurter Allgemeine Zeitung*, December 3, 1993.
47. For a brief description of the role of the supervisory board in German corporation law, including more extensive references, see Baums 1993.

agement. To this end, it is regularly informed by the management board and meets once a month.

In practice, the advisory function of the supervisory board has been at least as important as its control function.[48] The supervisory board is a way to institutionalize the exchange of information between the THA and different interest groups and to mediate between them. Figure 8-6 shows the composition of the supervisory board as appointed by the federal government by January 1, 1991. The regional interests (five of the twenty-two seats), expressed through the governments of the five East German states, and the trade unions (four seats) are both more strongly represented than the federal government. Dominant as a group are the employers (ten seats), with representatives from various industries (none yet from the banking sector).

On the operational level, the most effective control of the THA has probably been exterted by the Federal Accounting Office. The Federal Accounting Office examines all aspects of the THA's activity with respect to their financial correctness and economic responsibility on an ongoing basis. Its regular and special reports not only compile response information about mismanagement or fraud inside the THA, but also consider larger organizational issues. In particular, the proposed structure of the THA-successor institutions has been criticized extensively by the Federal Accounting Office on the grounds that it yielded too much to THA interests. The compromise that was agreed upon in May 1994 took these concerns fully into account.[49]

The role of Parliament in controlling the THA generally has been restricted to setting the legislative frame of THA activity and following this activity through a parliamentary committee. Given the high degree of formal independence of the THA, the Parliament has no legal authority over the THA's regular operations. Furthermore, in practice even the ex post control of the THA's activity through a special investigatory committee has turned out to be difficult. Backed by the government, the THA has been very reluctant to provide the informa-

---

48. Given the composition of the supervisory board, however, the dividing lines separating controlling, advising, and lobbying are not easy to draw.

49. See the interview with the office's president in *Frankfurter Allgemeine Zeitung*, May 17, 1994.

Figure 8-6. Composition of Treuhand Supervisory Board, January 1, 1991

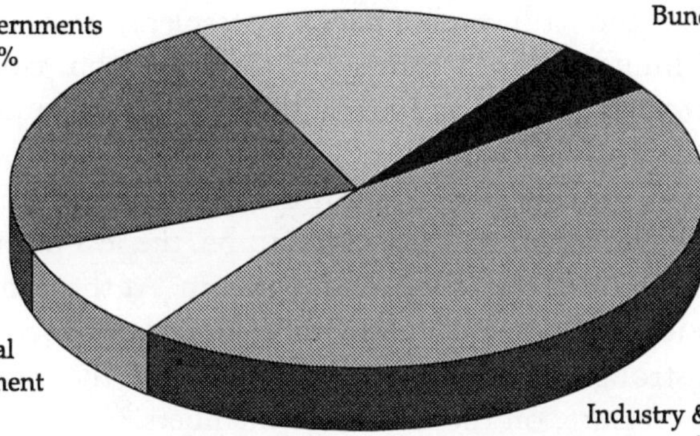

Source: Treuhandanstalt 1992.

tion the committee deemed necessary. In March 1994, members of the committee initiated a suit in the Constitutional Court to force the THA supervisory board to open its files to the committee.

The general picture that emerges from this analysis is one of almost complete operational independence and significant organizational freedom. Institutional independence has been an explicit goal of government policy toward the THA: "The THA can fulfill their tasks only if it can take the necessary decisions with great independence. . . I want to stress once more, and publicly stand up for it, that the Federal Government—and, most of all, I myself, as the chancellor of the Federal Republic of Germany—will do everything to guarantee this independence for the appropriate decisions" (Kohl 1992).

Hence, probably the most important control mechanism of the THA has been time. Although the Treuhand Act of June 1990 had not been specific about the timing of the THA's activity, a consensus soon emerged that the THA was to be an institution with a finite life. The Treuhand Credit Act of 1992 limited the THA's funding to the period of 1992–94. In May 1994, government and Parliament agreed on the institutional details that allow dissolution of the THA as planned at the end of 1994; a corresponding law was to be passed by Parliament in the summer of 1994. Although some THA activities—particularly contract management and the reorganization and sale of the remaining THA firms—will have to be continued for some years after 1994, this will be done by different agencies that will be directly subordinated to the Ministry of Finance.

In a first, and still preliminary, assessment, this institutional commitment limits the long-term gains available from collusion and lobbying of interest groups, and hence the "regulatory capture" of the institution (see Laffont and Tirole 1993). The less long-lasting the relationship between the privatization agency and its counterparts in business and administration is perceived to be, the less incentive there is to invest in mutually advantageous favoritism. At the same time, the longer an institution with such important distributional competencies operates, the stronger is the external pressure, and the temptation to yield to such pressure, on the side of its members.[50]

For such a commitment to terminate to be credible, it must be complemented by measures limiting the incentives for ex post renegotiation. In the case of the THA, career concerns and reputation seem to have played an important role in this respect. As Seibel (1993) has documented, much of the THA's top management below the board level has been in their late fifties and sixties, seeking a last challenge in their careers. For this group, the incentives for lobbying and influence activities (Milgrom 1988) to extend the life of the institution much beyond the planned duration seem to be naturally diminished.

For younger top managers, in particular some members of the board from West German industry, reputation seems to provide some incentives to accomplish the THA's task in time. Since the THA's overall task—to privatize "as fast and as far as possible"—has been clearly defined from the beginning, delays in the privatization process, and even more so an extended coexistence of the THA with its firms, would have a negative effect on the reputation of the THA's top management. The reaction of the THA's president to the draft bill enacting the THA's successor institutions has been very critical, on the grounds

50. An interesting empirical study by Czada (1993) substantiates this argument. For a sample of 165 higher-level managers of the THA, 58.8 percent stated that external influences on their activity had increased from 1991 to 1992; only 9.7 percent perceived decreasing external influences.

that the bill effectively prolongs the life of an institution that was designed to be transitional.

Decentralized Ownership: Postprivatization

For the problem of corporate governance, a decisive structural consequence of the transition process in East Germany has been the entailed decrease in firm size. As shown earlier, most of the employment in the GDR had been in the large *Kombinate*. By June 30, 1991, after the THA had become actively involved in the restructuring of the *Kombinate*, 72 percent of the approximately 2.2 million employees of THA-owned firms were employed in firms with more than 500 employees. By the end of 1993, however, more than 75 percent of employment in THA and ex-THA firms was in firms with fewer than 500 employees.[51]

This enormous leftward shift of the distribution of company size can largely be attributed to the restructuring activity of the THA, and in particular to its two policies of massive labor shedding and company splitting prior to privatization. The latter activity has been described above. With respect to the former, figure 8-7 provides quantitative evidence.

Between January 1, 1991, and December 31, 1993, THA firms lost between 40 and 50 percent of their total work force to unemployment, early retirement, publicly funded employment schemes, or withdrawal from the labor market.[52] During the first year of the privatization process, when the early bargains were made and the THA made little use of penalties in privatization contracts, buyers often reduced the work forces of the acquired firms substantially. Later, because of the drastic cuts by the THA prior to privatization, the new owners generally reduced employment only a little further and, in the longer run, more than met their contractually agreed upon employment targets.[53]

By March 31, 1994, with the breakup of the old firms largely completed (see "Political and Economic Development after 1989," above),

51. THA 1993b, 1994, *Monatsberichte.*

52. Nolte 1993 provides additional evidence and further references.

53. A first evaluation of contract fulfillment for 1991–92 (84 percent of all contracts) shows overfulfillment by 16 percent (THA 1994).

Figure 8-7. Evolution of Work Force of THA Firms, January 1, 1991

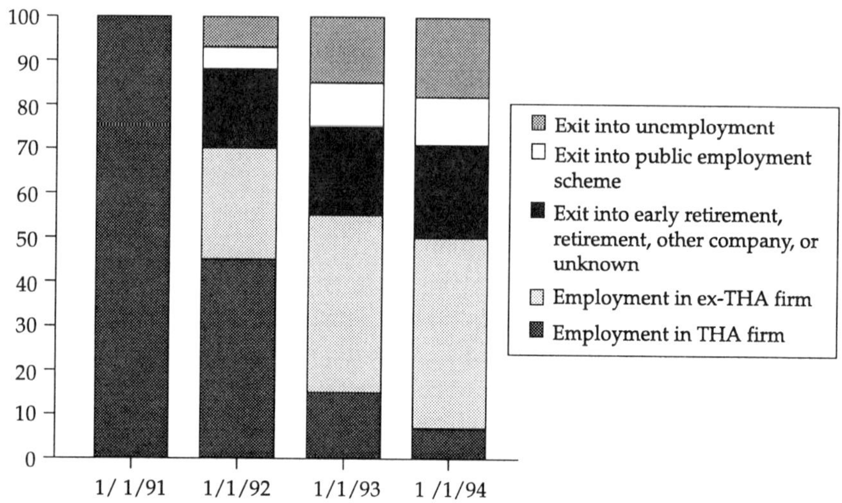

Note: Total = 2,922 million.
Source: Treuhandanstalt.

the THA had privatized or reprivatized 18,279 businesses or business parts. Of these new entities 14.5 percent were created by management buyouts, 23.6 percent were restitutions to former owners, 4.6 percent were bought by foreign firms, and the remaining 57.3 percent were almost exclusively purchased by West German firms. Figure 8-8 presents the size distribution of acquiring and acquired firms for the 1,426 acquisitions registered with the Federal Cartel Office between 1989 and 1992.

Despite the sample selection bias toward larger companies, the data clearly exhibit the extreme asymmetry between acquiring and acquired firms in this takeover wave. On the one hand, 78 percent of all acquired firms in the sample had annual turnover of less than DM 50 million. On the other hand, 79 percent of all acquiring firms had annual turnover of more than DM 2 billion. Taking into account that many of the smaller transactions not recorded in this sample were undertaken by small to medium-size West German firms, the general picture is that of a rather wide range of buying firms in the West purchasing a population of predominantly small firms in the East.

Figure 8-8. Size Distribution of Acquiring and Acquired Firms in East Germany, 1989–92, by Turnover
(in million DM)

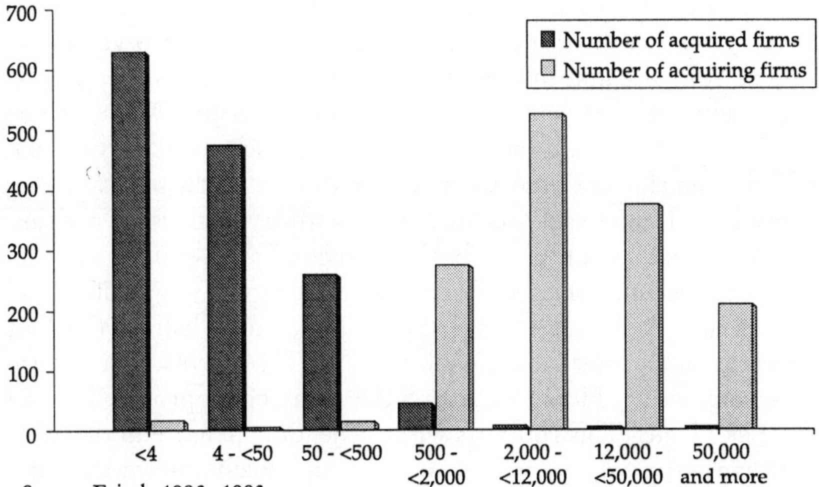

Source: Frisch 1992, 1993.

These data imply two kinds of corporate governance structures in posttransition East Germany. First, a significant fraction of privatized firms—including most management buyouts and reprivatizations—are owner-managed. In this group, corporate governance problems caused by the separation of ownership and control in larger firms are likely to be of secondary importance compared with direct agency costs of outside finance.[54] Second, most of the remaining privatized firms have become subdivisions of larger Western companies and are therefore subject to internal rather than external control problems.[55] Putting it crudely, one can characterize this second group of firms as one for which the problem of corporate governance has been shifted from the East to the West.

54. See, in particular, Jensen and Meckling 1976. See also Aghion and Bolton 1992; von Thadden 1990, forthcoming; Hellwig 1994.

55. See, for example, Williamson 1975, and Milgrom and Roberts 1992.

Of the institutions that are generally considered to be important in the privatization processes, in East Germany the stock market has played no role in the transition. Until the spring of 1994 only one East German firm attempted to go public, but this offering was ill-designed and the privatized firm ended in bankruptcy less than two years later.

The role of banks in the transformation process has been limited and has given rise to some controversy in Germany. While the big West German banks and the savings and loan institutions very quickly established an efficient branch network in the East,[56] the banks' lending activity lagged significantly behind the depository business. Only since 1992 has the volume of private bank lending in East Germany exceeded that of the deposits collected. Even then, lending was very cautious. As late as March 1992, after more than a year and a half in the East, 92 percent of all outstanding bank loans to THA firms were government-guaranteed.[57] Hence, even for THA firms, banks provided virtually no risky loans. This contrasts with the lending practice in the West, where approximately 30 percent of short- and medium-term lending is uncollateralized, let alone government-guaranteed (Drukarczyk, Duttle, and Rieger 1985).

The reluctance to provide risky finance points to deficiencies in monitoring and screening by banks in the earlier phase of the economic transition. This is consistent with the empirical finding by Brandkamp (1993), who reports for a sample of small business start-ups that banks played a relatively minor role in advising new firms. More than a quarter of all respondents obtained no consulting at all. Of the rest, most advice came from professional consultants, followed by local chambers of commerce, friends from the West, and, finally, banks.

Furthermore, throughout the transition process, banks showed extreme restraint with respect to equity participations. Under increasing public pressure, the president of the German Banking Association finally promised the German chancellor in January 1993 that the banks would buy THA firms worth DM 1 billion. One year later, banks had

56. By December 1990, Deutsche Bank and Dresdner Bank alone had established 263 branches in East Germany, mostly taken over from the former state bank. See Wagner 1993 for details.

57. See Bundesverband Deutscher Banken 1992.

bought just two firms. The banks often emphasized that they considered such engagements not to be their business.[58] In contrast, private banks contributed substantially to the restructuring of THA firms, primarily by consulting for THA branches and firms and through their representation on THA firm supervisory boards. In 1991 about 25 percent of THA firm supervisory board seats were held by bankers (Carlin and Mayer 1992). Yet, it is interesting to note that representatives of West German banks neither held seats on the THA supervisory board nor served on the THA management board.[59]

Conclusions

By the end of 1994 the transition from centrally planned socialism to capitalism in East Germany will be largely completed. The political and macroeconomic design of the transformation process has been criticized on several grounds, most prominently with respect to the allocation of property rights (Bundeswirtschaftsministerium 1991; Sinn and Sinn 1993), the extent of regulation of business activity (Bundeswirtschaftsministerium 1991), the emphasis on privatization by sale (Sinn and Sinn 1993; Bolton and Roland 1992), the centralized wage policy (Akerlof and others 1991; Begg and Portes 1992), and the implementation of monetary union (Pöhl 1993).

This chapter has ignored these issues and focused on privatization problems at the corporate level. Here, experiences in other Central or Eastern European countries have shown that loss of control and a resulting obstruction of corporate restructuring by insiders can create serious problems for the transition process. These dangers have been largely avoided in the German case. As discussed in the previous sections, this can be credited primarily to the form of transitional cor-

58. For a view from Deutsche Bank, see, for example, Krupp 1993: "It is not the primary task of banks to develop entrepreneurial activity. This would go against the classical division of roles in a market economy and, in the end, would be beyond the banks' capabilities."
59. G. Rexrodt, on the management board from September 1991 to January 1993, had been with Citibank since January 1990, after eight years in public service in Berlin.

porate governance imposed on the East German economy by the West. The main feature of this system has been that the state actually tightened control in the first phase of the transition by making significant investments into new control structures.

The major implication of this policy has been the possibility of tougher bargaining with entrenched management and of restructuring—particularly dismantling—large firms prior to privatization. Centralization thus has allowed the process to overcome the free-rider problem in the restructuring of loosely controlled firms in a manner comparable to the workings of hostile takeovers in competitive capital markets. Furthermore, and beyond the scope of this chapter, it has permitted those involved to address other, more structural, goals, such as the consideration of regional problems, industry structure, and ownership distribution.[60]

At least three elements of institution design have supported this process of centralized decentralization. First, as discussed earlier, heavy initial investment in the organizational and human capital of the privatization agency has created the structure necessary for the complex managerial tasks of control, bargaining, and restructuring during the privatization process. Second, the privatization agency has had a high degree of organizational independence, and even more operational freedom. Third, it has operated under an explicit time limit, which helped to limit collusion between the agency and its clients.

When asking what this specific transformation experience can imply for other economies in transition, it is useful to first identify what has been unique to the German case. There are three major elements. First, the large material transfers; second, the transfer of human capital; and third, the availability of an advanced and refined legal and administrative structure.

Of these three elements, the first sets the East German economy far apart from all other transitional economies in quantitative terms. However, the major part of the transfers from the West—which were

---

60. These issues are emphasized in Dornbusch and Wolf 1993 and Carlin and Mayer 1992. Carlin 1993, however, rightly points to the severe, and sometimes devastating, structural implications of the economic transition in East Germany.

between DM 150 and 200 billion a year, depending on the estimates—did not even involve the THA. Most of these transfers were either for consumption or for infrastructure investment, dictated by the constitutional and economic necessity to equalize living standards in both parts of Germany as fast as possible. The THA's total operating deficit between July 1990 and the end of 1994 was approximately DM 216 billion, an average of DM 48 billion a year. This deficit resulted almost exclusively from the obligation to honor firms' outstanding old debts; to finance the clean-up of environmental damages; to pay high wages, above productivity levels; and to finance social benefits for dismissed employees in keeping with West German precedents. Hence, it is safe to say that the "pure" costs of operating a strong, independent privatization agency have been relatively small, in particular in view of the large sums available internationally for the restructuring of Eastern Europe.

Another question is to what extent the large transfers from the West have facilitated the THA's privatization policy. Clearly, such enormous transfers would ease any privatization program. But it seems rather unlikely that these transfers were essential for the THA's policy. They seem to have had slight success in generating widespread support for economic reform in the population. Surveys by the Allensbach Institute, for example, show that the proportion of East Germans who were "quite satisfied" with the market-based West German economic system dropped from almost 80 percent in early 1990 to around 35 percent in late 1993.[61]

The other two elements clearly also had an important positive impact on the operations of the THA. There have, however, also been downsides to both of them. With respect to the third element, it has been argued that the provision of a large set of highly refined institutions and regulations may hinder rather than promote the emergence of entrepreneurial activity (see Bundeswirtschaftsministerium 1991). These concerns have often been voiced with respect to environmental or labor market regulations. A piece of legislation that directly impeded the activity of the THA concerns the management of firms governed by supervisory boards. Under German company law such management

61. See *International Herald Tribune*, April 20, 1994.

is responsible only to the supervisory board, and thus the owner has no direct means of imposing his or her will on the management. There have been several cases in which the THA had to go into lengthy legal procedures to obtain information from management or simply to sack managers that opposed THA plans.[62] The Splitting Act of 1991 is an example of a piece of legislation introduced to curb the rights granted to corporate insiders under existing legislation.

The strong inflow of human capital from the West—often provided for free or for only small fees by Western companies—has also had its downside. Because it was already common in 1990 for West German firms to establish business links with East German counterparts, send consultants, or advise on supervisory boards, West German firms often gained detailed information about potential Eastern competitors or acquisitions. This often put them in a strong bargaining position in negotiations with the THA, not only with respect to the takeover price, but also in regard to the restructuring or liquidation decisions included in the sales contract. In several cases negotiations broke down after protracted bilateral bargaining, and the Eastern firm, not having been able to establish alternative business contacts in the meantime, was liquidated.

Hence, although the East German transition took place under extremely privileged material conditions, it does not appear that its privatization strategy of centralized decentralization depended on these conditions. What seems to have been more important is the commitment to an independent, finitely lived privatization agency, with the capability to tighten control prior to privatization. The experience of the Hungarian "centralization" strategy of autumn 1991 (see Voszka 1994) shows that such policies are problematic if implemented only partially. In particular, if the privatization agency is controlled by the government, the "rights to hire, fire, and set the compensation of top-level managers" (Jensen and Ruback 1983) may easily degenerate into a source of government favoritism and party power. Similarly, if there is no clear commitment to the completion of the privatization program and "if the state proves to be a generous owner and permissive controller, this formal subordination may be more convenient for the man-

62. For relevant case studies see, for example, Die Wirtschaft 1993.

agers than strong private ownership" (Voszka 1994). Creating an environment in which managers know that such formal subordination is only a means to implement private control is an integral part of the design of transition processes.

Bibliography

Aghion, P., and P. Bolton. 1992. "An Incomplete Contracts Approach to Financial Contracting." *Review of Economic Studies* 59: 473–94.

Aghion, P., and W. Carlin. 1994. "The Economics of Enterprise Restructuring in Central and Eastern Europe." Nuffield College, Oxford. Mimeo.

Aghion, P., and J. Tirole. 1994. "Formal and Real Authority in Organizations." IDEI Toulouse. Mimeo.

Akerlof, G. A., A. K. Rose, J. Yellen, and H. Hessenius. 1991. "East Germany in from the Cold: The Economic Aftermath of Currency Union." *Brookings Papers on Economic Activity* 1: 1–105.

Albach, H. 1992. "The Transformation of Firms and Markets: A Network Approach to Economic Transformation Processes in East Germany." Wissenschaftszentrum Berlin. Mimeo.

Baums, T. 1993. "The German Banking System and Its Impact on Corporate Finance and Governance." Universität Osnabrück. Mimeo.

Begg, D., and R. Portes. 1992. "Eastern Germany since Unification: Wage Subsidies Remain a Better Way." Discussion Paper 730, Centre for Economic Policy Research, London.

Berg, A. 1993. "The Logistics of Privatization in Poland." In O. Blanchard, K. Froot, and J. Sachs, eds., *Transition in Eastern Europe*. Chicago, Ill.: National Bureau of Economic Research.

Bolton, P., and G. Roland. 1992. "Privatization Policies in Central and Eastern Europe." *Economic Policy* 15: 275–309.

Boycko, M., A. Shleifer, and R. Vishny. 1993. "Privatizing Russia." Harvard University. Mimeo.

Brandkamp, M. 1993. "Erfolgsaussichten von Unternehmensgründungen in den Fünf Neuen Bundesländern." *Zeitschrift für Betriebswirtschaft, Ergänzungsheft* 1/93: 109–44.

Bundesregierung. 1991. "Presse- und Informationsdienst." *Bulletin* 29: 213–14.

Bundesverband Deutscher Banken. 1992. "Aktivitäten der privaten Banken in den neuen Bundesländern." *Die Bank* 6: 357–61.

Bundeswirtschaftsministerium. 1991. "Gutachten des Wissenschaftlichen Beirats beim Bundesministerium für Wirtschaft." BMWI Studienreihe Nr. 73.

Carlin, W. 1993. "Privatization and Deindustrialization in East Germany." Discussion Paper 892. Centre for Economic Policy Research, London.

Carlin, W., and C. Mayer. 1992. "Restructuring Enterprises in Eastern Europe." *Economic Policy* 15: 311–51.

Czada, R. 1993. "Die Treuhandanstalt im Umfeld von Politik und Verbänden." In W. Fischer, H. Hax, and H. K. Schneider, eds., *Trenhandanstalt: Das Unmögliche Wagen*. Berlin: Akademe Verlag.

Die Wirtschaft, ed. 1993. *Kombinate: Was aus ihnen Geworden Ist.* Berlin: Verlag Die Wirtschaft.

Dittus, P. 1994. "Corporate Governance in Central Europe: The Role of Banks." Bank for International Settlements, Basel. Mimeo.

Dornbusch, R., and H. Wolf. 1993. "East German Economic Reconstruction." In O. Blanchard, K. Froot, and J. Sachs, eds., *Transition in Eastern Europe*. Chicago, Ill.: National Bureau of Economic Research.

Drukarcyk, J., J. Duttle, and R. Rieger. 1985. *Mobiliarsicherheiten.* Köln: Bundesanzeiger.

Dyck, A. 1992. "Privatization in Eastern Germany: A Response to Adverse Selection in the Managerial Labor Market." Stanford University. Mimeo.

Fischer, S., and A. Gelb. 1991. "The Process of Socialist Economic Transformation." *Journal of Economic Perspectives* 5: 91–105.

Fischer, W., H. Hax, and H. K. Schneider, eds. 1993. *Treuhandanstalt: Das Unmögliche Wagen*. Berlin: Akademe Verlag.

Frisch, T. 1992, 1993. "Privatisierung und Unternehmenskäufe in Ostdeutschland." HWWA-Institut für Wirtschaftsforschung, Hamburg.

Gless, S., and J. Schwalbach. 1993. "Sanierung von Unternehmen der Treuhandanstalt." Humboldt Universität Berlin. Mimeo.

Gray, Cheryl W., and Rebecca J. Hanson. 1993. "Corporate Governance in Central and Eastern Europe: Lessons from Advanced Market Economies." World Bank, Policy Research Department, Transition and Macro-Adjustment Division, Policy Research Working Paper WPS 1182. Washington, D.C.

von Gusinski, G. 1993. "Vom Plan zum Markt: Erfolge die Schmerzen." *Die Wirtschaft* 1993: 15–38.

Hellwig, M. 1994. "A Reconsideration of the Jensen-Heckling Model of Outside Finance." Universität Basel. Mimeo.

Hommelhoff, P., ed. 1991. *Treuhandunternehmen im Umbruch. Recht und Rechtswirklichkeit beim Übergang in die Marktwirtschaft*. Köln: Verlag Kommunikationsforum.

Hornich, S. 1993. "Das Gebrochene Rückgrat." *Die Wirtschaft* 1993: 9–14.

Jensen, M. C., and W. H. Meckling. 1976. "Theory of the Firm: Managerial Behavior, Agency Costs and Ownership Structure." *Journal of Financial Economics* 3: 305–60.

Jensen, M. C., and R. S. Ruback. 1983. "The Market for Corporate Control: The Scientific Evidence." *Journal of Financial Economics* 11: 5–50.

Kampe, D. 1993. *Nachruf auf die Treuhandanstalt: Wer uns Kennenlernt, Gewinnt-uns Lieb*. Berlin: Rotbuch Verlag.

Kloepfer, M. 1993. "Öffentlich-Rechtliche Vorgaben für die Treuhandanstalt." In W. Fischer, H. Hax, and H. K. Schneider, eds., *Treuhandstalt: Das Unmögliche Wagen*. Berlin: Akademe Verlag.

Kohl, H. 1992. "Rede zur Namensgebung des Detlev-Rohwedder-Hauses." In Treuhandanstalt, *Entschlossen Sanieren* (March): 21–28.

Kornai, J. 1979. "Economy-Constrained versus Demand-Constrained Systems." *Econometrica* 47: 801–19.

Krupp, G. 1993. "Die Aufgaben der Banken." *Zeitschrift für das Gesamte Kreditwesen* 46: 438–40.

Laffont, J. J., and J. Tirole. 1993. *A Theory of Incentives in Procurement and Regulation*. Cambridge, Mass., and London: MIT Press.

Manne, H. G. 1965. "Mergers and the Market for Corporate Control." *Journal of Political Economy* 73: 110–20.

Milgrom, P. 1988. "Employment Contracts, Influence Activities and Organization Design." *Journal of Political Economy* 96: 42–60.

Milgrom, P., and J. Roberts. 1992. *Economics, Organization, and Management*. Englewood Cliffs, N.J.: Prentice-Hall.

Müller, J. 1993, "Strukturelle Auswirkungen der Privatisierung durch die Treuhandanstalt." In W. Fischer, H. Hax, and H. K. Schneider, eds., *Treuhandstalt: Das Unmögliche Wagen*. Berlin: Akademe Verlag.

Nolte, D. 1993. "Zwischen Privatisierung und Sanierung: Die Arbeit der Treuhandanstalt." Wirtschafts- und Sozialwissenschaftsliches Institut des Deutschen Gewerkschaftsbundes. Dusseldorf. Mimeo.

Phelps, E. S., R. Frydman, A. Rapaczynski, and A. Shleifer. 1993. "Needed Mechanisms of Corporate Governance and Finance in Eastern Europe." EBRD, London. Mimeo.

Pöhl, K. 1993. Statements before the Investigatory Committee of Parliament. In *Untersuchungsausschuß Treuhandanstalt* 11. Sitzung.

Scherer, F. M. 1988. "Corporate Takeovers: The Efficiency Arguments." *Journal of Economic Perspectives* 2: 69–82.

von Schleinitz, F. 1993. "IFA-Kombinat PKW Karl-Marx-Stadt." *Die Wirtschaft*: 69–82.

Schuppert, G. F. 1992. "Die Treuhandanstalt—Zum Leben einer Organisation im Überschneidungsbereich zweier Rechtskreise." *Staatswissenschaften* und *Staatspraxis* 3: 186–210.

Seibel, W. 1993. "Die Organisatorische Entwicklung der Treuhandanstalt." In W. Fischer, H. Hax, and H. K. Schneider, eds., *Treuhandstalt: Das Unmögliche Wagen*. Berlin: Akademe Verlag.

Sinn, G., and H. W. Sinn. 1993. *Kaltstart*. München: Beck-dtv (first edition 1991). American edition: *Jumpstart*. Cambridge, Mass.: MIT Press.

Statistisches Bundesamt. Various years. *Zur Wirtschaftlichen und Sozialen Lage in den Neuen Bundesländern.*

Stigler, G. 1971. "The Economic Theory of Regulation." *Bell Journal of Economics* 2: 3–21.

von Thadden, E. L. 1990. "Bank Finance and Long-Term Investment." Universität Basel. Mimeo.

———. Forthcoming. "Long-Term Investment and Monitoring in Financial Relationships." In J. E. Roemer, ed., *Property Rights, Incentives, and Welfare*. London: Macmillan.

THA (Treuhandanstalt). 1992. *DM-Eröffnungsbilanz*. October.

———. 1993a. *Aufgabenspektrum und Lösungswege*. March.

———. 1993b. *Treuhandinitiative Mittelstand*. September.

———. 1993c. *Reprivatisierung von Unternehmen*. September.

———. 1994. *Dokumentation Vertragsmanagement*. March.

———. Various issues. *Monatsberichte.*

———. Various issues. *Treuhand Informationen.*

Voszka, É. 1994. "Centralization, Renationalization, Redistribution: The Role of the Government in Changing the Ownership Structure in Hungary, 1989–93." Discussion Paper 916. Centre for Economic Policy Research, London.

Wagner, H. 1993. "Reconstruction of the Financial System in East Germany: Description and Comparison with Eastern Europe." *Journal of Banking and Finance* 17: 1001–19.

van Wijnbergen, S. 1993. "Enterprise Reform in Eastern Europe." Working Paper Series 1068. World Bank, Europe and Central Asia Department, Washington, D.C.

Williamson, O. E. 1975. *Markets and Hierarchies*. New York: Free Press.

Womack, J. P., D. T. Jones, and D. Roos. 1991. *The Machine that Changed the World*. New York: HarperCollins.

Part III

Relevance and Lessons of the Japanese and German Experiences

Introductory Note

Masahiko Aoki

Chapter 1 designed the contingent governance structure in which the controlling rights reside in the insider when the financial state of the enterprise is without a problem, but the shift of control rights to the outsider (the lead bank) is triggered automatically when the enterprise is financially distressed. Theoretically, it is known that such a governance structure is effective in controlling insider's shirking when the team element is involved in production (Aoki 1994). Empirically, the model is reminiscent of an important aspect of the corporate governance practice in the Japanese economy in the heyday of the main bank system, between the mid-1950s and the mid-1970s (this aspect may be thought not to have yet disappeared in spite of the decline of bank credits in corporate financing). Comparatively, the model may be suggestive of the value of nurturing banking institutions as a device to control the emergent insider control in the transition economies.

Chapter 3, by Berglöf, conceptually distinguished two kinds of financing: arm's-length financing with monitoring by objective on one hand, and control-oriented financing with monitoring by intervention on the other. It was argued that monitoring by objective may be less effective in transition economies where the asset markets are thin and the property rights are only ambiguously defined. Therefore, complementary though these two kinds of financing may be in any economy, control-oriented financing with monitoring by intervention ought to play a more productive role in transition economies. This kind of financing and monitoring anticipates long-term relationships between the enterprise and the financial institutions, especially banks. The chapter specifically points to the Japanese experience of the main bank system as an example of a financial system in which monitoring by intervention is the dominant pattern.

The design of financial systems today in the transition economies must be consonant with the workings and conditions of the current international financial markets, as well as the evolutionary nature of the transition economies. Therefore, the Japanese experience cannot be a precise model for the transition economies to emulate. Nevertheless, the original situations preceding the establishment of the main bank system in the mid-1950s have some important characteristics in common with the transition economies: the failure of the competitive markets for corporate control to operate and the tendency toward insider control of, or at least a strong insider voice in, the governance of the enterprise. Therefore it may be a useful exercise to ask: what kind of historical conditions in Japan eventually facilitated the evolution of the main bank system as an effective external device to curb the ill-effects of insider control; to what extent those conditions were unique to the post–World War II situation facing Japan; whether there were any generic aspects in these conditions that may arise in other economies in other times, although concrete forms may appear diverse; and whether any public policy implications may be derived from the Japanese experience for the development of banking institutions as an important monitoring and financing device. Part III is added to consider these problems in depth.

Chapter 9 by Hoshi considers how Japan dealt with the insolvency and recapitalization problems of banks and enterprises in the immediate post–World War II period and how close bank-enterprise cooperation during the process eventually contributed to the establishment of the banks' capacity as effective corporate monitors. Chapter 10 by Miyajima describes how the original attempt by the occupation authority to democratize corporate control through the massive sales of "quasi-state-owned" stocks of ex-*Zaibatsu* companies to the insiders failed and how the main bank system evolved instead, as an alternative mechanism of corporate control. Chapter 11 by Teranishi describes how the main bank system evolved as an effective institution to funnel development funds from household savings to the industrial sector following the initial reconstruction of the economy. He points to the importance of the public policies of the mid-1950s in facilitating the maturity transformation of short-term deposit savings into long-term industrial financing.

The rest of this introductory note describes broad historical contexts in Japan between the prewar and postwar periods preceding the establishment of the main bank system, particularly the role of government. (For a comprehensive description and analysis of the Japanese main bank system and its possible relevance to transitional economies, see the report of a prior project undertaken under the auspices of the Development Institute of the World Bank, Aoki and Patrick 1994.)

The Role of the Government Preceding the Emergence of the Main Bank System

In the 1920s, the Japanese capitalist system did not exhibit any unique characteristics except for the unescapable manifestation of its backwardness and underdevelopment. The enterprises were firmly controlled by major stockholders, be they holding companies or individual entrepreneurs. The position of the managers as subordinate agents for major stockholders was clear. The banks, numerous in number as a consequence of a lax regulatory capital requirement, did not play an important role in investment financing of the enterprises. They played the more conventional roles of commercial banking and financing wealthy investors with securities as collateral. The formation of the bank-oriented financial system and the associated contingent governance structure in the post–World War II period did not autonomously evolve in the *laissez faire* framework. State intervention in the design of the financial system and national economic administration over the period from the late 1930s to the early 1950s was instrumental in its formation.

Beginning in 1937, the alliance of the military and the so-called "reformed" bureaucrats decisively enhanced its control over the government. In that year, the government introduced the three major economic control laws, including the Temporary Funds Adjustment Law, and created the powerful Planning Agency for the purpose of the centralization of economic planning and administration. By this law, important corporate decisionmaking—such as change in the Article of Corporation, new equity, and bond issues—required government approval. Subsequent government decrees deprived stockholders of the right to determine dividends payout (1939), and appoint managers (1943), and these decisions were placed under government control. The military-bureaucrat alliance went as far as to emulate some of the planning techniques used for the heavy industrialization of the Soviet Union in the early 1930s (see Okazaki 1994).

At the same time, the government promoted mergers of banks and established the legal authority of requiring banks to supply investment as well as working capital to enterprises prioritized by economic planning (1939, 1940). Major banks responded to such orders by the formation of loan syndicates (chapter by Teranishi in Aoki and Patrick 1994). Those syndicates were predominantly managed by the Industrial Bank of Japan.

In 1938 the government created the National Finance Control Association (*Zenkoku Kinvu Toseikai*) as an instrument to control funds flow, with the president of the Bank of Japan as the chairman and various associations of financial institutions as members. The Association mediated 2,200 syndications until June 1944, when the Munitions Financing Institution Designation System was introduced. Under this system, one major bank was designated to each munitions company under the Munitions Company Law (1944). The designated bank automatically became the lead manager of syndications. The syndicate loan was funneled through the designated bank as a sole nominal lender, and the designated bank maintained an exclusive payment settlement account for the munitions companies assigned to it. Because loans by designated banks to munitions companies were guaranteed by the War-Time Finance Public Corporation, there was no need for prudent monitoring by the designated bank. The tendency toward soft budgeting was rampant. At the end of World War II, the system had been applied to 2,240 munitions companies, of which 1,582 were assigned to one of five major *Zaibatsu* banks.

After World War II, government guarantees of bank credits to munitions companies, as well as government debts and insurance obligations to munitions companies, were canceled to control rising inflation. Also, cash holdings of enterprises were converted into new currencies and frozen at banks beyond a certain limit. These measures inevitably forced enterprises to become dependent upon banks for restructuring and recapitalization (see Hoshi's chapter). To lubricate money supply, the government introduced the "stamped" bills and trade bills system in August 1946. Under this system, bills drawn by enterprises on banks were stamped by the Bank of Japan (BOJ) and made eligible for rediscounting upon the bank's guarantee of their clearance. Bills drawn by export agencies on exporters were treated in a similar way. In spite of the depletion of banks' assets, the close bank-enterprise relationship was thus maintained.

In the end of 1946, the government introduced the famous Priority Production (*keisya seisan*) Method, in which funds and resources were to be directed into the strategic coal and steel industries for the recovery of the war-damaged economy. The Reconstruction Finance Bank (RFB) was created in 1947 for financing the strategic industries, as well as various public corporations. RFB loans in 1947 exceeded total private bank loans, although those in 1948 declined to about one-third of the latter. RFB financed its loans mostly by debenture issues, the majority of which (73 percent) were purchased by the BOJ. The value of BOJ purchase of RFB debentures amounted to 38 percent of the increase in BOJ note issues during the period of 1947-48, which was an obvious source of inflation. In 1949, the loan activity of the RFB was terminated. In parallel to massive RFB loans for long-term investment, industrial loans by city banks were guided by BOJ, according to priority guidelines set by the government. BOJ was also active in mediating loan syndication, mostly for working capital, involving itself in the credit evaluation of private projects. The number of syndications BOJ mediated during 1947–49 amounted to 5,387. BOJ's active involvement in syndication continued until 1949, when a steamrolling deflationary measure known as the Dodge Line was introduced to balance the government budget.

Even after the implementation of the Dodge Line, however, BOJ was active in supplying loanable funds to city banks through direct loans against eligible bonds as collateral, rediscounting of stamped bills and other eligible bills, or open-market operations with national bonds and RFB debentures as instruments. In 1949 the amount of the government budget surplus totaled 84.4 billion yen, but BOJ net credits topped 92 billion yen. In the end of 1948, the total bank credits outstanding were 381 billion yen, but jumped to 994 billion yen at the end of 1950. During the same period private bank deposits merely doubled. The pattern observed in the subsequent high-growth period—that the banks lent in concentration to large enterprises by borrowing from BOJ—was in the making (see the chapter by Teranishi for details).

The Japanese main bank system that emerged following the reconstruction of the economy came to exhibit the following characteristics in its heyday, between the mid-1950s and the mid-1970s (Aoki, Patrick, and Sheard 1994). Usually a single bank came to establish close relationships with each large enterprise through historical connections (for example, old *Zaibatsu* grouping, wartime designated bank connection, post–World War II syndicates) and to own the largest block of its shares among banks, within the legal limit of 10 percent (5 percent before 1951). This bank became widely known as the main bank (MB) for that enterprise. The formation of loan syndications gradually became informal and conventionalized. The MB took the initiative for long-term credits to those enterprises, but its share in the de facto syndicate normally remained less than 50 percent (around 20 percent, on average, in later periods). Other banks relied upon ex ante credit evaluation of the MB and followed its lead in loan arrangements. They also entrusted interim monitoring to the MB, which maintained major payment settlement accounts. In return, it was understood that it was the MB's responsibility to cope with possible financial distress of the enterprise. Depending on the situation, the actual risk-cost-bearing between the MB and other banks might become subject to ex post bargaining, but it is conventionalized that the MB bore a much higher share of risk cost than its loan share. The moral hazard behavior of the MB was believed to be severely punished by the regulatory authority.

If the above represents the concise stylized facts of the MB system, we may identify the following two factors essential to the evolution of the system. First, the government intervention to limit the number of qualified banks, as well as to promote and conventionalize syndication, may have played a crucial role. In order for reciprocal delegation of monitoring among MBs to be accountable, the number of banks qualified to be MBs needs to be limited so that the defection from responsible monitoring and ex post risk-cost-bearing must be easily identifiable and punishable. Around 1930 there were as many as 1,500 banks in Japan. By administrative guidance and coercion of the government, the number of commercial banks was reduced to sixty-five by 1945. Even among this group, more than fifty banks were regional banks, basing their activity within the limit of a prefecture, and only about ten banks eventually evolved as main banks for major enterprises. Further, as already noted, the government (and the IBJ) during the World War II period, and BOJ after the World War II period, were actively involved in the mediation of loan syndications. The convention of the MB system evolved only after such government intervention. Evolution of implicit trust relationships among member banks may not have been possible in the *laissez faire* framework.

The government intervention is double-edged, however. There is always danger of soft budgeting. If it is known that the government is using the banking system as an instrument for fulfilling its economic objective, be it the maximum production of munitions or the reconstruction of the war-damaged economy, the enterprise would develop incentives to extract more lending from the banks, as well as gain bargaining power to do so. The bank may, in turn, rely upon the creation of money by the central bank to meet such demands, and the weak central bank captured by the political control of bureaucrats and politicians may not be able to resist it. We have seen that such was indeed the case in the period of active government intervention between the late 1930s and the late 1940s.

A rigorous comparative institutional analysis indicates that, when the profitability of the enterprise is yet very low, moderate loss absorption by the bank rather than outright liquidation may be efficiency-compatible, although the worst performance is to be credibly punished to curb the moral hazard of insiders (see Aoki 1994). This may, in turn, imply that the bank needs to operate within the orbit of the government's assistance. Such arrangements, however, should be regarded as strictly transitory. The sound stabilization policy should be regarded as a prerequisite for the effective workings of any bank-oriented financial system. It is indeed only after the effective implementation of the Dodge Line and the termination of RFB loans that responsible monitoring by the bank emerged as a countervailing power to the insiders who were capturing the de facto and de jure control of the enterprise. This ought to be the most important, indisputable lesson drawn from the Japanese experience.

References

Aoki, M. 1994. "Contingent Governance of Teams: Analysis of Institutional Complementarity." *International Economic Review* 35: 657–76.

Aoki, M., H. Patrick, and P. Sheard. 1994. "The Japanese Main Bank System: Overview." In M. Aoki and H. Patrick, eds., *The Japanese Main Bank System: Its Relevance to Developing and Transforming Economies*. New York: Oxford University Press.

Aoki, M., and H. Patrick, eds. 1994. *The Japanese Main Bank System: Overview*. New York: Oxford University Press.

Okazaki, T. 1994. "The Japanese Firm under the Wartime Planned Economy." In M. Aoki and R. Dore, eds., *The Japanese Firm: Its Competitive Sources*. New York: Oxford University Press.

9

Cleaning up the Balance Sheets: Japanese Experience in the Postwar Reconstruction Period

Takeo Hoshi

During the initial stage of the postwar reconstruction, many Japanese firms faced a serious insolvency problem. The major cause of the insolvency problem was the repudiation of the large amount of wartime compensation that the government owed the munitions companies. Insolvency of the munitions companies implied financial troubles for financial institutions as well, because many were heavily exposed to munitions companies. To make the matter worse, the government also decided to withdraw its guarantee to corporate bonds, most of which were held by financial institutions, and to suspend compensation for the losses from uncollectible government-ordered loans to munitions companies.

The size of losses from the repudiation was enormous. According to estimates as of October 2, 1946, the total losses were 91.8 billion yen

An earlier version of this paper was prepared for the workshop on "The Corporate Governance Structure in Transforming Economies: with Special References to the Role of the Bank and Relevance of Japanese Experience," Stanford, California, April 22–23, 1994. The author thanks Masahiko Aoki, John McMillan, Hideaki Miyajima, and Yingyi Qian for helpful comments on the paper, and Mr. Yushin Yamamuro for stimulating conversation on this topic.

(66.9 billion yen from repudiation of wartime compensation, 19.8 billion yen from repudiation of government-guaranteed bonds, and 5.0 billion yen from the suspension of compensation for losses arising from government-ordered loans).[1] Since the gross national expenditure (GNE) in fiscal year 1946 was 474.0 billion yen, the losses amounted to almost 20 percent of GNE.[2]

This chapter examines how such an economywide solvency problem was resolved. Because many firms in Eastern Europe and the former Soviet Union face a similar solvency problem, the Japanese experience seems to offer some lessons. The following points are suggested by the Japanese experience.

- A viable alternative to bankruptcy courts for mass reorganization exists.
- Separation of the balance sheet allows the company (bank) to reorganize without interfering with the ongoing business.
- There are two alternative ways of debt restructuring: individual level or industry level. Industry-level debt restructuring is less time-consuming, but individual-firm-level debt restructuring spreads the cost more equally to many parties.
- Creation of reconciliation accounts allows reevaluation to continue after the merger of the new and old accounts.
- The reorganization process has a significant impact on the subsequent development of corporate governance.
- The reorganization process can be (and probably should be) coordinated with antitrust measures.
- The condition of the stock market influences the success of recapitalization.
- The debt-equity swap is a useful way of recapitalization.
- Inflation can reduce the creditors' (depositors') cost of reorganization. But, a reorganization plan that relies on this role of inflation may jeopardize the credibility of tough anti-inflationary policy.

---

1. Japan 1983, p. 699.
2. Japan 1978, pp. 26–27.

Each point is discussed in more detail after the Japanese experience is reviewed.

The chapter is organized as follows. The next section starts the examination of the Japanese experience in large-scale restructuring by looking at the reconstruction and reorganization of financial institutions. The third section studies the reconstruction and reorganization process of nonfinancial corporations. The following five sections are devoted to five case studies of restructuring presented to help us better understand the process. Included are the cases of the Industrial Bank of Japan (IBJ) and the restructuring of the Fuji Bank, which was called the Yasuda Bank during this period. The next three sections examine the reconstruction of nonfinancial institutions, including a manufacturing firm, Ajinomoto, Nippon Steel, and NEC. The final section concludes by discussing the nine lessons listed above from the Japanese experience.

Bank Reorganization and Recapitalization

The process of cleaning up the balance sheets of financial institutions followed three steps. First, the balance sheet was separated into a new account and an old account. Second, the financial institutions were allowed to continue their business using their new accounts, while their old accounts were reorganized. Finally, after the reorganization, the old accounts were merged back with the new accounts, and the financial institutions were recapitalized. This section reviews the process of bank reorganization in detail.

Separation of the Balance Sheet

As of 0:00 a.m. on August 11, 1946, the balance sheet of each financial institution was separated into two parts following *Kin'yu Kikan Keiri Ohkyu Sochi Ho* (the Financial Institutions Accounting Temporary Measures Act) promulgated on August 15, 1946.[3] Table 9-1 shows how major balance sheet items were separated into two parts: a new account

3. The text of *Kin'yu Kikan Keiri Ohkyu Sochi Ho* is found in Takaishi 1966b, pp. 681–90.

Table 9-1. Major Items in the New and the Old Accounts of Financial Institutions

Category	*Assets*	*Liabilities*
Old account	(A1) Loans (except those for governments and other financial institutions)	(L1) Second-line frozen deposits
	(A2) Bonds and equities (except government and municipal bonds)	(L2) Special deposits[b]
	(A3) Unpaid capital[a]	(L3) Retained earnings
	(A4) Other assets (including tangible assets)	(L4) Capital
	[(A5) Receivable from new account]	[(L5) Payable to new account]
New account	(a1) Cash	(l1) Free deposits
	(a2) Interbank loans (credits)	(l2) First-line frozen deposits
	(a3) Government and municipal bonds	(l3) Interbank loans (liabilities)
	[(a4) Receivable from old account]	(l4) Tax obligations
		[(l5) Payable to old account]

a. According to the old commercial code in Japan, shareholders were allowed to leave a portion of the capital not paid in. Thus this item can be considered as receivable from shareholders and is recorded on the assets side. During the occupation period, the Allies questioned this practice, and all the unpaid capital must have been paid in when the old and new accounts merged at the end of reorganization.

b. Toward the end of the war, the government introduced a "special settlement system," in which the government pays the private party in the form of deposits that cannot be withdrawn for several years. The special deposits are the payments through the special settlement system and were accumulated until the end of the war without being withdrawn (see Japan 1978, pp. 10–13).

Source: Teranishi 1991, p. 33; Japan 1983, pp. 225–27, 1991, p. 5; Takaishi 1966b, pp. 681–84.

and an old account. The idea behind the separation was to clean up bad loans without interfering with ongoing banking business. Thus all assets that were expected to be uncollectible because of suspension of wartime compensation were assigned to the old account, which was frozen and expected to go through reorganization. A portion of deposits and the bank's entire capital were put in the liabilities side of the old account, and they were at risk of being canceled to cover the bad loans. Differences between assets and liabilities in one account were recorded as an unsettled account against the other. For instance, for financial institutions the liabilities of the new account often exceeded its assets, and the difference was entered as a credit against the old account.

There are several points worth noting about the way the bank balance sheets were separated. First, interbank loans were assigned to the new account. There were disputes about whether interbank loans should be treated in the same way as any other loans, but eventually the government decided to treat interbank loans differently, arguing that the bank that directly lent to the munitions firms should be held responsible for the decision.[4] It is unclear if such an argument is convincing, but this decision created another problem: how to deal with the bank debentures. Initially the bank debentures held by financial institutions (and government) were assigned to the new account, while the bank debentures held by individuals and nonfinancial corporations were put into the old account. Thus, depending on the identity of the owner, the bank debentures were treated differently. The Supreme Commander, Allied Powers (SCAP), however, later criticized this treatment as unfair and possibly unlawful, and ordered that all the bank debentures be reassigned to the old account on March 12, 1948, just a few weeks before the planned merger of new and old accounts.[5] As we will see later in the chapter, when the reorganization of IBJ is discussed, the reassignment of bank debentures to the old account enormously helped IBJ.

Second, in order to protect depositors, a substantial proportion of deposits was put into the new accounts. Because the government started to freeze deposits in February of 1946 to combat inflation, 86 percent

4. Takaishi 1966, pp. 660–61, and Japan 1983, p. 227.
5. Japan 1983, pp. 268–83, documents the negotiations between SCAP and the Japanese government on the bank debentures issue.

of the total deposits were frozen at the end of July 1946, just before the separation of balance sheets.[6] On August 11, the frozen deposits were separated into the first-line frozen deposits and the second-line frozen deposits. The first-line frozen deposits were put in the new account and protected from the reorganization. A household was usually entitled to have first-line frozen deposits of between ¥15,000 and ¥32,000.[7] Because the monthly consumption expenditure of a typical household was estimated to be ¥2,125 (Japan 1979, pp. 132–33), the level of first-line frozen deposits amounted to seven to fifteen months of living expenses. The second-line frozen deposits were at risk of being canceled to cover the bad loans. At the end of August 1946, the second-line frozen deposits at banks were about 37 percent of the total frozen deposits, as table 9-2 shows. The proportion of the deposits assigned to the old account (second-line frozen deposits and special deposits) were 47 percent of the total deposits (including free deposits).

Reorganization of Old Accounts

The next step was reorganization of old accounts, guided by *Kin'yu Kikan Saiken Seibi Ho* (the Financial Institutions Reconstruction and Reorganization Act), promulgated on October 18, 1946.[8] There were

---

6. The anti-inflation policy was formalized by two laws: *Kin'yu Kinkyu Sochi Rei* (Finance Emergency Measure Act) and *Nihon Ginko-ken Azukeire Rei* (Bank of Japan Notes Deposit Act). Both acts took effect on February 17, 1946. The Bank of Japan Notes Deposit Act declared that new yen notes would replace existing yen notes, which would lose acceptability on March 2, and required people to deposit all the cash by March 7. The Finance Emergency Measure Act froze deposits and prohibited the people from withdrawing more than deemed necessary for living. The deposits in new yen notes were called "free deposits," and the withdrawals from such deposits were not restricted.

7. Japan 1976, p. 125.

8. *Kin'yu Kikan Saiken Seibi Ho* subsequently went through numerous revisions. The whole text of the law before the revisions is found in Takaishi 1966c, pp. 61–90. The major revisions of the law are discussed in Takaishi 1966c, pp. 99–187. A brief discussion of the law in English is found in General Headquarters, Supreme Commander for the Allied Powers (GHQ/SCAP henceforth) 1951a, pp. 21–22.

Table 9-2. The Amount of Each Kind of Deposit at Banks
(million yen)

Month and year	*First-line frozen deposits*	*Second-line frozen deposits*	*Special deposits*	*Free deposits*
March 1946	94,450	—	26,782	14,518
April	93,080	—	27,571	14,578
May	84,740	—	37,430	17,118
June	89,587	—	33,557	18,072
July	87,679	—	34,964	19,936
August	53,372	31,255	35,851	21,944
September	60,984	22,457	35,960	25,830
October	62,862	21,005	35,799	30,227
November	73,194	21,819	21,948	32,847
December	82,507	20,936	1,675	39,751
January 1947	78,619	20,026	414	46,955
February	77,792	19,691	393	47,792
March	69,619	19,515	369	59,140
April	63,512	19,414	358	63,197
May	60,230	19,314	273	70,088
June	58,779	16,862	183	78,981
July	55,294	16,779	151	86,864
August	53,054	16,730	119	97,634
September	52,360	16,706	112	115,288
October	49,349	16,687	98	121,752
November	47,447	16,673	82	133,783
December	49,714	14,519	75	170,065
January 1948	40,325	14,320	60	182,957
February	34,836	14,350	30	189,897
March	31,695	5,349	10	220,020

— Not applicable.
Source: Japan 1978, p. 129.

several issues to be resolved before starting this step. The first problem arose from the interdependence of credits between financial institutions and industrial firms. Financial institutions cannot start calculating the value of loans until industrial firms determine the value of their assets. In order for the firms to calculate the value of their assets, however, they need to know the value of the second-line frozen deposits they hold, and the value cannot be known until financial institutions finish reorganizing their old accounts. The government initially planned the following three steps to restructure the old accounts of both financial institutions and industrial firms in a few months.[9]

- Industrial firms give their estimates of the losses from the repudiation of wartime compensation to their creditors.
- Financial institutions restructure their balance sheets based on the estimates supplied by industrial firms, and publish the results.
- Industrial firms reestimate their losses, using the information supplied by financial institutions and other industrial firms.

Thus, the plan assumed that industrial firms should first estimate the amount of losses from the suspension of wartime compensation, because financial institutions cannot start their reorganization without that. Then the financial institutions follow by cleaning up their balance sheets and publishing them, so that industrial firms can use the numbers to improve their estimates. Theoretically, this process can be reiterated to further improve the estimates, but, for practical reasons, the plan stopped after one iteration.

The three-step plan, however, did not materialize because antitrust issues substantially delayed the reorganization of industrial firms, as we will see in the next section. The delay of the corporate reorganization necessitated that banks start evaluating items in the old accounts without estimates of losses at nonfinancial firms. Both SCAP and the Japanese government seem to have believed that speedy reorganization of financial institutions was important.[10]

The second problem concerned whether unrealized capital gains on fixed assets in the old account should be offset against losses. Such unrealized capital gains were believed to be substantial, because inflation was very high during the postwar period. If the unrealized capital gains are ignored, the losses paid by depositors and shareholders increase. If the capital gains are taken into account, however, it creates

9. Japan 1991, p. 8.
10. Takaishi 1966c, p. 20, and Japan 1983, p. 300.

another problem. Because inflation will increase the capital gains and reduce the losses suffered by depositors and shareholders, the government faces the temptation to stop fighting inflation. The government found this credibility problem very important and eventually decided to let the banks ignore the unrealized capital gains on fixed assets.[11] This practice was also helpful in increasing the capital of new banks that emerged when the old accounts were merged with the new accounts, which was another policy goal.

Finally, how to evaluate the assets and liabilities in foreign countries was another important issue. Here, the banks were ordered to assume the worst case and attach no value to the foreign assets. Foreign liabilities were calculated at face value.[12]

As banks started estimating the values of assets in old accounts, it became clear for some banks that they would never have to cancel all the second-line frozen deposits. Those banks were allowed to move the second-line frozen deposits that would not be at risk into the first-line frozen deposits in December 1947. Out of sixty-four special and ordinary banks, forty-eight went through this interim settlement. None of the major banks, however, was able to make interim settlement, because they suffered from so many bad loans that almost all the second-line frozen deposits were at risk.

Table 9-2 shows that the second-line frozen deposits fell by about 2 billion yen in December 1947, and the first-line frozen deposits increased by about the same amount. This reflects the interim settlements by many banks. We also find that by December 1947, the second-line frozen deposits had already shrunk to about a half of the initial amount. This is because some payments were allowed from the second-line frozen deposits, as the Ministry of Finance (Japan 1976, pp. 124–33) discusses. Most important, depositors were allowed to use the second-line frozen deposits to pay some taxes and to pay back the bank loans that were collateralized by the second-line frozen deposits. Thus, the second-line frozen deposits quickly fell from 31 billion yen in August 1946 to 22 billion yen in September, and eventually to 17 billion yen just before the interim settlements.

---

11. Takaishi 1966c, pp. 22, 188–99.
12. Takaishi 1966b, pp. 664–77.

Plans for final settlements were submitted to the minister of finance on January 10, 1948, and were approved. But at this point, SCAP ordered reclassification of bank debentures as discussed above, and banks were asked to resubmit revised plans. Finally, on May 15, 1948, the final settlement plans were retroactively approved as of March 31. In a final settlement, the assets were evaluated (realized), capital gains were calculated, and the losses from suspension of wartime compensation were canceled out. The following prioritization of write-offs was used in the process of cancellation.

- Capital gains on assets (realized gains) and other profits in the old account
- Retained earnings in the old account
- Up to 90 percent of the bank's capital
- Up to 70 percent of the second-line frozen corporate deposits that exceed 5 million yen per account
- Up to 50 percent of the second-line frozen corporate deposits that exceed 1 million yen per account
- Up to 30 percent of the second-line frozen corporate deposits that exceed 100,000 yen per account
- Up to 70 percent of the remaining second-line frozen deposits
- Remaining 10 percent of the capital
- Remaining 30 percent of the second-line frozen deposits
- Designated deposits (frozen deposits designated for tax payments).

If the losses still remained after the cancellation discussed above, the government compensated for the losses. Old accounts were merged with new accounts after the reorganization.

For the banking sector as a whole, the total losses amounted to 27.5 billion yen.[13] Capital gains and profits (6.2 billion yen), retained earnings (1.3 billion yen), capital (1.6 billion yen), and deposits (18.0 billion yen) were all used to cancel the losses. Thus, many banks were forced to significantly reduce capital and to cut into the frozen deposits. Out of sixty-four ordinary and special banks, fifty-seven banks reduced

---

13. The numbers in this paragraph and the next are from Japan 1983, pp. 302–5.

capital by more than 90 percent and had to default on some deposits. Collectively, 19.6 billion yen (or 71 percent) of the total losses were borne by depositors and shareholders. Few banks (one ordinary bank and no special banks) needed the government compensation, and the government spent only 0.4 billion yen to cancel the losses of the banks.

Many agricultural banks and insurance companies, however, received government compensation. The total losses for the financial institutions other than banks amounted to 16.6 billion yen, of which 1.7 billion yen were canceled with capital gains and profits, 0.2 billion yen were canceled with retained earnings, 0.4 billion yen were canceled with capital, and 2.9 billion yen were canceled with deposits. Thus, the government paid the balance of 11.4 billion yen for the protection of small deposits. This amount was much more than SCAP initially hoped.

Recapitalization and Reconciliation Account

To replenish the capital lost to cancel the losses, many banks had to issue new shares. SCAP initially ordered banks to increase the risk assets ratio (the ratio of capital to the risk asset that is defined to be total assets - government bonds - cash - Bank of Japan deposits) to 5 percent, and eventually to 10 percent. Expecting the difficulty the banks would face in selling a large amount of shares in a short period of time, the Ministry of Finance negotiated with SCAP to lower the initial target risk assets ratio from 5 percent to 3 percent.[14]

The former creditors whose credit was canceled against the losses had first priority in the purchase of a set number of shares at par value. The former shareholders had the second priority. The third priority went to employees of the financial institution. Finally, the residents of the local community of the financial institution received the priority before the general public.

Contrary to the Japanese government's initial concern, most issues were well subscribed, and many banks succeeded in achieving a risk assets ratios higher than 5 percent. The major reason for the success of bank recapitalization can be found in the fortunate stock market condi-

14. Japan 1983, pp. 309–15.

tion. When the banks issued the shares in late 1948 and early 1949, people were eagerly waiting for the reopening of the Tokyo Stock Exchange. The Ministry of Finance started requesting SCAP's approval of reopening in April of 1948, and the reopening was finally approved in January 1949.[15] When the Tokyo Stock Exchange was finally opened in May 1949, the shares were very actively traded and the prices rose sharply. This favorable condition in the stock market seems to be the most important reason that bank shares were so successfully subscribed.

SCAP hoped that Japanese banks would recapitalize again so that the risk assets ratio would exceed 10 percent. Unfortunately, this did not happen. Figure 9-1 shows the risk assets ratio calculated from the balance sheets for city banks from 1948 to 1992. The risk assets ratio here is defined as the ratio of (capital + reserves + retained profits) to (total assets – cash – deposits – government bonds). Thus, the definition of capital includes reserves and retained profits.[16] The deposits include all deposits held by the banks and is larger than the amount of deposits at the Bank of Japan. Hence our estimates of the risk asset ratio are upwardly biased. Figure 9-1 shows that the risk asset ratios for city banks have been consistently lower than 5 percent, even when we use an upwardly biased measure. Thus, the city banks as a whole never achieved the initial goal of 5 percent that SCAP set, let alone the ultimate goal of 10 percent.

The major reason for the failure of the banks to increase their capital ratios was that the favorable condition in the stock market mentioned above did not continue for long. Primarily because of the tight macroeconomic policy of the Dodge plan, the stock market collapsed in October 1949, making new share issues extremely difficult. Even after the recovery of stock prices, the Ministry of Finance (MOF) was not strict about imposing the capital ratio requirement envisioned by SCAP. Even though MOF issued the directive in 1954 and notified

15. Japan 1979, pp. 389–97.

16. This definition of capital corresponds to the "narrowly defined capital" (Yokoyama 1989, p. 96). The "broadly defined capital" also includes reserves classified under liabilities. Even when the broadly defined capital is used, asset ratios for Japanese banks were low and falling in the 1980s (Yokoyama 1989, pp. 105–7).

Figure 9-1. Risk Assets Ratio for City Banks

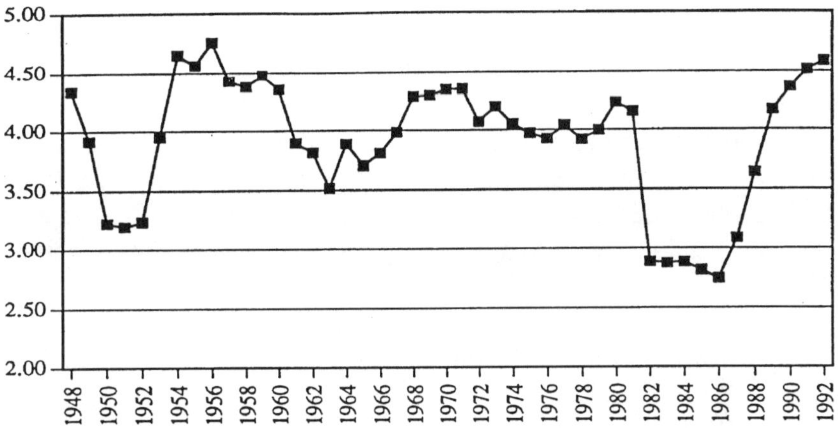

Note: The risk assets ratio is calculated as (Capital + Reserves + Retained Profits)/(Total Assets – Cash – Deposits – Government Bonds). Since the deposits include not only the deposits at the Bank of Japan but also those at other financial institutions, the risk assets ratio is overestimated.
Source: Bank of Japan 1971, 1993.

the banks to hold the broadly defined capital (see footnote 16) above 10 percent of the total deposits, most banks did not achieve this goal.[17]

Instead of relying on the capital ratio regulation, MOF seems to have chosen to intervene directly in bank management to secure sound banking. For example, from 1949 to 1968, MOF required the banks to hold the ordinary costs below a certain fraction of the ordinary income. Initially, the fraction was 90 percent, but the regulation was gradually tightened, and by 1954 the ratio was lowered to 78 percent, which continued to be the standard until 1968. Thus, the capital ratio regulation never became an important part of Japanese bank regulation until after the Basle Accord of 1988.

17. Yokoyama 1989, pp. 101–5.

Finishing the reorganization of the old account and recapitalizing through new share issues, Japanese banks made a fresh start. We should note, however, that reorganization of financial institutions was based on the estimates about the value of loans to the munitions companies. Thus, the balance sheets of new banks still involved some uncertainty, which was captured in the "reconciliation account."[18]

Because the value of assets in the old accounts was often estimated conservatively, the reconciliation accounts typically began to show profits as uncertainty about the value of assets was gradually resolved. The reformed Financial Institutions Reconstruction and Reorganization Act of July 1948 declared that such profits should be returned to the creditors whose claims were wiped away in the reorganization process. The following prioritization was used in distributing profits from reconciliation accounts.

1. Government compensation and interest
2. Principal of the designated deposits that were canceled
3. Principal of the frozen deposits that were canceled (in the reverse order of the priority of cancellation)
4. Interest on the frozen deposits
5. Interest on the designated deposits.

It took a long time to evaluate and distribute profits from the reconciliation accounts, because the progress in reorganizing industrial firms was very slow. Banks did not start to make distributions until 1953.

Between February and July of 1953, many regional banks paid out at least a portion of profit from the reconciliation account ("interim distribution"). Major banks such as Mitsubishi, Sumitomo, Fuji, Sanwa, Daiwa, Mitsui, and Dai-Ichi did not make interim distribution because they still had a significant amount of foreign assets and liabilities that were not yet evaluated. As we will see, IBJ made interim distribution to pay back some canceled debentures in February, which facilitated interim distribution of other financial institutions that held IBJ debentures.

---

18. Takaishi 1967, chapter 254; Japan 1983, pp. 315–27; Japan 1959, pp. 173–88.

By 1958 banks had a fairly accurate evaluation of the reconciliation accounts, including the values of foreign assets and liabilities, and almost all banks made a "final distribution" and closed their reconciliation accounts. For many banks, the profits in reconciliation accounts were sufficient to pay back all the canceled deposits, including the interest. Out of sixty-five banks (including former special banks), only one bank failed to pay back the principal of the canceled deposits and another five banks failed to pay the interest on the canceled deposits as of March 1959.[19] Many insurance companies also paid back canceled debt successfully. Many agricultural banks, however, failed to do so, and they failed to pay back even the government compensation.

Thus, thirteen years after the separation of the balance sheets, the reorganization and reconstruction of financial institutions were finally complete. Although the process cost the depositors and shareholders, financial institutions succeeded in cleaning up their balance sheets. The costs for the depositors eventually turned out to be much less than expected, because the profits of reconciliation accounts were sufficient to pay back the principal and the interest for all the depositors at many banks.

Corporate Reorganization and Recapitalization

The restructuring of the nonfinancial corporations was done in a parallel fashion. The process began with the government letting the companies that were expected to be damaged by suspension of wartime compensation declare themselves *tokubetsu keiri gaisha* (special account companies). Then, special account companies were to go through the following three steps, similar to those taken by financial institutions to clean up their balance sheets. First, their balance sheets were separated into new accounts and old accounts. Second, the firms were allowed to continue their business using their new accounts, while their old accounts are reorganized. Finally, after the reorganization, the old accounts were merged back with the new accounts, and the firms were expected to be recapitalized.

---

19. Japan 1959, p. 188.

Separation of the Balance Sheet

As of 0:00 a.m. on August 11, 1946, the special account companies had their balance sheets separated into new and old accounts. The items that should be included in the new account and those in the old account were specified in *Kigyo Kaikei Ohkyu Sochi Ho* (Corporations Accounting Temporary Measures Act) promulgated on August 15, 1946.[20] Table 9-3 shows how major balance sheet items were classified into new and old accounts. Again the idea was to avoid interfering with the continuation of current business while the balance sheets were cleaned up. The rules about separation were much simpler than those for financial institutions. The assets of the new account included only the assets that were deemed necessary to "continue the current business and promote the postwar development."[21] All the other assets and the firm's liabilities were moved into the old account, and the total value of assets in the new account was recorded as the liabilities of the new account against the old account. The special account companies were prohibited from settling liabilities incurred before August 11 and were protected from seizure of their assets in the old account. The companies were also forbidden to declare bankruptcy.

The process of restructuring nonfinancial firms involved an important role for banks. Each firm was required to select a set of *tokubetsu kanrinin* (special managers), who would oversee the restructuring process. As a rule, the special managers were two of a company's own executives and two representatives of the firm's creditors. The special managers were central decisionmakers in the restructuring process. For instance, it was their responsibility to determine which assets should be included in the new account. They were also required to draw up a restructuring plan and submit it to the finance minister for approval. Miyajima (1992, pp. 229–30) reports that drafting a restructuring plan required the special managers to assess the value of assets, make plans for future production and finance, and create forecasts of balance sheets and income statements. Accordingly, the restructuring of special account companies gave the special managers an excellent opportunity to accumulate information about the companies. Hoshi, Kashyap, and

20. The whole text of *Kaisha Keiri Ohkyu Sochi Ho* can be found in Takaishi 1966c, pp. 220–35.
21. Japan 1983, p. 734.

Table 9-3. Major Items in the New and the Old Accounts of Nonfinancial Corporations

Category	*Assets*		*Liabilities*	
Old account	(A1)	Assets other than (a1)	(L1)	All liabilities
	(A2)	Receivable from new account	(L2)	Capital
New account	(a1)	Assets that were deemed necessary to continue the current business	(l1)	Payable to old account

Source: Japan 1983, pp. 734–36; Takaishi 1966c, pp. 223–25.

Loveman (forthcoming) and Hoshi (1993) argue that this experience increased the banks' monitoring capability and enabled the banks to play an important role in corporate governance in Japan.

According to Takaishi (1966b, p. 271), there was a movement that requested participation of a labor representative in the reorganization process as a special manager. This was the period when the labor movement was very active. Okazaki (1993a,b) argues that the power of corporate control had shifted from shareholders to mangers, employees, and banks during the war. After the war, encouraged by SCAP's labor democratization policy, including the introduction of the Labor Union Law in 1946, the labor movement became extremely militant and fought for corporate control with the other strong contenders, banks.[22] The issue of inclusion of labor representatives in special management teams is one aspect of the battle over corporate control between labor unions and banks. Thus, the decision by the Japanese government and SCAP not to allow labor representation through special managers had an impact in shaping the postwar system of corporate governance in Japan.

It would be exaggerating to suggest that the exclusion of special managers eliminated the chance for the workers to win control of cor-

22. Teranishi 1993, pp. 81–83.

porations. During this period (1946–47), the labor unions had great influence on the management of corporations, even though they were not formally represented by special managers. According to Hideaki Miyajima, we can observe that representatives of labor unions often signed the reconstruction and reorganization plan presented for approval.[23] As we will see later in the chapter, the labor union of NEC repeatedly requested wage increases during this period. The power of labor unions started to decline as the focus of U.S. occupation policy started to shift from the democratization of Japan to its economic recovery in 1948, and the Dodge stabilization policy of 1949 made it almost impossible for the management to accommodate wage increases. Thus, by late 1949, when many corporations started reorganizations, management (with the help of banks) was powerful enough to impose reorganization plans that often involved massive layoffs. Exclusion of labor from special management teams did not immediately reduce the influence of labor unions, but, combined with other important factors such as the change in the occupation policy and the implementation of the stabilization plan, it played a role in forming the postwar system of corporate governance.

Let us go back to the discussion of the Corporations Accounting Temporary Measures Act. Table 9-4 shows the proportion of assets placed in the old account as of August 11, 1946, by industry. For this sample of 266 firms, an average of 64.21 percent of total assets and 59.67 percent of fixed assets were assigned to the old account. There is substantial cross-industry variation in the figure, as one would expect. The proportion of assets placed in the old account is high for a heavy industry that was greatly involved in war-related production, and low for light manufacturing. In an extreme case—airplane and weapon industries—about 95 percent of assets were classified into the old account.

Reorganization of the Old Account

Special managers led the reorganization of the old accounts of special account firms. The process was guided by *Kigyo Saiken Seibi Ho* (Cor-

---

23. Personal communication.

Table 9-4. Size of Old Account by Industry

Industry	*Number of firms*	*Proportion of total assets assigned to old account (percent)*	*Proportion of fixed assets assigned to old account (percent)*
Agriculture[a]	7	39.42	24.02
Coal	6	46.23	40.54
Other mining	12	76.66	69.58
Construction	9	27.61	32.09
Metal	22	72.68	74.95
Machinery	84	71.56	70.14
Electric machinery	9	60.60	50.79
Communication equipment	11	63.95	50.37
Transportation, durable	19	71.33	70.35
Precision machinery	7	74.00	76.35
Airplanes and weapons	11	93.13	96.45
Other machinery	27	61.20	57.45
Chemical	42	59.70	48.95
Cotton spinning	10	62.04	54.35
Other textile	14	32.31	37.15
Other manufacturing	26	43.19	28.11
Distribution and services	34	61.97	63.00
Total	266	64.21	59.67

a. Includes lumber and fisheries.
Source: Japan 1983, pp. 762–73.

porations Reconstruction and Reorganization Act), promulgated on October 18, 1946.[24] About the same time, SCAP started to implement numerous antitrust measures to "democratize" Japanese business, and these measures seriously complicated and delayed the process of corpo-

24. The text of *Kigyo Saiken Seibi Ho* can be found in Takaishi 1966c, pp. 291–310. This law also went through numerous revisions. The major revisions are discussed in Takaishi 1966c, pp. 338–73. A discussion of the process in English is found in GHQ/SCAP 1951b.

rate reorganization and reconstruction. Among numerous antitrust measures, the Elimination of Excessive Concentration of Economic Power Law was the most important in influencing the reorganization process.

Discussion of breaking up large firms in Japan started when the U.S. government submitted the Policy on Excessive Concentration of Economic Power in Japan (FEC-230) to the Far Eastern Committee on May 12, 1947.[25] This document identified "an excessive concentration of economic power" as "any private enterprise conducted for profit, or combination of such enterprises, which, by reason of its relative size in any line or the cumulative power of its position in many lines, restricts competition or impairs the opportunity for others to engage in business independently, in any important segment of business," and argued that controls exercised by such economic power "have been a major factor in fostering and supporting Japanese aggression." SCAP initially planned to include the elimination of excessive concentration in the reorganization and reconstruction process of corporations. Thus, firms that were considered to be too big were required to include a plan to break up in the reorganization plan. The reorganization process was substantially delayed because now industrial firms had to wait and see whether they would be ordered to split up before they could draw up a reorganization plan.

On December 18, 1947, the Elimination of Excessive Concentration of Economic Power Law was promulgated, and SCAP started the investigation to determine which companies should be broken up. By February 1948, SCAP came up with a list of 325 companies to be split up. At about the same time, however, the U.S. policy toward the occupation of Japan started to change, reflecting escalation of the Cold War. The United States is believed to have decided that the occupation must be geared more toward reconstruction of the Japanese economy rather than its thorough democratization. The implementation of the Elimination of Excessive Concentration of Economic Power Law was greatly influenced by this policy change, and, in the end, only eighteen of the designated companies were actually split up.

25. For the development leading to the Elimination of Excessive Concentration of Economic Power Law and its consequences, see Japan 1982a, pp. 456–77. Japan 1982b contains the FEC-230 (pp. 350–61).

As we saw in the last section, the Japanese government initially planned to coordinate the reorganization processes of financial institutions and industrial firms by using the three-step approach, in which the industrial firms first came up with the estimates of losses. Because it was clear that the antitrust issues described above substantially delayed the reorganization of nonfinancial corporations, the three-step approach was abandoned. The financial institutions reorganized their old accounts without waiting for the industrial firms to reorganize, and the industrial firms evaluated their old accounts using the estimates supplied by financial institutions.

The nonfinancial corporations also faced the same evaluation problems that financial institutions encountered. Unrealized capital gains on fixed assets and the value of foreign assets were treated in much the same way they had been in financial institutions. The value of foreign assets was totally discounted, while the liabilities were valued at face value. Firms were prohibited from adding unrealized capital gains on fixed assets to the profits of the old account. The inventories were, however, evaluated at the market values, enabling firms to include the unrealized capital gains in the profits.

There was also a problem unique to the industrial firm. The problem arose from the uncertainty concerning reparations policy. Many industrial firms had industrial plants that were initially expected to be seized for reparation payment. During the reorganization process, such assets were evaluated at zero value. As the U.S. policy toward Japan changed, reflecting the start of the Cold War in the late 1940s, its reparation policy also changed, and the seizure of industrial plants for reparation did not happen. The restrictions placed on designated plants for reparation during the reorganization period, however, caused many managerial as well as accounting problems for the firms.

As in the case of the financial institutions, the losses from suspension of wartime compensation were canceled out with the capital and the liabilities according to the following prioritization.

1. Profits accrued to the old account before August 10, 1946
2. Retained earnings in the old account
3. Profits of the old account after August 10, 1946, and before the merger of new and old accounts

Table 9-5. Special Losses by Industry
(million yen)

Industry	*Number of firms*	*Special losses*	*Retained earning, etc.*	*Capital gains*	*Capital canceled*	*Credit canceled*	*Capital cancellation ratio (percent)*
Agriculture[a]	11	466	359	40	47	17	9
Coal	21	4,040	2,170	489	315	851	11
Metal	53	11,280	4,856	2,258	1,649	2,490	52
Communication equipment	19	2,057	800	716	154	387	32
Electric machinery	16	3,986	2,256	1,631	31	69	1
Transportation, durable	39	9,785	3,293	2,484	1,689	2,265	53
Airplanes and weapons	21	8,686	1,896	1,582	689	4,518	71
Other machinery	91	2,697	1,186	897	251	362	33
Chemical	69	5,006	2,549	1,069	577	746	19
Textile	42	4,730	3,757	596	48	6	1
Other manufacturing	39	1,246	767	349	39	31	3
Shipping	33	2,400	1,940	83	253	123	38
Commerce and service	45	1,226	736	144	162	137	26
Total	499	57,604	26,563	12,339	5,904	12,002	24

a. Includes lumber and fisheries.
Source: Japan 1983, pp. 904–5.

4. Capital gains on assets in the old account[26]
5. Up to 90 percent of the capital
6. Up to 70 percent of the debt
7. Remaining 10 percent of the capital
8. Remaining 30 percent of the debt.

The restructuring of nonfinancial companies took much longer than that of financial institutions, and all the special account companies had submitted their restructuring plans only in 1950. The implementation of the plans took even longer, and more than 20 percent of special account companies were still undergoing restructuring at the end of 1952. About 12 percent of the companies seem to have disappeared without completing the restructuring.[27]

The losses incurred by shareholders and creditors were not as large as expected. The profits of the old account, which included the proceeds from sales of assets, were sufficient to cover 45.9 percent of the total losses of 91.3 billion yen. The capital gains of assets covered another 21.3 percent. Postwar inflation turned out to be very helpful by increasing the gains of the old accounts, and the losses of shareholders and creditors were limited to 32.8 percent of the total losses, or about 30 billion yen.[28]

The total losses for each industry are reported in table 9-5 for the sample of 499 companies. The losses for these 499 companies (57.6 billion yen) explain about 63 percent of the economywide losses. One can observe that the amount of total losses, and hence the burden on shareholders and creditors, was especially large for the war-related heavy industries.

Recapitalization of Nonfinancial Corporations

After the merger of new and old accounts, each special account company had to decide whether the current firm would continue business or disband. If the company decided to disband itself, it was allowed to

26. This includes capital gains on inventories and evaluation gains on fixed assets for which accelerated depreciation was claimed in the past.
27. Japan 1983, pp. 899–900.
28. Japan 1983, p. 902.

set up a new company (*daini gaisha*, meaning second company), which could acquire productive assets from the current company by giving shares. As we will see later in this chapter, when the case of Nippon Steel is discussed, many companies that were split up according to the Elimination of Excessive Concentration of Economic Power Law chose to disband the company and set up several new companies.

To assure the financial health of the continuing companies or new companies, SCAP ordered that the level of capital must be "no less than the amount of fixed capital and normally fixed working capital" in the Standards for Reorganization.[29] Thus, many companies have to issue new shares to raise their capital levels. The delay of the reorganization process for industrial firms created a serious problem in their recapitalization because of the stock market collapse of October 1949. Unlike the recapitalization of financial institutions, the recapitalization of nonfinancial corporations encountered difficulty from the very beginning. Miyajima (1993) reports the examples of Hitachi and Toshiba, both of which had trouble selling shares because their share prices dropped below their par values. Observing the difficulty of issuing new shares in the depressed market, the Standards for Reorganization was revised in December 1949 to require "as much recapitalization as possible given the market conditions."[30]

As Miyajima (in this volume) argues, the collapse of the stock market posed another serious problem to the managers of Japanese companies: the threat of takeovers. The arrangement of cross-shareholdings started to develop to solve the problems of the difficulty of new share issues and the takeover threats. The main banks played an important role in developing cross-shareholdings, as Miyajima (in this volume) discusses. According to Mr. Yushin Yamamuro, who was a banker at Mitsubishi Bank during this period, the main banks often financed share purchases of customer companies by friendly individuals.[31]

29. Japan 1983, p. 876.
30. Japan 1983, p. 887.
31. Personal interview, December 8, 1993.

Like the new shares issued by financial institutions, new shares of a special account company were preferentially allocated to the former shareholders and the former creditors whose credit was canceled against the losses.[32] They had the right to buy a set number of shares at par value. Because nonfinancial corporations were prohibited from holding shares in other companies by the Anti-Monopoly Law, they could not exercise such a right, but they were allowed to sell the right or to request the refund of the premiums they would have enjoyed. Following the former shareholders and the creditors, employees of the firm received priority to buy new shares. The residents of the community where the company was located received the third priority and could buy new shares before they were sold to the general public.

When a company decided to create a new company from the new account, shares in a new company were initially used to pay for the assets provided by the (old) special account company. When the special account company was disbanded, the shares in the new company were sold to (a) individuals and financial institutions who were the former shareholders or the creditors, (b) executives and employees of the new company, (c) local residents, and (d) the general public, in this order. Nonfinancial companies that were former shareholders could sell their right to buy new shares at par value.

The benefits enjoyed by the former shareholders and the creditors must have substantially reduced the cost of their losses, and their losses must have been well below 30 billion yen.

After the reorganization, many firms were required to create reconciliation accounts. Because the estimates of the value of assets in the old account were extremely conservative, firms often realized capital gains when those assets were actually sold off after the reorganization. Such capital gains were put into the reconciliation account, and the accumulated "profits" of the reconciliation account were later distributed to the former creditors and the former shareholders whose claims had been canceled during the reorganization. Thus, the reconcil-

---

32. The discussion of the rules concerning share issues by special account companies and the new companies follows Japan 1983, pp. 877–80.

iation account of an industrial firm played very much the same role as it did for a financial institution.

Case Study 1: Industrial Bank of Japan

In this section and the next, two cases of bank reorganization are examined to aid in the understanding of the process. This section studies the case of IBJ, and the next section looks at the experience of Yasuda Bank, which later changed its name to Fuji Bank.

IBJ (*Nihon Kogyo Ginko*) was established in 1903 as a bank that specialized in long-term industrial financing. The bank raised funds by selling debentures and made long-term loans. Although IBJ was not owned by the government, its directors were appointed by the Ministry of Finance.[33] Thus, IBJ was considered to be a *de facto* government financial institution. This semigovernmental nature of IBJ is important in explaining the massive exposure that IBJ had to have for the war industries.

By the end of the war, IBJ was heavily involved in war financing, and the war-related loans of IBJ reached 76.1 percent.[34] As of August 11, 1946, IBJ's balance sheet was separated into a new account and an old account, and the restructuring process started. Table 9-6 shows how the balance sheet was separated. At this time, IBJ debentures held by other financial institutions and the government were classified into the new account. As we can see from the table, IBJ debentures assigned to the new account amounted to 92.4 percent of the total IBJ debentures outstanding.

After evaluating the value of asset items in the old account, IBJ submitted a reorganization plan to the finance minister on January 10, 1948. According to the plan, the total losses of the old account were estimated to be 6.839 billion yen. The capital and liabilities that could be used to cancel the losses were estimated to be the following.

33. Packer, forthcoming, p. 3.

34. The discussion in this section draws on Takaishi 1966c, chapter 248; IBJ 1982, pp. 113–23; Takasugi 1990, chapters 9 and 12.

Category	*Amount (million yen)*
Capital gains in the old account	35
Retained earnings	62
Capital	200
Deposits in the old account	281
IBJ debentures in the old account	479
Other liabilities in the old account	106
Total	1,163

Thus, IBJ expected to have losses of 5.676 billion yen that would remain even after the cancellation of capital and debts. As discussed earlier, the government was to compensate for losses if the entire capital and liabilities in the old account were not sufficient to cover losses. As of January 1948, the limit of the government compensation was set at 10 billion yen. IBJ estimates suggested that 57 percent of the planned rescue fund must be used for IBJ alone. Later in 1948, the limit was increased to 16.5 billion yen and the government ended up spending 16.4 billion yen for compensation, as we saw earlier. Even compared with these larger numbers, IBJ was expected to use up 34 percent of government funds.

Thus, it was fortunate for IBJ that SCAP found the treatment of bank debenture "unfair and unlawful." On March 27, 1948, the Financial Institutions Accounting Temporary Measures Act was partially reformed, and all the bank debentures held by financial institutions were moved from the new account to the old account. This substantially increased the liabilities in the old account of IBJ, which could be wiped away.

On May 15, 1948, the final plan of IBJ reorganization was accepted by the government, and the old account was restructured retroactively to March 31, 1948. The final estimate of the losses amounted to 7.593 billion yen, which exceeds the estimate of January 10 by about 10 percent, mainly because the new number includes the operational costs between August 10, 1946, and March 31, 1948 (0.637 billion yen). Most of the losses were from the write-off of bad loans (6.625 billion yen). Table 9-7 shows how the capital and liabilities in the old account were used to cover the losses. The difference between the amount of total

Table 9-6. Separation of IBJ's Balance Sheet, August 11, 1946
(thousand yen)

Item	*Before separation*	*Old account*	*New account*
[Assets]			
Cash and deposits	254,335	—	254,335
Loans	17,420,930	17,829,945	130,985
Securities	710,634	154,426	556,208
Unpaid capital	112,500	112,500	—
Other assets	1,436,040	972,961	463,079
Unsettled accounts	—	—	13,285,755
Total	19,934,439	19,069,832	14,690,362
[Liabilities]			
Deposits	3,925,450	3,762,067	163,383
Debentures	7,752,167	590,666	7,161,501
Borrowing	7,724,936	476,132	7,248,804
Other liabilities	813,586	696,912	116,674
[Capital]			
Capital	200,000	200,000	—
Reserves	58,300	58,300	—
Unsettled accounts	—	13,285,755	—

— Not applicable.
Source: Takaishi 1966c, p. 579.

cancellation and the losses, which amounted to 1.597 million yen, was transferred to the reconciliation account (discussed later). The shift of bank debentures held by other financial institutions from the new account to the old account created the most dramatic difference between these numbers and the estimates on January 10. The amount of deposits, debentures, and other liabilities in the old account jumped from 0.866 billion yen to 10.617 billion yen, of which 6.514 billion yen was canceled to cover the losses. Thus, the average cancellation ratio of liabilities for IBJ was 61.35 percent, which favorably compares with the cancellation ratios for other large banks, as we will see in the next section.

The final step of the restructuring was recapitalization. As we saw earlier, the banks were ordered to have a risk assets ratio of more than

Table 9-7. Cancellation of Liabilities in the Old Account (IBJ) *(thousand yen)*

Item	*Amount canceled*
Capital gains and retained earnings	819,017
All reserves	61,474
90 percent of capital	180,000
70 percent of corporate deposits that exceed 5 million yen per account	60,545
50 percent of corporate deposits that exceed 1 million yen per account	27,278
30 percent of corporate deposits that exceed 0.1 million yen per account	17,033
70 percent of remaining deposits and bank debentures	5,607,790
10 percent of capital	20,000
Up to 30 percent of remaining deposits and bank debentures	801,090
Total	7,594,227

Source: IBJ 1982, p. 116.

3 percent (and ideally more than 5 percent). Because IBJ was estimated to have 14.32 billion yen of risk assets, it had to raise between 430 million yen (3 percent of the risk assets) and 710 million yen (5 percent of the risk assets) through new share issues.[35] When IBJ was about to start the process of recapitalization, SCAP ordered all the special banks abolished, which included IBJ.

On June 30, SCAP ordered that the special bank system in Japan be discontinued and that each special bank decide whether it would transform itself (a) into a commercial bank or (b) into a debenture-issuing nonbank. Faced with the choice of "a or b," IBJ started to draft a reconstruction plan assuming that alternative a would be chosen; at the same time, it began negotiating with SCAP.[36] IBJ argued that

35. Takasugi 1990, p. 74.

36. Takasugi 1990, which is a novel based on the postwar history of IBJ, includes a vivid description of the negotiation, which involved IBJ, SCAP, the Bank of Japan, and the Ministry of Finance (chapters 9 and 12).

debenture-issuing banks that specialize in long-term project financing would be indispensable for the reconstruction and growth of the Japanese economy. With the help of the Bank of Japan, IBJ finally succeeded in convincing SCAP, and it was allowed to survive as a bank that specializes in long-term industrial financing. Finally, the reconstruction plan of IBJ submitted on November 22, 1948, was approved by the finance minister on November 27, and IBJ was able to start selling the shares on December 2.

IBJ planned new share issues of 500 million yen, which amounted to 3.4 percent of the risk assets. SCAP requested that IBJ sell its shares to other financial institutions as much as possible. Because many financial institutions suffered from the cancellation of IBJ debentures, which were moved from the new account to the old account at the latest stage of reorganization, IBJ had difficulty selling them the shares. (Takasugi 1990, pp. 291–306, gives a colorful account of the IBJ's effort to convince regional banks to hold IBJ shares.) New share issues were complete by December 23, and IBJ succeeded in selling all 500 million yen of shares. About 58 percent of shares were bought by financial institutions, and most of the remaining shares were held by the general public. Although the former shareholders, creditors, and the employees had the priority right to subscribe to new shares, they collectively bought only 2.21 percent of IBJ shares.

IBJ created a reconciliation account, as did many financial institutions. On February 2, 1953, IBJ became one of the first financial institutions to distribute a portion of profit of the reconciliation account to the former creditors of canceled debentures and deposits. The amount distributed reached 1.269 billion yen, which was 20 percent of the total amount of canceled credits. By November 29, 1958, when IBJ closed the reconciliation account, the cumulative profits amounted to 6.456 billion yen, and all the former creditors could reclaim their principal.[37]

37. The number is 99.12 percent of the exact amount of canceled debentures and deposits that we can calculate from table 9-7 (6. was billion yen). Because there must have been some creditors who failed to show up to receive the distribution, we can say that IBJ was able to pay back all the canceled credits.

The profits, however, were not enough to cover the interest on those debentures and deposits, and the interest income was lost forever.

Case Study 2: Yasuda Bank to Fuji Bank

Yasuda Bank, the central company in the Yasuda *zaibatsu*, had the largest deposits among Japanese banks when the war ended.[38] Like other major banks, Yasuda Bank grew rapidly through numerous mergers during the war.[39] The rapid growth during the war also meant a heavy involvement with war financing. Thus, when the Japanese government decided to repudiate wartime compensations, it was clear that Yasuda Bank had to go through a massive reorganization.

The reorganization process was started by the separation of the balance sheet into old and new accounts as of 0:00 a.m. on August 11, 1946. Table 9-8 illustrates how the balance sheet was separated into the two accounts. The table shows that 52.7 percent of the deposits were classified into the old account. This proportion is a bit higher than that for the aggregate banking industry (47 percent), and probably reflects the high proportion of corporate deposits at Yasuda Bank compared with the average financial institution. The proportion was even higher for the other *zaibatsu* banks. Mitsubishi Bank put 60 percent of deposits into the old account, and the proportions at Sumitomo Bank and Mitsui Bank were even higher, at 76 percent and 83 percent, respectively.[40]

A major part of the assets in the old account included loans (and discounts), some expected to be uncollectible. The table shows that the proportion of the loans in the total amount of assets in the old account was 85 percent for Yasuda Bank. The ratio was also high for other

---

38. This section draws on Fuji Ginko 1960, pp. 215–19, 248–49, 314–35, 568–73; and Takaishi 1966c, pp. 773–77.
39. See Teranishi 1982 for details on the concentration process of the Japanese banking industry.
40. Mitsubishi Ginko 1954, p. 398; Sumitomo Ginko 1979, p. 391; and Mitsui Ginko 1957, p. 319.

Table 9-8. Separation of Yasuda Bank's Balance Sheet, August 11, 1946 *(thousand yen)*

Item	*Before separation*	*Old account*	*New account*
[Assets]			
Cash and deposits	728,152	34	728,118
Interbank loans (credit)	0	—	0
Loans and discounts	13,364,160	13,328,921	35,239
Securities	3,245,899	429,882	2,816,017
Foreign exchange	13,514	13,514	—
Tangible assets	20,348	20,348	—
Other assets	1,840,026	1,782,452	57,574
Unpaid capital	67,300	67,300	—
Unsettled accounts	—	—	7,621,483
Total	19,279,408	15,642,457	11,258,434
[Liabilities]			
Deposits	14,096,033	7,430,204	6,665,829
Interbank loans (debt)	3,859,918	—	3,859,918
Foreign exchange	8,645	8,645	—
Other liabilities	1,002,759	270,073	732,686
[Capital]			
Capital	170,000	170,000	—
Reserves	137,092	137,092	—
Retained earnings	4,956	4,956	—
Unsettled accounts	—	7,621,483	—

— Not applicable.
Source: Fuji Ginko 1960, p. 316.

zaibatsu banks: 92 percent for Mitsubishi, 86 percent for Sumitomo Bank, and 93 percent for Teikoku Bank.[41]

On January 10, 1948, Yasuda Bank submitted the restructuring plan. It was initially accepted, but was returned for recalculation in February because the bank debentures had to be shifted from the new account to the old account, as we have discussed. On May 15, Yasuda

41. Sumitomo Bank 1954, p. 391; Mitsubishi Bank 1979, p. 398; and Mitsui Ginko 1957, p. 319.

submitted a revised reorganization plan, and it was approved on May 17. According to the plan, Yasuda evaluated the old account as of March 31, compensated the losses using the capital and liabilities in the old account, and merged the two accounts.

The total losses were estimated to be 1,621,462 thousand yen. Table 9-9 shows how the losses were compensated. The difference between the total amount of cancellation (1,631,543 thousand yen) and the losses, which amounted to 10,081 thousand yen, was put into the reconciliation account. As the table shows, Yasuda did not go as far as IBJ did: 10 percent of the shares remained intact and the cancellation ratio of the deposits was less than 70 percent. The other *zaibatsu* banks were not as fortunate as Yasuda, as table 9-10 shows. Many banks had to cut 100 percent of the capital and more than 70 percent of the deposits.

Table 9-11 shows how the old and the new accounts were merged on March 31, 1948. At this time, the reconciliation account showed profits of 21,419 thousand yen.

Recapitalization of Yasuda Bank was delayed because SCAP had not decided whether the Elimination of Excessive Concentration of

Table 9-9. Cancellation of Liabilities in the Old Account, Yasuda Bank *(thousand yen)*

Item	*Amount canceled*
Capital gains and retained earnings	310,786
All reserves	129,168
90 percent of capital	153,000
70 percent of corporate deposits that exceed 5 million yen per account	32,305
50 percent of corporate deposits that exceed 1 million yen per account	43,861
30 percent of corporate deposits that exceed 0.1 million yen per account	60,890
Up to 70 percent of remaining deposits and bank debentures (Actual cancellation ratio = 61.0 percent)	901,533
Total	1,631,543

Source: Fuji Ginko 1960, pp. 318–20.

Table 9-10. Amount of Losses and How They Were Covered, Five Major Banks
(million yen)

Bank	*Losses*	*Capital gain*	*Retained earnings*	*Capital*	*Deposit*
Sumitomo	1,518	349	90	74 (100%)	1,005 (79%)
Teikoku	2,391	400	224	220 (100%)	1,548 (79%)
Mitsubishi	1,975	442	151	126 (93%)	1,256 (74%)
Yasuda	1,621	311	129	153 (90%)	1,039 (64%)
Sanwa	1,503	231	84	138 (90%)	1,051 (64%)

Note: The numbers in parentheses show the ratios to the total amount available in the old account.

Source: Sumitomo Bank 1979, p. 392.

Economic Power Law should be also applied to large financial institutions. But the delay was much shorter than that experienced by IBJ. On July 30, 1948, the Holding Companies Liquidation Committee announced that the Excessive Power Law would not be applied to financial institutions, and on August 21 the government approved recapitalization of Yasuda Bank.

New issues that started on August 23 initially aimed at raising 953 million yen. Adding 17 million yen of capital that survived the reorganization, the new level of capital was to be 970 million yen, which was 5 percent of the risk assets of Yasuda Bank. As we have seen, the priority to buy new shares was given to (a) the former creditors, (b) the former shareholders, (c) the employees, and (d) the local residents, in this order. Shares were subscribed surprisingly well, and the bank raised 1,333 million yen. On October 1, 1948, the bank started with a new capital level of 1,350 million yen, which was 6.9 percent of the risk assets. The name of the bank was changed to Fuji Bank at the same time.[42]

42. Other *zaibatsu* banks also changed their names. For instance, Sumitomo Bank became Osaka Bank; Mitsubishi Bank changed its name to Chiyoda Bank.

Table 9-11. Merger of Yasuda Bank's Balance Sheets, March 31, 1948 *(thousand yen)*

Item	*New account*	*Old account*	*After merger*
[Assets]			
Cash and deposits	6,328,674	—	6,328,674
Interbank loans (credit)	250,000	—	250,000
Loans and discounts	12,564,444	5,019,471	17,583,916
Securities	6,027,844	56,316	6,084,160
Tangible assets	52,167	—	52,167
Other assets	1,532,681	438,383	1,971,064
Unsettled accounts	4,718,235	—	—
Total	31,474,050	5,514,173	32,256,597
[Liabilities]			
Deposits	25,368,821	698,857	26,067,678
Interbank loans (debt)	3,348,938	—	3,348,938
Foreign exchange	—	3,135	3,135
Other liabilities	2,704,123	33,323	2,737,446
[Capital]			
Capital, reserves, and retained earnings	52,167	39,200	91,367
Reconciliation account	—	21,419	21,419
Unsettled accounts	—	4,718,235	—

— Not applicable.
Source: Fuji Bank 1960, p. 321.

On November 28, 1955, seven years after the merger of new and old accounts, Fuji Bank closed the reconciliation account by distributing the profits to the former creditors and the former shareholders. Fuji Bank returned 1,034 million yen to the former creditors to cover the principal they lost (1,039 million yen according to table 9-9) during the reorganization. In addition, Fuji was also able to pay them 169 million yen of interest. The former shareholders received 176 million yen to cover the lost principal (153 million yen) and the interest. The profits that remained after the distribution to the former creditors and shareholders were put into the reserves on the balance sheet of Fuji (the amount was 27 million yen). Thus, the depositors and the shareholders of Yasuda Bank were eventually able to reclaim what they lost during the reorganization process.

Case Study 3: Ajinomoto

In this section and the next, we look at two cases of the restructuring and reorganization of industrial firms. This section studies the experience at Ajinomoto, a food company that was forced to expand into war supplies production during the war; the next section discusses the case of Nippon Steel, which became one of the eighteen companies that were actually split up by the Elimination of Excessive Concentration of Economic Power Law.

Ajinomoto is famous for its monosodium-glutamate (MSG) based chemical seasoning, named *ajinomoto*.[43] Ajinomoto has been producing and marketing MSG since 1908. During the war, however, Ajinomoto was involved in the production of war supplies. In 1942, Ajinomoto started to produce butanol for airplane fuels and acetone for nitrocotton. In that year, the company changed its name to Dai Nippon Kagaku Kogyo (Great Japan Chemical Industries), and it was designated as a munitions company in January of 1944. During the last eighteen months of the war, the company had to stop producing *ajinomoto* and exclusively produce war supplies.

Although Dai Nippon Kagaku Kogyo was not a major *zaibatsu*, such as Mitsubishi or Mitsui, it could be considered to be a part of a small *zaibatsu*. The Suzuki family, who founded the company, had a holding company that held a substantial number of shares in Dai Nippon Kagaku Kogyo. The holding company decided to sell off the shares in Dai Nippon Kagaku Kogyo before it would be forced to do so under the *zaibatsu* dissolution. Moreover, the name of the company was changed back to Ajinomoto.

Involvement in war supplies production made Ajinomoto vulnerable to the repudiation of wartime compensation. Ajinomoto was designated as a special account company and started reorganization. As of 0:00 a.m. on August 11, the balance sheet was separated into old and new accounts. Table 9-12 shows how the balance sheet was separated.

---

43. This section draws on Ajinomoto 1971, 1972, and especially Ajinomoto 1972, pp. 26–35.

Table 9-12. Separation of Ajinomoto's Balance Sheet, August 11, 1946
(thousand yen)

Item	*Before separation*	*Old account*	*New account*
[Assets]			
Inventories	31,201	384	30,817
Other liquid assets	8,080	3,239	4,840
Financial assets	18,568	18,114	454
Land	2,201	1,280	1,163
Buildings and structures	2,753	74	2,679
Machines and equipment	9,495	—	9,495
Construction in progress	28,853	11,042	17,811
Deferred cost	312	—	312
Unpaid capital	16,875	16,875	—
Other assets	1,861	1,861	—
Wartime compensation	15,288	15,288	—
Foreign assets	1,782	1,782	—
Unsettled accounts	—	67,572	—
Total	137,511	137,511	67,572
[Liabilities]			
Short-term debt	6,011	6,011	—
Long-term debt	30,024	30,024	—
Other liabilities	44,266	44,266	—
[Capital]			
Capital	45,000	45,000	—
Reserves	10,069	10,069	—
Retained earnings	1,864	1,864	—
Unsettled accounts	—	—	67,572

— Not applicable.
Source: Ajinomoto 1972, pp. 26–35.

As we have discussed, the process of separating the balance sheet of nonfinancial institutions is more straightforward than that for financial institutions. The liabilities and capital are all classified into the old account. Only assets that are considered to be necessary to continue the current business are classified into the new account. The total value of the assets in the new account is recorded as the unsettled account that is payable from the new account to the old account. This unsettled account is the only item on the liabilities side of the new account.

The table shows that the size of the new account was roughly the same as that of the old account at the time of separation. This is a sharp contrast to the case of Nippon Steel, which we will consider in the next section, where the majority of assets were assigned to the old account. Perhaps more important for the production capability of Ajinomoto, 100 percent of machines and equipment and 97.3 percent of buildings and structures were put into the new account. This must have helped Ajinomoto enormously to restart production of *ajinomoto* without interference from the reorganization process.

There were five special managers for Ajinomoto. Two were selected from the management of Ajinomoto, and the other three were sent by the large creditors: Shimizu-gumi, Toyo Seikan, and Mitsubishi Bank, which was the designated financial institution for Dai Nippon Kagaku Kogyo.

The reorganization plan was submitted to the government on November 9, 1948, and approved on December 31 of that year. The total losses in the old account reached 96.273 million yen, itemized in table 9-13. Note that 66 percent of the losses were due to the repudiation of wartime compensation.

The special loss was canceled by (a) profits (1,864,000 yen), (b) retained earnings (10,426,000 yen), (c) profits of the old account (70,589,000 yen), and (d) capital gains on inventories (13,393,000 yen). Thus, Ajinomoto did not have to cut into its capital or debt to clean up the balance sheet, and it did not have to create a reconciliation account. Ajinomoto was not required to recapitalize, but it increased the capital through several private placements. As a result, the capital increased from 45 million yen in November 1948 to 400 million yen in May 1952.

Table 9-13. Itemized Losses for Ajinomoto, December 1948
(yen)

Item	*Amount of loss*
Wartime compensation special tax	63,501,539
Loss of foreign assets	1,505,871
Loss of second-line frozen deposits	1,668
Loss of credit against other companies	4,350,910
Loss of equities in other companies	463,182
Payment of unpaid capital to other companies	259,500
Deferred losses	1,790,046
Taxes and retirement payment	301,148
Fees for special managers	100,000
Management costs	14,518
Realized capital losses	1,307,155
Evaluation losses (from change of use, etc.) of assets	1,236,093
Others	21,441,470
Total	96,273,098

Source: Ajinomoto 1972, p. 27.

Case Study 4: Dissolution of Nippon Steel

In 1934 Nippon Steel was created as the result of a government policy to concentrate the steel industry.[44] The government solicited many private steel firms to merge with the government-owned Yawata Steel. Five companies (Fuji Steel, Kyushu Steel, Mitsubishi Steel, Kamaishi Mining, and Wanishi Steel) responded, and they merged with Yawata Steel to form Nippon Steel. Later in 1934, Toyo Steel and Osaka Steel also joined, and Nippon Steel became by far the largest steel company in Japan. As of the end of 1934, Nippon Steel produced 96 percent of

44. This section draws on Nihon Seitetsu Kabushiki Kaisha-shi Henshu Iinkai (Nihon Seitetsu henceforth) 1959, pp. 153–232, 915–92; Takaishi 1966a, pp. 498–510, 955–66.

the pig iron, 52 percent of the crude steel, and 44 percent of the steel materials that were made in Japan.

Observing that the international trade system was breaking down, the Japanese government created Nippon Steel to assure a reliable supply of domestic steel. During the war, Nippon Steel was obviously involved in war efforts. It invested a huge amount in the Japanese colonies (including Korea) to expand production. By the end of the war, the foreign assets held by Nippon Steel reached 1.1 billion yen. Because Nippon Steel did most of its business with the government and the military, it was seriously influenced by the repudiation of wartime compensation. Nihon Seitetsu (1959, p. 875) lists fifteen production facilities that the government ordered Nippon Steel to build and never paid for. The total cost for the fifteen facilities reached 76 million yen. In addition to these losses, Nippon Steel lost many factories to air raids and artillery attacks (from fleets) of the U.S. forces.

Nippon Steel started planning reconstruction and reorganization in late 1945. Their initial draft included the idea of liquidating the existing company and creating a new company, which is essentially what eventually happened. On August 11, 1946, Nippon Steel became a special account company, and its balance sheet was separated into new and old accounts. Table 9-14 shows how the balance sheet was separated into the two accounts. More than 99 percent of the assets were assigned to the old account at this time. Nihon Seitetsu (1959, pp. 218–19) suggests that the separation was modified in June 1947 under the guidance of the special managers, and the assets in the new account came to include the following:

Inventories	450,459,942 yen
Other liquid assets	63,592,319 yen
Fixed assets	12,248,034 yen
Other assets	15,376,893 yen
Total	541,677,189 yen

Even with this larger new account, its proportion to the amount of assets before the separation is less than 15 percent. As for the fixed assets, only 1.8 percent of the total amount was assigned to the new account.

Table 9-14. Separation of the Balance Sheet of Nippon Steel, August 11, 1946
(thousand yen)

Item	*Before separation*	*Old account*	*New account*
[Assets]			
Inventories	492,760	188,292	304,468
Other liquid assets	599,634	536,042	63,592
Financial assets	71,454	71,454	—
Fixed assets	691,989	691,989	—
Other assets	1,501,418	1,486,041	15,737
Deferred loss	487,759	487,759	—
Unsettled accounts	—	383,437	—
Total	3,845,013	3,845,013	383,437
[Liabilities]			
Short-term debt	1,238,990	1,238,990	—
Long-term debt	1,464,967	1,464,967	—
Other liabilities	17,945	17,945	—
[Capital]			
Capital	1,123,112	1,123,112	—
Unsettled accounts	—	—	383,437

— Not applicable.
Source: Nihon Seitetsu Kabushiki Kaisha-shi Henshu Iinkai 1959, p. 926.

As we discussed earlier, a special account company had to select special managers, who supervised the reorganization process. In the case of Nippon Steel, the special managers included a representative of IBJ, a representative of Teikoku Bank, a representative of the Closed Organizations Liquidation Committee (which dealt with the liquidation of closed organizations such as Chosen Bank or Taiwan Bank), and three representatives from Nippon Steel management. IBJ, Teikoku, and the Closed Organizations Liquidation Committee were large creditors of Nippon Steel.

On February 8, 1948, the Elimination of Excessive Concentration of Economic Power Law was applied to Nippon Steel, and it was ordered to be split up into smaller entities. Nippon Steel opposed the idea of a split-up, arguing that the company was not and would not be anti-competitive, but could not convince SCAP. Although the outbreak of the Cold War changed the U.S. occupation policy toward Japan, and the number of companies broken up under the Excessive Power Law was substantially reduced, Nippon Steel became one of the eighteen companies that were actually split up.

Thus, Nippon Steel had to come up with a reconstruction plan that included liquidation of the current company and establishment of new (smaller) companies. Such a plan was submitted to the government on May 16, 1949, and, after some revisions, approved on December 31 of that year. In this plan, the total losses of the old account were estimated to be 1,823 million yen, which was canceled with 90 percent of the capital (720 million yen) and 47.51 percent of the debt (1,103 million yen). Thus the situation at Nippon Steel was much more serious than that at Ajinomoto. Both shareholders and creditors of Nippon Steel suffered losses.

On April 1, 1950, the assets of the new account were distributed to four new companies: Yawata Steel, Fuji Steel, Nittetsu Steamship, and Harima Firebrick. In return, Nippon Steel received shares in the new companies. Table 9-15 shows how the assets of Nippon Steel were allocated to the four companies. Nippon Steel was expected to sell off the shares and the remaining assets (in the old account) and liquidate the company.

Nippon Steel initially planned to start selling shares on April 15, 1950. But the start was delayed three times, mainly because the stock market was so stagnated after the Dodge stabilization plan that it did not seem to be able to handle massive sales without depressing prices. While Nippon Steel was hesitating to sell shares in the new companies, the Korean War erupted on June 25, 1950. The start of the Korean War raised the expectation of boom in the Japanese economy and the stock prices, especially those for heavy industry, started to appreciate. Thus, Nippon Steel started selling shares in July, and shares of all four companies were priced above their par values.

As was previously discussed, the shares in the new companies had to be allocated to the former shareholders, the former creditors, the

Table 9-15. Dissolution of Nippon Steel into Four New Companies, April 1, 1950
(thousand yen)

Item	*Nippon Steel*	*Yawata Steel*	*Fuji Steel*	*Nittetsu Steamship*	*Harima Firebrick*
Fixed assets	4,187,601	2,209,725	1,719,370	252,911	5,595
Inventories	7,484,256	3,710,394	3,748,218	3,000	22,644
Liquid assets	11,167,693	6,872,697	4,222,224	59,802	13,059

Source: Nihon Seitetsu Kabushiki Kaisha-shi Henshu Iinkai 1959, pp. 926, 956–58.

employees, the local residents, and the general public, in this order of preference. A problem for Nippon Steel was that the government was both a large shareholder and large creditor. Because SCAP prohibited the government from holding shares of the new companies, Nippon Steel had to sell the shares that would have been allocated to the government and refund the premium to the government. About 44 percent of shares were supposed to be allocated to the government, but Nippon Steel was able to sell all of them to financial institutions and paid a premium (sales value minus par value) to the government.

The proceeds from share sales were used to repay the remaining debts in the old account. The remaining debts of Nippon Steel were 1,261 million yen, including the interest. When shares in the new companies were sold to the former creditors, they were often allowed to pay using the remaining part of their claims. Of 5,967,600 shares sold to the former creditors, 4,377,490 (73 percent) were sold through such debt-equity swaps, and this reduced the liabilities by 219 million yen. The remaining debts were paid off using (a) proceeds from sales of assets, (b) collected loans to the other companies, (c) receipts from reconciliation accounts of financial institutions, (d) receipts from reconciliation accounts of other industrial firms, and (e) proceeds from share sales. Table 9-16 shows how the debt was repaid. The importance of proceeds from share sales is clear. The sum of the revenues used to repay the debts is estimated to have exceeded the amount of debt by 177 million yen, which was put into the reconciliation account.

Because Nippon Steel eliminated 90 percent of the capital and canceled a portion of debt (48 percent), it had to set up a reconciliation

Table 9-16. Repayment of Debts in the Liquidation of Nippon Steel *(yen)*

Item	*Amount*
Total debts	1,261,153,048
Swapped with equities	218,874,500
Proceeds from asset sales	30,455,467
Collected loans to other companies	158,850,318
Distribution from reconciliation accounts (banks)	8,317,161
Distribution from reconciliation accounts (industrial firms)	18,992,215
(A Part of) Proceeds from share sales[a]	1,003,125,500

a. The author's estimate: each share is evaluated at par value (¥50).
Source: Nihon Seitetsu 1959, pp. 962–79.

account. When the profits from the account were redistributed in August 1956, the former creditors received 267 million yen, which is about 26.3 percent of the canceled amount.

Case Study 5: NEC

NEC (Nippon Electronic Corporation) started in 1898 as a limited partnership with Western Electric Company.[45] Starting as a manufacturer of telephones, NEC gradually expanded the business into other communication devices, such as radios. In 1920, NEC tied up with the electric cable subsidiary of Sumitomo, and this started a relationship between NEC and Sumitomo Zaibatsu. In the 1930s, as the Japanese military started to attack the foreign capitals, NEC, which had International Standard Electric (which includes the former Western Electric Company) as the majority shareholder, decided to delegate their management to Sumitomo Zaibatsu, becoming de facto a Sumitomo company. NEC changed its name to Sumitomo Tsushin Kogyo (Sumitomo Telecommunication) in 1943, and was designated as a munitions company in 1944.

45. This section draws on Nihon Denki Kabushiki Kaisha-shi Hensan-shitsu (Nihon Denki henceforth) 1972, especially pp. 219–36 and 240–46.

Soon after the war, NEC changed its name back to Nippon Electronic Corporation (November 1945) and started to shift back to nonmilitary production. NEC faced a problem common to all the munitions companies: cancellation of wartime compensation. NEC went through a reorganization under the Corporations Accounting Temporary Measures Act and the Corporations Reconstruction and Reorganization Act. The balance sheet was separated into new and old accounts as of August 11, 1946. But the reorganization process was delayed because on February 8, 1948, NEC was designated as one of 325 companies to be split up under the Elimination of Excessive Concentration of Economic Power Law. Fortunately for NEC, the U.S. occupation policy toward economic concentration dramatically changed as I described earlier, and NEC was removed from the list as of February 18, 1949. On April 30, NEC submitted the reconstruction plan to the government.

The total losses of NEC amounted to 478 million yen, as table 9-17 shows. The losses from the repudiation of wartime compensation were the largest item, explaining 66 percent of the total losses. Compared with table 9-12, we can observe that the losses at NEC, which was an important munitions company supplying communication equipment for military use, were about five times larger than the losses at Ajinomoto, which was inherently a food producer.

Of the total losses of 478 million yen, 182 million yen were canceled against the retained earnings and profits in the old account. The rest of the loss was canceled with evaluation gains on inventories (165 million), evaluation gains on fixed assets (15 million), and realized capital gains on fixed assets (115 million). Thus, NEC did not have to cancel any of its equities or debts. Unlike Ajinomoto, however, NEC had to use realized capital gains from the sales of several plants. This meant massive layoffs and relocation of workers, and the labor union naturally was opposed to this plan. The negotiation between the management and the labor union took more than three months, and finally, in August 1949, the labor union accepted the plan.

Let us look at the role of the labor union at NEC during this period more carefully. After labor unions were legalized under the Labor Union Law, unions started to form at the plant level of NEC. Initially, separate labor unions were formed for white-collar workers and blue-collar workers at each plant, but eventually the two unions merged, and plant-based unions merged into a single enterprise-level

Table 9-17. Itemized Losses for NEC, April 1949
(thousand yen)

Item	*Amount of losses*
Wartime compensation special tax	317,214
Loss of foreign assets	14,265
Loss of second-line frozen deposits	623
Loss of credit and equities in other companies	7,407
Deferred losses	16,552
Losses in the old account (including evaluation losses, etc.)	107,574
Others	13,948
Total	477,583

Source: Nihon Denki 1972, p. 241.

union. Thus, in June 1946, the NEC Labor Union, which included both white-collar and blue-collar workers at all the plants, was formed. The labor union frequently demanded wage increases and often went on strike. For example, in September 1947, following failed negotiations on a wage increase, the union went on a strike that lasted for forty-five days. By the end of strike, the labor union succeeded in getting wage increases comparable to the initial request. Thus, the labor union at NEC seems to have been very powerful during this period.

The environment surrounding the labor union movement started to change in 1948, as the United States began to shift the focus of its occupation policy from the democratization of Japan to its economic recovery. In March of 1948, SCAP ordered a stop to a general strike planned by major labor organizations, and in July government employees were deprived of their right to go on strike. Reflecting the change in the general environment, the power at NEC seems to have started to shift from labor to management. In September of 1948, the management demanded that the labor union accept a plan to increase productivity, which involved relocation of workers and restraints on wage increases. After the negotiation, the labor union finally accepted management's demand in October.

Thus, by the time management and the labor union started negotiation on the reconstruction plan in April of 1949, NEC's management seems to have gained substantial power against the union. Because the plan involved the layoff of 3,600 workers, the labor union fiercely opposed the plan. The management, however, did not show any sign of yielding to the union's pressure and, after a negotiation of more than three months, the labor union accepted the management plan with little change. When the plan was implemented, the number of workers at NEC shrank by more than 40 percent (including those who chose to retire), from about 12,000 to 6,750. This was just one-fourth of the wartime peak of 26,840 workers.

The case of NEC suggests a pattern of development of the postwar system of corporate governance in Japan. During the war and the postwar democratization, workers gained substantial power in corporate control. In 1946 and 1947, many Japanese companies seem to have been effectively controlled by insiders (Aoki 1994). After 1948, however, SCAP's policy toward the labor movement started to change, and the management appears to have started to gain more power over workers. By 1949, when many corporations started to implement their reorganization plans, the managers were able to convince the labor union to accept massive redundancies. Of course, we should be careful about generalizing from just one case study, and hope for future studies along this line.[46]

In the reorganization of NEC, its main bank, Osaka Bank (now Sumitomo Bank), played an important role. The massive layoffs required the company to pay a large amount in severance payments. Osaka Bank formed a lending consortium with seven other banks and lent NEC 100 million yen in late 1949 and 1950. In January of 1950, Osaka Bank sent Iwao Iwata to become the director of accounting at NEC and strengthened the main bank relationship.

Lessons from the Japanese Experience

The measures discussed above solved a large-scale insolvency problem of postwar Japan. This section concludes the paper by deriving some

46. We should also note that some labor unions stayed militant well into the 1950s and continued to influence management.

lessons from the Japanese experience that are useful for other economies that face similar insolvency problems, including China, Russia, and the economies in Eastern Europe and the former Soviet Union.

Lesson #1

A viable alternative to bankruptcy courts for mass reorganization exists.

As van Wijnbergen (1993) argues, "(u)se of bankruptcy procedures would inevitably overload the system and lead to interminable delays" (p. 12). Thus, relying on formal bankruptcy procedures to solve a large-scale insolvency problem is impractical. The Japanese experience suggests a viable alternative to bankruptcy courts to solve the problem.

Lesson #2

Separation of the balance sheet allows the company (bank) to reorganize without interfering with the ongoing business.

By separating the balance sheet into a new account and an old account, a firm (bank) can isolate the healthy part of the balance sheet from the part plagued by bad assets (loans). This measure allowed the firm (bank) to continue the business while the old account was reorganized. Moreover, by shielding the healthy assets from the bad assets, the problem of debt overhang was eliminated.

Note that, after the separation of the balance sheet, the new account and the old account may not have to belong to the same firm (bank), although they did belong to the same company and were later merged in postwar Japan. It is possible to come up with a reorganization process that transfers the new account to a totally new firm (bank). This scheme would be similar to the case of Nippon Steel, where new companies were established and the old company was liquidated, and also similar to the way some Eastern European economies, such as Hungary, handled the bad loans of state banks (Dittus 1993, pp. 12–13). The idea of setting up a new institution may be attractive to the transforming socialist economies, where the existing former state firms are operating with soft budget constraints. Phelps and colleagues (1993) favor creating new banks out of the state banking sector following a similar procedure, arguing that "the new banks would not operate according to the old rules" (p. 29).[47]

Lesson #3

There are two alternative ways of debt restructuring: individual-level or industry-level. Industry-level debt restructuring is less time-consuming, but individual-firm-level debt restructuring spreads the cost more equally to many parties.

In Japan, all the interfirm debts that involved a nonfinancial corporation were put in the old accounts, but the interbank loans were assigned to the new accounts. As Takaishi (1966b, pp. 660–61) points out, this means that debts were restructured at the industry level for financial institutions and at the individual level for nonfinancial institutions. Industry-level debt restructuring seems to be less time-consuming than firm-level debt restructuring, because iterations of assets revaluation within the industry are not necessary. At the same time, firm-level debt restructuring disperses the cost of shock (repudiation of wartime compensation in the case of Japan) over many firms, and may be considered fair. The Japanese government ended up choosing an eclectic plan: industry-level restructuring for banks and individual-level restructuring for nonfinancial corporations. This solution had one advantage. It speeded up the process of reorganization of banks by avoiding repeated reevaluation of interbank loans, and it allowed the banks to lead the reorganization process of industrial firms.

Lesson #4

Creation of reconciliation accounts allows reevaluation to continue after the merger of the new and old accounts.

---

47. The plan described in Phelps and others 1993 (pp. 28–29) does not create the new bank out of the new account. Using our terminology, they propose to create new banks out of the old accounts of the existing banks. The government takes up some deposits of a bank in return for the bank writing off the equivalent amount of bad loans. Then, the government transfers the deposits to a new bank with a sufficient amount of treasury bills.

Evaluation of interfirm debts requires iterated calculations. Setting up reconciliation accounts permits this iterative process to continue even after the reorganization is complete. In other words, people can call an end to the reorganization process at an early stage if they know the reevaluation process will continue in reconciliation accounts.

Lesson #5

The reorganization process has a significant impact on the subsequent development of corporate governance.

Restructuring and reorganization of a firm provide a nice opportunity for the involved parties to acquire valuable information about the firm. In the case of Japan, the banks were involved in the reorganization process of industrial firms as their special mangers and they accumulated knowledge that later became very useful in the main bank relationship. Labor failed to join the reorganization process as special managers. Although this was not the most important factor contributing to the decline of labor union power, labor eventually lost the battle over corporate governance to banks.

This episode suggests that the reorganization process has important implications for the corporate governance of the future. If there is a vision of the desirable corporate governance for the economy, the restructuring process may be designed to allow corporate governance a better chance to evolve in the desired direction. For instance, if the banks are expected to play an important role in corporate governance, they will benefit from involvement in the restructuring.

Lesson #6

The reorganization process can be (and probably should be) coordinated with antitrust measures.

Coordination with antitrust issues substantially delayed the reorganization of industrial firms in postwar Japan, but I believe the idea of utilizing the reorganization process to achieve deconcentration of industries is ingenious. Many transforming socialist economies have heavily concentrated industries. Restructuring and reorganization processes can be designed to achieve two goals at once: healthy firms and competitive industrial organization.

A general point here is that a reorganization of firms can involve more than accounting procedures. One can use the reorganization process to change other aspects of the firms. Most important, the organization of the firms should be changed if it is closely related to the causes of the insolvency problem. In the Japanese case, the cause of the insolvency problem was clear. The devastation in the war and the repudiation of wartime compensation made many firms and banks insolvent. Assuming that the occupation forces would successfully disarm Japan, the problem would never occur again. It is important to find out the sources of the insolvency problem in the economies in Eastern Europe and the former Soviet Union. If some organizational aspects of state firms are to be blamed, the reorganization is an excellent opportunity to correct the problems.

Lesson #7

The condition of the stock market influences the success of recapitalization.

This idea may seem obvious, but the Japanese experience confirms its validity. Recapitalization is useful and sometimes necessary to make firms (banks) healthy again, and the success of new share issues depends on the condition of the stock market. The banks did not really have trouble finding buyers for their shares because they were issued before the stock market collapsed in October 1949. Many industrial firms that tried to issue shares after the crash had trouble selling them. This may suggest that the restructuring and recapitalization of firms in the Eastern European economies should be done before the enthusiasm for their emerging stock markets is lost.

If there is a limit for the stock market to finance recapitalization, the question arises of which kind of companies should get priority in issuing shares—banks or industrial firms? In Japan, banks first recapitalized themselves, and industrial firms followed. This allowed the banks to play an important role in the reorganization of nonfinancial corporations, and subsequently in corporate governance. Starting with bank recapitalization seems to be a natural policy if the government tries to establish a bank-led system of corporate governance.

Lesson #8

The debt-equity swap is a useful tool of recapitalization.

As we saw in the last section, Nippon Steel used debt-equity swaps to distribute shares in the new companies and avoided dumping shares in the stock market. Thus, the debt-equity swap is a useful tool of recapitalization when the stock market is not well capitalized. This condition applies to almost all the emerging stock markets in the Eastern European economies, and hence the debt-equity swap is likely to be a useful instrument for recapitalization.

Lesson #9

Inflation can reduce the creditors' (depositors') cost of reorganization. But a reorganization plan that relies on this role of inflation may jeopardize the credibility of a tough anti-inflationary policy.

As we saw earlier, many banks eventually paid almost all the canceled deposits (and the interest) back to the depositors by distributing from the reconciliation accounts. One may argue that the cost for depositors was still substantial because they could not access these deposits when they really needed them in the immediate postwar period, and because the deposits they could recover in the end had lost their original value because of inflation. But the distribution from the reconciliation accounts nonetheless substantially reduced the costs of reorganization borne by depositors. Because postwar inflation created large capital gains in the reconciliation accounts of many firms and banks, we can give the credit for cost reduction to inflation.

There was a tradeoff, however, between this benefit of inflation and the possibility of losing government credibility to be tough on inflation, as the Japanese government correctly observed. Thus, the Japanese government initially decided to ignore unrealized capital gains to maintain credibility. This is likely to be a tradeoff encountered by the policymakers of the countries in Eastern Europe and the former Soviet Union. If there is a government that has already achieved a reputation for stable macroeconomic policy, it will be able to enjoy the benefits of the past inflation.

Bibliography

Ajinomoto. 1971. *Ajinomoto Kabushiki Kaisha Sha-shi. (Ajinomoto's Company History)*, vol. 1. Tokyo.

————. 1972. *Ajinomoto Kabushiki Kaisha Sha-shi. (Ajinomoto's Company History)*, vol. 2. Tokyo.

Aoki, Masahiko. 1994. "Controlling the Insider Control: Corporate Governance Issue in Transitional Economies." Stanford University, Palo Alto, Calif. Mimeo.

Bank of Japan. 1971. *Economic Statistics Annual, 1970*. Tokyo.

————. 1993. *Economic Statistics Annual, 1992*. Tokyo.

Dittus, Peter. 1993. "Corporate Governance in Central Europe: The Role of Banks." Bank for International Settlements, Basel. Mimeo.

Fuji Ginko. 1960. *Fuji Ginko Hachiju Nenshi (The Eighty-Years History of the Fuji Bank)*. Tokyo.

GHQ/SCAP (General Headquarters, Supreme Commander for the Allied Powers). 1951a. *History of the Nonmilitary Activities of the Occupation of Japan*, vol. 13. Part C, *Money and Banking*. National Archives, Washington, D.C.

————. 1951b. *History of the Nonmilitary Activities of the Occupation of Japan*, vol. 13. Part D, *Financial Reorganization of Corporate Enterprise*. National Archives, Washington, D.C.

Hoshi, Takeo. 1993. "Evolution of the Main Bank System in Japan." CEPR Working Paper Series, the Network in Financial Markets No. 46, London.

Hoshi, Takeo, Anil Kashyap, and Gary Loveman. Forthcoming. "Lessons from the Japanese Main Bank System for Financial System Reform in Poland." In Masahiko Aoki and Hugh Patrick, eds., *Japanese Finance and the Main Bank System*. Oxford, U.K.: Oxford University Press.

IBJ (Industrial Bank of Japan). 1982. *Nihon Kogyo Ginko Nanajugo Nenshi (The 75-Year History of the Industrial Bank of Japan).* Tokyo.

Japan, Ministry of Finance. 1959. *Dai 8 Kai Ginko-kyoku Kin'yu Nenpo (The 8th Financial Annual of the Banking Bureau).* Tokyo: The Ministry of Finance.

———. 1976. *Showa Zaisei-shi: Shusen kara Kowa made*, vol. 12, *Kin'yu (1) (The Financial History of Japan: The Allied Occupation Period, 1945–1952*, vol. 12, *Finance [1]).* Tokyo: Toyo Keizai Shimpo-sha.

———. 1978. *Showa Zaisei-shi: Shusen kara Kowa made*, vol. 19, *Tokei (The Financial History of Japan: The Allied Occupation Period, 1945–1952*, vol. 19, *Statistical Data).* Tokyo: Toyo Keizai Shimpo-sha.

———. 1979. *Showa Zaisei-shi: Shusen kara Kowa made*, vol. 14, *Hoken, Shoken (The Financial History of Japan: The Allied Occupation Period, 1945–1952*, vol. 14, *Insurance, Security).* Tokyo: Toyo Keizai Shimpo-sha.

———. 1982a. *Showa Zaisei-shi: Shusen kara Kowa made*, vol. 2, *Dokusen Kinshi (The Financial History of Japan: The Allied Occupation Period, 1945–1952*, vol. 2, *Anti-Monopoly).* Tokyo: Toyo Keizai Shimpo-sha.

———. 1982b. *Showa Zaisei-shi: Shusen kara Kowa made*, vol. 20, *Eibun Shiryo (The Financial History of Japan: The Allied Occupation Period, 1945–1952*, vol. 20, *English Documents).* Tokyo: Toyo Keizai Shimpo-sha.

———. 1983. *Showa Zaisei-shi: Shusen kara Kowa made*, vol. 13, *Kin'yu (2), Kigyo Zaimu, Mikaeri Shikin (The Financial History of Japan: The Allied Occupation Period, 1945–1952*, vol. 13, *Finance [2], Corporate Finance, and Assistance Funds).* Tokyo: Toyo Keizai Shimpo-sha.

———. 1991. *Showa Zaisei-shi: Showa 27-48 nendo*, vol. 10, *Kin'yu (2) (History of Fiscal and Monetary Policies in Japan: 1952–1973*, vol. 10, *Finance [2]).* Tokyo: Toyo Keizai Shimpo-sha.

Mitsubishi Ginko. 1954. *Mitsubishi Ginko-shi (History of the Mitsubishi Bank).* Tokyo.

Mitsui Ginko. 1957. *Mitsui Ginko Hachi-Ju-Nen-shi (Eighty Years History of the Mitsui Bank).* Tokyo.

Miyajima, Hideaki. 1992. "Zaibatsu Kaitai" (Zaibatsu Dissolution). In Juro Hashimoto and Haruto Takeda, eds., *Nihon Keizai no Hatten to Kigyo Shudan (The Development of the Japanese Economy and Industrial Groups).* Tokyo: University of Tokyo Press.

————— . 1993. "The Transformation of *Zaibatsu* to Post-war Corporate Groups—From Hierarchical Integrated Group to Horizontally Integrated Group." Waseda University, Tokyo. Mimeo.

Nakamura, Takafusa. 1986. *Showa Keizai-shi (Economic History of Showa).* Tokyo: Iwanami Shoten.

Nihon Denki Kabushiki Kaisha-shi Hensan-shitsu. 1972. *Nihon Denki Kabushiki Kaisha Shichi-Ju-nen-shi (70 Years History of Nippon Electric Corporation).* Tokyo: Nihon Denki Kabushiki Gaisha.

Nihon Seitetsu Kabushiki Kaisha-shi Henshu Iinkai. 1959. *Nihon Seitetsu Kabushiki Kaisha-shi, 1934–1950 (Nippon Steel Company History, 1934–1950).* Tokyo: Nihon Seitetsu Kabushiki Kaisha-shi Henshu Iinkai.

Okazaki, Tetsuji. 1993a. "The Japanese Firm under the Wartime Planned Economy." *Journal of the Japanese and International Economies* 7: 175–203.

————— . 1993b. "Kigyo Sisutemu" (The Corporate System). In Tetsuji Okazaki and Masahiro Okuno, eds., *Gendai Nihon Keizai Sisutemu no Genryu (The Origins of the Contemporary Japanese Economic System).* Tokyo: Nihon Keizai Shimbun-sha.

Packer, Frank. Forthcoming. "The Role of Long-Term Credit Banks within the Main Bank System." In Masahiko Aoki and Hugh Patrick, eds., *Japanese Finance and the Main Bank System.* Oxford, U.K.: Oxford University Press.

Phelps, Edmund S., Roman Frydman, Andrzej Rapaczynski, and Andrei Shleifer. 1993. "Needed Mechanisms of Corporate Governance and Finance in Eastern Europe." European Bank for Reconstruction and Development Working Paper #1, London.

Sumitomo Ginko. 1979. *Sumitomo Ginko Hachi-Ju-nen-shi (Eighty Years History of the Sumitomo Bank)*. Tokyo.

Takaishi, Suekichi. 1966a. *Oboegaki Shusen Zaisei Shimatsu*, vol. 14, *Mochi-Kabu Gaisha Seiri Iinkai no Katsudo (Notes on Post-War Fiscal and Monetary Situation*, vol. 14, *Activities of the Holding Companies Liquidation Committee)*. Tokyo: The Ministry of Finance.

———. 1966b. *Oboegaki Shusen Zaisei Shimatsu*, vol. 15, *Shusen-go ni okeru Kin'yu Mondai (Notes on Post-War Fiscal and Monetary Situation*, vol. 15, *Post-War Financial Problems)*. Tokyo: The Ministry of Finance.

———. 1966c. *Oboegaki Shusen Zaisei Shimatsu*, vol. 16, *Kin'yu Kikan to Kigyo no Saiken Seibi (Notes on Post-War Fiscal and Monetary Situation*, vol. 16, *Reconstruction and Reorganization of Financial Institutions and Corporations)*. Tokyo: The Ministry of Finance.

———. 1967. *Oboegaki Shusen Zaisei Shimatsu*, vol. 17, *Kin'yu Kikan Saiken Seibi-go no Kin'yu (Notes on Post-War Fiscal and Monetary Situation*, vol. 17, *Finance after the Reconstruction and Reorganization of Financial Institutions)*. Tokyo: The Ministry of Finance.

Takasugi, Ryo. 1990. *Shosetsu Nihon Kogyo Ginko Dai 2-bu (Industrial Bank of Japan: A Novel, Part 2)*. Tokyo: Kodansha Bunko.

Teranishi, Juro. 1982. *Nihon no Keizai Hatten to Kin'yu. (Economic Development and Finance in Japan)*. Tokyo: Iwanami-shoten.

———. 1991. "Financial System Reform after the War." Hitotsubashi University, Institute of Economic Research, Working Paper #244, Tokyo.

———. 1993. "Mein Banku Sisutemu" (The Main Bank System). In Tetsuji Okazaki and Masahiro Okuno, eds., *Gendai Nihon*

Keizai Sisutemu no Genryu (The Origins of the Contemporary Japanese Economic System). Tokyo: Nihon Keizai Shimbun-sha.

van Wijnbergen, Sweder. 1993. "Enterprise Reform in Eastern Europe." Working Paper Series 1068. World Bank, Europe and Central Asia Department, Washington, D.C.

Yokoyama, Akio. 1989. *Kin'yu Kikan no Risuku Kanri to Jiko Shihon (Risk Management and Capital of Financial Institutions)*. Tokyo: Yuhikaku.

10

The Privatization of Ex-Zaibatsu Holding Stocks and the Emergence of Bank-Centered Corporate Groups in Japan

Hideaki Miyajima

The task of this chapter is to investigate the economic reform of postwar Japan—the *zaibatsu* dissolution and the resulting changes in Japanese corporate governance structure. The implications of this process for the current economic reform in Central and Eastern Europe are then considered.

There are many differences between the Japanese postwar experience and current Central and Eastern European reform. Apart from dissimilar external circumstances, it is clear that the internal structure to be reformed and the purpose of the reform are quite different in the two cases. It has often been pointed out that the period of wartime national planning in the operation of the Japanese economy was relatively short, and that this planned economy was based on private ownership (Teranishi and Kosai 1993, p. 6). Although the problem of establishing a new corporate governance system is the crucial issue in

The author thanks Jishay Jafeh, Lee G. Branstetter, Ernst-Ludwig von Thadden, and Takeo Hoshi for helpful comments on an earlier draft.

Central and Eastern Europe, the main purpose of economic reform in Japan was to eliminate war potential, at least before 1948, when the purpose of rapid construction of the Japanese economy began to be emphasized.[1]

It is also important to pay attention to the similarity of the two cases: although Japanese postwar reform was small in magnitude, *zaibatsu* dissolution had some of the same characteristics as the privatization of state-owned companies. The number of companies targeted for *zaibatsu* dissolution reached approximately half of big businesses (as I will explain in detail, using a new data set composed of the 100 mining and manufacturing companies that were the largest in either 1937 or 1955). On average, nearly 50 percent of the issued stock of these ex-*zaibatsu* companies was transferred to the Holding Company Liquidation Commission (HCLC) as the liquidation agency. Furthermore, these companies' behaviors were strictly controlled by the government and the ownership rights of these stocks were held by HCLC. Thus, during postwar reform Japanese ex-*zaibatsu* companies were somewhat similar to state-owned companies. In addition, top Japanese management during wartime—and even during postwar reform—tended to operate companies inefficiently because of the soft budget constraint under the planned economy. That is, insider control prevailed. Therefore, economic reform in postwar Japan faced a similar task to that of economic reform in Central and Eastern Europe: to create an effective monitoring system.

It is true that the creation of a system of corporate governance, in the sense of the system disciplining top management, was not an explicit goal of GHQ/SCAP (General Headquarters, Supreme Commander for the Allied Powers, hereafter GHQ) officials, in comparison with the clear goal of economic reform in Central and Eastern Europe. Nevertheless, the measures entitled "economic democratization," generally designed to eliminate war potential in Japan, affected the corporate governance of Japanese companies. Instead of the former *zaibatsu* model—holding companies with a central, hierarchical ownership structure—the corporate governance system the GHQ tried to establish in

---

1. About the reorientation of occupation policy, see Miwa 1989 and Hadley 1970, Chapter 9.

Japan eventually amounted to an Americanization of the Japanese corporate system. An Anglo-Saxon style of corporate governance structure—that is, market corporate control—was seen as the most desirable system, and the "radical" idea of employee control for management was added to it. In this sense, the Japanese case was the first large-scale experiment of the privatization of state-owned companies modeled by an Anglo-Saxon form of corporate governance structure.

The corporate governance structure that emerged in the mid-1950s was quite different from what GHQ originally intended. It was the bank-centered corporate group system, although in an early, formative stage.

Thus, the questions this chapter investigates are:

- When an individual-centered ownership structure with employee ownership, equity finance, and a market corporate control were viewed as the most desirable corporate system by GHQ, why and how did a drastically different system of institution-centered ownership with cross-shareholding, debt (*keiretsu*) financing, and a main-bank-delegated monitoring system emerge in Japan?
- Who played a positive role in forming this structure in the postwar reform period?
- What functions did this corporate governance structure play in the reconstruction and early rapid growth period through monitoring of management and the provision of proper incentives?

The first section of this chapter discusses the GHQ's concept of a desirable corporate system, comparing it with the corporate governance structure and government policy that existed in Japan both before and during World War II.

The second section examines major measures of postwar reform, focusing on the dissolution of the holding-company-centered ownership structure and the purge of top management. The effects of these measures on Japanese corporate structure will be clarified. The third section examines the privatization of ex-*zaibatsu* stock, focusing on the liquidation policy of HCLC. The fourth section clarifies the drastic changes that occurred in ownership structure after the stabilization policy in early 1949. From this time on, the original policy had to be changed, and institution-centered ownership, including cross-shareholding, gradually emerged. The task of this section is to outline the process and clarify the causes. The fifth section briefly sketches corporate finance. Based on previous research and using a new data set, the reasons for the emergence of the main bank system will be summarized, and several new facts about main bank competition will be offered.

Last, I will summarize the corporate governance structure of 1955, when rapid growth of the Japanese economy began. Through an investigation of the correlation between turnover of top management and firm performance, it will be demonstrated that the newly established bank-centered corporate governance structure had an effective function in disciplining the top management team from the viewpoint of shareholders as well as debtholders.

GHQ's Design for Japanese Corporate Governance Structure

GHQ had no clear sense of the agency problem in corporate governance, which is being considered explicitly in regard to the recent economic reform in Central and Eastern Europe. It is also true that there were contradictions between GHQ and the State Department in the United States—and even within GHQ—about *zaibatsu* dissolution policy. Nevertheless, it is possible, and necessary, to rebuild GHQ's idea for corporate governance. I will summarize this idea using the reference documents supplied to GHQ officials when they designed concrete measures.[2]

The view of GHQ was that dispersion of stock to individuals (widespread ownership of securities) should be a pillar of economic democratization, because they understood that the concentration of

---

2. This summary is based primarily on the following documents: JCS (Joint Chiefs of Staff) 1380/50 in November 1945; SCAPIN (Supreme Commander of Allied Powers, Instruction to Japanese Government) No. 244, "Dissolution of Holding Companies"; and FEC (Far Eastern Commission) 230, "Policy on Excessive Concentration of Economic Power in Japan" in May 1947. I will also use "Edward Mission Report" of 1946.

ownership in *zaibatsu* families or with other large shareholders was a characteristic of the prewar economic system and had a close relationship to militarization. Therefore, GHQ designed an individual-centered, widespread ownership system that could monitor management through the market and general meetings of shareholders. The kind of "market corporate control" conceived by GHQ, however, was not the same as the current practice of takeover bids playing a significant role (Fama 1980; Jensen and Ruback 1983), although stock price fluctuation was given an important role. Rather, GHQ programs implied that top management would be disciplined by competition with other companies in the product market, since a market of top management as well as deconcentration policy were emphasized.

Not only was the ownership structure dispersed into the public, but also insider ownership, especially employee ownership, was highly recommended. The expected function is twofold: employee ownership motivated employees to commit to a company's activities, and it also made it possible to prevent top management from abusing their powers over labor conditions. This indicates that GHQ originally thought not only of external control, or a market for corporate control, but also that a certain kind of internal control should exist as a desirable ownership pattern.

At the same time, large shareholders were excluded in order to avoid the reconcentration of control rights. This was not only true for family ownership, but also for ownership by entities such as banks or other financial institutions, as well as manufacturing companies. These institutions were originally excluded from the list of desirable owners. For this purpose, the Anti-Trust Law enacted in 1947 prohibited industrial companies from holding stock and restricted financial institutions from holding more than 5 percent of the stock of a given company. The Securities Trade Act of 1947, modeled after the Glass Steagall Act in the United States, prohibited banks from underwriting or holding and dealing in corporate securities, either directly or through securities affiliations. The concern behind this exclusion was that direct commercial bank involvement with corporate securities was detrimental to the stability of the financial system.

The position of top management would be occupied by salaried managers, who were promoted from within companies and engaged in nonmilitary industries. Large shareholders, or *zaibatsu* family members, were eliminated from the executive boards. Imperial Ordinance No. 567 stipulated that a shareholder who owned more than 10 percent of a company had to resign. The theory behind this provision is "any large shareholders should not have any definite influences on a company's decision" (GHQ/SCAP 1951b).

The corporate governance structure summarized above corresponded to "equity-based corporate finance." The model of the desired corporate financial structure envisioned by GHQ was that of a company that raised its investment funds through the securities market and retained earnings; thus, the capital structure was mainly composed of equity. These ideas were institutionally complementary to a financial system that separated commercial banking from investment banking. From the viewpoint of three stages of monitoring (Aoki 1993), this division of labor among financial institutions following the GHQ model could be summarized as follows: "ex ante monitoring" about a project was delegated to an investment bank, "interim monitoring" was delegated to the commercial bank, and "ex post monitoring" was delegated to the equity market.

In short, the concept behind GHQ's idea of corporate governance encompassed widespread ownership, with internal ownership, equity finance, and the market for corporate control. What relationship did the GHQ policies have with previous government policies and existing corporate governance structure in Japan?

Although this point is often neglected, the corporate governance structure of Japanese companies and related government policy was transformed during World War II. As a result, there was some consensus between GHQ and the Japanese concerning what the desirable corporate governance structure should be.[3] This contrasts sharply with views of the policy of deconcentration of economic power, which led to contradictory opinions among the Japanese government, Japanese business circles, and the GHQ.

---

3. Former officer of the Ministry of Commerce and Industry and the Wartime Planning Agency (Kikakui-in), Yôji Minobe reviewed that "our purpose was somehow realized by *zaibatsu* dissolution measures of GHQ" ("Senji Keizai no Kaiko" ["Retrospect of Wartime Economy"], Minobe Papers, Tokyo University Ga-1).

In wartime there was a broad consensus among business leaders and government officials about the appropriateness of autonomy for professional managers and the restriction of shareholders' rights. The new economic movement begun in the mid-1940s, which was intended to reform firms to change their goal from the maximization of profit to the maximization of production, suggested setting companies free from shareholders' control. In 1940 the restriction of the dividend was introduced to aid in the transformation. The Munitions Companies Law enacted in 1943 officially declared the appropriateness of managerial autonomy instead of the control of large shareholders and authorized the restriction of shareholders' rights through exceptional treatment of commercial law (Okazaki 1993a). It is important that this policy was also supported by big companies' top management, who had been salaried managers independent on the large shareholders' control. The Juyô Sangyô Kyôgi-kai (Association of Important Industries), a trade association of big companies in wartime, investigated corporate control and requested the restriction of shareholders' rights (Miyajima 1993).

Furthermore, this idea developed after World War II. The Ministry of Commerce and Industry (MCI) proposed to introduce employee ownership to get a positive commitment from employees to rebuild the companies. This idea was shared by a part of the business circle. Keizai Doyu-kai, a managers association newly established in the early postwar period by young top management, suggested the participation of employees in management, suggesting that the corporation be seen as a cooperative body of labor and shareholders, intermediated by management (Keizai Doyu-kai 1951).

There were also crucial differences in views about the corporate governance to be created. The first concerned the rights of shareholders. GHQ tried to stress the rights of small shareholders, suggesting various devices for protecting shareholders' rights, while the Japanese preferred to restrict the rights of shareholders in general. The individual-centered ownership designed by GHQ conflicted with the ideas of the Japanese government in this area, although they shared a similar view of the desirability of the elimination of *zaibatsu* family control.

There was another conflict concerning institutional ownership. GHQ wanted to minimize institutional ownership to eliminate undesirable intercorporate security ownership, while the Japanese thought that ownership by institutions was desirable, or at least inevitable.

Corresponding with this point, the third difference of opinion concerned corporate finance. GHQ favored corporate finance based on the equity market, while the Japanese were skeptical about equity finance, and thought that intermediation by banks was inevitable for the rapid revival of production.

The *Zaibatsu* Dissolution: Transfer of Ex-*Zaibatsu* Stock and the Managerial Revolution

Dissolving the Hierarchical Ownership Structure

Considering the views of the GHQ and the contradictions between GHQ and the Japanese, how did the process of *zaibatsu* dissolution advance? The main step toward *zaibatsu* dissolution was to eliminate family control through dissolving its hierarchical ownership structure.[4] This process was accomplished through HCLC.

The procedure was to designate *zaibatsu* families, holding companies, and subsidiary companies to be dissolved and to transfer their stock to HCLC. The process has been described in detail in previous research (Hadley 1970; MOF 1982). It included the following steps.

Ten families, such as Mitsui, Sumitomo, Iwasaki (Mitsubishi), and so on were designated as *zaibatsu* families and their holding stock was transferred into HCLC on the basis of SCAPIN 1363. The amount of stock held by these ten families, and fifty-six persons, was estimated at 0.5 billion yen (Hadley 1970).

The designation of holding companies dissolved the hierarchical holding relationship between holding companies and subsidiary companies. The important point is that this designation of holding companies was drastically enlarged after Edward Mission's report in mid-1946.[5] Originally, applying a narrow definition of *zaibatsu*, which focused on

---

4. The percentage of the economy controlled by the big-ten *zaibatsu*-affiliated companies in capital was estimated at 35 percent. Affiliated companies were defined as the companies with more than 10 percent of issued stock held by designated holding companies.

5. Edward Mission was sent to design the *zaibatsu* dissolution and deconcentration policy. Although GHQ criticized the recommendations' too academic tone, it accepted the basic ideas (GHQ 1951b, pp. 23–27).

the family concern and therefore the ownership relationship of family holding companies and their subsidiaries, GHQ tried to dissolve only the original ten family concerns. Edward's report, however, suggested enlarging the dissolution by applying the broader definition of *zaibatsu* as the holding-company-centered hierarchical ownership structure in general. As a result, the number of holding companies to be dissolved was enlarged from the original ten family concerns to eighty-three companies by mid-1947.

These eighty-three companies included several kinds of companies, as is shown in table 10-1: (a) pure holding companies, which were composed of not only holding companies of big family concerns, but also holding companies of relatively small, local family concerns; (b) large subsidiary companies of the big-ten *zaibatsu*, such as Mitsubishi Heavy Industry, Inc., and Sumitomo Metal, Inc.; and (c) relatively independent big companies such as new *zaibatsu* and the textile companies.

The stock owned by these designated holding companies was a major part of the transfer in *zaibatsu* dissolution, estimated at 7 billion yen. These shares were transferred into HCLC on the basis of the decree of HCLC. At the same time, thirty-one companies out of the designated eighty-three holding companies, including Mitsui, Mitsubishi, and Sumitomo Honsha (holding companies), were dissolved. The control center completely disappeared.

In November 1946, the imperial ordinance known as the Ordinance of Restriction of Companies' Stockholding severed the stockholding relationship among subsidiaries. Designating the *zaibatsu* subsidiaries, the ordinance required the transfer of their shares to HCLC and prohibited them from holding the affiliated companies' stock in the future. The number of companies designated by this ordinance totaled 615, and the transferred stock to HCLC based on this ordinance amounted to 1.5 billion yen.

The amount of shares transferred as a part of *zaibatsu* dissolution to HCLC totaled 9 billion yen, which was estimated to be 21 percent of the economy's capital.[6] Including the stock disposition of other insti-

6. The estimate of Bank of Japan (BOJ) is somewhat different from Hadley's figure, slightly larger. The transferred stock held by designated family was listed at 0.9 billion; designated holding companies, 7.9 billion; the restricted concerns, including related companies, 0.9 billion.

Table 10-1. Designated Holding Companies

Designation	*Securities transferred to HCLC (million)*	*Company type*	
First (5 companies)	2,231		
Second (40 companies)	2,914		
Third (20 companies)	1,637		
Fourth (2 companies)	66		
Fifth (16 companies)	183		
Total	7,026		
All designations			
		Pure holding companies	23
		Trading companies	4
		Mining companies	9
		Heavy industries	13
		Textile	14
		Communication	10
		Others	10
Total			83

Source: Hadley 1970; GHQ/SCAP 1951b.

tutions, 14.4 billion shares were to be dissolved, which amounted to 34 percent of paid capital (MOF 1986, p. 379).

Because these figures were aggregate figures of transferred stock, it is important to figure out to what extent each company's issued stock had to be transferred. For this purpose, table 10-2 examines large companies, which are ranked as the top one hundred either in 1937 or in 1955. In this table, the companies whose issued stock was held by designated holding companies are defined as big ex-*zaibatsu* companies. The number of big ex-*zaibatsu* companies is 62 out of 127. These are composed of (a) subsidiaries of the big-three *zaibatsu*, (b) subsidiaries of big-ten *zaibatsu*, and (c) the big companies with stock held by a local family and operating companies with a holding function. The percentage of transferred stock out of whole issued stock according to these categories is summarized in table 10-2. It shows that the average of all categories

Table 10-2. The Impact of Stock Disposal
(thousand units)

Category	*Number of companies*	*Average issued stock*	*Issued stock transferred to HCLC (percent)*		
			Simple average	*Weighted average*	*Standard deviation*
Big-three *zaibatsu*	23	3,251	44.1	44.4	26.5
Big-ten *zaibatsu* except big three	22	2,522	47.8	32.8	30.0
Other companies (quasi-*zaibatsu*)	17	2,684	41.0	35.0	31.6
Ex-*zaibatsu*, total	62	2,837	44.6	38.5	29.1
Independent	65	1,905	7.2	4.8	9.8
Total	127	2,360	26.1	24.6	28.7

Note: Top one hundred companies in mining and manufacturing industries either in 1937 or 1955 are picked up according to assets. Big-three means first-line subsidiary companies of Mitsui, Mitsubishi, and Sumitomo. Big-ten *zaibatsu* means subsidiary companies of Nissan, Yasuda, Furukawa, Asano, Okura, Nomura, and Nakajima. Other companies (quasi-*zaibatsu*) are companies whose issued stock was held by designated holding companies, such as Kurashiki Spinning, Inc., held by the Ohara family and Kokusaku palpu, Inc., held by Oji Paper, Inc. Mitsui line investment companies such as Toshiba, Maruzen Oil, and Onoda Cement are also included here.
Source: HCLC 1951.

of ex-*zaibatsu* is nearly 50 percent, while the independent companies' average is under 10 percent. Therefore, it is safe to say that *zaibatsu* dissolution targeted more than half of the big companies for reform, and these companies were forced to disperse nearly 50 percent of their issued stocks.

In addition, the following two points are important in the understanding of corporate governance under postwar reform. First, the voting rights of transferred stock were also delegated to HCLC. Imperial Ordinance No. 233 not only authorized HCLC to exercise supervision over the disposal of the securities, but also to exercise voting power of such securities until their disposition (GHQ/SCAP 1951c, p. 146; HCLC 1951, p. 259). As a result, HCLC became the largest shareholder in these ex-*zaibatsu* companies until its share was liquidated.

Second, the companies designated as "restricted concerns" by Imperial Ordinance No. 657 of November 1945 were widely restricted by GHQ and government in such matters as dividends and rewards.[7] The number of designated restricted concerns reached 1,350 companies, which included all the big businesses mentioned above.[8] As a part of the restrictions (which included increases of capital and borrowing money), the restricted concerns were prohibited from paying dividends to shareholders and rewarding executives over the level prevailing in June 1945. These dividend and reward regulations were slightly relaxed later—for instance, the former was revised to allow a 5 percent dividend (payment of the dividend by borrowing, however, was consistently prohibited), and the latter was altered according to subsequent inflation (GHQ/SCAP, 1951b, p. 71). Thus, the regulations affecting stockholders and management were much more severe than in wartime.

In short, the half-stock of ex-*zaibatsu* companies was held by a quasi-government agency and their financial decisions, including disposition of profit, were completely restricted by government. Furthermore, because ex-*zaibatsu* companies' operational decisions were restricted in all spheres—including their purchasing, production, and marketing—they were in some ways similar to state-owned or nationalized companies.

The Managerial Revolution from above

Zaibatsu dissolution included the goal of eliminating the top management appointed by the *zaibatsu* family and the interlocking relation-

---

7. The purpose of this designation was to maintain the status quo for *zaibatsu* dissolution. When companies were designated as the "restricted concerns," their property and assets were frozen, their security records impounded, and the sale or transfer of securities, as well as their participation in stock ownership of nonrestricted companies, were prohibited (MOF 1982, pp. 181–90).

8. The number included 1,203 companies designated as "restricted concerns" and 147 "related companies." The latter is a second-line subsidiary of a restricted first-line subsidiary, which was designated by Imperial Ordinance No. 567 of November 1946, based on SCAPIN 1238.

ships between holding companies and subsidiary companies. Severing of personnel relationships was mainly realized through the "economic purge," originally different from *zaibatsu* dissolution. Technically, the purge resulted from the expansion of the January 1946 directive calling for the removal of "militarists and ultra-nationalists." This category included all those who occupied key positions in 245 major companies before September 2, 1945.[9] As a result of the economic purge, at least 2,000 executives resigned from their former positions. Another measure that was closely related to the *zaibatsu* dissolution program was the Law for Termination of *Zaibatsu* Family Control, enacted in January 1948. This law called for the removal of affected officers of the big-ten *zaibatsu* companies. In addition to the officers removed by the economic purge, 145 additional officers were forced to resign through this law (MOF 1982, pp. 312–20; Miyajima 1993b).

Thus, the top management of big businesses had to be changed. As for big businesses, in 112 out of 122 cases, top management was changed through these measures. Especially in the case of the big-ten *zaibatsu* subsidiaries, not only the president but also every executive member had to resign, because they were all regarded as *zaibatsu* appointees who were influenced by *zaibatsu* families. Instead of former executives, the salaried and professional managers now took over top management. The economic purge and the elimination of *zaibatsu* control brought Japan "managerial revolution from above." The new managers were promoted from within the companies. There were only four cases of new managers recruited from outside. This trend was more pronounced for board members. All the members of the executive board were professional managers promoted from within companies, and even among auditors at least one position was occupied by a salaried manager promoted from within the company. The majority of new top management came from former factory managers who were qualified as engineers. This happened in 56 out of 122 cases, compared with 21 out of 98 cases in 1937 (Miyajima, forthcoming).

There were several reasons for this pattern. The relative position of engineer was improved during wartime. The skill needed by new top

9. These major companies were defined as (a) companies over 100 million yen in capital, (b) companies designated as having an "excess concentration of economic power," and (c) companies with monopoly power and so on.

management at that time was not marketing or financial skill, but the ability to maximize the production level. Government also encouraged companies to give decisionmaking rights to factory managers and to raise their position in the management team. Thus, while the power of board members as the representatives of the shareholders decreased, the factory managers began to take part in the board's decisionmaking.

A more important reason for this trend is that the appointment of new top management after the purge required the approval of labor unions and HCLC as the largest shareholder, and the new top management was chosen according to the preference of these groups. As an agency of *zaibatsu* dissolution policy, HCLC disapproved of the top management represented by shareholders, unlike a regular shareholder. If a company did not appoint an appropriate person, HCLC intervened. For instance, despite being a relative of the founding family, Mori, who was the president of Showa Denko, Inc., was asked to resign by HCLC. At the same time, HCLC asked the Reconstruction Finance Bank (RFB) to select an appropriate candidate (HCLC 1951, p. 249).

During a time of frequent labor strikes, it was relatively easy to get labor unions to agree to the promotion of former factory managers. For instance, in Mitsubishi Electric, Inc., after former top management was purged, board members selected two candidates for president, one of whom was a former factory manager and the other from Mitsubishi Bank. The board then asked the labor union who was appropriate as the top manager. The labor union preferred the first candidate, and he undertook the rehabilitation of the company (Nihon Keizai Shinbunsha 1980).

This turnover under *zaibatsu* dissolution exerted two important influences on the corporate governance structure of Japanese big businesses. First, it completely eliminated the outside director, who played an important role in the control of the manager in the Anglo-Saxon system (Fama 1980). As business historians have noted, the managerial enterprise that emerged in the 1930s and 1940s in the United States had representatives of large shareholders and investment companies as board members (Chandler 1977; Lazonick 1992). In prewar Japan, salaried managers were monitored by executives of holding companies in big *zaibatsu* or by large shareholders in independent enterprises. There were no longer outside directors who could play the important role of monitoring the top management team and replacing it when necessary. The postwar managerial revolution from above was associated with eliminating the internal control of shareholders.

Second, new top management did not have much managerial experience. The number of new top managers who had served as president, vice president, or managing director before World War II was only 16 out of 122. The top management who did not have any prior management experience numbered 26 (Miyajima, forthcoming). The remaining 80 were new top managers who had taken part in the executive board as "plain" directors in the last phase of war or immediately after the war. As "plain" directors they did not normally take part in strategic decisions, but engaged in operational decisions at the factory or branch level and attended general board meetings once a month; they did not have a great deal of management experience.[10]

*Liquidation Process: Privatization of Ex-*Zaibatsu *Stock*

The liquidation of *zaibatsu*-related stocks began in early 1948. The liquidation was carried out by the Securities Coordinating and Liquidation Committee (SCLC), the liquidating agency established in 1947. According to the original policy, designed to create the individual-centered ownership structure, the priorities and procedures of stock disposal were decided in April 1948. The established priorities were as follows:

- The first priority of purchase of liquidated shares was given to employees of the company and then to the residents of localities in which the company operated.
- No individuals were allowed to purchase more than 1 percent of a given company's shares (MOF 1979; HCLC 1951).
- In addition, the reconcentration of ownership was strictly avoided. If *zaibatsu*-affiliated companies, either manufacturing companies or financial institutions, were designated as restricted concerns, they were prohibited from buying stock of affiliated companies on the basis of Imperial Ordinance No. 567. The manufacturing companies were prohibited from holding stock by the Anti-Monopoly Law in 1947, although they were not restricted companies and were former stockholders or creditors.

10. Yafeh (1993) reports a negative effect of the economic purge on firm performance in this period.

Concerning sales procedures, the three most important methods of transfer were public tender, underwriting sales, and employee sales. The appropriate sale price was carefully considered in all cases. Using public tender, securities were auctioned off to the highest bidder, down to a minimum price set by the agency. Through underwriting sales, large blocks of securities were offered to underwriting groups of securities dealers on a competitive bid basis for resale to the public at a fixed price. In the case of employee sales, including local residents in the area of the head or factory office, the sales price needed to be approved by SCLC—in practice, the sales price was set by SCLC.[11]

The liquidation of stock through these methods advanced smoothly. By July 1949, 80 percent of the stocks transferred to HCLC were liquidated, although the liquidation of big ex-*zaibatsu* companies, which were targeted by deconcentration policy, was not accomplished yet. This progress was greater than GHQ and SCLC had expected. It is therefore important to examine the reasons for this smooth liquidation, when we consider the current economic reform in Central and Eastern Europe.

One of the important factors was the inflationary macroeconomic situation. Rapid inflation raised the advantage of stocks as an inflation hedge. Small investors preferred stocks to savings deposits in spite of their high transaction costs and risk. Securities companies also positively underwrote stocks, expecting their price to increase.

The measures taken by government to promote widespread ownership also contributed to smooth liquidation. A kind of educational movement, called "securities democratization," was promoted. This movement, which began at the conference for "Promoting Securities Democratization," held in December 1947, disseminated information to small investors who had no knowledge or experience of securities investment. Along with this movement, financial assistance for purchasing funds was introduced. One of these measures was to allow the payment of frozen deposits for the purchase of stock disposed by SCLC in

---

11. United States of America, National Archives, Economic and Scientific Section, Antitrust and Cartel Division, "Policies and Procedure of Securities Program." File (F.) 28, Washington, D.C.

August 1947; another was to enlarge the supply of loans to securities companies (MOF 1979, p. 356).

To encourage employee ownership, provision was made for the financial support of stock purchases by employees. The ordinance of May 1948 (No. 83) specified that funds could be supplied to the employee by the bank that handled their company's transactions up to a limit of either 70 percent of the purchase or 2,500 yen (MOF 1979, p. 369). This financial support was ineffective; the percentage of purchasing funds borrowed from financial institutions was very low (see table 10-3).

More important for promoting employee ownership was the company's support. In this context, the important point is that new top

Table 10-3. Sample Research, Employee Stockholding

Item	*Percent*
Purchasing funds	
Own funds	53.4
Borrow from company	22.5
Borrow from financial institution	2.4
Own funds plus borrow from company	5.8
Others[a]	15.9
Will continue to hold	50.8
Will sell whenever price goes up	6.9
Will sell	17.2
No idea	16.7
Unknown	8.4
Do you think that production or business efficiency increase when employees become stockholders of the company?	
Yes	61.6
No influence	32.6
It decreases	1.9
Unknown	3.9

a. Others includes unknown.

Source: SCLC Registration Office: "Democratization of Securities Holding after the War," National Archives.

management of ex-*zaibatsu* companies was very active in promoting employee ownership to stabilize their companies. For instance, Tokyo Kaijyô (marine insurance, former Mitsubishi line) allotted 30–150 shares for each employee, according to their length of service, and wholly financed their purchases (Tokyo Kaijô 1982, p. 226–30).

These activities were very common, because stock to be sold to an employee was normally transacted between HCLC and the company, as the agent of employees, and the company temporarily paid purchasing money to HCLC instead of employees (MOF 1982, p. 370–73). According to SCLC's sample survey, it was estimated that less than 30 percent of the purchase funds came from companies (table 10-3).

As a result of these promotion measures, coupled with the inflationary macroeconomic situation, the stock disposition advanced much more smoothly than expected. Who, then, became the new shareholders of liquidated stock and what kind of ownership structure was established?

According to table 10-4, which summarizes the percentage of stock disposal by marketing methods in September 1949, 27 percent of whole disposed stocks were sold to employees and 7.5 percent to local resi-

Table 10-4. The Figure of Disposition, 1 September 1949

Method	*1,000 units*	*Percent*
Employee sales	41,762	27.1
Public tender (nationwide)	41,543	27.0
Local tender	11,617	7.6
Fixed price sales, public	12,080	7.8
Fixed price sales, local	711	0.5
Consignment sales	673	0.4
Underwriting sales	45,285	29.5
Off-market sales	35	0.0
Total	153,706	

Source: U.S. National Archives, Economics and Scientific Section, "History of the Securities Branch."

dents.[12] Securities companies also played an important role. Through the underwriting sales of securities companies, approximately 30 percent of disposed stock was held by securities companies, and then sold to the public. It was reported that "in the case of listed stock the disposition was made mainly through dealers and brokers;" this is especially true of big companies (GHQ/SCAP 1951b, p. 158).

As a result of this securities democratization, the ownership structure completely changed. Instead of a holding-company-centered hierarchical ownership structure, an individual-centered widespread ownership structure emerged as a result of *zaibatsu* dissolution. Nearly 70 percent of stocks were owned by individuals, and 13 percent were owned by securities companies (see table 10-5).

At the same time, when the liquidation of *zaibatsu*-related stocks was nearly completed, the constraints on "restricted concerns" began to be relaxed. In March 1949, the Supreme Commander of Allied Powers (SCAP) relaxed the restrictions, including restraints imposed on dividends and executive pay (MOF 1982, p. 213). Thus, the privatization of ex-*zaibatsu* companies was accomplished and new top management was in charge, representing the interests of widespread (small) shareholders again.

Emergence of Institution-Centered Ownership Structure

In early 1949, Japanese economic reform entered into the next stage. Real gross national product (GNP) recovered 85 percent of the prewar level (1934–36 = 100) in 1948, and inflation settled down from the peak level of late 1948.

The Stock Market Collapse and Price Stabilization Policy

At this time, a series of stabilization programs was introduced. Three principles of enterprise operation released at the end of 1948 prohibited

---

12. The percentage of stock sold to employees out of whole disposed stock increased slightly later, because public tender was postponed from the end of 1949. Final composition according to sales method in 1950 was as follows: employees, including local residents, 42.7 percent; competition bids, 26.9 percent; fixed price sales, including underwriting, 30.4 percent (HCLC 1951, p. 455).

Table 10-5. Ownership Structure of Postwar Period, Listed Companies
(percent)

Category	*1945*	*1949*	*1951*	*1953*	*1955*	*1960*
Number	631	677	714	774	786	785
Government	8.3	2.8	1.8	0.7	0.4	0.2
Financial institution	11.2	9.9	18.2	22.9	23.6	30.6
Trust bank	—	—	5.2	6.7	4.1	7.5
Securities companies	2.8	12.6	9.2	7.3	7.9	3.7
Other companies	24.6	5.6	13.8	13.5	13.2	17.8
Foreign	—	—	1.8	1.7	1.7	1.3
Individual	53.1	69.1	57.0	53.8	53.2	46.3

— Not available.
Source: BOJ 1970.

(a) provision of subsidies, (b) increases in controlled prices, and (c) raising wages through loans. The Dodge Line of 1949 required the establishment of fixed exchange rates to replace the former multiple exchange rate and the suspension of new loans from the RFB (Reconstruction Financing Bank). This policy represented a great change from the previous operations of companies; thus far, top man- agement had accepted the requests of labor unions, expecting increases on controlled prices and subsidies that mainly depended on loans from the RFB, while they avoided real reconstruction (Okazaki 1993b). Hence, top management of companies was required to reconstruct their businesses on a free market basis, instead of the soft budget constraints of a controlled economy.

In the adjustment process from a planned economy to a market economy, the new corporate governance structure, regarded by GHQ as desirable, confronted several difficulties. The most noteworthy challenge was the stock market collapse in August 1949. There were several reasons for the stock price collapse.

On the supply side, an excess of stock existed. In addition to the *zaibatsu*-related stock to be redistributed, there was the increased capital of the "special accounting companies" (explained by Hoshi, in this volume).[13] This increase in capital began at the end of 1948 and reached a peak in 1949.[14] Because the increased capital under the reorganization plan would be sold with the same priority as the liquidation of *zaibatsu*-related stock, "special accounting companies issuing new shares were competing for buyers with the SCLC" (GHQ/SCAP 1951b, p. 64).

Furthermore, company profits and dividends were still low. Only 250 of 453 listed companies paid dividends in 1949 (BOJ 1970). At the same time, as real interest rates went up under tight fiscal-monetary policy and simultaneously inflation was brought down, the preference of the small investor shifted from securities to deposits.

The stock price collapse caused by these events exerted a great influence on the ownership structure that emerged through the liquidation of ex-*zaibatsu* stocks.

Employee ownership decreased, because employees sold their stock during the stock market collapse (how long employees held their companies' stocks is illustrated in table 10-6). It is noteworthy that the percentage of stocks held for more than five months or one year decreased rapidly after mid-1949, when the stock market collapsed. On average, only 50 percent of employees who bought their companies' stocks from January 1948 to June 1949 continued to hold their stock for more than two years. According to table 10-3, employee shareholders had a willingness to sell their stock, while they did not seem to realize a positive effect from holding their companies' stock, such as increasing production. Quoting this sample research, a document of SCLC noted that "disposition of stocks to employees may have a different result from what had originally been designed."[15]

---

13. At the same time, they were pressed to decrease their capital on behalf of disposing of the special loss in old accounts. This increase in capital was particularly needed at the former big *zaibatsu* companies (see Miyajima 1994).
14. The criteria for approval of a reorganization plan mandated that companies keep "the financial soundness." It means that the amount of paid in capital could not be less than the total amount of fixed assets and operating funds, which were also normally fixed (GHQ/SCAP 1951c, p. 41).
15. SCLC Registration Bureau, "Democratization of Securities Holding after the War," September 30, 1951.

Table 10-6. How Long Did Employees Hold Liquidated Stocks? *(thousand units)*

Item	*1948 Jan.–June*	*July 1948– June 1949*	*July 1949– June 1950*	*July 1950– April 1951*	*Whole period*
Number of companies	161 (13.2%)	727 (59.7%)	249 (20.5%)	80 (6.6%)	1,217 (100.0%)
Disposed stocks	3,688	27,846	15,702	19,359	66,595
Two months	3,440 (93.3%)	25,610 (92.0%)	14,359 (91.4%)	17,721 (91.5%)	61,130 (91.8%)
Five months	3,185 (86.4%)	22,791 (81.8%)	13,210 (63.4%)	(4,995) —	44,141 (80.1%)
One year	2,775 (75.2%)	18,890 (67.8%)	10,939 (69.7%)	— —	32,605 (69.0%)
Two years	2,166 (58.7%)	14,010 (50.3%)	— —	— —	16,177 (51.3%)

— Not available.

Note: Concerning five-month disposition, total figure is only available until December 1950.

Source: SCLC, "Democratization of Securities Holding after the War."

The securities companies, which played a significant role in securities disposition, also suffered from serious problems. They were immobilized by their high inventories and precarious financial condition. Large capital and operational losses were experienced by securities companies that depended on purchasing funds using high-interest, short-term loans.[16]

16. The loss of securities companies, which was composed of capital loss of holding securities and operational loss, reached 1,189 million yen and their bank loans were 2,633 million yen, compared with their securities holdings of 2,989 million yen (ESS/AC, "Provision of Capital for Japanese Enterprise," December, 1949).

At the same time, the stock market collapse created two critical problems for the new top management of big business, while it induced them to take care of shareholders by giving up their previous management policy, which had placed too much stress on the insiders' (employees') interest.

First, the companies faced serious difficulties in increasing capital. Former munitions companies were especially obliged to raise large amounts of capital to gain approval of their reorganization plans. Moreover, they had other needs to increase capital. They faced a liquidity crisis and their high debt-equity ratio made it difficult for these companies to borrow from banks, because their capital composition was showing undercapitalization because of decreasing capital under the reconstruction plan.

Second, a decline in price heightened the threat of takeover bids and buyouts. This was especially valid for ex-*zaibatsu* companies, whose issued stock was heavily liquidated. Several former *zaibatsu* companies suffered from takeover bids (Miyajima 1994). These takeover bids, however, did not target the poorly performing companies, but those such as real estate companies whose market value was much lower than the actual resale value of their assets because of undercapitalization. At the same time, this stock price collapse gave the top management team strong incentives to keep their managerial autonomy.

Top management teams tried to maintain their stock price, eventually through measures similar to the "company buyout," which was prohibited under Japanese commercial law.

The first step companies took in stabilizing their stockholdings was to delegate securities companies to hold their stocks. In this case, the purchasing fund came from the company, and securities companies just lent their names to it as stockholders. It is reported that these activities were fairly common (FTC 1955; Suzuki 1992). Second, the management asked people outside the company to hold their company's stock through an unofficial contract. Although this activity was not verifiable, the case of Mitsui Real Estate, Inc., was famous in regard to the practice (Mitsui Real Estate 1986). Third, top management delegated other financial institutions to hold their issued shares and affiliated companies' shares they once held, in exchange for deposits to these financial institutions.

These stabilizing activities prevailed in late 1949 and early 1950.[17] Seeing that Japanese companies' behavior was undesirable from the viewpoint of the original plan, GHQ and HCLC began to strengthen surveillance over sales as well as to warn of the illegal actions. For instance, beginning in May 1949, a report system was introduced to prevent companies from retaining their control power (GHQ/SCAP 1951b, p. 156).[18]

The Japanese government simultaneously suggested various ways to maintain equity prices. GHQ also realized that it was not relevant for rapid rehabilitation of the Japanese economy to continue to push the original plan.

As a measure to avoid an excess supply of securities, SCLC decided to indefinitely postpone the selling of *zaibatsu*-related stocks by public tender after October 1949, and this measure was continued until SCLC dissolved (MOF 1979, pp. 381–83, 408). In concert with this action, adjustment of the mandated schedule of the capital increases was introduced through establishing a "Conference on Adjustment of Capital Increases" in December 1949. This adjustment could be seen as restrictive, since the actual increased capital of early 1950 was only 40 percent of proposed increased capital (MOF 1979, p. 409). The original program of the reorganization plan was also modified. In April 1949, the Ministry of Finance (MOF) announced that it would give up maintaining the original priority principle, which stressed individual and employee ownership. In the summer of 1950, the standard for Approval of Reorganization Plan, which required a high equity level, was revised (GHQ/SCAP 1951c, p. 71).

More important, several positive measures for maintaining stock prices were also introduced. In this process, GHQ officially began to admit the significance of institutional ownership. First, the financial

17. GHQ admitted that manufacturing companies "illegally acquired their own shares" in late 1949 and early 1950 to support the market and complete their capital composition. U.S. National Archives, ESS/AC, "Brief Report of Current Stock Market Activities," 21 July 1950.

18. Legislation required that all joint companies capitalized at more than 100 million yen must report to the SCLC all stockholders that were holding more than 5,000 shares on 31 May 1949.

institution's shareholding was encouraged by the Japanese government. By the end of 1949, life insurance companies purchased substantial numbers of stocks, using funds supplied by the Bank of Japan (BOJ), which purchased national bonds from the life insurance companies. At the same time, BOJ requested that "the city banks cooperated in the financing of security purchases and encouraged purchasing for their own account."[19]

Second, various plans of stockholding institutions were proposed both within and outside the government for the purpose of raising the price level of shares. These plans, however, were halted because of GHQ opposition. Instead of such a stock-price-stabilizing organization, the Investment Trust Act was enacted in 1951. The Investment Trust was developed as a group of trust banks that would act as trustees engaged in securities operations according to the circumstances of the securities companies that represented their entrustees. In this case, the restrictions on shareholding by financial institutions no longer applied to trust banks if they gave up their voting power. This institution allowed the funds of small investors to flow to the equity market by decreasing the high transaction costs and risks of securities (MOF 1979, pp. 495–502).

Last, the original antitrust statutory framework was revised. In 1949 the prohibition against industrial companies' shareholding in antitrust law was revised. Although the primary purpose of this revision was to promote the inflow of foreign capital into the Japanese market, it also made it possible for industrial companies to hold other companies' stocks, if it were not judged to substantially restrain competition. When the Japan–United States Peace Treaty went into effect, a series of laws and orders, which restricted ex-*zaibatsu* companies' shareholding, were repealed. The abolition of Imperial Ordinance No. 567 was especially important, because it made cross-shareholding among ex-*zaibatsu* companies possible. In 1953 the substantial revision of the Antitrust Law included the revision of article 13, which raised the limit of a financial institution's ownership from the previous 5 percent to 10 percent.

---

19. U.S. National Archives, ESS/AC, "Measures Taken to Encourage Stock Purchase."

Emergence of Institutional Ownership

With this policy change, ownership structure drastically changed from individual-centered ownership to institution-centered ownership. The ownership structure of 1955 is shown in table 10-5 for listed companies and table 10-7 for big businesses.

From 1949 to 1955, the percentage of individual owners decreased from 69 percent to 53 percent, and the securities companies holding shares, which was partly a temporary holding prior to reselling to the public, also decreased, from 13 percent to 8 percent. Financial institutions increased their share. Ex-*zaibatsu* stocks, which had been held completely by individuals, were now held by institutional owners again.

Another important point is that the ownership structures of Japanese companies were extremely homogenous after economic reform. In prewar Japan, ownership structures of big businesses were quite heterogeneous, ranging from the concentrated *zaibatsu* form of ownership structure to a more diffused structure, such as the managerial enterprise structures represented by the big cotton spinning companies (Miyajima, forthcoming). Through ownership dispersion of ex-*zaibatsu* companies, both independent and ex-*zaibatsu* companies' ownership structures became quite similar in the share of the largest ten shareholders, as well as the composition of shareholders, as is shown in table 10-7.

It is already clear that the motivation of the share-issuing side was to preserve the stock price to promote the increase of capital, stabilize stockholding, and thus maintain management autonomy. Then what is the incentive of the stockholding side?

The largest contributors to this change in ownership structure were financial institutions, especially insurance companies and trust banks. The top ten shareholders of big businesses were generally insurance companies, trust banks, and securities companies. The investment policy of trust banks was: (a) the market value of a purchased company should exceed its face value over the previous three years, (b) an actual dividend was paid or a dividend was certainly expected, and (c) 8 percent yield rate was expected (Okazaki 1993b). The insurance companies' investment policy was similar (Yamanaka 1986, pp. 330–40). This investment policy is confirmed in table 10-8, which demonstrates the cor-

Table 10-7. Ownership Structure of Big Business in 1955
(percentage)

Category	*Total*	*Ex-zaibatsu*	*Independent*
Number	122	63	59
Issued stock (1,000 units)	38,614	40,515	36,306
Standard deviation	31,788	29,562	33,802
Financial institutions	28.5	26.9	30.0
Securities companies	7.9	8.7	6.9
Industrial	7.0	7.6	6.2
Foreign	2.9	2.9	2.8
Individuals	53.7	53.9	53.6
Ten large shareholders	25.6	26.1	25.4
Standard deviation	12.8	14.4	10.7
Bank	3.0	2.2	3.9
Trust bank	7.5	7.9	7.1
Insurance	6.2	6.3	5.9
Financial institutions, total	16.7	16.4	16.9

Note: Definition of ex-*zaibatsu* companies and independent is the same as in table 10-2. The share of trust banks included Daiwa Bank, since it engaged in the operation of an investment trust.

Source: TEC 1956, Yamaichi 1956.

relation between the shareholding of each institution and the dividend rates of companies controlled by industry average (dividend) in order to measure to what extent investment was driven by simple profit maximization. There is a positive, significant correlation between dividend and the share of trust banks, including insurance companies (SH-TR/INSU).

It is also important that the cross-shareholding of ex-*zaibatsu* companies advanced during 1949–55. The cross-shareholding ratios of three big ex-*zaibatsu* companies and Furukawa line companies in 1954 were: Mitsubishi (twenty-three companies), 14.8 percent; Sumitomo (twelve companies), 15.8 percent; Mitsui (twenty companies), 7.9 percent; and Furukawa (ten companies), 20.9 percent, and the number of

Table 10-8. Factor Analysis of Shareholding Ratio
(N=122)

	SH-TR/INSU	*SH-BANK*	*SH-INS*	*SH-SEC*
Dispos	—	—	—	0.056 (3.788)[a]
Dividend	0.003 (3.088)[a]	0.000 (0.820)	0.003 (1.882)[c]	-0.006 (-1.202)
Ex-*zaibatsu*	—	—	0.059 (2.156)[b]	—
Borrowing Ratio	0.031 (0.538)	0.045 (1.717)[c]	0.202 (1.934)[c]	—
Profit Ratio	-0.076 (-0.697)	-0.081 (-1.629)	—	-0.009 (-0.142)
Adjusted *R2*	0.07	0.05	0.05	0.32

— Not available.

Note: Dependent variable is share of each institution. Numbers in parentheses are *t* statistics.

Dependent variables are defined as follows: SH-TR/INSU = Share of trust banks and insurance companies in large ten shareholders. Daiwa Bank is included (see table 10-7, note). SH-BANK = Share of bank in large ten shareholders. SH-INS = Share of all institutional holdings, including financial institutions and other companies. SH-SEC = Share of securities companies.

Independent variables are defined as follows: Dispos denotes the percentage of the transferred stock to HCLC out of total issued stock in 1945. Dividend is calculated as follows: *Di* – *Dij*; *Di* = average dividend rate from 1951–54 of *i* companies; *Dij* = average dividend rate at the same time of *j* industry that *i* company belongs to, based on the three-digit industrial code. Profit ratio is calculated the same way as dividend, using average profit rate (net profit after tax/sales), 1951–54. Ex-*zaibatsu* is dummy variables if the companies belong to former Mitsui, Mitsubishi, Sumitomo, and Furukawa *zaibatsu*. The number of these companies is twenty-seven. Borrowing ratio is borrowing/assets in 1955. SH-TR/INSU and SH-BANK are based on ten large shareholders, while SH-INS and SH-SEC are based on all shareholders. All regressions are controlled by issued stock, foreigner shareholding, and subsidiary companies dummy, which is two companies.

a. Significant at the 1 percent level.
b. Significant at the 5 percent level.
c. Significant at the 10 percent level.

Source: HCLC 1951; TSE 1950–56.

companies that experienced takeover bids was high (Miyajima 1994; Tôyô keizai 1955). This rise was primarily the result of the transfer of stocks stabilized by the measures described above back to the same line companies. In these cases, the financial institutions, especially banks, played the core role of cross-shareholding through supplying purchase money to the same line companies. The residents' clubs of corporate groups played a coordinating role in defending against takeover bids by coordinating member companies' repurchases.

These intentional stockholder stabilizing policies are also detailed in table 10-8. An ex-*zaibatsu* dummy, which denoted the big-three and Furukawa line companies, has a positive significant correlation with all institutions' shareholding (SH-INS). The management team of the big-three ex-*zaibatsu* and Furukawa companies, which suffered from large-scale liquidation and faced hostile takeovers, tried to defend their management autonomy.

Last, although the percentage has been decreasing, the share of securities companies (SH-SEC) cannot be neglected—8 percent in listed companies and 9 percent in ex-*zaibatsu* companies. There is no significant correlation between the dividend and SH-SEC, while there is a positive, significant relationship between the percentage of the transferred stock to HCLC out of issued stock (Dispos) and SH-SEC. It indicates that ex-*zaibatsu* companies still depended on securities companies for stabilizing their shareholders. In other words, the stabilized ownership structure was not completely redesigned according to ex-*zaibatsu* management views.

Emergence of Main Bank System as Delegated Monitor

New money for reconstruction, which companies no longer raised from the equity market, was supplied by city banks. The percentage of money supply coming from bank loans increased after 1950 in contrast to the rapid decline of equity finance. These loans came exclusively from private financial institutions because of the suspension of RFB loans. The city bank loans were supported by BOJ loans. The loans from BOJ to private institutions increased three times in 1949–50 (table 10-9).

Table 10-9. Money Supply to Industries

		Composition (percent)					
Period	*Money supply (billion yen)*	*Equity*	*Bonds*	*Borrowings*	*Private financial institutions*	*RFB JDB (percent)*	*Loan from BOJ (billion yen)*
1937–45	123.4	21.3	8.6	72.0	70.0	—	—
1946	59.2	7.6	-2.1	94.4	94.8	—	50.4
1947	133.3	6.8	0.0	93.2	60.1	33.1	32.3
1948	437.7	13.6	0.0	86.4	71.3	15.3	51.9
1949	491.8	22.1	3.0	74.9	73.8	-0.1	88.6
1950	512.9	6.2	8.5	85.3	72.6	-3.6	114.5
1951	857.8	8.1	4.2	87.7	74.7	1.5	223.0
1952	1,021.3	12.0	3.6	84.4	78.0	2.6	223.2
1953	1,063.3	15.6	3.9	80.5	69.2	7.8	298.8
1954	612.0	23.2	2.9	73.8	66.2	16.3	243.4
1955	676.5	14.1	3.9	82.0	68.9	11.0	32.0

— Not applicable.
Source: MOF 1978.

The loans from city banks had a unique lending pattern, which is often called *keiretsu* financing. *Keiretsu* financing is an expression of one aspect of the main bank system, that is, loan behavior of city banks. It means the big-six (Mitsui, Mitsubishi, Sumitomo, Fuji, Daiichi, and Sanwa) banks and the Industry Bank of Japan (IBJ) supplied nearly half of the monetary demands of affiliated companies by borrowing large sums of money from BOJ, with the rest being supplied by the (de facto) syndicate loans of other banks. As already has been demonstrated, this loan promoted reconstruction of ex-*zaibatsu* line companies in early the 1950s (Miyajima 1994).

As for how and why these relationships between city banks and companies—that is, the main bank system—emerged in Japan, excellent research has already been done. It is sufficient to mention the following points, using table 10-10, which summarizes the emergence of the main bank system by focusing on its four features (Aoki, Patrick, and Sheard 1993).

First, it was through the syndicate loans of 1939–41 that these relationships began to form. As money demands from munitions companies increased, it became difficult and risky for city banks to lend to them individually. City banks began to organize syndicate loans, with a manager bank in each syndicate that was responsible for monitoring the munitions companies.

Second, when the designated financial institution (hereafter DFI) system was introduced in 1943, the close ties between banks and companies were established. Under the DFI system, city banks were designated to exclusively supply money to certain companies. In this phase, the close relationships between companies and banks concerning loans and settlements emerged, while the monitoring of companies by banks was diminished because of the guarantee of debt by government.

Third, after World War II, GHQ realized that the banks held powerful "interrelated solvency" over affiliated companies.[20] GHQ, however, was not willing to dissolve the bank-firm ties as it had dissolved

20. Interrelated solvency was defined by GHQ as follows: "arising from the fact that a large part of the banks' investment and loans went to their affiliated enterprises, while the major part of the affiliates' deposits resided in their related banks" (GHQ/SCAP 1951c, pp. 111–13).

Table 10-10. Broad Concept of Emergence of Main Bank System

Element	*I* *1939–43* *Syndicate*	*II* *1944–45* *DFIS*	*III* *1946–49,* *Special supervisor*	*IV* *1950–55,* *Main bank*
Payment settlement	///	***	***	***
Shareholding	---	///	+++	///
Loan relations				
Close ties, or correspondent relations	///	***	***	***
Reciprocal monitoring system	///	+++	///	***
Dispatching managers	---	---	---	***

Note: --- Did not exist; /// formation; *** establishment; +++ diminishing. DFIS means the designated financial institution system.

Source: Teranishi 1994; Hoshi 1993; Aoki, Patrick, and Sheard 1993.

the ties between holding companies and firms. The reason for this was that GHQ feared a financial crisis if it pursued such policies. In addition to that, it is important that the bank-firm ties were strengthened at that time through banks collecting borrowers' information, because city banks as the largest debtholders of "special accounts" companies supervised their reorganization (MOF 1983, pp. 740–44).

Fourth, under this precondition, it was quite natural that loans were mainly supplied by former designated financial institutions, ex-*zaibatsu* banks, which organized de facto syndicates again for risk diffusion and efficient money allocation. The emergence of *keiretsu* financing was institutionally supported by BOJ policy. BOJ organized the Loan Coordinating Committee, composed of nineteen city banks and BOJ officials, in July 1948. The committee coordinated syndicate loans, particularly to companies suffering from low liquidity (BOJ 1959). GHQ permitted the bank loans because it seemed a necessary measure for economic rehabilitation, although it warned against too great a concentration of loans to affiliated companies (MOF 1976, pp. 427–28, 570–71).

It is worth noting that main bank status was not firmly established at that time; instead, there was severe competition for this designation. This point is clear in table 10-11, which follows the relation between a DFI and the largest private debtor in 1948 and 1955. The change of largest private debtor between 1948 and 1955 was more frequent than that of DFI in 1948. This is the case of non-ex-*zaibatsu* companies, while ex-*zaibatsu* companies, especially Sumitomo; Mitsubishi; and, to a degree, the Daiichi line companies, showed unchanged relationships.

The following situation existed during this frequent changing of largest private debtor. On the one hand, Sumitomo Bank and Mitsubishi Bank tried to enlarge their client lists beyond former affiliated companies (same line companies) in order to maximize their loans and diffuse loan risk.

On the other hand, Fuji (former Yasuda), Sanwa, and Daiichi, which had relatively small numbers of big companies as clients thus far, tried to look for large clients. For this purpose, Fuji enlarged its inspection division in 1949 and so did Sanwa (Fuji Bank 1982; Sanwa Bank 1974). Both companies were enthusiastic about making close ties with new clients, suggesting a new policy that stressed big clients. Mitsui Bank suffered from a relative shortage of loan money and had difficulties in supplying the money needed by formerly affiliated companies, because Daiichi Bank was split again during the postwar reform. As a result, severe loan competition, or main bank competition, began after the Dodge Line, with former Mitsui-affiliated companies as one of the focal points (see table 10-11, parentheses).

Thus, *keiretsu* financing prevailed among ex-*zaibatsu* and non-ex-*zaibatsu* companies. Similarly, just as the ownership structures of ex-*zaibatsu* companies and non-ex-*zaibatsu* companies began to converge, the corporate finance pattern of both became convergent.

In this emergence of a main bank system with severe loan competition, a monitoring system by a main bank was established. This system, in which a main bank had an informational advantage through loans and payment settlement, was also supplemented by two elements.

First, dispatching executives from banks to manufacturing companies prevailed during 1949–52. There was a clear tendency for the

Table 10-11. The Relations of the Largest Private Debtholder

Category	*DFI and largest debtor in 1948*		*Largest debtor, 1948 and 1955*	
N	61		108	
Unchanged	54	88.5%	52	75.0%
Unchanged	—		29	
Change	7		27(13)	
Ex-*zaibatsu*				
N	38		55	
Unchanged	35	92.1%	29	90.9%
Unchanged′	—		21	
Change	3		5(4)	
Non-ex-*zaibatsu*				
N	23		53	
Unchanged	19	82.6%	23	58.4%
Unchanged′	—		8	
Change	4		22(9)	

Note: This table investigates the continuous relationships of the largest private debtholder. Therefore, the government financial institutions (RFB and JDB) are excluded. Unchanged′ is the case that the largest debtholder of a private financial institution in 1948 is the same as that of 1955, except long-term financial institutions (Industry Bank of Japan and Long-Term Credit Bank). In this case, the city bank is the second or third largest debtholder of private financial institutions. DFI means designated financial institution. Parentheses in 1955 signify that the Teikoku Bank as a largest debtholder in 1948 was taken over by the other city bank without the Mitsui and Daiichi Bank.

Source: FTC 1948; TSE 1956.

big-six banks and IBJ to send their executives to the boards of companies whose borrowing ratio was high and to whom it lent large amounts of money (Miyajima 1994; Tôyô-keizai 1953, 1955). This is in contrast with the practice of insurance companies and trust banks, which rarely sent their members to companies they had lent a large amount or in which they had invested. Using Aoki's definition of the three types of monitoring (Aoki 1993), this dispatching of executives to the boards contributed not only to "ex ante" monitoring, which means evaluation of the project to be loaned, but also "interim monitoring," which means supervising the advancement of the project and correcting the clients' behavior when necessary.

Second, the big-six banks had a tendency to hold their client companies' stocks, although they were not the largest shareholder of client companies. It has been shown that for the big-three ex-*zaibatsu* companies there was a significant positive correlation between the loans and shareholding (Miyajima 1994).[21] This point is confirmed by a positive significant correlation between the borrowing ratio and share of banks (SH-BANK), although the coefficient of determination and *t* statistics are still low, because this regression is biased by only picking up the ten largest shareholders (table 10-8). At the same time, there was no significant positive correlation between dividend and SH-BANK, as seen in the trust bank shareholding. Furthermore, a negative correlation between the profit ratio and SH-BANK exists. In short, the higher the default risk was, the more the bank held their client's share. This tendency indicates that the purpose of a bank's investment was not to maximize the dividend or to realize portfolio profitability in the normal sense, but to maintain close relations with borrower companies—in other words, to prevent an opportunistic action by a large borrower. It is consistent with the behavior of banks that a city bank calculate its loss and profit from each client comprehensively, including the transaction commission, loan interest, compensation deposit, dividend of holding shares, and so on (Prowse 1990). Therefore, the apparently low profits realized by the main banks could be adjusted by the compensation ratio and loan interest.

Effective Monitoring through Bank-Centered Corporate Groups

The corporate governance structure established in the postwar era was not the same as GHQ originally planned. The institutional combina-

21. Initially, this increase of shareholding by city banks advanced through so-called debt-equity swaps, although the magnitude is still unclear. The former president of Sumitomo Bank stated that "*zaibatsu* related shares were naturally allotted to concerned financial institutions according to their credit amount" (Hyûga 1975).

tion of an individual-centered ownership structure with employee ownership, equity finance, and a market for corporate control with employee control was replaced by a drastically different system. Internal corporate control was not realized because of the exit of employee-shareholders during the stock market collapse. The market for corporate control through market price and takeover bids did not correctly evaluate the companies' performance, although it functioned to discipline management that neglected shareholder interests. Furthermore, individual-centered ownership had to be changed through the shareholder stabilization operation by the top management team. A corporate finance system depending on internal funds and equity finance was almost impossible with the stock market collapse and the low income level. Thus, instead of the institutional set designed by GHQ, a new system—including institution-centered ownership with cross-shareholding among ex-*zaibatsu* companies, debt financing with *keiretsu* financing, and a corporate monitoring system by main banks—emerged after the Dodge Line.

The main organizer in this process for a new institutional combination was the city bank. It supplied rehabilitation money to ex-*zaibatsu* companies as well as non-ex-*zaibatsu* companies by organizing syndicate loans as a manager bank. It held client companies' stocks according to default risk, and regardless of yield level. It also contributed to the supply of money to purchase stock, increasing ex-*zaibatsu* companies' cross-shareholding in the case of the big-three ex-*zaibatsu* and Furukawa. At the same time, it is important to note that banks played an exclusive monitoring role for their client companies. The main bank, which was the large debtor as well as one of the largest shareholders, sent its executives to client companies. By doing so, it monitored its clients' behavior not only ex ante and ex-post, but also interim.

Last, I should ask whether this corporate governance structure based on bank-centered corporate groups was effective for monitoring top management teams. As I mentioned before, the new top management team of big businesses, composed of salaried managers promoted within companies, had a potential tendency to represent their employee's interests. Some individuals may not have enough appropriate managerial capability to reconstruct their businesses. Did the main bank effectively discipline these management teams promoted within companies? Whose interest did the main bank represent?

In order to answer this question, we investigate the correlation between management turnover and firm performance, using a method developed by recent research (Kaplan 1992). Here turnover is identified as the case in which the top management (president) in 1955 was different from the top management of 1950. During 1950–55, management turnover occurred in 35 out of 122 companies. These turnovers were of two kinds. *Turn 1* denotes turnover by new management promoted within companies. Out of our sample of 122, 20 cases belong to this category. *Turn 2* denotes the turnover by new management who came from outside companies. This is divided into two subtypes. One includes (TURN 2) nine cases in which the new top management came from outside companies such as banks or other companies. The other case (TURN-2′) is TURN 2 plus cases of turnover by a new president who was purged during the postwar reform period and returned as president after the Peace Treaty was in effect.

Table 10-12 tries probit regression analysis, using TURN 1-2 as independent variables and selecting the growth rates of assets and sales, dividends, and profit control for industry as firm performance variables. From table 10-12, several points are clear.

While relative sales and relative assets did not necessarily have a significant correlation with management turnover, in all categories of turnover it has a negative significant correlation with relative dividend rate. Wrong performance in terms of dividend encouraged the turnover of top management. It indicates that an effective monitoring system functioned in the interests of stockholders in the early 1950s. It is interesting that even TURN 1 has a significant negative correlation with dividend rate. Top management who did not care about dividends had to resign earlier and were taken over by other board members promoted within companies. Monitoring systems under bank-centered corporate groups functioned according to the shareholder interest, although in TURN 1 some cases could not be confirmed by bank intervention, while the other cases could be.

Examples (TURN 2) of top management being taken over by persons outside companies have a significant negative correlation with profit rate as well as dividend rate. Because bank intervention was con-

Table 10-12. Probit Analysis of Turnover and Company Performance (*N=122*)

Item	*TURN 1 PROMOTION*	*TURN 2 OUT*	*TURN 2′ +RECOVER*	*TURN2″ +CHAIR*	*TURN 1+2′*	*TURN 1+2″*
Number of turnovers	20	9	15	22	35	42
Relative dividend	–0.047	–0.075	–0.064	–0.576	–0.074	–0.080
	–2.614[a]	–2.829[a]	–2.806[a]	–2.997[a]	4.114[a]	–4.371[a]
Relative profit	1.261	–12.8	–11.96	–9.156	–2.049	–2.310
	0.507	–2.839[a]	–2.986[a]	–2.703[a]	–1.192	–1.354
Relative sales	–0.301	–0.717	–0.813	–0.053	–0.604	–0.218
	–0.982	–1.293	–1.672[b]	–0.208	–0.984	–0.929
Relative assets	–0.529	0.075	–0.285	–0.062	–0.553	–0.396
	–1.066	0.134	–0.545	–0.132	–1.271	–0.954

Note: All variables are calculated on relative terms, *vi – vij*; *vi* = *i* companies variables; *vij* = the average *v* of *j* industry at same time, which *i* companies belong to. Relative dividend and relative profit are the same as in table 10-8. Relative sales is calculated by using sales in 1955/sales in 1951. Relative assets is calculated by using assets in 1955/sales in 1951. Lower row is *t* statistics.

a. Significant at 1 percent level.

b. Significant at 10 percent level.

Source: TSE 1951–56; Yamaichi 1956.

firmed in almost every case of TURN 2 and TURN 2′, this negative correlation indicates that, if the default risk increased because of the management teams' bad performance, the bank clearly intervened in personnel matters.[22]

22. It is the contingent relationship between the main bank and manufacturing companies that was formalized by Aoki (1993). The influence of banks on companies did not affect the decisionmaking of the borrowers, as long as their management was satisfactory. Banks intervened substantially, however, in the personnel matters of the borrowers and requested changes when the profitability of borrowers decreased and the lack of management ability became obvious.

For example, IBJ intervened in the personnel matters of Nihon Yakin (Metal Company), which suffered from financial distress in 1953. An experienced person who had run other smaller companies was appointed as president by IBJ as part of a rescue package (Tôyô-keizai 1953). When Mitsui Chemical, Inc., faced serious liquidity problems under the new top management in 1951–52, Mitsui Bank intervened in personnel matters. Ishida ken, who was a former Mitsui Mining executive and was purged during the postwar period, was appointed as the new president (Tôyô-keizai 1951).

It is noteworthy that, as is shown in the Mitsui Chemical case, the former purged top management as well as bank members or outside companies' candidates were recruited as new top management by main banks immediately after the Peace Treaty was effected. Generally speaking, the cases in which purged former presidents or executive board members could return to their positions after the Peace Treaty were rare (Miyajima 1993). If the companies showed bad performance from the viewpoint of debtholders, however, banks considered the former purged top manager as a possible candidate. This point is strengthened because TURN 2″ also had a negative significant correlation with profit, if the case of the former purged manager returning as a chairman is included in the regression.

It has been pointed out that the main bank was delegated to monitor their clients' companies by debtholders such as nonmain banks, insurance companies, and trust banks, as well as shareholders (Aoki 1988). The result in table 10-12 that turnover correlated to profit level as well as dividend ratio historically supports this view. Instead of the originally expected monitor—the market and the employees—the main bank, which dispatched executives to clients' companies and at the same time remained one of the large shareholders, exclusively monitored the top management team, being delegated by other debtholders as well as shareholders. Thus, the bank-centered corporate groups that emerged in the mid-1950s had an effective monitoring system for disciplining the top management team.

Bibliography

Aoki, M. 1988. *Information, Incentives, and Bargaining in the Japanese Economy*. Cambridge, U.K.: Cambridge University Press.

———. 1993. "Monitoring Characteristics of the Main Banks System: an Analytical and Historical View." In M. Aoki and H. Patrick, eds., *The Japanese Main Bank System: Its Relevancy for Developing and Transforming Economies*. Oxford, U.K.: Oxford University Press.

Aoki, M., H. Patrick, and P. Sheard. 1993. "The Japanese Main Bank System: An Introductory Overview." In M. Aoki, and H. Patrick, eds., *The Japanese Main Bank System: Its Relevancy for Developing and Transforming Economies*. Oxford, U.K.: Oxford University Press.

BOJ (Bank of Japan). 1970. *Meiji-ikô Honpô Shuyô Keizai Tokei (Economic Statistics since Meiji Era)*. Tokyo.

———. 1959. "Yushi Atsusen no Enkaku (Brief Summary of Loan Syndication)." In *Nihon Kinyu-shi Shiryo (The Document of Japanese Financial History)*. Tokyo.

Chandler, A. 1977. *The Visible Hand: The Managerial Revolution in American Business*. Cambridge, Mass.: Harvard University Press.

Fama, E. 1980. "Agency Problem and the Theory of the Firm." *Journal of Political Economy* 88.

FTC (Fair Trade Commission) 1948. *The Record of the Elimination of Law of Excess Economic Power*. National Archives, Box 8520–8535, Washington, D.C.

———. 1955. *Shôken Shijô ni okeru Kinyû-shihon no Shihai to Shûtyû (Control and Concentration of Financial Institution in Security Market)*. Tokyo.

Fuji Bank. 1982. *Fuji Ginkô Hyaku-Nenshi (Fuji Bank Centennial History)*. Tokyo.

GHQ/SCAP (General Headquarters, Supreme Commander for the Allied Nations). 1951a. *History of the Nonmilitary Activities of the Occupation of Japan (1945 through September 1949), Money and Banking*. GHQ. National Archives, Washington, D.C.

———. 1951b. *History of the Nonmilitary Activities of the Occupation of Japan*. Vol. 24. *Elimination of Zaibatsu Control*. GHQ. National Archives, Washington, D.C.

————. 1951c. *History of the Nonmilitary Activities of the Occupation of Japan*. Vol. 25. *The Reorganization of Enterprise*. GHQ. National Archives, Washington, D.C.

Hadley, E. 1970. *Antitrust in Japan*. Princeton, N.J.: Princeton University Press.

HCLC (Holding Company Liquidation Commission). 1951. *Nihon-zaibatsu to Sono Kaitai (Japanese Zaibatsu and its Dissolution)*. Tokyo.

Hoshi, T. 1993. "Evolution of the Main Bank System in Japan." University of California at San Diego. Mimeo.

Hyûga, H. 1975. "Kigyô Hihan ni Kotaeru (The Answer to Company Criticism)." *Shûkan Tôyô-keizai*, March, 22.

Jensen, M., and R. Ruback. 1983. "The Market for Corporate Control." *Journal of Financial Economics* 11.

Kaplan, S. N. 1992. "Internal Corporate Governance in Japan and the USA: Difference in Activities and Horizons." University of Chicago. Mimeo.

Keizai Doyu-kai. 1951. *Keizaidoyu Kai 5 nen-shi (Five-year History of Keizai Doyu-kai)*. Tokyo.

Lazonick, W. 1992. "Controlling the Market for Corporate Control: the Historical Significance of Managerial Capitalism." *Industry and Corporate Change* 1: 445–88.

Mitsui Real Estate. 1986. *Mitsui Fudôsan Yonjû Nen-shi (Mitsui Real Estate 40 Years History)*. Tokyo.

Miwa, R. 1989. "Sengo Minshuka to Keizai-saiken (Postwar Democratization and Economic Reconstruction)." In T. Nakamura, ed., *Nihon-Keizai Shi 7 Keikakuka to Minshuka (Japanese Economic History 7)*. Tokyo: Iwanami-shoten.

Miyajima, H. 1993a. "Senji Keizaika no Jiyushugi Keizai-ron to Tosei keizai-ron (Liberalism-based Policy versus Control-based Policy in the Wartime Economy)." In *Shirizu Nihon Kin-gendai shi 3: Gendai Shakai e no Tenkei (The Transformation to Contemporary Society)*. Tokyo: Iwanami-shoten.

———— . 1993b. "Postwar Reform in Enterprise Management: Managerial Revolution from above and the Emergence of the 'Japanese-type' Firm." *Japanese Yearbook on Business History* 10: 53–82.

———— . 1994. "The Transformation of *Zaibatsu* to Postwar Corporate Groups: From Hierarchical Integrated Group to Horizontally Integrated Group." *Journal of the Japanese and International Economies* 8: 293–328.

————. Forthcoming. "Nihon ni okeru Keieisha Kakumei (The Managerial Revolution in Japan)." In H. Yamazaki and T. Kikkawa, eds., *Nihon Keieishi Koza (The Series of Business History in Japan)*. Tokyo: Iwanami-shoten.

MOF (Ministry of Finance). 1976. *Shôwa Zaiseishi-shi Shûsen kara Kôwa made: 12 Kinyû (1) (Financial History of Shôwa: War's End to Peace Treaty, Vol. 12: Finance)*. Tokyo: Tôyô-keizai Shinpô-sha.

———— . 1978. *Shôwa Zaisei-shi Shûsen kara Kôwa made: 19 Tokei (Financial History of Shôwa: War's End to Peace Treaty, Vol. 19: Statistics)*. Tokyo: Tôyô-keizai Shinpô-sha.

———— . 1979. *Shôwa Zaisei-shi Shûsen kara Kôwa made: 14 Hoken/Shôken (Financial History of Shôwa: War's End to Peace Treaty, Vol. 14: Insurance and Securities)*. Tokyo: Tôyô-keizai Shinpô-sha.

———— . 1982. *Shôwa Zaiseishi-shi Shûsen kara Kôwa made, 2 Dokusen-Kinshi (Financial History of Shôwa: War's End to Peace Treaty: Anti-Trust)*. Tokyo: Tôyô-keizai Shinpô-sha.

Nihon-keizai Shinbun-sha, ed. 1980. *Watashi no Rireki-sho; Keizai-jin (My Personal History; Businessman)*. Nihon-Keizai Shinbun-Sha.

Okazaki, T. 1993a. "The Japanese Firm under the Wartime Planned Economy." *Journal of the Japanese and International Economies* 7: 175–203.

———— . 1993b. "Kigyo (Corporation)." In T. Okazaki and M. Okuno, eds., *Nihon Gata Keizai Shisutemu no Genryu (The Origin of the Japanese Economic System)*. Nihon-Keizai Shinbunsha.

Prowse, S. 1990. "Institutional Investment Patterns and Corporate Finance Behavior in the U.S. and Japan." *Journal of Financial Economics* 27: 43–66.

Sanwa Bank. 1974. *Sanwa Ginko no Rekishi (The History of Sanwa Bank).* Osaka.

Suzuki K. 1992. "*Zaibatsu* kara Kigyo-shudan, Kigyo-*keiretsu he* (From *zaibatsu* to Corporate Groups)." *Tochi Seido Shigaku* 135: 1–18.

Teranishi, J. 1993. "Emergence of Loan Syndication in Wartime Japan—An Investigation into the Historical Origin of the Main Bank." In M. Aoki and H. Patrick, eds., *The Japanese Main Bank System: Its Relevancy for Developing and Transforming Economies.* Oxford, U.K.: Oxford University Press.

Teranishi, Juro, and Yutaka Kosai, eds. 1993. *The Japanese Experience of Economic Reform.* London: Macmillan.

Tokyo Kaijô-Cessio. 1982. *Tokyo Kaijô Cessio-kabushiki Kaisha Hyakunen-shi (History of Tokyo Marine and Fire).* Tokyo.

TSE (Tokyo Stock Exchange). 1950–56. *Jôjô-Kaisha Sôran (The Yearbook of Listed Companies).* Tokyo: Tôyô-keizai Shinpô-sha.

Tôyô-keizai. 1953. "Ginkô-shihai no Kyôka to *Zaibatsu* Saihensei no Hôkô (The Control of Banks and Direction of *zaibatsu* Reorganization)." *Tôyô-keizai Shinpô*, Oct. 24.

————. 1955. "*Zaibatsu* no Saihensei to Kin-yû Shihairyoku no Jitsutai (Reorganization of *Zaibatsu* and their Financial Control)." *Tôyô-keizai Shinpô*, June 1.

Yafeh, Y. 1993. "Corporate Ownership, Profitability and Bank-Firm Ties: Evidence from American Occupation Reforms in Japan." Harvard University. Mimeo.

Yamaichi Shôken. 1956. *Kabushiki Kaisha Nenkan (The Yearbook of Companies).* Tokyo.

Yamanaka, H. 1986. *Seimei-hoken Kinyu Hattenshi (The History of Life Insurance Institutions).* Tokyo.

11

Savings Mobilization and Investment Financing during Japan's Postwar Economic Recovery

Juro Teranishi

Japan's war against the Allied Forces ended in 1945. The Japanese high-growth era (1957–73), with an average annual growth rate in the gross national product (GNP) of 9.99 percent and an investment/GNP ratio of 31.6 percent, started between 1955 and 1957. It thus took ten years to rebuild the war-torn economy and put it on a trajectory of sustained growth. The first five of these years (1945–50), a subphase known as the period of reforms and stabilization (Teranishi 1994b), were spent fighting inflation. The near hyperinflation, which reached a peak monthly consumer price index (CPI) growth rate of 32.8 percent, was overcome by 1949. Yet despite achieving macroeconomic stability, the GNP growth rate and investment ratio stayed rather low during the next five years (1950–55), the subphase of institutional adjustment (Teranishi 1994b). The high growth rate and high investment ratio of the high-growth era seem to be closely related to the low growth rate and low investment ratio of the preceding period, 1950–55.

The author is grateful for the comments from Takeo Hoshi, Hideaki Miyajima, and other participants at the World Bank conference, "Corporate Governance in Transitional Economies," held at Stanford University, April 22–23, 1994.

Let us call the periods 1945–50, 1950–57, and 1957–73 periods I, II, and III, respectively. This chapter examines time series data on investment financing, saving mobilization, and financial intermediation. Special emphasis is given to period II, an era that was characterized by (i) the onset of a dramatic increase in capital intensity, (ii) a low share of investment to GNP, and (iii) a heavy reliance by large manufacturing firms on financing through retained earnings.

The second section of the chapter briefly examines the first two characteristics of the period, and then turns to a close investigation of the third. This focus is especially useful in view of the high dependence on bank borrowing for corporate financing during wartime, period I, and period III, and it is apparently closely related to the first two characteristics. The third section of the chapter discusses the reasons for the heavy reliance of large manufacturers on retained earnings. First we will consider the borrower's side and the possible role of inactive investment behavior. Second, we turn to the lender's side and discuss related factors, such as the possibility of low levels of saving mobilization, bank lending behavior, and the adequacy of the maturity of funds mobilized.

Our analysis is still tentative and inconclusive. Nevertheless, it will be suggested that the low level of investment in period II is closely linked to the low level of bank borrowing through the increased capital intensity of production technology. In other words, we suggest that the relative scarcity of long-term funds, essential for active investment in capital-intensive equipment, prevented the general level of investment from rising during period II.

In the fourth section we calculate a time series of the indexes of the degree of maturity transformation carried out by the financial sector. The estimated series shows a medium-term cycle of about ten years duration, moving in close correspondence to the share of long-term corporate financing. The chapter concludes with a discussion of the reasons for the prominence of indirect financing during the high-growth era.

Three Characteristics of Period II

Let us first briefly compare the macroeconomic data of the three periods. As seen in table 11-1, the high investment ratio in period I is

Table 11-1. Macroeconomic Characteristics of the Three Periods

Period	$\Delta P/p(\%)$	$\Delta Y/Y(\%)$	$I/Y(\%)$	$\Delta I/\Delta Y$
I, 1946–51	57.21	9.8	31.1	0.10
II, 1952–57	4.64	7.1	19.7	0.37
III, 1957–62	1.04	9.5	26.1	0.39
1962–67	4.55	9.8	31.4	0.43
1967–72	4.96	10.8	37.3	0.44

Note: P = GNP deflator, Y = real GNP, I = gross capital formation. Until 1951, fiscal year and 1934–36 prices; after 1952, calendar year and 1950 prices.

Source: Statistical Bureau of Japan 1988, pp. 363, 367–69.

noteworthy in view of the turmoil and confusion of the day. The basic reason for this is that the fight against inflation mainly relied on supply-side measures such as the Priority Production System (concentrated lending and subsidies to important intermediate goods industries) and price anchoring.[1] Financed by new money, these measures were in themselves inflationary, and they were eventually replaced by the orthodox stabilization measures of tight fiscal and monetary policy. Even so, the supply-side measures effectively encouraged investment and reduced consumption through compulsory saving. Since this investment comprised mainly the repair of capital equipment and its conversion from military to peaceful use, the incremental capital-output ratio (ICOR—$\Delta I/\Delta Y$) was a very low 0.1, and production was free to increase at the considerable rate of 9.8 percent (see table 11-1). The rebound in production also owed much to the gradual resumption of the import of energy and basic material.

After the initial phase of recovery, however, ICOR rose considerably ($\Delta I/\Delta Y$ = 0.37),[2] making further production gains difficult without investment in foreign technology imports to modernize obsolete equipment (the Industry Rationalization Policy). Table 11-1 shows that,

1. On these points, refer to the chapters by Masahiro Kuroda, Hiroshi Yoshikawa and Tetsuji Okazaki, and Teranishi, in Teranishi and Kosai 1993.
2. See Kosai 1986.

at the same time, the investment ratio *I/Y* settled to a comparatively low 19.1 percent during period II. These characteristics are quite remarkable because both ICOR and the investment ratio were high during period III. In table 11-1, *I/Y* in period III is about 30 percent and ICOR approximately 0.40, a level comparable to period II. In other words, in period II ICOR reached levels as high as it did during the high-growth era, but the investment ratio declined to a low level.

The two characteristics of investment during period II—low *I/Y* and high ICOR—seem closely related to the pattern of investment financing. It will be shown that in a remarkable contrast to the high dependence on bank borrowing during periods I and III, during period II the corporate sector financed its investment mainly through retained earnings.

Let us investigate this point with the corporate financial data compiled by the Ministry of Finance in *Hojinkigyo Tokei Nenpo (Annual Statistics of Corporate Firms).* Coverage varies by firm size and changes slightly from year to year. As an example, in 1960 the ratios of sampled firms to total firms (the sampling ratio) are as follows: for firms with paid-in capital of less than 2 million yen, 1/200; for firms between 2 and 5 million yen, 1/50; for firms between 5 and 10 million yen, 1/10; for firms between 10 and 50 million yen, 1/5; for firms between 50 and 100 million yen, 1/2; and for firms over 100 million yen, coverage is 100 percent. For each category, figures for total firms are estimated by multiplying the number of sample firms by the inverse of the sampling ratio.[3]

Figure 11-1 compares various methods of financing as ratios to the sum of fixed tangible assets and inventories. Borrowings from financial institutions (hereafter, borrowing) are net of compensating deposits (assumed equal to time deposits)[4] for all manufacturing

3. For more detail and for changes over time, refer to Ministry of Finance, *Hojinkigyo Tokei Shuran (FY 1960–1974)*, vol. 1, pp. 1–2.

4. Because the *Hojinkigyo Tokei Nenpo* does not give separate figures for time deposits, the ratio of time deposits to the sum of total corporate time deposits, demand deposits, and cash was calculated from Bank of Japan, *Flow of Funds Accounts* and from Ministry of Finance (1978) and was multiplied with the total value of cash and deposits found in *Hojinkigyo Tokei Nenpo.*

Figure 11-1. Financing of the Corporate Sector, Total Manufacturing

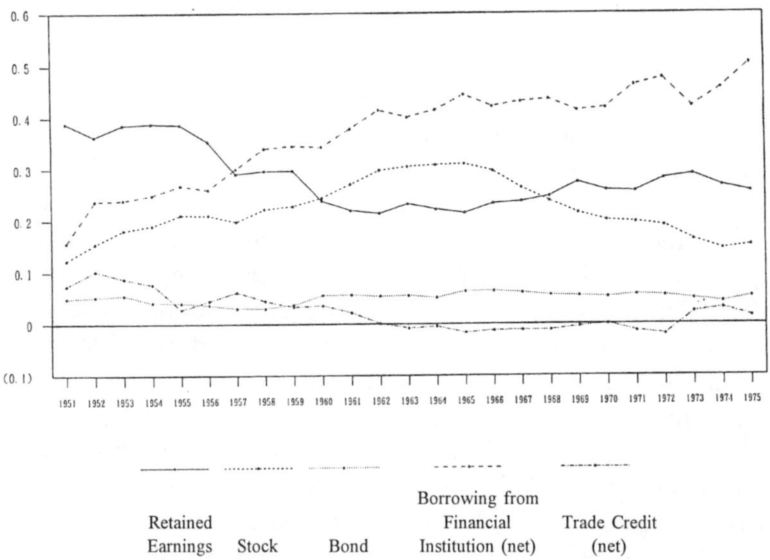

Note: Until 1959, calendar year; after 1960, fiscal year (begins April and ends March of next year). Borrowing from other sources is not shown for the sake of simplicity.

Source: Ministry of Finance, *Hojinkigyo Tokei Nenpo*, various issues.

firms.[5] Trade credits are also net figures (accounts and bills receivable minus accounts and bills payable). This procedure roughly follows Colin Mayer (1990, p. 311) in calculating the unweighted average net financing of nonfinancial enterprises, 1970–85 (see table 12.1 in Mayer 1990).

5. For the period 1951–55, the *Hojinkigyo-Tokei Nenpo* does not give figures for the entire manufacturing sector, so figures for the following industries were summed up: food, textiles, spinning, paper products, chemicals, fertilizer, glass and clay products, primary metals, steel, metal products, machinery (including electric and transportation machinery), and shipbuilding.

One of the noteworthy features of figure 11-1 is the high ratio of retained earnings in period II and its decrease through the early years of period III, until about 1960. Borrowing rose correspondingly in period III and stayed very high through the later years of period III, in accordance with an often noted characteristic of the high-growth era financial system: the dominance of indirect financing.[6]

Figures 11-2 and 11-3 offer information for large manufacturing firms (firms with paid-in capital over 100 million yen before 1960, and over 1 billion yen thereafter) and smaller manufacturing firms (the rest). Figure 11-2 shows movements of retained earnings and borrowing similar to those in figure 11-1, but figure 11-3 does not. The retained earnings and borrowing of smaller firms remained rather stable until the mid-1960s, and rose gradually thereafter.[7]

The high share of retained earnings during period II has thus far gone relatively unnoticed, and further confirmation through other methods is in order. To begin with, table 11-2 shows an index similar to that in figures 11-1–3, but calculated on a flow basis for five periods—1951–56, 1956–60, 1961–66, 1966–71, and 1971–76—for large and small firms. Table 11-3 provides flow financing ratios based on gross figures and as ratios to total assets. In both tables one can see that during 1951–56 large manufacturing firms depended heavily on internal funds for financing; their reliance on borrowings is relatively slight compared with later periods.

The percentage composition of the flow of funds to all industries as compiled by the Bank of Japan is shown in figure 11-4. These data show the flow of total lendings by private and government financial institutions, issuance of corporate bonds, issuance of stocks, and corporate savings in national accounts. The percentage share of retained earnings rises from 1945 to the early 1950s, thereby confirming our earlier findings. Because this figure refers to total industry, the share of retained earnings is not so high. According to calculations based on

---

6. Although the share of retained earnings stays rather low during period III, it begins to surge in the mid-1970s and reaches more than 70 percent in the mid-1980s. This corresponds to the rather high share of retained earnings in the data for 1970–85 compiled by Mayer (1988, 1990).

7. As of the end of FY 1960, total gross assets of large and small manufacturing firms were 6,599 and 6,452 billion yen, respectively.

Figure 11-2. Financing of the Corporate Sector, Large Manufacturing Firms

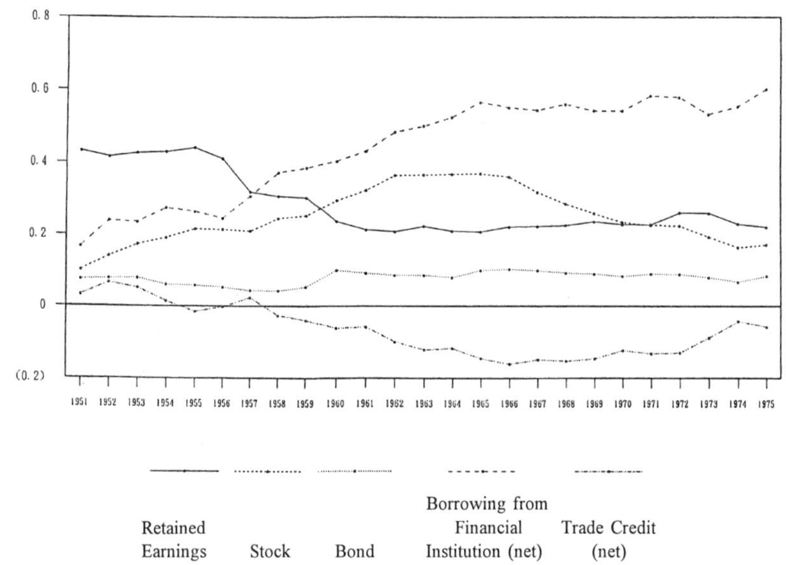

Source: Ministry of Finance, *Hojinkigyo Tokei Nenpo.*

data from the *Hojinkigyo Tokei Nenpo*, the percentage of the increase in retained earnings to the increase in total assets (to the increase in the sum of fixed tangible assets and inventories) during 1951–56 is 13.3 percent (26.7 percent) for total industry, 15.2 percent (32.7 percent) for to-total manufacturing, 23.0 percent (39.5 percent) for large manufacturing firms, and 5.7 percent (13.9 percent) for small manufacturing firms. The percentage of the increase in borrowings is 27.4 percent (42.9 percent) for total industry, 24.2 percent (34.1 percent) for total manufacturing, 20.8 percent (30.2 percent) for large manufacturing firms, and 31.0 percent (44.9 percent) for small manufacturing firms.

Corporate Finance in the Recovery Period

What explains the high share of retained earnings and relatively low share of borrowing among large firms? Both borrower's and lender's conditions play a role.

Figure 11-3. Financing of the Corporate Sector, Small Manufacturing Firms

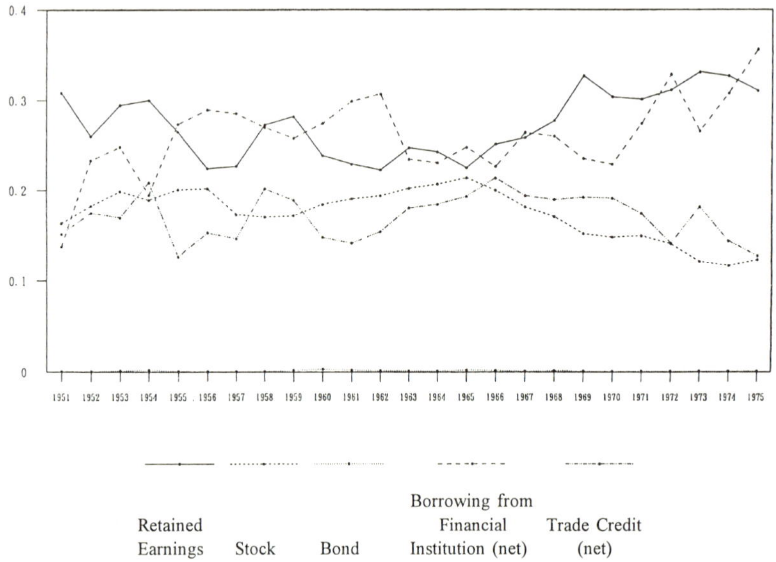

Source: Ministry of Finance, *Hojinkigyo Tokei Nenpo*.

An explanation from the borrower's side is that low levels of investment activity led to a high reliance on internal funding. The reasons that entrepreneurs reduced investment during the period are powerful—for example, the instability in the corporate governance structure of firms at the time (Teranishi and Kosai 1993). Owing to the "democratization" of securities, large companies came to be held by small stockholders with individual stakes insufficiently large to justify extensive monitoring, and managers faced constant takeover threats. At the same time, managers were locked in a fierce struggle for corporate control with powerful, militant labor unions. The absence of an adequate system of investment coordination also may have affected investment behavior. As suggested by the increased capital intensity, further investment was not possible without the introduction of foreign technology, especially in the case of large firms. Because the import of

Table 11-2. Composition of Corporate Manufacturing Financing (Flow)
(percentage of fixed tangible assets and inventories)

Category and period	*Retained earnings*	*Capital*	*Bonds*	*Net borrowing from financial institutions*	*Net trade credit*
(A) Large manufacturing corporations					
1951–56	39.5	29.0	3.8	30.2	–0.3
1956–60	–1.0	40.9	16.7	63.4	–14.7
1961–66	23.3	41.8	12.2	75.0	–32.1
1966–71	23.2	12.6	7.9	61.0	–10.9
1971–76	25.3	10.4	7.6	65.0	0.0
					–3.8
(B) Small manufacturing corporations					
1951–56	13.9	24.1	0.0	44.9	15.4
1956–60	24.5	17.7	0.4	27.7	14.6
1961–66	28.5	21.5	0.1	13.4	32.6
1966–71	34.4	10.8	0.0	31.9	14.2
1971–76	32.3	9.5	0.1	39.9	11.8

Table 11-3. Composition of Corporate Manufacturing Financing (Flow)
(percentage of total assets)

Category and period	*Retained earnings*	*Capital*	*Bonds*	*Gross borrowing from financial institutions*	*Gross financing by trade credit*
(A) Large manufacturing corporations					
1951–56	23.0	16.9	2.2	20.8	17.0
1956–60	-0.5	19.9	8.2	40.4	13.2
1961–66	7.8	14.0	4.1	39.9	16.6
1966–71	10.2	5.5	3.5	40.4	17.4
1971–76	10.1	4.2	3.0	35.9	23.2
(B) Small manufacturing corporations					
1951–56	5.7	9.9	0.0	31.0	35.4
1956–60	12.0	8.6	0.2	29.4	29.4
1961–66	10.2	7.7	0.0	27.3	37.4
1966–71	13.8	4.3	0.0	33.1	29.2
1971–76	11.6	3.4	0.0	31.8	32.0

Source: Statistical Bureau of Japan 1988.

Figure 11-4. Flow of Funds to Total Industry, Bank of Japan Data

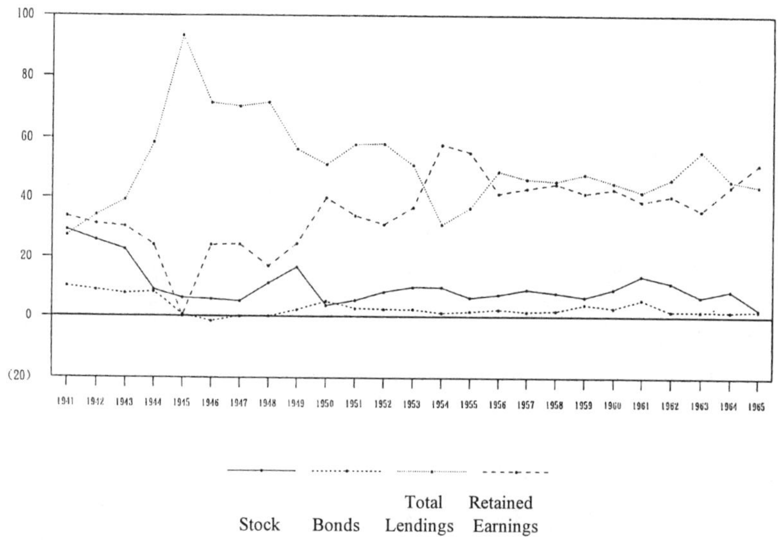

technology and the concomitant learning process has technical external effects throughout industry, proper coordination by the government can be effective in encouraging individual activity. In postwar Japan, the government's coordinating role formed gradually during period II. With respect to technological externalities, for example, industrial policy was adopted as a formal development measure when the government embarked on the Industry Rationalization Plan in 1951, targeting the coal and steel industries. Nevertheless, the first postwar economic plan—"Five-Year Plan for Economic Self-Support"—was published only in 1955.

Taken as a whole, these conditions discouraged investment during period II. Agency cost of internal funds was at its lowest, investment could be financed mainly by internal funds, and dependence on external funds could be quite low.

Incidentally, figures 11-1 and 11-2 show a rising share of equity (capital) financing during period II, which needs additional explanation. One of the reasons for this is the compulsory new issue of equity. Hoshi (in this volume) shows that wartime losses were mainly offset by the stockholders' burden (*Kigyo Saiken Seibiho*). But after reorganization, firms were encouraged to increase their capital base with new stock issues at least equal to the sum of their fixed assets and fixed operating capital (Miyajima 1992).

Another reason for the increase in equity financing is rooted in the character of new stock issues. Table 11-4 shows that shares of new capitalization with no payment comprised about 19.9 percent of new issues during 1951–54. These are nothing but a shift of funds from retained earnings to paid-in capital, however, and they do not represent new financing in any sense. In addition, over 90 percent of new capitalization with payment was subscription by existing stockholders. Since existing stockholders are corporate insiders, such financing is quite similar to financing with retained earnings, and is free from agency problems (Horiuchi 1993).

Yet low investment activity cannot be the sole reason for the high corporate reliance on internal funds. If it were, firms with low levels of investment should rely on internal finance to a greater extent than other firms. A comparison between large and small manufacturing firms shows that this is not the case. As figures 11-2 and 11-3 and tables 11-2 and 11-3 show, dependence on internal funds was definitely higher for large firms during period II, but the increase in fixed tangible assets during 1951–56 was 3.40 times for large firms and 2.26 times for small firms.

Let us move on to lender-side sources of high levels of internal financing among large firms. First, it could be argued that a low level of financial saving mobilization forced reliance upon internal funds for corporate investment. Figure 11-5 shows the composition of assets beginning in period I in the personal sector (households plus unincorporated businesses, such as farms and small firms). Data are drawn from tables by the Ministry of Finance (1978) for the period 1946–52 and from the Bank of Japan's *Flow of Funds Accounts* for the period thereafter. The composition of personal sector assets in period I reflects wartime financing. Because war financing was done through new currency issues, the proportion of cash to total assets was high during period I. The ratio was further increased during 1947–48, when Reconstruction Bank activity was financed by Bank of Japan note issues. The high share of cash persisted throughout period II, long after the containment of inflation (around 1949), although it gradually decreased.

Table 11-4. New Equity Issues of Listed Firms
(percentage)

Period	*New capitalization without payments*	*New capitalization with payments*	*Subscription rationed to existing shareholders*	*Public offering*	*Rationing to new shareholders*
1951–54	19.9	81.1	—	—	—
1955–59	20.1	79.9	96.5	3.4	0.1
1960–64	10.7	89.3	92.9	6.5	0.5
1965–69	14.7	85.3	93.3	5.3	1.4

— Not available.

Note: The percentage of new capitalization with and without payments refers only to listed companies of the first section of Tokyo Stock Exchange. New capitalization without payments includes others, such as dividend payments in the form of stocks.

Source: Bank of Japan 1964 (p. 187), 1973 (p. 172); Ministry of Finance 1983 (p. 602); and Horiuchi 1993.

Figure 11-5. Composition of Personal Sector Assets

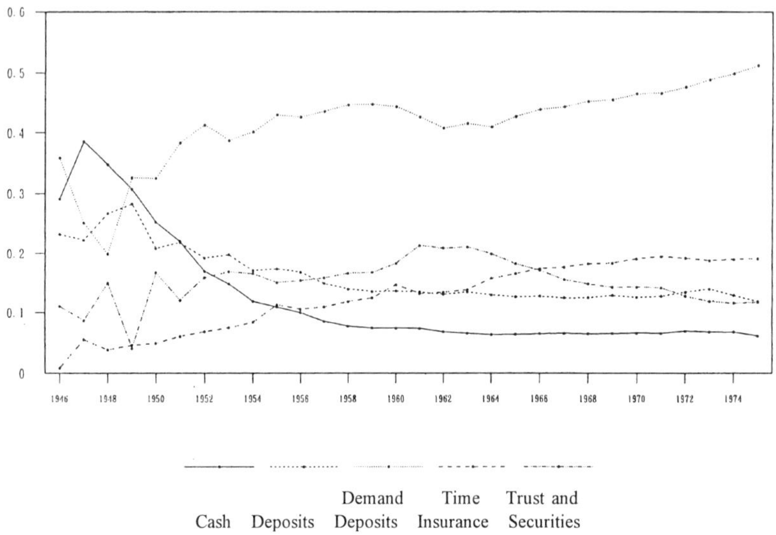

Source: Bank of Japan, *Flow of Funds Accounts.*

The slow speed of decrease in the share of cash to total assets implies a low share of deposits to total assets. It could be argued that the relatively feeble mobilization of bank deposits was one of the reasons for the low dependence of large firms on bank borrowings. The low level of mobilization can be explained by inflationary expectations, which reduce the real interest rates on deposits. Figure 11-6 indicates a very close relationship between the real deposit rate (the interest rate on six-month time deposits less the rate of increase in the GNP deflator) and the rate of increase in real deposits balance (total deposits in the banking sector divided by the GNP deflator). In light of the experience of the preceding years, it is reasonable to expect that a strong concern about inflation prevailed during period II, and that the expectation of falling real deposit rates induced people to hold cash in preparation for a shortage of goods.

Figure 11-6. Real Interest Rate and Rate of Increase of Real Deposits

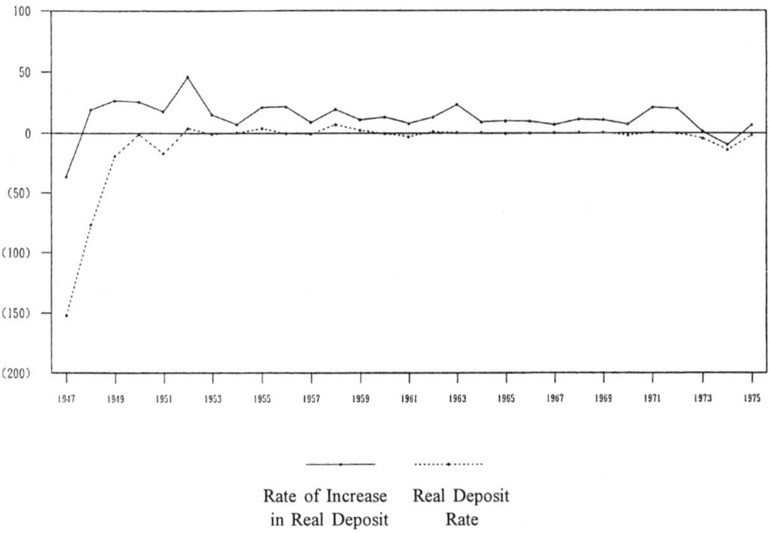

Note: Deposits are total deposits of Zenkoku Ginko.
Source: Statistical Bureau of Japan 1988.

Another element that might be responsible for the low share of bank borrowing by large firms during period II is bank lending behavior. If banks were reluctant to lend to large firms, plagued as they were with labor disputes and lacking a long-term perspective on technology imports, firms might have been obliged to rely on internal funds. This conjecture, however, does not seem to be correct. As table 11-5 illustrates, the ratio of lending to deposits is quite high during period II for every group of banks. Moreover, city banks relied rather heavily on Bank of Japan borrowing, as well as interbank money markets. (The lending/deposit ratio of the Sogo banks is rather low, but this is because of the reorganization of the Sogo bank system, which included a dramatic increase in the number of branches.) It must also be noted that during period II many ex-*zaibatsu* firms tried to borrow from banks outside their corporate group, indicating an inability of

Table 11-5. Lending-Deposit Ratio (a), Borrowings from Bank of Japan-Deposit Ratio (b), and Net Money Market Borrowing Rate (c)

	City bank			*Local bank*			*Sogo bank (Daini-Chingin)*		
Year	*(a)*	*(b)*	*(c)*	*(a)*	*(b)*	*(c)*	*(a)*	*(b)*	*(c)*
1945	93.3	—	-0.1	28.4	—	0.2	36.0	—	—
1946	119.4	—	0.4	36.6	—	1.4	31.0	—	—
1947	75.7	—	0.7	44.9	—	0.5	33.3	—	—
1948	74.7	12.6	0.1	66.3	1.6	0.2	37.3	—	—
1949	83.2	12.7	-0.3	78.1	4.7	0.3	45.7	—	—
1950	90.1	15.3	-0.4	86.3	7.3	0.0	51.9	—	—
1951	100.0	19.3	-1.3	82.4	2.0	1.5	—	—	0.6
1952	92.8	13.3	-2.2	81.7	1.7	1.7	45.2	—	0.7
1953	96.4	14.7	-2.2	82.8	1.4	2.0	50.2	—	0.5
1954	91.6	11.2	-2.9	81.2	0.6	2.9	53.7	—	1.6
1955	77.3	1.2	-2.7	78.7	0.0	3.1	52.0	—	1.6
1956	77.5	3.7	-2.5	78.2	0.0	2.9	52.4	—	1.5
1957	85.4	14.6	-3.4	79.0	0.1	2.9	55.5	—	2.8
1958	82.7	8.0	-4.3	77.3	0.2	3.7	58.8	—	3.6
1959	84.6	6.2	-4.8	77.9	0.2	4.2	66.0	—	1.6

1960	84.3	7.8	–4.2	78.5	0.2	3.9	68.6	—	1.8
1961	88.2	19.3	–3.0	78.2	0.3	1.9	70.6	—	2.2
1962	90.0	16.4	–5.2	77.5	0.2	3.6	72.5	—	1.9
1963	87.5	11.4	–5.8	78.2	0.2	2.5	74.9	—	1.5
1964	89.3	8.7	–10.0	77.5	0.2	3.1	75.9	—	3.0
1965	86.8	9.1	–7.4	77.8	0.3	3.5	78.2	—	2.1
1966	85.9	9.5	–5.7	78.0	0.3	2.6	80.4	—	1.6
1967	88.7	7.5	–7.1	78.7	0.4	3.4	81.1	—	2.0
1968	87.1	7.5	–5.5	78.6	0.3	3.1	80.4	—	2.0
1969	87.8	8.0	–6.9	79.0	0.3	3.2	80.7	—	2.3
1970	89.5	8.7	–8.4	81.1	0.3	3.8	81.8	—	2.8
1971	85.4	1.7	–1.4	82.3	0.2	3.3	81.8	—	2.0
1972	84.5	4.8	–6.8	83.0	0.4	1.9	83.0	—	1.4
1973	90.0	4.7	–12.1	81.9	0.3	2.0	80.4	—	1.6
1974	92.7	3.1	–15.6	81.7	0.2	2.6	78.5	—	2.9

— No borrowing.

Note: Net money market borrowing rate is ([call loan + bills receivable + lendings to financial institutions] – [call money + bills payable + borrowings from financial institutions]) / (deposits and financial debentures).

Source: Ministry of Finance, *Ginko-kyoku Nenpo*, various issues.

large banks to satisfy the demand for loans by the firms of their own group (Miyajima 1992), and this tendency seems to have continued until around 1956 (Kitsukawa 1992, table 6-9).

Third, it is possible that the short-term nature of available funds, rather than simply the paucity of mobilized funds, retarded corporate investment. Since large-firm investment required capital-intensive imported technology, but many small firms still relied upon investment through second-hand equipment purchases, the shortage of long-term funds may have had more severe effects on large firms than on small firms. When investment by large firms is constrained by a lack of long-term borrowing, their investment must be financed by internal funds or decline.

Whether there was a shortage of long-term funds during period II is a delicate issue. Let us discuss a couple of points, beginning with the supply of long-term assets by the personal sector. Figure 11-7 depicts the composition of the sum of long-term assets (time deposits, trust and insurance, and securities) and the ratio of time deposits to total deposits. The rapid rise of these two indexes during period I and the deceleration of the rise during period II is impressive. It could be argued that the supply of long-term funds decelerated when it was most needed. Second, we must touch upon the effects of the closure of the Reconstruction Bank, which mainly supplied investment funds. At the end of March 1949, private banks had lent 28.7 billion yen for equipment and capital investment and 397.5 billion yen as working capital. Reconstruction Bank loans included 85.6 billion yen for equipment and capital investment and 28.2 billion yen for working capital. Adding the two, the share of loans for equipment and capital investment was 21.9 percent. After the suspension of Reconstruction Bank activity in 1949, the share of loans for equipment in total private bank lending was only 7.2 percent, 12.2 percent, and 16.6 percent at the end of 1949, 1955, and 1960, respectively. It can be conjectured that although firms demanded long-term loans for fixed capital investment, banks could not accommodate this demand because of the short-term nature of the funds at hand.

Figure 11-8 shows two indexes of long-term financing for large firms. (Data sources and the definition of large firms are the same as in figures 11-1 and 11-2). The long-term funds ratio, (a), is the ratio of the

Figure 11-7. Composition of Personal Sector, Long-Term Assets

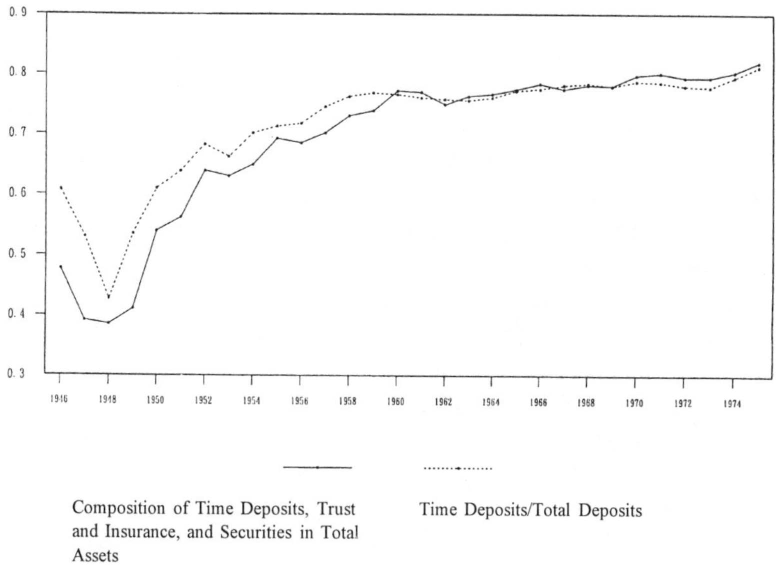

Figure 11-8. Long-Term Funds Ratio, Large Manufacturing Firms

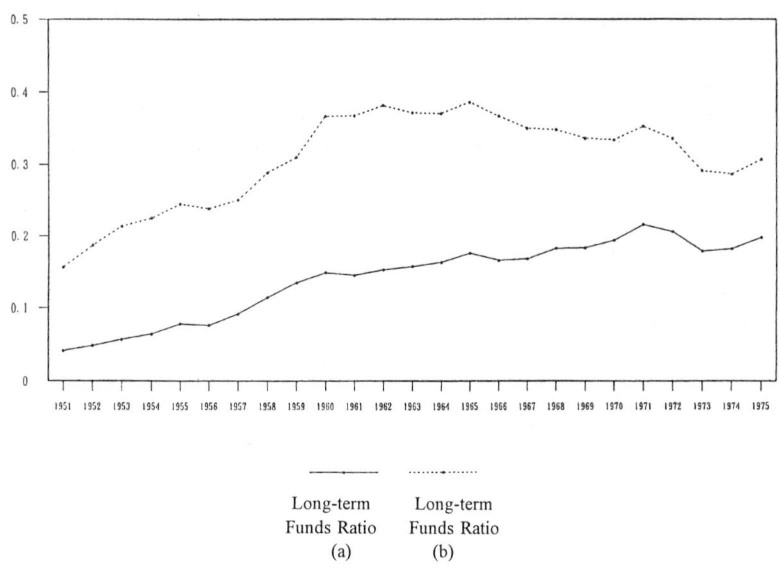

sum of long-term borrowing and bonds to total assets, while (b) is the ratio of long-term borrowing to total assets. One impressive phenomenon is the relative stability in ratios (a) and (b) during period II, and an extremely rapid rise thereafter until 1960. This phenomenon can be seen not only for large firms, but also for small firms (not shown). Since most bonds were rationed to financial institutions (in 1951, 84.6 percent; 1960, 89.9 percent; and 1970, 90.9 percent),[8] and institutions were obliged to hold them until maturity, bonds were another form of long-term lending, at least during the period under consideration. Consequently, ratios (a) and (b) show the long-term funds supply by financial institutions.

In sum, corporate investment in period II was constrained by the low level of mobilization of funds and by the short-term quality of bank deposits. Mobilization of savings was retarded by the expectation of goods shortages and inflation. The share of long-term assets in the portfolio of the personal sector increased rapidly during period I, but this increase decelerated in period II. The shortage of long-term funds was especially serious for large firms, which were asked to invest in capital-intensive imported technology. Consequently, large firm investment relied mainly on retained earnings, and the ratio of investment to GNP became rather low during the period.

Maturity Transformation by Financial Institutions

Given the rather poor conditions in corporate financing in period II, what explains the high level of investment in capital-intensive technology during period III? The reasons lie both in real and monetary factors. On the monetary side, this section suggests that the financial system's increased ability to transform the maturity of monetary instruments is one reason for the surge of investment during period III. Let us start from a comparison of figures 11-7 and 11-8 immediately after period II (1958–61). The share of long-term funds in the portfolio of the personal sector was rising at a decelerating speed, while the rising share of long-term funds in the financing of the corporate sector accel-

8. The reasons for and functions of bond rationing are explained in the next section.

erated. How could this happen? The answer can be found in an investigation of the behavior of financial institutions with respect to maturity transformation.

Let us combine the information from the *Hojinkigyo Tokei Nenpo* (on which figures 11-1 through 11-3 are based) with that from the *Flow of Funds Accounts* (on which figure 11-5 is based) to calculate indexes of maturity transformation. The first source contains data for the ratio of long-term borrowing to total borrowing for all industries. By multiplying this ratio with the sum of corporate and personal sector borrowing from the *Flow of Funds Accounts*, one estimates *total long-term private sector borrowing* (LB). Furthermore, by adding this to the bonds held by financial institutions, *total long-term private sector debt from financial institutions* (LD) is obtained. Estimated in this way, LB and LD comprise the borrowing from and the bonds held by both private and government financial institutions. By subtracting from LB the lending of government financial institutions, all of which is long term, we obtain *long-term private sector borrowing from private financial institutions* (LBP). Furthermore, by subtracting from LD the sum of government financial institution lending and bondholdings, we obtain *long-term private sector debt from private financial institutions* (LDP).

Turning from firm liabilities to financial institution liabilities, we derive another four indexes of long-term funds. The first is the *gross long-term funding of private financial institutions* (GLFP), defined as the sum of time deposits, trust funds, insurance, and financial debentures. Some financial debentures issued by long-term credit banks were held by financial institutions such as city banks. By subtracting these, an index for *net long-term funding of private financial institutions* (NLFP) is obtained.[9] By adding to GLFP the funds from government financial institutions in the form of postal savings and government insurance, *gross long-term funding of financial institutions* (GLF) is obtained. Finally, by subtracting financial debentures held by government finan-

9. Ministry of Finance (1983) *Flow of Funds Tables* gives only figures for the sum of financial debentures and corporate bonds. Financial debentures are estimated by multiplying the average ratio of financial debentures to the sum of financial debentures and corporate bonds during 1953–55. The same procedures were applied in the calculation of NFL.

cial institutions from GLF, we derive *net long-term funding of financial institutions* (NLF).

Figure 11-9 shows the indexes of maturity transformation by private financial institutions. LBP/GLFP and LDP/GLFP indicate ratios of private long-term lending and long-term lending plus bonds, respectively, to gross private long-term funds. LBP/NLFP and LDP/NLFP show similar ratios to the net long-term funds obtained by private financial institutions. Figure 11-10 shows corresponding indexes with respect to all financial institutions, including governmental financial institutions.

All the indexes suggest a similar pattern. First, transformation ratios gradually rise. Second, shifts in the transformation ratios evince a clear cyclical pattern. For the postwar period, these cycles are closely related to medium-term business cycles (Juglar cycles). Troughs of the cycles match troughs in the growth rate of the GNP and in corporate profit rates in 1955, 1965, and 1975, and transformation ratios tend to rise with increase in GNP and profits.

Figure 11-9. Maturity Transformation by Private Financial Institutions

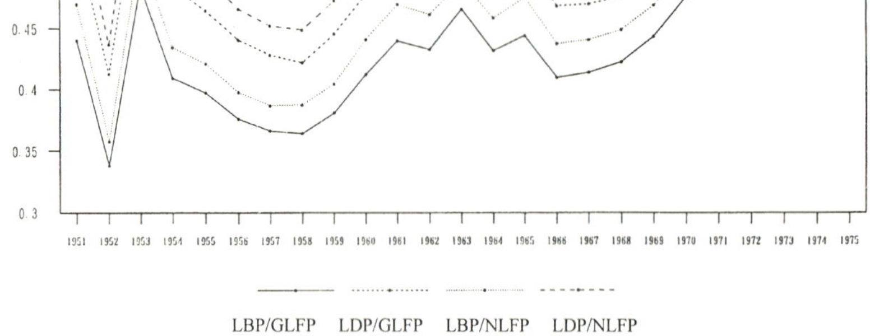

The indexes also show that around 1958–61 there was a upward surge in the maturity transformation ratio. This seems to be closely related to the sharp rise in the corporate sector's long-term financing ratio during period II, despite slow growth in the long-term assets ratio of the personal sector at the same time. An additional, unexplained, peak in the transformation ratios comes around 1953; the economic boom caused by the Korean War is a highly plausible explanation.

Our analysis of maturity transformation is still only preliminary, and much more needs to be done. It is pertinent to add a brief explanation of the financial institutions' maturity transformation mechanism, which we call *Strategic Intervention in Maturity Transformation* (SIMT) of the banking sector, following Teranishi (1993), and to discuss the emergence of this mechanism during period II.

The mechanism of strategic intervention in bank maturity transformation has two parts: the rationing system of corporate bonds and financial debentures and the accommodating supply of Bank of Japan (BOJ) credits at below-market rates. During the high-growth era, most

Figure 11-10. Maturity Transformation by Private and Government Financial Institutions

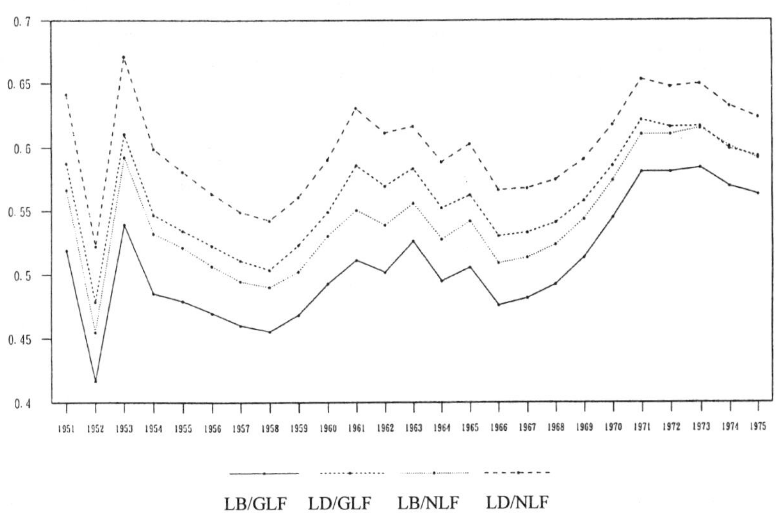

bonds were issued at above-market prices and were rationed to banks. As of the end of 1960, 693 billion yen in corporate bonds were outstanding, of which 614 billion yen was held by private financial institutions (216 billion by city banks), 7 billion by the government financial institutions, and only 71 billion by the private nonbank sector. The outstanding amount of financial debentures was 1,054 billion yen, of which 603 billion was held by private financial institutions (307 by city banks), 175 billion by the government financial institutions program, and 278 billion by the private nonbank sector. Because these bonds were sold at above-market prices, the rate of return for subscribers was lower than the market rate.

In 1960 (the latter half of fiscal year 1960), the average cost of funds for city banks was 6.43 percent and their average lending rate (opportunity cost) was 7.67 percent. Since a subscriber's rate of return on corporate bonds (*ichiryu-jigyosai*) and financial debentures (*ritsuki-kinyusai*) was 7.95 percent and 7.61 percent, respectively, it was not optimal for city banks to hold financial debentures, although it did not cause losses in their current account. Moreover, since banks purchased bonds and financial debentures at above-market prices, selling them on the secondary market would have caused losses to the banks. To avoid losses, banks held bonds and financial debentures until maturity, with a considerable reduction in the liquidity of their portfolios.

Why did banks (especially city banks) hold corporate bonds and financial debentures even though their rates of return were less than the opportunity cost and they had unfavorable effects on their liquidity position? The answer to this question lies in the second part of the SIMT mechanism, the strategic role of BOJ credits. First, the subscriber's rate of return is less than the borrowing rate from BOJ. Because banks are permitted to use corporate bonds and financial debentures as collateral for BOJ borrowing, they can obtain *de facto* subsidies by borrowing from BOJ on this collateral, and compensate for the difference between the opportunity cost and the subscriber's rate of return on bonds and debentures. Second, the BOJ took an accommodating stance in the supply of BOJ credits to city banks. On every business day, *ex post* demand and supply at the call market is reported to the BOJ at 3 P.M., and the BOJ in principle supplied the difference by lending directly to city banks, who were the major borrowers at the call market. Whenever BOJ felt it necessary to tighten the money supply, however, it had the option of reducing the supply of BOJ credits by requesting that city banks reduce their bank deposits at BOJ. Since reserve deposit rate requirements limited the extent of possible adjustment, however, by and large BOJ passively followed city bank demand for borrowing. In other words, the BOJ credit served as liquid assets or implicit reserves for city banks, thereby enabling city banks to hold illiquid corporate bonds and financial debentures during the high-growth era without liquidity risk.

It should now be clear that the SIMT mechanism, composed of bond rationing and an accommodating supply of cheap BOJ credits to city banks, was designed to convert short-term city bank deposits, together with deposits siphoned to the city banks from specialized financial institutions through the money markets, into the long-term debt of the corporate sector and the long-term credit banks. Most of the funds obtained by long-term credit banks were lent to the corporate sector at maturities of three to five years.

Note that this system of transforming short-term deposits into long-term lending was based on transfer of income between city banks and government in the form of implicit subsidies and taxation. The implicit subsidies to city banks could be calculated as the call market rate less the BOJ discount rate, multiplied by outstanding borrowing from the BOJ. The implicit tax on city banks can be calculated as the market rate of return on bonds and debentures less the subscriber's rate of return on bonds and debentures, multiplied by the bonds and debentures held by city banks. It can be shown that financial debentures issued by long-term credit banks comprised the largest component of the implicit tax on city banks.

An important property of the SIMT can be identified in a comparison of estimates of tax and subsidies for the period 1966–77, reported in Teranishi (1993). The entire implicit subsidy amounted to 2,470 hundred-million yen, comparable in magnitude to the estimated value of the implicit tax of 2,255 hundred-million yen. In other words, the medium-term average of implicit subsidies to city banks from the maturity of transformation of short-term deposits to long-term lending almost balanced the average of implicit taxes on city banks. What does this mean? The equality implies the following:

> (call market rate – BOJ discount rate) x city bank borrowing from BOJ = (market rate of return on bonds and debentures – subscriber's rate of return on bonds and debentures) x bonds and debentures held by city banks.

Since call market rate of return $\geq$ market rate of return
$>$ subscriber's rate of return
$>$ BOJ discount rate,
city bank borrowings from BOJ $<$ bonds and debentures held by city banks.

In other words, through the SIMT, the amount of short-term deposits transformed into long-term lending (equal to the bonds and debentures held by city banks) is larger than the BOJ credits.

The importance of this proposition can be seen by contrasting the SIMT with the direct purchase of bonds and debentures by BOJ. In the case of direct purchases, BOJ must issue high-powered money equal to the amount of long-term funds to be created, at the risk of creating inflationary pressure. The well-known stability of the price level, especially wholesale prices, during the high-growth era suggests one additional role played by the SIMT.

Finally, let us touch briefly upon the process of the introduction of the SIMT during period II. The bond rationing system was established during periods I and II through a complicated political process including bankers, security companies, bureaucrats, and the occupation forces. The law on long-term credit banks whose financial debentures play a crucial role in the SIMT was promulgated in 1952. The Bank of Japan began its accommodating stance in lending and credit rationing in 1955. (These points were closely examined in Teranishi and Kosai 1993.)

Concluding Remarks

We have discovered and analyzed the rather heavy dependence on retained earnings of large manufacturing firms during period II, a period after the initial recovery from wartime confusion and before the onset of rapid economic growth. This phenomenon stands in clear contrast with the financing structure of the high-growth era, especially in its early days when corporate firms were heavily dependent on bank borrowings.

Our analysis suggest three reasons for the dominance of indirect financing during the high-growth era. First, the mere existence of high rates of investment explains the high dependence on external financing, part of which is financed by financial institutions. The concentration of mobilization of financial savings in the banking sector is also important. One reason for this concentration is the disappearance of informal credits in the inflation and reforms immediately after the war. Another cause lies in the regulation of the bond market by bureaucrats, which also became possible in the postwar confusion (Teranishi and Kosai 1993). Finally, the establishment of an effective system of maturity transformation (SIMT) is also responsible for the dominance of indirect financing, because the SIMT mechanism spurred the supply of long-term funds without resorting to the securities market.

It is important to note that these three factors are a product of postwar conditions. The origin of the postwar financial system does not necessarily lie in the wartime system. Although we do not deny that the postwar financial system inherited various aspects of the prewar financial system and was influenced by the shock of World War II and defeat, we oppose the thesis that the postwar financial system is a simple inheritance or continuation of the wartime system. Incidentally, those who emphasize the continuity of the wartime and postwar financial systems often argue that once a banking system attains dominance during wartime, it tends to maintain its dominance over nascent securities markets through its favored access to and internalization of information. This theory, however, does not apply to the Japanese case for two reasons.[10] First, under the system of the Wartime Designated Financial Institution for Munition Financing, the information-related capabilities of banks were completely neglected. Second, the renewed accumulation of information by the banking sector began through the process of rehabilitating the corporate balance sheets (*Kigyo saiken seibi*) immediately after the war and did not arise as a result of its previous dominant financing position.

10. These points were clarified through the recent research by Hoshi and others. Refer to Hoshi, in this volume.

Bibliography

Aoki, Masahiko. 1988. *Information Incentives and Bargaining in the Japanese Economy*. Cambridge, U.K.: Cambridge University Press.

Bank of Japan. 1964. *Honpo Keizaitokei* (Economic Statistics Annual).

———. Various years. *Flow of Funds Accounts. Keizai Tokei-geppo.*

Horiuchi, Akiyoshi. 1993. "A Survey on Corporate Financing in Japan" (in Japanese). *Finanshiaru Revyu* June (28): 3–33.

Kitsukawa, Takeo. 1992. "The Formation of Post-War Type Business Groups" (in Japanese). In Juro Hashimoto and Haruto Takeda, eds., *Nihonkeiza no Hatten to Kigyoshudan*. Tokyo: Tokyo Daigaku Shuppankai.

Komine, Takao. 1993. *The Role of Economic Planning in Japan*. In J. Teranishi and Y. Kosai, eds., *The Japanese Experience of Economic Reforms*. London: Macmillan.

Kosai, Yutaka. 1986. *The Era of High-Speed Growth—Notes on the Postwar Japan Economy*. Tokyo: University of Tokyo Press.

Mayer, Colin P. 1988. "New Issues in Corporate Finance." *European Economic Review* 32: 1167–89.

———. 1990. "Financial Systems, Corporate Finance, and Economic Development." In R. Glenn Hubbard, ed., *Asymmetric Information, Corporate Finance, and Investment*. Chicago, Ill.: University of Chicago Press.

Ministry of Finance. 1978. *Showa Zaiseishi*, vol. 13.

———. 1983. *Showa Zaiseishi*, vol. 19.

———. Various years. *Hojinkigyo Tokei Nenpo*. Tokyo.

———. Various years. *Ginko-kyoku Nengo (Annual Report of the Banking Bureau)*. Tokyo.

Miyajima, Hideaki. 1992. "Zaibatsu Dissolution" (in Japanese). In Juro Hashimoto and Haruto Takeda, eds., *Nihonkeizai no Hatten to Kigyoshudan*. Tokyo: Tokyo Daigaku Shuppankai.

Murphy, Kevin M., Andrei Shleifer, and Robert W. Vishny. 1989. "Industrialization and the Big Push." *Journal of Political Economy* 97 (5): 1003–26.

Okazaki, Tetsuji. 1994. "Evolution of the Financial System in Postwar Japan." Discussion Paper 94-F2, University of Tokyo.

Statistical Bureau of Japan. 1988. *Nihon Choki Tokei Soran* 3. Japan Statistical Association.

Teranishi, Juro. 1993a. "Emergence and Establishment of the Financial System in Postwar Japan—Government Intervention, Indirect Financing and the Corporate Monitoring System." A background paper for the World Bank project, *The East Asian Miracle—Economic Growth and Public Policy* (Oxford University Press).

———. 1993b. "The Financial System of High Growth Era Japan." A paper prepared for the project, *A Study of Financial Policies of Selected DMCS*, by the Asian Development Bank, Manila.

———. 1994a. "Emergence of Loan Syndication in Wartime Japan: An Investigation into the Historical Origin of the Main Bank System." EDI Working Paper 94-3. World Bank, Washington, D.C.

———. 1994b. "(Gradualism) in the Japanese Experience of Economic Reforms." A paper prepared for the conference, "Economic Reform in the N.I.S. and the Crisis in Ukraine," Kiev, May 19–21, 1994.

Teranishi, Juro, and Yutaka Kosai, eds. 1993. *The Japanese Experience of Economic Reforms*. London: Macmillan.

Ueda, Kazuo. 1993. "Institutional and Regulatory Frameworks for the Main Bank System." EDI Working Paper 94-3. World Bank, Washington, D.C.

12

Shareholder Voting and Corporate Governance: The German Experience and a New Approach

Theodor Baums and Philipp v. Randow

The rapid expansion of the private sector in transition economies, particularly the corporatization of enterprises, poses problems of corporate governance. To provide large, publicly held corporations with equity capital, investors need assurance that they are protected against the detrimental side-effects of a separation of ownership and control. In this chapter we propose a tentative market solution to some of the governance problems in large, publicly held corporations and compare it with the "German experience"—that is, the role of banks in corporate governance.

Shareholder Voting and Collective Action

Shareholder voting is an integral part of the governance structure of publicly held corporations. Requiring shareholder consent for any fundamental change in corporate policy is a safeguard for the residual riskbearers of a corporation against ex post expropriation by the management. The right to vote assures the shareholders that the basic terms of their investment cannot be altered without their approval. In essence, then, voting rights are to stockholders what covenants are to bondholders: by limiting managerial discretion, they serve as a protection against moral hazard (Easterbrook and Fischel 1990, p. 186). Unlike bondholders, however, shareholders receive most of the marginal costs and benefits of fundamental corporate decisions. Thus, shareholders as residual risk-bearers have the appropriate incentives to decide on those matters (Easterbrook and Fischel, 1991, pp. 67, 69). Also, vesting voting rights in shareholders is the only feasible method to implement major improvements of corporate policy that affect the terms of their investment. Because of the dispersion of equity holdings, renegotiations are impossible to organize (Bebchuk 1989). Moreover, renegotiations would require unanimity, thus giving veto power to all shareholders, including those who hold only a small fraction of shares. By allowing a majority to implement fundamental changes of corporate policy, however, veto power can only be exerted if a shareholder holds a substantial proportion of the shares—thus, a vetoing shareholder is forced to internalize at least part of the impact of his decision on firm value.

Unfortunately, voting as a decision mechanism suffers from collective action problems. Widely dispersed shareholders are likely to be "rational-apathetic" when it comes to acquiring information on changes of corporate policy proposed by management. The cost of informing oneself in order to cast an intelligent vote on a management proposal will exceed the expected benefits, even if one assumes that their own vote will be decisive. Therefore, voters that hold only a small fraction of shares will remain rationally ignorant. If the management controls the agenda, as it does in most legal systems, shareholders will give their approval, assuming that the management acts on superior knowledge (Easterbrook and Fischel 1991, p. 67). Moreover, even if some shareholders have determined that a particular proposal will result in a loss in share value, "free-rider" problems will discourage formation of an opposition. Each shareholder may gain from opposition, but each will gain more if other shareholders bear the costs. Shareholders are not rewarded for contributing to decisionmaking. Thus, while it is better for all if everyone contributes, it is better for everyone not to contribute, with the result that the activities (information gathering, casting votes) will not be undertaken. *There is no cost-sharing mechanism that forces all the shareholders who gained from the efforts of forming an opposition to pay for these activities* (Gordon 1989).

As a result, changes of corporate policy might be adopted even though they are value-decreasing. Selling shares is not a viable alternative; informed traders would anticipate the approval of a value-decreasing change of corporate policy, and they would lower their willingness to pay accordingly. Thus, investors cannot escape the detrimental effects of their collective action problems by selling shares. True, if a buyer acquires large blocks of shares, he can change the course of action of a particular firm and dismiss the incumbent management. Under these circumstances, his expected payoff from informed voting may warrant efforts to evaluate the proposals of the incumbent management. Voting rights, then, help to provide incentives to the management to work hard on behalf of the shareholders because a poorly performing firm may become a target for a takeover. But large equity holdings come at a cost—they reduce liquidity in the market and thereby limit the informational content of share trading (Holmström and Tirole 1993). This cost is ultimately borne by the shareholders themselves, because reductions in market liquidity make performance evaluation of the management more difficult (Holmström and Tirole 1993).

The question we want to address is whether there exists a less costly mechanism to eliminate the collective choice problems mentioned above. We will try to evaluate the costs and benefits of a market solution where there are *entrepreneurs, who can earn profits by lowering the costs that dispersed shareholders must bear to exercise informed, coordinated voting power.* Allowing for entrepreneurs to cast a vote for dispersed shareholders would be advantageous to the group as a whole. The cost of informed voting by the entrepreneur would be lower than the sum of the personal costs of all shareholder monitoring as well as the costs of nonmonitoring by individual shareholders. Unlike dispersed shareholders, an entrepreneur can economize on the fixed costs of collecting information about firms. Moreover, it is plausible to assume that there are economies of scope as well if a specialist casts votes for shareholders of different firms of the same industry.

In what follows, we shall argue that *it is possible to establish a market that functions well for voting services, where firms offer to engage in monitoring and voting on behalf of the equity owners of large, publicly held corporations.* To accomplish this, however, a new regulatory framework for proxy voting needs to be implemented. We will outline its main components, some of its potential pitfalls, and compare it to the German experience—that is, proxy voting by universal banks. Banks' proxy voting power is often assumed to be a substitute for the activism of large shareholders because they can exploit economies of scale and scope in information collection, evaluation, and exercise of shareholder voting rights (Cable 1985, p. 121). Our analysis, however, will cast some doubts on the well-known notion that German banks act as delegated users of equity control rights.

A Market for Voting Services

To start the analysis, let us very briefly describe the main reasons why markets that function well for proxy voting services may not emerge.

First, there would be *free-rider effects* on the demand and the supply sides of voting services. To see this, let us assume for a moment that a voting company could collect the proxies of the majority of shareholders. While this majority would have to pay for the monitoring and voting services, its benefits would also accrue to the minority shareholders who did not give their proxies to the voting company. Clearly then, instead of paying for the services provided, shareholders will try to take a free ride on the efforts of a voting agent. Moreover, there may be free-rider incentives on the supply side of voting services as well. The management of voting companies may want to rely on the monitoring efforts of their competitors and vice versa, resulting in undermonitoring of the company to be controlled.

Second, there is a problem of *asymmetric information*. Again, assume that there are competing firms, offering their monitoring and voting services to shareholders. Yet because of the small investment, a single shareholder will devote almost no resources to ascertaining the quality of their services. Voting agents that offer good quality cannot charge higher prices than those who offer voting services of inferior quality. Thus, bad firms may drive out the good (Akerlof 1970). Even if a shareholder learns that the voting services from a particular agent are of inferior quality, he will still not know whether its competitors provide quality of a higher standard. Therefore, his costs of switching to another company may be higher than the expected benefits.

We thus are led to conclude that there are major obstacles to the establishment of a well-functioning market for voting services. Because of problems of collective action and asymmetric information, there is no reason for an individual investor to hire an agent to cast an informed vote on his behalf at the shareholder's meeting. The German experience, however, tells us a different story. Equity owners in Germany give proxies to their banks and let them exercise voting rights at their discretion. Is there a German solution to the problems of collective choice in shareholder voting?

The German Experience

In Germany (Baums 1992, 1993; Köndgen 1994), private investors do not have access to the stock exchanges. Instead, listed stock is acquired and sold through intermediaries, such as banks.[1] Because of high transaction costs, investors generally choose not to hold the documents themselves; in most cases they "deposit" their shares with a bank. The bank holds an account at a special deposit company (*Deutscher Kassenverein*), where the shares are certified in a global document.[2] According to the Stock Corporation Code (Aktiengesetz 1965), banks that offer to hold shares on "deposit" for their customers are obliged to furnish them with the corporation's information on shareholders' meetings (for example, the agenda, the recommendations of the management board, the proposals of other shareholders as to resolutions of the meeting). Although the banks are refunded for this service by the company itself,[3] they charge their customers for keeping the shares in custody; they also offer to vote these shares.[4] If a bank offers to vote the shares to any shareholder of a company, it is obliged to accept each client's request to cast their vote as well (§ 135 [10], Aktiengesetz). Banks do not, however, charge their clients an additional fee for their voting ser-

1. Wolfgang Hefermehl speaks of a monopoly position of the banks in this respect (Schlegelberger 1977).
2. Most shares of German stock corporations are bearer shares, not registered shares.
3. See "Verordnung über den Ersatz von Aufwendungen der Kreditinstitute vom 18. Juni 1968," *Bundesgesetzblatt* I, S. 720.
4. Apart from the depot banks, two incorporated associations of shareholders (Schutzvereinigung deutscher Wertpapierbesitz; Schutzgemeinschaft der Kleinaktionäre) act as proxies on behalf of their members.

vices.[5] They ask for a flat rate for the depository service only. Soliciting proxies and voting their clients' stock is one of the few financial services that German banks offer "for free."[6]

The latest statistical data on shareholder representation by banks show that the main banks in Germany have acquired control of a substantial proportion of voting rights in publicly held corporations. According to a study conducted by Perlitz and Seger (forthcoming), in nine out of fifty-seven major "top one-hundred" German industrial corporations, proxy voting rights provided the main banks with the blocking minority, in another six companies with the majority, and in eleven corporations with a majority of over 75 percent of the shares present at the shareholders' meeting, thus enabling them to change statutes (see tables 12-1 and 12-2). The voting power of the main banks is even more impressive if their own shareholdings are taken into account. The combined voting power from shareholdings and proxy voting rights amounts to a blocking minority in five companies, a majority in nine companies, and a qualified majority (over 75 percent of the shares represented at the shareholders' meeting) of seventeen corporations (see tables 12-3 and 12-4).

According to a further study, conducted by Fraune (forthcoming), the accumulated voting power of banks from their *own shareholdings, proxy votes, and shares held by investment companies where banks hold more than 50 percent of nominal equity capital* accounted in 1992, on average, for more than 82 percent of the votes present in general meetings in twenty-four of the "top one-hundred" publicly owned corporations in Germany (the average presence of all shares being 58 percent). This voting power amounted to a blocking minority in four corporations, a majority in three, and a qualified majority in seventeen corporations of the sample.

In a further study, from a list of the one hundred largest firms in 1984, Gottschalk (1988) selected firms with more than 50 percent of

---

5. Overview in *Capital* 7/92 at p. 100 f. The three "big" banks with the largest number of proxies do not belong to the banks with the lowest depositary fees.

6. Banks are refunded for communicating notices and so forth by the company. These refunds do not, however, cover the costs of asking for proxies and voting.

Table 12-1. Proxy Votes of German Banks, 1990
(percent of shares present)

	Number of corporations			
Proxy votes	*Deutsche Bank AG*	*Dresdner Bank AG*	*Commerz-bank AG*	*Other banks*
< 10	40	45	56	28
10–25	9	10	1	15
25–50 (blocking minority)	6	2	0	11
> 50 (majority)	2	0	0	3
Total cases of bank proxies	57	57	57	57

Note: $N = 57$.
Source: Perlitz and Seger, forthcoming, p. 16.

Table 12-2. Proxy Votes of German Banks, 1990
(percent of shares present)

Total bank proxies	*Number of corporations*	*Percentage of total number of corporations*
< 10	20	35.1
10–25	11	19.3
25–50 (blocking minority)	9	15.8
50–75 (majority)	6	10.5
> 75 (extraordinary majority)	11	19.3

Note: $N = 57$.
Source: Perlitz and Seger, forthcoming, p. 17.

their stock either widely held or owned by banks. These thirty-two companies, with a (nominal) equity capital of DM 29.5 billion, represented about a quarter of the nominal capital of all German stock corporations. Gottschalk aggregated the voting power of the banks' own shares, their custodial shares, and shares held by investment companies that are bank subsidiaries. He found that, on average, banks represented

Table 12-3. Shareholdings plus Proxy Votes of German Banks, 1990
(percent of shares present)

	Number of corporations			
Shareholdings plus proxy voting	*Deutsche Bank AG*	*Dresdner bank AG*	*Commerz-bank AG*	*Other banks*
< 10	35	43	56	26
10–25	10	8	1	13
25–50 (blocking minority)	8	4	0	13
50–75 (majority)	1	2	0	4
> 75 (extraordinary majority)	3	0	0	1

Note: $N = 57$.
Source: Perlitz and Seger, forthcoming, p. 17.

Table 12-4. Total Shareholdings plus Proxy Votes of German Banks, 1990
(percent of shares present)

Total banks' shareholdings plus proxies	*Number of corporations*	*Percentage of total number of corporations*
< 10	17	29.8
10–25	9	15.8
25–50 (blocking minority)	5	8.8
50–75 (majority)	9	15.8
> 75 (extraordinary majority)	17	29.8

Note: $N = 57$.
Source: Perlitz and Seger, forthcoming, p. 18.

more than four-fifths (82.67 percent) of all votes present at meetings (the average presence of all shares was 64 percent). With one exception, they represented at least a majority (more than half) of the votes present. Consequently, banks were able to elect the members of the supervisory board chosen by shareholders and changes in the corporate statutes could not be effected against their votes. In twenty-two, or two-thirds, of the firms, the banks voted more than three-fourths of the stock present and thus could change the statutes. No other shareholder could block these decisions. Note that many of these corporations (by the votes of the banks) have provisions in their statutes that no one shareholder may vote more than (typically) 5 percent of all shares of the company. This rule does not, however, apply to banks voting proxies. The aggregated voting power of banks, added to rights based on their own equity holdings or rights transferred to them by mutual funds run by a subsidiary, thus provide a comfortable and stable power base at shareholder meetings. Furthermore, Gottschalk's study shows that the voting power is highly concentrated in the three largest private banks (Deutsche Bank, Dresdner Bank, and Commerzbank). Together they voted an average of approximately 45 percent of the stock represented at the general meetings of the thirty-two companies. In almost half the cases (fifteen firms), they held the majority; in another third (ten firms) they had a blocking minority. In individual cases, one or another of the big banks dominates. In most cases the votes are distributed roughly equally among them, or two banks together have about the same number of votes as the third alone. Also, according to a survey conducted by the *Gesslerkommission*, the proxy rights of the three big banks together in 1974 constituted the voting majority in five companies and the blocking minority or voting majority in another sixteen companies (out of seventy-four) (Bericht der Stüdienkommission 1979, p. 436).

To sum up, our overview shows that the banks accumulate and wield considerable voting power at shareholder meetings (Baums 1992, table 1, 1994, table 12-3). This is most visible in the number of seats they hold on the supervisory boards of companies with a fragmented ownership structure. Banks sent eighty-five representatives (managers and directors) into the board rooms of the one-hundred largest industrial firms in 1990 (on personal interlocks between firms and banks, see Baums 1992, table 4), placing banks at the center of corporate interlocks. Perlitz and Seger confirm this data in their recent study: in a sample of 110 large industrial companies, the credit institutions are represented by 162 members; this accounts for 12 percent of all the 1,355 members that were chosen by the shareholders; moreover, in 29 corporations the chairman of the supervisory board is a bank representative (see tables 12-5 and 12-6; Perlitz and Seger, forthcoming). Also,

Table 12-5. Banks' Representation in the Supervisory Boards of German Companies, 1990
(number)

	Corporations			
Bankers on supervisory boards	*Deutsche Bank AG*	*Dresdner bank AG*	*Commerz-bank AG*	*Other banks*
1	45	22	12	43
2	7	1	2	7
3	0	0	0	2
Total cases of representation	52	23	14	52
Chairmanships	15	3	0	11

Note: $N = 110$.
Source: Perlitz and Seger, forthcoming, p. 18.

Table 12-6. Total Banks' Representation in the Supervisory Boards of German Companies, 1990

Bankers on supervisory board	*Number of corporations*	*Percentage of corporations*
None	18	16.4
1	51	46.4
2	19	17.3
3	17	15.4
4 or more	5	4.5

Note: $N = 110$.
Source: Perlitz and Seger, forthcoming, p. 19.

according to a survey conducted by the *Monopolkommission* in 1978, bank representatives occupied 145 seats on the supervisory boards of the largest one-hundred publicly held corporations in Germany (Edwards and Fischer 1994). The main banks (Deutsche, Dresdner, and Commerzbank) accounted for 94 of the 145 representatives (Edwards and Fischer 1994).

The enormous success of German banks in soliciting proxies is easy to explain: there is a factual compulsion to use the banks as trading institutions and depositories. Because banks do not charge their clients a fee for the additional service of casting votes on their behalf, it is easy for them to solicit proxies from their clients. Thus, the *free-rider problem* on the demand side of voting services has been overcome. The question then arises: do banks exercise their voting power in the best interest of their clients? But before we turn to this question, let us describe briefly the extent to which banks are allowed to cast the votes of their clients at their own discretion.

In order to cast a vote for its clients, the bank needs a special written power of authority or proxy, which may not be included in the general standard form contract governing the bank-customer relation. This proxy cannot be given for more than fifteen months, and it is revocable at any time (§ 135 [1], [2], Aktiengesetz). Before a shareholder meeting, banks have to recommend to their customers how to vote, and they must ask for special instructions. To enable the client to make an informed decision, the bank has to submit its own proposals of how it intends to vote in case it does not receive any instruction. In such a case the bank may then vote the client's stock in accordance with its previous proposals (§§ 128 [2], 135 [5], Aktiengesetz). In most cases, a bank votes the proxy on the basis of a carte blanche and in accordance with proposals that are of its own making. Apart from extraordinary cases, banks usually take sides with the proposals of the management (which does not exclude the possibility that management has checked in advance with the major deposit institutions to determine if certain proposals will have a chance to pass; see Bericht der Studienkommission 1979). Banks usually content themselves with mailing a proxy form sheet, routinely suggesting that the vote should be cast in accordance with the proposals of the management if the shareholder has not given other instructions. Empirical surveys have shown that customers give directions of their own in only 2 to 3 percent of all cases (Immenga 1978, p. 103). Any vote that departs from either the customer's guidelines or the bank's own proposals has to be reported and accounted for to the client (§ 135 [10] Aktiengesetz). Apart from the provision that banks follow the explicit instructions of their clients, the Stock Corporation Code does not say much about the duties of the depository banks when voting their clients' stock (Köndgen 1994). Provision

§ 128 [2] of the Aktiengesetz requires that the bank's proposals for voting be in the best interest of the client-shareholder. Only two provisions address conflict of interest. First, if a bank has been given a proxy to vote the stock of its own company, it may do so only if it has been given explicit instructions regarding specified items on the agenda (§ 135 [1] Aktiengesetz). Second, the bank has to disclose if one of its managers is a member of the supervisory board of the issuing company or vice versa (§ 128 [2] Aktiengesetz).

From the above analysis it should be clear that banks have a *substantial degree of discretion* when they exercise the voting rights of shareholders. Since banks are able to vote at their discretion to a large extent, the question remains of whether this voting power is exercised exclusively in their clients' interest. Recall first that there is a problem of asymmetric information inherent in markets for voting services. Again, if shareholders that hold small equity claims do not care about their right to vote, why should they try to evaluate whether a voting agent acts to their best interest? And why then should a bank as voting agent provide for good quality?

We can look at this question from two different angles. First, potential conflicts of interest have to be identified when a bank exercises voting rights in other corporations. The multiple roles of German banks as advisers, lenders, equityholders, and voting agents have to be taken into account. This analysis, however, would rely on the assumption that the management of banks will try to maximize the value of the *banking corporation.* But banks very often are large, publicly held corporations themselves. Thus, we also need an understanding of the *particular objectives of bank's managers* as the decisionmakers of large, publicly held corporations when they decide on how to vote their customers' shares in other companies (Edwards and Fischer 1994, p. 237). Specifically, we are led to ask whether the unique combinations of proxy voting power and equity holdings between banks and other corporations in Germany are a device that enables self-interested managers to protect each other against the threat of dismissal by dissatisfied equity owners and to establish a "cooperative shirking equilibrium." Although there is some anecdotal evidence that proxy voting power is exercised to the detriment of the clients' interests in single cases (Wenger 1992), there are no systematic studies on the voting behavior and policies of depositary banks and their managements. But if we look at the incentive structure of these intermediaries and their managements, and keep in mind that there is considerable discretion to use their positions as proxies in their own rather than in their clients' interest, the guess is certainly that this monitoring device comes at an additional agency cost for the shareholders. The agency cost of the monitoring system that we analyze is the sum of the investments borne by the shareholders in limiting shirking or opportunistic behavior of the depository, plus the costs associated with remaining or residual suboptimal behavior. Since small shareholders *are rationally apathetic as shown* above, the amount of the investment of the shareholders themselves to limit shirking or opportunistic behavior will probably be low, or even zero, whereas the residual cost may be high if there are no mechanisms to reduce this cost.

There are only a few legal provisions that address conflict of interest and try to ensure that depository banks pursue the interests of their clients. The provision that banks comply with express directions from their clients is certainly not an innovation. In addition, Aktiengesetz (§ 128 [2]) requires that the bank's own proposals for voting the proxy be in the best interest of the shareholder. This broad phrasing gives way to almost any interpretation (see Köndgen 1994, p. 552). Courts have never tried to specify the meaning of this rule because shareholders have not brought suits against depot banks so far.[7] The provision that banks may vote their own stock only if they have been given express instructions on how to cast the vote (§ 128 [1] Aktiengesetz) covers only a small range of possible conflicts of interest. The banking supervisory authorities do control the deposit and proxy voting business of banks to a certain extent; this control, however, is merely formal. It is confined to checking whether the depository institutions complied with the provisions of the Stock Corporation Act. In addition it provides that a bank has to document the reasons and deliberations that led to its voting proposals.[8] The most effective control is probably exerted *by the financial press and the public debate* on the role and eco-

7. With only one exception; see Köndgen 1994, p. 545.
8. See Nos. 14 and 15 of the "Richtlinien für die Depotprüfung," as of December 16, 1970, in *Bundesanzeiger* 239, December 23, 1970.

nomic power of banks.[9] Banks are responsive to this critique because abuses could lead to adverse public or political reactions.

Now, let us look at the main reasons that banks might be interested in soliciting proxies from individual shareholders. This analysis will reveal a number of conflicts of interest for banks that might adversely affect the interests of small shareholders.

Banks could try to *protect and enhance the value of their own equity investments*. As we mentioned above, German banks may, and do, hold, in addition to their position as proxyholders, considerable equity stakes in firms. The 4,191 banks that are supervised by the Federal Banking Supervisory Agency (Bundesaufsichtsamt für das Kreditwesen) held 4,802 direct participations in other firms of more than 10 percent of the capital of these firms in November 1993 (Federal Banking Supervisory Agency 1993). Proxy voting power may enable a bank to influence the management of a particular corporation to deal with other companies where the bank has substantial *equity holdings*. If these business transactions with other bank-controlled companies benefit the bank's shareholders but are not in the best interest of the shareholders of the controlled corporation, close and ongoing monitoring on behalf of these shareholders does not pay off for the bank.

Also, as a *creditor* commanding over half the votes at a shareholder meeting because of its own holdings and proxy voting rights, a bank can choose who manages the firm. It will choose people who implicitly promise not to harm the interests of the creditor by engaging in overly risky projects, distributing assets to shareholders, and the like, without the bank's approval. In case of misbehavior it can punish management—clearly, the incumbent management will anticipate this possibility. The addition of custodial shares to its own equity holdings seems to be a perfect arrangement to get the necessary leverage on a firm's management to protect the bank's own credit investment without sharing the risks. Because proxy voting rights yield disproportionate voting power, the bank will not bear the residual losses from an overly risk-

9. On December 8, 1993, the Committee on Economic Affairs of the federal Parliament held a public hearing, the "Power of Banks and Insurance Companies." Depository voting was one of the issues (some of the statements are published in *Zeitschrift für Bankrecht und Bankpolitik*, 1994, issue 1, p. 69.

averse investment strategy commensurate with its control over the company. It does not matter that this power usually has to be shared with other banks; as creditors they have largely parallel interests in dealing with the firm's management.

A bank does have incentives to act as a depository and get as many proxies as possible in order to be able to cast votes and send representatives into board rooms, because this will increase the likelihood that the bank will get a share of the respective firm's financial business. The main banks that command the most votes at the general meeting of a given firm will most likely be among the (leading) members of an underwriting syndicate for the issuing company (Böhm 1992). There remain complaints about the stable structures of these syndicates and the low degree of competition in the market, although things seem to be changing in issues on the national market (Verband der Auslandsbanken in Deutschland 1993). Furthermore, banks may want to hold proxy voting power in order to maintain their dominant role as leaders of a syndicate when new shares are issued. Since the existing equity owners usually get the right to purchase the shares of a new issue, a bank with a great number of shares on deposit is in a good position to arrange the sale of shares to the existing shareholders (Edwards and Fischer 1994, p. 216).

Banks may also prefer projects that need (higher) external (credit) finance to projects with a comparatively higher net present value for the firm and greater benefit for the shareholders (Böhm 1992). If the assertions of the managerialists are correct, corporate managers do not pursue profit maximization, but rather seek size or growth maximization (Klein and Coffee 1990, pp. 161–62). This means that there may be a common interest between managers and custodial banks at the expense of shareholders. The evidence, however, is mixed. Credit finance does not play a more important role in firms where banks exercise substantial proxy voting power than it does in firms that do not have banks in a comparable position. Large corporations with banks as proxyholders raise significantly less bank finance than the German corporate sector as a whole ("Monatsberichte der Deutschen Bundesbank" Oct. 1992, p. 31; Mayer and Alexander 1990). A related issue concerns the dividend policy of firms. Management may prefer to retain earnings rather than distribute them to shareholders. This makes the firm less dependent on external finance and provides a way to conceal fluctuations in future reported earnings, and thus reduces management's accountability for losses. Banks are said to support this restrictive dividend policy when casting their clients' votes to protect their credit extensions or to get a share of the firm's financial business (Böhm 1992, pp. 139–40, 143, 149; Immenga 1978, p. 121). At the same time, retaining dividends means that management becomes increasingly independent and "emancipated" from external finance as the internal funds grow. But perhaps banks tend to neglect this long-term development in order to pursue their present interests.

Still another *incentive* to get proxies exists *for management* of banks that are publicly held corporations with widely distributed shares. Mutual proxy or capital interlocks between two banks, a bank and an insurance company, or a bank and an industrial firm can dilute the respective managements' ability to control each other when exercising the voting rights of third parties. If managements can punish each other because both firms hold a sufficient amount of either the stock of the other firm or its shareholders' proxies, they will probably refrain from being a nuisance to the other side. Such mutual proxy and capital interlocks ensure that the respective managements can support as well as punish each other.[10] In the past, banks have helped the management of other banks and large firms whose stock they vote protect themselves against unwanted takeovers by changing the target firm's corporate statutes to dilute the voting power of a possible challenger.[11] Admittedly, this incentive does not play a role in cases where the ownership structure of the deposit bank looks different—as is the case, for example, at a privately held bank or at savings banks (Sparkassen) owned by a municipality. To sum up, there are a number of conflicts

---

10. For example, according to Gottschalk's study (1988), in the shareholders' meeting of Commerzbank in 1986. Commerzbank's management commanded 34.58 percent, whereas 26.22 percent of the votes were cast by the other two big banks (Deutsche and Dresdner Bank). In Dresdner Bank's general meeting the numbers were 47.08 percent and 16.98 percent, respectively. In order to get the majority of votes each side depended on the other.

11. See Lutter and Lammers 1990. It has to be mentioned, however, that the views on such anti-takeover provisions and the interests of the target's shareholders are not unanimous in the academic literature (see Baums 1990; for a different view see Zöllner and Noack 1991).

of interest for banks exercising proxy votes that might adversely affect the interest of small shareholders. Apparently, the German system of depositary voting is in need of a change. In the following, we will try to evaluate the costs and benefits of a market where there are entrepreneurs, who can earn profits by lowering the costs that dispersed shareholders must bear to exercise informed, coordinated voting power.

A New Approach

Let us now turn to a proposal that might help to establish a market in voting services despite the problems mentioned above. The main requirements are outlined below.

Voting agents offer their services to the corporation and declare the prices they intend to charge for their services. Eligible as voting agents are auditors and auditing companies only. Any business links between the voting agents and the corporation and/or the shareholders of the corporation are prohibited by law. These restrictions do not apply to other parties that exercise shareholder voting rights on the basis of specific instructions.

- Shareholders will be furnished with the all relevant data concerning these offers. *Voting agents will be elected by the active shareholder*: the votes may be cast by postal vote, by representatives on the ground of specific instructions, and by shareholders who attend the general meeting. The voting agents will be elected for a certain period of time. After each period—say, three years—there will be a new election. In this election the incumbent voting agents are not allowed to represent shareholders. Moreover, a term limit prohibits reelection of a voting agent for more than two consecutive terms. After such a break, however, voting agents are free to campaign for a new election.
- *There is a limit on the number of voting agents that may be elected*, depending on the ownership structure of the corporation. In corporations that are listed on a stock exchange there may be no more than three (3) voting agents at a time; unlisted corporations with a nominal equity capital of more than DM 1 million may not have more than two (2) voting agents. In

corporations with a nominal equity capital of less than DM 1 million, voting agents may not be elected.

- In order to be elected, *voting agents need to get at least 5 percent of the votes cast or votes representing more than DM 500,000 of the nominal equity capital of the corporation.*
- *The voting agents represent all shareholders except those who attend the general meetings during their tenure or are represented by a person that has been given specific instructions or a special proxy.* For example: if, say, 60 percent of the shareholders attend the general meeting or are represented by third parties on instructions, the voting agents will automatically cast 40 percent of the votes not present. *Thus, there will be a 100 percent rate of shareholder representation in any general meeting.*
- *The voting agents declare in advance how they plan to decide the issues of the general meeting's agenda.* If shareholders want to vote otherwise, they have to attend the general meeting or send their specific instructions to the bank that holds their shares in custody.
- *The voting agents cast votes of nonactive shareholders according to their success in the election.* Thus, if two voting agents have been elected, and voting agent *A* received 40 percent of the votes, while voting agent *B* got 20 percent, *A* represents two-thirds and voting agent *B* one-third of the inactive shareholders in the general meeting. Shareholders, of course, are free to choose whether to attend the general meeting, let third parties decide on specific instructions, or to rely on the voting agent.
- *The voting agents are paid by the corporation.*
- *Voting agents will be supervised by a regulatory authority.*

This regulatory framework should assure that a well-functioning market for voting services will emerge. First, recall that there may be free-rider effects on the demand side if firms will offer voting services. *By requiring the corporation to remunerate the voting agents, however, a cost-sharing mechanism will be introduced that forces all the shareholders who gain from the effort of informed, coordinated voting to pay for this activity through the corporation.* (Kallfass 1992a,b). True, if the active shareholders hold only a small proportion of the shares, they will bear only a small fraction of the cost of their choice. Thus, they might be led to vote for an expensive voting agent. Hiring an unduly expensive voting agent, however, would lower the value of the shares as well. Therefore, the incentives to externalize costs on the inactive majority are mitigated.

Second, the problem of asymmetric information has to be managed. Shareholders, who hold only small fractions of shares, will devote almost no resources to ascertaining the quality of the services of a particular voting agent.[12] Again, the cost of informing oneself will exceed the expected benefits. Thus, we need a mechanism that allows for an informed choice of voting agent. Enter the general meeting: Voting agents should be elected by active shareholders. Basically, then, *active shareholders elect voting agents on behalf of the inactive shareholders*. By allowing only active shareholders to cast a vote, the problem of asymmetric information will be overcome.

Active shareholders are—almost by definition—interested in corporate matters, and their interests, as far as profit-maximization is concerned, align with those of inactive shareholders. Therefore, they will carefully scrutinize the quality and prices of the voting companies that stand for election. This quality control by active shareholders and limited tenure will provide a voting trust with an incentive to work hard on behalf of the shareholders it represents. Only by providing monitoring efforts that benefit shareholder interests can the voting agent hope to get reelected. The role of active shareholders in electing a voting agent for inactive shareholders, however, might raise some concern. Let us address two potential objections. First, active shareholders might try to preserve their disproportionate voting power in the general meeting by refraining from casting a vote altogether. Because the election of voting agents requires the participation of only a very small group of active shareholders (5 percent of the votes cast or votes representing more than DM 500,000 of the nominal equity capital

12. Kallfass (1992a,b) wants shareholders to choose voting agents on the market. Voting agents then are remunerated by the corporation according to the number of proxies they solicited. This approach, however, does not take into account the rational ignorance of small shareholders. There is no reason to assume that small shareholders will devote more resources in ascertaining the quality of voting agents than to controlling the management's agenda.

of the corporation), however, this risk will be minimized. Second, voting agents may go with the proposals of active shareholders in order to be reelected, when these proposals are disadvantageous to the inactive equityowners. Leaving potentially adverse reputational effects of such collusive behavior aside, there is good reason to assume that active shareholders and voting agents will not collude to the detriment of the group of inactive shareholders. If a shareholder wants value-decreasing changes of corporate policy in order to pursue his short-term interests, he will not be interested in holding the shares of the corporation for a long time. Thus, a voting agent cannot necessarily improve his chances of getting reelected by going with the short-term interests of a shareholder. Moreover, the competition between corporations for investors' money has to be taken into account. If, for example, an influential shareholder elects a voting agent who favors his interests over those of other shareholder groups to the detriment of the corporation as a whole, then, as a consequence, investors will be reluctant to provide additional equity capital to this firm. In other words: the shareholders' meeting choice of voting agents will become an important decision variable for (institutional) investors. Term limits and liability rules, as well as the prohibition of any business links between the voting agent and shareholders and the corporation to be controlled, should alleviate the problem. Also, by allowing for more than one voting agent at a time in bigger companies, a balance of power will be reached. Agents will be watching each other, thereby reducing any risk of collusion between an active group of shareholders and one of the voting agents.[13] Nevertheless, if we allow active shareholders to elect a voting agent for inactive shareholders, why not do away with proxy voting completely? Indeed, because our proposal relies essentially on a convergence of interests between large, active shareholders and dispersed, inactive shareholders, it seems logical that votes would only be cast by the former. But there is a significant difference: if active shareholders only are allowed to cast a vote, the extent of their control is limited to the amount of their shares; therefore, undermonitoring is inevitable. But hiring a voting agent brings another strong monitor into the gover-

---

13. Also, by allowing for only for a limited number of voting agents, the *free-rider* problems of the supply side of voting services should be mitigated.

nance structure of the corporation. Thus, control will increase. Moreover, this arrangement might attract institutional investors, who do attend the shareholder meetings, but do not want to engage in close monitoring of the corporation.

Summary

Allocating voting rights on fundamental corporate matters to the shareholders as the residual claimants of the firm represents a commitment by the corporations' decisionmakers not to act to the detriment of the investors after the investment is made. Problems of collective action, however, diminish the value of this bonding device. Holders of small equity claims lack the incentive to acquire and to act on information about the impact of the management's proposals on firm value. Proxy voting and takeovers are costly alternatives. We propose another mechanism—active shareholders should be allowed to elect a single voting agent for a specified period of time. The voting agent acts on behalf of the shareholders who do not attend the general meetings in this period. After each period there will be a new election. Because of limited tenure, a voting agent has an incentive to work hard on the behalf of the shareholders he represents. The voting agent is paid by the corporation. In order to avoid potential conflicts of interest, personal interlocks and business links between the voting agent and the corporation or the active shareholders have to be prohibited.

Bibliography

Akerlof, G. A. 1970. "The Market for Lemons: Quality, Uncertainty, and the Market Mechanism." *Quarterly Journal of Economics* 84: 488.

Baums, Theodor. 1990. "Höchststmmrechte." *Die Aktiengesellschaft* 221.

————. 1992. "Corporate Governance in Germany: The Role of Banks." *American Journal of Comp. L.*

————. 1993. "Takeovers vs. Institutions in Corporate Governance in Germany." In D. D. Prentice and P. R. J. Holland, eds., *Contemporary Issues in Corporate Governance*. Oxford, U.K.: Clarendon.

———— . 1994. "The German Banking System and Its Impact on Corporate Finance and Governance." In Aoki and Patrick, eds., *The Japanese Main Bank System: Its Relevance for Developing and Transforming Economies*. Oxford, U.K.: Oxford University Press.

Bebchuck, Lucian A. 1989. "Limiting Contractual Freedom in Corporate Law: The Desirable Constraints on Charter Amendments." *Harvard Law Review* 102: 1820.

Bericht der Studienkommission. 1979. "Grundsatzfragen der Kreditwirtschaft." Schriftenreihe des Burdesministeriums der Finanzen, Heft 28. Frankfurt/main.

Böhm, Jürgen. 1992. "Der Einfuß'der Banken auf Großuternehmen." In *Duisburger Volkswirtschaftliche Studien 13*. Hamburg: Steuer-Und Wirtschaftsvevlag.

Cable, J. R. 1985. "Capital Market Information and Industrial Performance: The Role of West German Banks." *Economic Journal* 95: 118.

Easterbrook, Frank H., and Daniel Fischel. 1990. "The Corporate Contract." In L. Bebchuck, ed., *Corporate Law and Economic Analysis*.

———— . 1991. *The Economic Structure of Corporate Law*.

Edwards, J. S. S., and K. Fischer. 1994. *Banks, Finance, and Investment in Germany*. Cambridge, U.K.: Cambridge University Press.

Federal Banking Supervisory Agency. 1993. Written statement for the hearing before the Committee on Economic Affairs, Federal Parliament, Bonn, November 26, 1993.

Fischer, Klaus. 1990. "Harbankbeziehungen als Instrument der Bindurg zwischen Banken und Unternehmen. Eine theoretische und empirische Analyse." Dissertation. OEC, Bonn.

Fraune, C. Forthcoming. "Der Einfluss Institutioneller Anleger in der Hauptversammlung." Dissertation. Osnabrück.

Gordon, Jeffrey N. 1990. "Ties that Bond: Dual Class Common Stock and the Problem of Shareholder Choice." In L. Bebchuck, ed., *Corporate Law and Economic Analysis.*

Gottschalk, Arno. 1988. "Der Stimmrechtseinfluß der Banken in den Aktionarsversammulurgen von Broßunternehmen." *YUSI-Milteiliurgen.*

Holmström, Bengt, and Jean Tirole. 1993. "Market Liquidity and Performance Monitoring." *Journal of Political Economy* 101: 678.

Immenga, Ulrich. 1978. *Beteilgungen von Banken in andeven Wirtschaftsweigen*, 2d ed. Baden-Baden: Nomos Verlag.

Kallfass, H. H. 1992a. *Kapitalmarktkoordination.* Göttingen: Vandenhoeck and Rupprecht.

———. 1992b. "Managementkontrolle in Publikumsgesellschaften." *Hamburger Jahrbuch für Wirtschafts- und Gesellschaftspolitik* 37: 277.

Klein, William A., and John C. Coffee, Jr. 1990. *Business Organization and Finance, Legal and Economic Principals*, 4th ed. Westbury, New York: Foundation.

Köndgen, Johannes. 1994. "Duties of Banks in Voting their Clients' Stock." In T. Baums, Baxbaum, and Hopt, eds., *Institutional Investors and Corporate Governance.* New York and Berlin: Walter de Gruytev.

Lutter, Marcus, and Brigitte Lammers. 1990. "Hostile Takeovers: Possibilities and Limitations According to German Law." In J. M. M. Maeijer and K. Greens, eds., *Defensive Measures against Hostile Takeovers in the Common Market.* Dordrecht: Martinus Nijhoff and Graham & Trotman.

Mayer, Colin, and Ian Alexander. 1990. "Corporate Financing in Germany and the United Kingdom." *Journal of Japanese and International Economies* 4: 457.

Perlitz, M., and F. Seger. Forthcoming. "Regarding the Particular Role of Universal Banks in German Corporate Governance." *Journal of Business and the Contemporary World.*

Schlegelberger, X. 1977. *Handelsgesetzbuch*, 5th ed., vol. 6. Munich: Vahlen Verlag.

Verband der Auslandsbanken in Deutschland. 1993. Written statement for a hearing before the Committee on Economic Affairs, Bonn, November, 1993.

Wenger, Ekkehard. 1992. "Universalbankensystem und Depotstimmrecht." *Der Markt für Unternehmenskontrollen, Schriften des Vereins für Socialpolitik* 124.

Zöllner, Wolfgang, and Ulrich Noack. 1991. "One Share—One Vote?" *Die Aktiengesellschaft* 117.

Index

(Page numbers in italics refer to nontext material.)